D0847894

Adolescence and Youth in Early Modern England

Adolescence and Youth in Early Modern England

Ilana Krausman Ben-Amos

Yale University Press
New Haven and London 1994

To my mother and in memory of my father

Set in Aster by Best-set Typesetter Ltd., Hong Kong
Printed and bound in Great Britain by St Edmundsbury Press

Library of Congress Cataloging-in-Publication Data

Ben-Amos, Ilana Krausman.
Adolescence and youth in early modern England / Ilana Krausman Ben-Amos.
p. cm.
Includes bibliographical references and index.
ISBN 0-300-05597-8
1. Youth—England—History. I. Title.
HQ799.G72E53 1994
305.23'5'0942—dc20 93-38314
CIP

A catalogue record for this book is available from the British Library.

Contents

Acknowledgements

My first debt is to the many historians and scholars working in the fields of family history, historical demography, urban and rural history, whose publications in the past two decades are referred to in the notes and the bibliography. Their work provided many insights and was essential in writing what would otherwise have remained a much less integrated book. The research for the book began when I wrote my doctoral dissertation, and I am grateful to the staff at the Bristol Record Office for providing assistance and hospitality during my trips to the Archive in the course of the past decade. I am also grateful to the staff at the Public Record Office and the Bodleian Library, where I spent many summers between busy semesters of teaching.

In the course of writing the book I have incurred many debts. Paul Seaver read the entire manuscript with great care. He saved me from many errors, posed pertinent questions, and over the years has been a constant source of inspiration and enlightenment. He also shared generously some of his own material with me. I would also like to express my gratitude to Keith Wrightson, who encouraged me to pursue this topic since I first conceived of it as a book. He read the whole typescript and provided many valuable comments and suggestions which also made the book more readable and comprehensive. The remaining faults and errors, of course, are mine.

Tamar Rapoport helped me to formulate the conceptual framework of the book, and her expertise in the sociology of youth helped me find my way in what is by now a vast sociological literature. Zvi Razi provided help and advice at various stages, and Shulamit Shahar allowed me to consult her book while it was still in manuscript form. I owe special thanks to Shmuel Galai and Elena Lourie, whose encouragement and friendship were especially valuable during the years I was writing the book. Dov Barak, Michael Heyd, Yanni Nevo, Adi Parush, Iris Parush, and Vered Slonim each contributed in his own way. Catherine Logan helped improve my style; and a grant from Ben-Gurion University helped at a final stage of the writing. Robert Baldock and the production team at Yale University Press were helpful and patient, and I am grateful to them for that. My greatest debt is to my husband, Avner, whose support, companionship, and affection contributed more than can easily be expressed to the completion of this book.

Abbreviations

All cited works were published in London unless otherwise noted.

Bangs	*Memoirs of the Life*: Bangs, Benjamin, *Memoirs of the Life and Convincement of Benjamin Bangs* (1757).
Barlow's Journal	Barlow, Edward, *Barlow's Journal of his Life at Sea in King's Ships, East and West Indiamen, and other Merchantmen from 1659 to 1703* (1934), transc. Basil Lubbock, Vol. I.
Coxere	*Adventures by Sea*: Coxere, Edward, *Adventures by Sea* (1945), ed. E.H.W. Meyerstein.
Disney	*Some Remarkable Passages*: Disney, Gervase, *Some Remarkable Passages in the Holy Life and Death of Gervase Disney* (1692).
Evans	*An Eccho to the Voice*: Evans, Arise, *An Eccho to the Voice from Heaven. Or a Narration of the Life, and Manner of the Special Calling, and Visions of* (1653).

Fretwell	*A Family History*: Fretwell, James, *A Family History*, in *Yorkshire Diaries and Autobiographies in the Seventeenth and Eighteenth Centuries* (Surtees Society, Vol. LXV, 1877).
Houlbrooke	*English Family*: Houlbrooke, R.A., *The English Family 1450–1700* (1984).
Ingram	*Church Courts*: Ingram, M., *Church Courts, Sex and Marriage in England, 1570–1640* (Cambridge, 1987).
Kussmaul	*Servants in Husbandry*: Kussmaul, A., *Servants in Husbandry in Early Modern England* (Cambridge, 1981).
McIntosh	'Servants and the household unit': McIntosh, M.K., 'Servants and the household unit in an Elizabethan English community', *Journal of Family History*, 9 (1984), 3–23.
McIntosh	*A Community Transformed*: McIntosh, M.K., *A Community Transformed: The Manor and Liberty of Havering 1500–1620* (Cambridge, 1991).
Life of Adam Martindale	Martindale, Adam, *The Life of Adam Martindale, Written by Himself* (Chetham Society, Vol. IV, 1845), ed. R. Parkinson.
Norwood	*Journal of*: Norwood, Richard, *The Journal of Richard Norwood, Surveyer of Bermuda* (New York, 1945).
Rappaport	*Worlds Within Worlds*: Rappaport, S., *Worlds Within*

	Worlds: Structures of Life in Sixteenth-Century London (Cambridge, 1989).
Smith (ed.)	*Land, Kinship and Life-Cycle*: Smith, R.M. (ed.), *Land, Kinship and Life-Cycle* (Cambridge, 1984).
Autobiography of William Stout	Stout, William, *The Autobiography of William Stout of Lancaster (1665–1752)* (Manchester, Chetham Society, 3rd. series, Vol. XIV, 1967), ed. J.D. Marshall.

Archives

BRO	Bristol Record Office
PRO	Public Record Office

‘A man among children will be long a child, a child among men will be soon a man.’

Thomas Fuller, *Gnomologia: Adagies and Proverbs* (1732)

Introduction

On the day in March 1657 that Edward Barlow left his native village of Prestwich in Lancashire, he went early in the morning to do his routine duty of fetching a loaf of bread from the bakehouse. Then he went into his chamber, put on his best clothes, and came down the stairs of the house to say goodbye to his sister and mother. His mother still tried to persuade him not to go to London, but to remain nearer home, in Manchester, where he had been apprenticed for a while. But Barlow would not be persuaded. He went to take his leave of his father, who was working in the fields of the parish clerk. His father gave him six shillings, bid him farewell, and prayed for God's blessing for his son. Barlow himself came away 'with tears in [his] eyes' – as he remembered it later on – and then went to Manchester, where his mother had arranged with the carrier for his trip. Some five or six years later, when Barlow was already a seaman's apprentice and had begun to write his diary, he recorded his recollections of these early events in the first pages of his journal. To give them greater visual impact, he drew a picture of himself walking on a road leading away from his parents' home, and of his mother beckoning to him, as if asking him to stay.[1]

Barlow's life and career as a seaman were in many ways unique. Yet his social background, his childhood experiences before he left home, his departure in his mid-teens, and his migration to and apprenticeship in a large town were all well within the broad outlines of the patterns of childhood and youth in the early modern period. Unlike in most pre-industrial societies, young people in England were single and often in what historians have called life-cycle service. This term refers to a range of practices: domestic service, farm service and apprenticeship in various trades and crafts. Variations between these practices through time and from place to place were many, but common to all was a living-in arrangement for a specific period of time and the coincidence of this arrangement, or series of arrangements, with the period of adolescence and youth. One entered service some time in the course of one's teens, and left it still unmarried.[2] As an institution, service goes back to the Middle Ages, and available evidence suggests that in some medieval communities as much as a fifth of the population were servants.[3] In the late sixteenth century, parish listings show 60 per cent or more people in the age category of 15–24 living outside their parental homes.[4] There were fluctuations in the incidence of service throughout the period, and its decline was a protracted process which varied greatly across time and place. But overall, service remained an integral part of the social and economic life of the period, and its final phase of decline was delayed well into the late eighteenth and nineteenth centuries.[5]

This book is about young people, men and women in a broad spectrum of middling and lower groups of society, who, in the period between 1500 and 1700, spent at least part of their adolescence and youth away from their homes as farm servants, domestic servants, or apprentices. Although it begins with an overview of the ways adults in early modern English society thought about youth – what it was or what it should have been – the book concentrates on the experience of growing up; of moving from childhood to adolescence, youth, and then to early and mature adult life.

Two conflicting models have been used in descriptions of the transition from childhood to adult life in the pre-industrial and early modern past. In the first model, emphasis is placed on the short duration of adolescence; in the second, on its prolongation over several years or more. The first model, formulated in sociological literature on adolescence and youth, describes an early, fast, and relatively simple transition to adult life in the past. Sociological thinking on these issues goes back to the late nineteenth century and the first decade of the twentieth, when adolescence as a social phenomenon gained prominence in the emergent fields of social psychology, psychiatry, and a wide range of socioeconomic studies which were motivated by the need for social reform. In many of these early writings, various aspects of adolescence were interpreted in the context of the industrial and urbanised world and the social problems they generated, especially among the young.[6] The earliest, and still valuable and informative, book on the history of child labour and its deterioration in the industrial world was written with this perspective in mind, and it emphasised the relative security which characterised juvenile labour in the pre-industrial past.[7] Other writers assumed that 'city lads' were wilder, more reckless and disorderly than their village counterparts.[8] The latter, by impliction, represented a vanishing past in which the transition to adult life was supposedly healthier, more secure, and shorn of tensions and turmoil. The belief that in the pre-industrial past the transition to adult life was quite short and free of complications was expressed in Pollock and Maitland's *The History of English Law*, in their remark that 'in past times [i.e. the early medieval period] boys and girls had soon attained full age; life was simple and there was not much to learn'.[9]

Most influential in elaborating ideas about the relative smoothness of the transition to adulthood in the pre-industrial past were sociologists who analysed age divisions and their role in social organisation and the transition from one generation to the next. In his classic essay on social generations, published in 1928–29, Karl Mannheim made the important distinction between 'youth' and 'generation': while youth was a universal phenomenon – a 'mere collective fact', as he referred to it – a generation was created by specific historical circumstances, and consisted of people who shared not only age, but also a set of attitudes which placed them apart from society at large.[10] His analysis implied that in past societies the young were integrated into adult society without ever developing a distinct generational consciousness because change in pre-industrial society was extremely slow. In such 'static' societies, the attitudes of the young were characterised by 'piety', and they adapted themselves to the older generation 'even to the point of making [themselves] appear older'.[11] Also influential in these formulations was S.N. Eisenstadt, who argued that in so-called traditional society, the impact of peer groups on young people was shallow and of short duration. Instead, family and kin had the most formative influence, overcoming whatever differences there were between the young and the old in a village community. Youthful manifestations like sports, games and dancing remained 'silent' and largely under the control of adult kin, who ensured a relatively peaceful transition from one generation to the next.[12]

Like other sociologists, Eisenstadt believed that the transition to adult life in the past was gradual, relatively secure, and allowed no personal autonomy and liberty of choice for the young. In a technologically undeveloped society in which the unit of production was the family, little room was thought to be left for the young to decide about their occupations and careers.[13] Assumptions about so-called traditional societies and their effect, in one way or another, on the smooth and relatively short transition to adulthood have continued to form the basis of most sociological thinking about adolescence and youth in past times. It is assumed that, not unlike primitive societies in which the transition to adult life is short and marked by a series of rites that extend for up to several months,[14] the transition to adulthood in the pre-industrial past was smooth and of relatively short duration. Simple technologies, early entry into the workforce and short training, little division of labour, the strength of the family and lack of compulsory schooling all are thought to encourage a lack of age segregation and this fast and smooth entry into adult life. By contrast to the modern world, when adolescence is perceived as having become a longer, complex and distinct psychological and sociological phenomenon, in pre-industrial societies adolescence appears a relatively simple process if only because it was short, lasting no more than three or four years or even less.[15]

Among historians, the first and most influential to explore these issues and adopt the model of the fast transition to adult life was Philippe Ariès in his famous study on the history of childhood.[16] Ariès presented a somewhat extreme version of the short-duration hypothesis, arguing that before the nineteenth century the period of adolescence was virtually unknown, in theory as well as in practice: 'Once he had passed the age of five or seven, the child was immediately absorbed into the world of adults.'[17] In his view, it was only from the seventeenth and eighteenth centuries that the prolongation of childhood began, and new phases of youth and adolescence were acknowledged, first among the upper classes, and then gradually among the middle and lower sections of society. Ariès's conception of an early and abrupt transition to adult life in the medieval past had some affinity with anthropological descriptions of the transition to adulthood in tribal societies, but it also accentuated and brought into sharper focus ideas current among sociologists, especially regarding the invisibility of the young and lack of marked differences between youths and adults in the pre-industrial past. This partly explains why his thesis was adopted more readily by sociologists than by historians, who while praising his new and imaginative entry into the forays of family life in the past, expressed reservations and a great deal of scepticism about his ideas and historical methodology.[18] Similar assumptions about the short duration of adolescence in the past permeated early writings on the history of youth in the twentieth century. J. and V. Demos emphasised urbanisation and the disintegration of the family economy in late nineteenth-century American society as the catalysts of the emergence of adolescence as a distinct phase in the life cycle, and Joseph F. Kett argued that in a stable agrarian society (referring to early colonial America), the range of occupational and religious choices open to young people was so narrow as to preclude a period of 'doubt and indecision'. One generation supposedly passed quietly into the next, and only from the 1860s on did the prolongation of adolescence through the postponement of career choices become prominent.[19] As one historian who wrote on adolescents in modern Britain has observed, these suppositions on the absence or short duration of adolescence in the past raised one serious difficulty: they hardly accorded with what English historians of the early modern period were beginning to reveal about youth in the pre-industrial past.[20]

Historians of early modern English society have indeed diverged from the idea of the short duration of youth in the past. They have applied, or tacitly assumed, a model in which emphasis is placed on the longevity and extension of that stage in the life cycle. They all stress that in early modern English society full participation in adult life was retarded, and legal, social and economic rights and obligations were accorded to the young only many years after they had reached puberty. The 'prolongation of childhood', as Keith Thomas has called it, or the 'extension of puberty', aptly summarise some of the findings about the lives of the young in the early modern period.[21] This model of the transition to adult life through an extended period has been formulated, or indirectly reinforced, by three fields of historical investigation.

The first, and in some ways the most important, has been historical demography, whose findings about family structure and age at marriage have altered our perceptions of social life during the period under review in many different ways. It has been established that most people in early modern England – in consonance with parts of western Europe – married only in their late twenties, between the ages of 27 and 29 for males, and around 26 for women. Upon marriage, couples created separate residential units, rather than becoming integrated into domestic groups involving their parents or other multiple and extended forms of co-residence with kin. This gave the act of marriage itself an added significance in terms of the assumption of responsibilities for offspring and of adult authority and rule. Since the family was also a unit of production, marriage and the formation of a household were by far the single most important criterion of entry to adult life in early modern English society. All this implied that the period of adolescence and youth was tremendously long rather than short, for if life expectancy was 35 or 40, most people spent nearly half of their lives in a position of 'youth', during which time they were barred from assumption of the primary role of adults; namely, household headship.[22]

The second group of historians who have contributed to our view of early modern youth as an extension of childhood are those who study the family – in particular, those who focus on the patriarchal nature of the early modern family. Assumptions about the patriarchal structure of the early modern family go back to studies in the political thought of the period, and to the first major studies of family life by Peter Laslett, and especially by Lawrence Stone, who has presented a particularly radical interpretation of the patriarchal and authoritarian nature of parental rule in the period between the medieval and the modern era.[23] According to Stone, the sixteenth and first half of the seventeenth century was a period characterised by strict patriarchal rule, which was exercised not only over younger children but also over older servants and apprentices by masters who acted *in loco parentis*. Stone's interpretation, especially regarding the lack of affection of parents for their children, has been subject to a great deal of criticism by historians like Alan Macfarlane, Keith Wrightson, Lynda Pollock, Ralph Houlbrooke and others, who have all pointed out the parental care and the emotional and material investment parents made in their offspring. The relationship between parents and children during this period was in fact affectionate and less authoritarian than Stone envisaged.[24] Ann Kussmaul, who brought to light the lives of servants in husbandry, pointed to the ambiguities in the position of the farm servant, and to some aspects of the activities of servants, who escaped the immediate bounds of patriarchal authority. Houlbrooke also commented on the independence young people might have achieved by the time they made their decision to marry.[25] Yet overall, life-cycle service has continued to be viewed first and foremost in the context of the subordination and dependency of the young, and the limits this placed on the assumption of adult responsibilities. In the case of apprenticeship, this position of dependency is assumed to have been particularly long, since apprenticeship to a craft or a trade was based on a long period of service with a single master, and was subject to municipal rules and national legislation which ensured that apprentices remained in a status of dependency and subordination well into their mid-twenties and beyond. Whether depicted as authoritarian or simply as paternal towards their apprentices, masters in these studies were viewed as acting *in loco parentis*, and the view of the position of their apprentices as passive – somewhat akin to that of a child – has thus been amplified.[26]

A third group of historians who have contributed to our thinking about youth as a prolongation of adolescence are those who examined various forms of adolescent and youth culture in the early modern period. Partly in reaction to Ariès's suppositions about the non-existence of the adolescent phase in the past, they have examined distinct dimensions in the lives of the young. Of substantial influence was Natalie Zemon Davis's seminal and innovative article on youth groups – abbeys and kingdoms, as they were called – in France.[27] These abbeys had social roles and obligations which expressed the distinct position of the young in villages, as well as in towns. Some historians of English society have followed in her footsteps, and although similar types of abbeys and kingdoms – with jurisdiction, hierarchy and permanency – in England were hard to find, they have still elaborated on other forms of expression distinct to the young, and the manifestation of these in religion, politics, leisure and the social relations between peers.[28]

In spite of their importance to our enhanced understanding of various aspects of social life in the early modern past, these studies have fostered a picture of the prolongation of childhood or adolescence which appears inadequate, and, on occasion, somewhat misguided. Something of this inadequacy comes through in descriptions of a 23-year-old apprentice as an adolescent or even a boy or a child, and in suggestions that the transition to adulthood could begin only when apprentices finished their formal terms, when they might have been as old as 26, or even older.[29] Laslett and Kussmaul have observed ambiguities about the position of servants: in some ways they were treated as children, but in others they were not children at all.[30] Yet much of the historical literature has so far overlooked this latter aspect in the lives of the young, and instead has alluded to the former: the passivity and dependency of servants, and their teenage tendency towards rebellion, insubordination and turmoil. The possibility that people in their early twenties could act as responsible adults is normally ignored, so that examples of young people aged 23 or 24 who took responsibility for the conduct of extensive businesses or the management of farms on their own have been noted as exceptionally impressive for people of 'only' 24 years.[31]

Arguably, the two models described above capture the life of the young in the past in an insular and fragmentary way. While both touch on some aspects of the lives of the young, they leave others neglected, unexplored, or simply view them through erroneous assumptions. The model which describes a short transition to adulthood rightly emphasises the importance of early entry to work, but it fails to capture the very long transition to full adult life: the complexities, demands, not to speak of the hardships, involved in becoming an adult in early modern English society. A series of assumptions long held by sociologists regarding the absence of autonomy and choice in the past do not quite fit with what has become, to historians, a familiar picture of the economic and occupational scene of the early modern period, which, as we shall see, was bound to have a profound effect on the life of young people and the range of choices they were encouraged, or forced, to make. Even the assumption of the security of the young is little understood, for, as will be seen in Chapter 7, the relative security of the young derived neither solely from the strength of the kin or domestic group, nor from the protection provided by the guilds or by individual masters, but rather from a series of social ties and the intricate ways in which these ties interacted. Early modern historians have discovered unknown facets of family life during this period and have illuminated a range of questions regarding life-cycle service, but in their portrayal of the prolongation of adolescence and youth they have overlooked some of the most critical aspects in the lives of the young, and the ways these undermined the extension of childhood or even adolescence. Despite the findings and enhanced understanding of youth in the past, the experience, apprehensions and preoccupations involved in growing up and in the process of maturation during many years of service away from home have remained vague and unexplored.

In what follows, adolescence and youth in early modern English society is viewed as a long and dynamic phase in the life cycle – a phase which consisted of a series of mental, social and economic processes through which the young were transformed into adults. These involved major events such as separation from parents, entry into and exit from service or a series of service arrangements, setting up in business or on the land and marriage; but they also involved more subtle transformations which forced the young into mature, independent adult lives. Maturation, therefore, did not occur at a specific point in the lives of the young, nor was it a steady, uniform set of gradual stages. It involved various transformations which differed in pace and intensity, and which varied along gender lines, between social groups, and to some extent also across time. Examination of these transformations forms the substance of the various chapters of the book, and it should be pointed out that, in this respect, the book is less a comprehensive account of youth and more an investigation of its major features as a transitional stage in the life cycle.[32] Chapters 2–6 deal with the maturation involved in separation from parents, the working lives of the young, their adjustment to different households, and their acquisition of a wide range of skills as they grew up from childhood to adolescence and then youth. Chapters 7–9 explore the widening social ties of adolescents and youths, their leisure activities, values and preoccupations, as well as the responsibilities many of them had assumed before they married and formed households of their own.

Throughout the book the terms 'adolescence' and 'youth' are used to denote the years between the early teens and the mid-twenties: adolescence refers to the first stage – the years around puberty, in the early and mid-teens – while youth denotes people in their mid-teens and upwards. This conforms broadly to modern sociological terminology,[33] and it covers what early modern Englishmen referred to, for the most part, as youth and young adulthood. The term 'adolescentia' was well known to early modern writers and commentators, but on the whole it was less frequently used, although 'youth' itself was sometimes divided into distinct stages or sub-categories, as will also be pointed out in Chapter 1.

1 Images of Youth

'All the world's a stage, and all the men and women merely players', declares Jacques in *As You Like It*, in his famous speech on the various parts played by a man throughout his life. Following the infant who is 'mewling and puking in the nurse's arms', and the schoolboy who is 'creeping like snail unwillingly to school', there comes the lover, 'sighing like furnace, with a woeful ballad made to his mistress' eyebrow'. The fourth act belongs to the soldier, 'full of strange oaths . . . sudden and quick in quarrel, seeking the bubble reputation even in the cannon's mouth'. The fifth scene belongs to the justice, 'with eyes severe and beard of formal cut', followed by the old man with his 'big manly voice, turning again toward childish treble', he 'pipes and whistles in his sound'. And 'last scene of all, that ends this strange eventful history, is second childishness, and mere oblivion, sans teeth, sans eyes, sans taste, sans every thing.'[1]

In his book on the theme of the ages of man in medieval thought, J. A. Burrow showed that Shakespeare's evocation through Jacques's speech of the Ages of Man had a long pedigree in medieval learning, going back to the Ptolemaic system of the universe.[2] Ptolemaic astrology, which was revived during the Renaissance, divided human life into seven ages, each corresponding to a planet in an order unfolding from the earth to Saturn, and each associated with specific qualities: the moon (infancy) with chastity and purity, Mercury (childhood) with learning and eloquence, Venus (adolescence) with softness and sensuality, the sun (young manhood) with power and substance, Mars and Jupiter (manhood) with anger and ferocity, and Saturn (old age) with heaviness and gravity.[3] As Burrow shows, astrology was not the only theory on which Englishmen could draw for their discussion of human life during the Renaissance. There were other traditions which divided life into three, four and six ages, as well as seven and even eleven and more, and they all go back to medieval and ancient times: to Aristotelian biology, in which human life, like that of other organisms, was divided into three phases of growth, maturity and decay; to Galenic physiology, in which the four body humours controlled human life; and to theology and the analogy it made between the ages of man and the six historical ages of the world.[4]

Early modern writings and opinions on these themes derived from this variety of learned, Latin and vernacular, religious and literary sources.[5] Within the various schemes of human life, adolescence and youth were accorded a special place, although their boundaries were not clear-cut. Adolescence – the blossoming or lustful age, as it was more frequently referred to – could begin at the age of 9 but also at 14; youth could span the years between 14, or 18, and up to 25, 28, or simply until marriage.[6] Like their medieval ancestors, early modern Englishmen did not hold a single theory of youth, but more a series of images and attributes of young age, which were made explicit in various writings: quasi-scientific discussions, religious manuals, educational theories and literature – each presenting a view of youth from a particular, sometimes insular, point of view.[7] This chapter will deal with some of the most common images of young age as they recur in this variety of sources, as well as in autobiographies in which contemporaries remembered their youth and referred to themselves and other people when they were young. Some consideration will also be given to the degree to which the ideas and images that appear in the various texts were current among their readers and audiences, and to the degree to which they reflected something of the reality of the lives of young people during this period.

Sin and Piety

Recognition of physical maturation during the period of adolescence, as well as its denigration, were as old as attempts to explain the course of human life. Aristotle acknowledged that 'young men have strong passions', but soon added that they 'tend to gratify them indiscriminately' and that 'of the bodily desires, it is the sexual by which they are most swayed and in which they show absence of self control'.[8] According to Ptolemy, Venus, 'taking charge of the third age', when maturity begins, brings an 'activity of the seminal passages' and 'an impulse toward the embrace of love' as well as 'incontinence', 'desire for any chance sexual gratification', 'guile' and 'blindness'.[9]

But conceptions of youthful sins, of the sins to which a man was born and into which he was drawn more powerfully as he grew up to adolescence and youth, were rooted in Augustinian theology, which was steeped with suspicion of the imperfections and shortcomings of children in general and of adolescents in particular. Augustine's *Confessions*, in which he wrote of his childhood and youth, described in detail his idleness, playfulness, ambition, pride, his habits of lying, stealing, frequenting stage-plays, and, above all, his tendency to 'impure lustfulness', 'unchaste desires', and 'oversight' of the Truth of God during his youth.[10] Medieval preachers stressed that human predilection to sin became particularly marked in children who reached seven years, and that as they grew up to adolescence and youth their tendency to sin, to a lack of control over sexual passions, and to indulgence in bodily pleasures grew. In pre-Reformation preaching young people were likewise depicted as singularly attached to the 'pleasure of this bodye', to the 'voluptye and carnal desires of this bodye', and youth was described as a period in which indulgence in carnal lust, lasciviousness and sensual delights reigned.[11] The educational theories of the humanists were based on similar assumptions. Erasmus, Vives and Thomas Elyot expressed the conviction that human instincts tended towards wrongdoing, evil and vice, which were especially marked in infants, children and youth. Without constant and diligent nurturing, strict discipline, and a proper education, young people would succumb and be doomed to do wrong, and 'the frute [i.e. the child] may growe wylde, and conteine in it fervent and mortal poyson, to the utter destruction of a realme'.[12]

Paradoxically, Protestant theology, with its emphasis on the totality of human sins from which God alone could provide salvation, served to mute, to some extent, contemporary conception of the propensity to sin in the age of youth. 'The mind of a man or a child is like a restless Mill, that cannot stand still,' preached Thomas Gataker, reflecting the view that sin was embedded in all men and women, regardless of biological age. Advice literature for the young, in which the sins awaiting them were mentioned repeatedly, was explicitly based on the assumption that sins were not confined to the young.[13] Domestic manuals also made it clear that parents, no less than their children, were vulnerable to sin and consequently had to be reminded of their obligations and duties.[14] Among the sins parents were likely to commit were over-indulgence of children,[15] neglect of their needs as infants and small children, and neglect of their proper education when they grew up.[16] Parents were condemned for sending their children away from home to become servants or apprentices, instead of keeping them under their instruction, care and control.[17] When they acknowledged that sending children away was at times inevitable, preachers reproached parents for sending them away at too early an age, for not giving due thought to the qualities of the master they chose, or for binding children away from home for the wrong reasons altogether.[18]

Nevertheless, Protestant preachers and writers of guides for moral conduct, like the Catholics before them, gave strong expression to the idea that young people were particularly prone to sin and to indulgence in immoral activities, especially sins of the flesh.[19] Not only was the child born evil, but his tendency to evil deeds increased as he grew up; youths were by nature 'brutish and devilish'.[20] This belief in the young's increased tendency to sin was conveyed in spiritual autobiographies, of which the best example is John Bunyan's *Grace Abounding to the Chief of Sinners*. As a young child, John was captivated by the Devil and was drawn into cursing, swearing, lying and 'blaspheming the holy Name of God'. At the age of nine he became distressed and despaired of life, but his sinful behaviour continued; adolescence brought more sin, 'wherefore with more greediness, according to the strength of nature, I did still let loose the reins to my lust, and delighted in all transgression against God. So that until I came to the state of marriage, I was the very ring leader of all the Youth that kept me company, in all manner of vice and ungodliness.'[21]

Not all spiritual autobiographers described their youth as a continuous path of devilish immoralism, as we shall see shortly. But some authors, like Bunyan, provided abundant descriptions of the sins they committed in their early years, and these sins were often described as common among, and characteristic of, youth. 'Youthful sins', 'youthful follies', 'childish vanities' were some of the most common ways in which these sins were described. Sexual desire was viewed as a mark of youth, regardless of biological age; 'young Men tho old Sinners', 'old in age yet Young in lewdness', as some writers of autobiographies referred to themselves and others.[22] The list of youthful sins was long, and it included anything a young man or woman was likely to do in their time of leisure: drinking wine, spending money, and engaging in sports, games, dancing, and other recreations.[23] Different human qualities were associated with these sins: idleness and vanity, thoughtlessness, inconsiderateness, an incapacity to sustain deep feelings, intolerance, indulgence in useless things, such as cheap and insubstantial 'tale-books, Romances, Play-books, and false or hurtful History'. In the biography of Margaret Baxter, written by her husband Richard, the author asserted that in her 'vain youth, Pride, and Romances', she had no other interest except 'glittering herself in costly apparel, and delighting in her Romances'.[24] Mary Rich, Countess of Warwick likewise recalled that in her youth – when she was about 14 years old – she was enticed by her sister-in-law into being 'very vain and foolish' by spending time 'in seeing and reading plays and romances'. Young women were singled out for their vanity, as well as their seductive skills 'in arreigning of mens affections, at their flattering faces'.[25]

Historians of Puritanism and of the family have long been aware of these negative portrayals of youth with which didactic writings of the early modern period were replete.[26] Such moralising and the view of young people it expressed were well established in Augustinian theology and medieval preaching tradition.[27] But it is also important to stress that religious assumptions about young age in this period were not solely grounded in conceptions of sin and human pitfalls, and, again like their medieval counterparts, Puritan writers could occasionally employ an altogether different image of the age of youth. Along with the Augustinian portrayal of youthful lusts, medieval authors and hagiographers harboured the belief, based on St Matthew, that children were the fittest souls for entry into heaven; they were pure, innocent, joyful, their faith was wholesome, and their instincts for apprehending the Truth were deeper than those of adults. Some medieval biographers of saints depicted their heroes as particularly fond of the company of children, and Jesus himself, of course, was portrayed as the innocent infant. Some tales in the hagiographic literature also depicted Jesus as a handsome and elegant youth.[28] This traditional depiction of the child as a pure soul, and of the youth as full of piety, continued to have its influence. Some authors in the seventeenth century thought that children between the ages of 7 and 14 were 'pure and free from a certain natural strength and facultie arising about that age';[29] others believed that children were untainted with sin and were therefore more likely to be saved than adults,[30] while yet others claimed that youths were especially receptive to spiritual things. Oliver Sansom thought that during his childhood and his youth he had been absorbed with a particular religious awe of God. 'So that even in my childhood, and more in my youth, there was a fear in my heart of offending the Lord'; and Richard Norwood spoke about the 'Lord ... shining into the heart with a favourable and loving countenance' not only in childhood but during adolescence, explaining that 'it is said of our Saviour "He looked upon the young man and loved him"'.[31]

There were, of course, differences between the depiction of the pious child by medieval hagiographers and the portrayal of childhood and youth in post-Reformation autobiographies. In medieval biographies of saints, the hero was pictured as having been born, or drawn early in his life, into exceptional spirituality and holiness.[32] By contrast, the spiritual autobiographer of the seventeenth century normally focused on his all-too-human childhood, from which only God's blessing had saved him, and in accordance with Protestant theology, God's grace and human sin were thus exemplified. Instead of describing a small, wise and dignified child – the 'wise Samuel' portrayed by some medieval hagiographers – the Puritan autobiographer recalled a sudden encounter with God or with divines who had to explain, show and guide the spiritual journey of a young man or woman, so that these became conversion stories rather than accounts of the miraculous. There were few saints – unusual people born with the mark of holiness – in such autobiographies. Yet this difference need not be pushed too far, for attitudes and pronouncements in which the spirituality of young age was extolled are evident in post-Reformation autobiographies as well. Gervase Disney eulogised his sister and brother, who both died very young, in terms which had more in common with the medieval child-angel – pure, beautiful, pious – than with the depiction of the infant born into sin of Protestant sermons and moral guides. He described his sister Sarah at her death as

> very young, yet had a good savour of Spiritual Things upon her Heart; ... She was esteemed one of the beautifullest children that ever was seen, her Hair being Milk white, and Complexion pure white and red; yet it was judg'd her greatest Beauty lay within ... and from the abundance of her Heart, her Mouth did often speak, to the great Comfort and Refreshment of weeping Friends that stood about her.

Gervase's brother was likewise described as a 'good young Samuel' who was admired by his father for his 'pious Talk, his strange questions in Divinity; which sometimes he [i.e. the father] was astonished at'.[33]

Other spiritual autobiographies reflected similar attitudes towards young age. While many authors were at pains to catalogue all the sins of their young and pre-reformed years, others portrayed themselves as having been inclined to piety and spiritual things in childhood or during their teens, even before they fully converted. 'In my very young years,' George Fox wrote in his autobiography, 'I had a gravity and stayedness of mind and spirit, not usual in children.' When he grew up his inclination towards serious things and purity increased. 'I never wronged man or woman in all [my apprenticeship], for the Lord's power was with me to preserve me . . . people had generally a love to me for my innocency and honesty.'[34] Unlike other autobiographers, Fox was, throughout his youth and before he fully converted, adamant in his dislike of activities such as games, sports and drinking. Samuel Bownas also remembered that he 'was never given to swearing, nor any gross vice', and that his involvement in youthful games gave him a 'heavy heart'. Other autobiographers portrayed themselves as having struggled, from early childhood and through their youthful years, between an 'inclination to seek God', and the 'suggestions of Satan'; and while their tendency to sin was evident, at the same time they exhibited the type of spirituality which had the effect of producing religious piety, the remembrance of which 'is sweet to a man many years after,' as Richard Norwood put it.[35]

Insubordination

Some of the most potent images of youth used by Englishmen during this period had roots in Galenic medicine, which associated youth with heat and with hot temper. Although recognising that every human being had his own balance of four bodily humours – his natural complexion – Galenic physiology was based on the premiss that human life had a universal course, passing through four separate ages, each governed by a specific humour. Small infants were dominated by the blood humour; mature persons were governed by the black choler; and old age by the phlegm. Youth was governed by the red choler, which was also associated with hotness and dryness, with the summer season, and with fire.[36] This theory was still current in the seventeenth century, and Henry Cuffe referred to the link between youth and summer, the period in human life when the 'sun's lively operation' was most marked, and when the humour of the body was hot and dry.[37] The notion of youth as a period governed by hot temper, or humour, or fire – a 'sighing furnace', as Shakespeare portrayed it – could be used to evoke a variety of qualities: boldness, arrogance, excessive activity, rashness, a spirit easily drawn to quarrelling and vengence, and especially to disobedience, riot and rebelliousness. As Bede had explained long before, 'red cholers make [young] people . . . bold, irritable, and active'.[38] In the seventeenth century, young years were associated with a quarrelsome and vengeful spirit, and the natural heat of youth was linked with immoderate temper and rashness. The 'humour' of most young people, as William Fleetwood put it, made them 'grow wanton, insolent and head-strong'.[39]

The emphasis on the rashness of the young and their propensity to disobedience and insubordination was, like conceptions of sin, also well within the tradition of Christian morality and medieval preaching, which took it for granted that young people were proud and insubordinate.[40] Protestant and Puritan writers associated youthful instincts (or 'diseases', as Daniel Williams called them), with rashness, lack of restraint, and insubordination.[41] Young apprentices were suspected of 'poisonous weeds of pride and arrogance', which could easily lead to subversion of the social order; and all servants were accused of being 'bold, nasty, and ignorant', easily drawn to impudence and licentiousness.[42] Catholic preachers explained the spread of Protestantism in the early decades of the sixteenth century as a result of youthful predilections, and blamed Protestant subversiveness on the 'conceits of these younglings', who found in Protestantism an appropriate expression of their tendency to disobedience.[43] A century later, Richard Baxter, who grew weary of the strife and disorder of the Civil War, thought that young people were responsible for the great animosities and schism he had witnessed during that period.[44]

Disobedience, insubordination, reckless and riotous living were encapsulated in the traditional theme of the Prodigal Son. Based on St Luke and well utilised in medieval morality and preaching, the story was used by humanists and dramatists who by the mid-sixteenth century were staging plays for performance by pupils and professional actors.[45] Thereafter it appeared in numerous forms: in dramatic works and plays, in ballads, pictures and prints, in stories about insubordinate children and misspent youth,[46] and in sermons on the youth who 'grew weary' of his parents, 'resolves to stay no longer', and goes to a remote place 'where he should have none to check or curb him in his reveling and riot'.[47] Many spiritual autobiographies were also modelled on the parable of the Prodigal Son. Bunyan, Croker and Norwood all presented themselves as sinners who left the parental roof, lived riotously and grew wanton, underwent many trials and tribulations, and then came back to their homes, like 'a prodigal son now returning thither'.[48] Others reproached themselves for their adventurous spirits which led them away from their parents towards unknown, difficult and immoral destinations. Richard Norwood described his decision to become an apprentice at sea, against his parents' will, his consequent hardship at sea during which he came near to embracing Catholicism, and his eventual repentance and reconciliation with his father.[49]

The moral of it was quite obvious. 'Obey your parents, ply your book, and worship God,' as the mid-sixteenth-century dramatist put it.[50] Early modern Englishmen believed in a divinely ordained social order, and authority and obedience were central to its very survival.[51] It was a conviction strongly advocated by men in authority, and by ministers, preachers and other educational writers and moralists, and it tended to spotlight the propensity for disorder associated with the period of youth, for in the universal order of things the young were expected to be subordinate to the authority of parents, masters, ministers and other adults. In such a framework, alarm at the threat youth posed to the social order was only natural. But since the predilections and hot temper of the young were assumed to be a stage in the natural course of life, such predilections were sometimes also regarded as the acceptable forms of youth's behaviour, which would inevitably disappear in time. Nathaniel Barnardiston was reported to have led a godly life during his youth, the time when, according to his biographer, other young people behaved wantonly, 'pretending that the heat of nature produces a sufficient apology and discharge for the same'.[52] Again this was not altogether a novel attitude. Apologies for youthful follies and indiscipline, buttressed with the biblical saying that 'All things have their season: and in their times all things pass under heaven', were common in the Middle Ages, generating the accusation that adults' attitude towards the young was too lenient.[53]

Such attitudes surfaced clearly in popular stories and ballads, even in ones that had didactic messages similar to those in religious writings and sermons. An example is a ballad on the Prodigal Son theme. This told the usual story of the youth who between the ages of 15 and 30 lived extravagantly and did everything the 'devil could think or create', involving himself in excessive drinking, wenching, swearing and games, until in the end he wasted all his inheritance. The list of sins and follies ascribed to the youth was very much in line with those condemned in moral guides and sermons, and his subversion was made explicit and no less straightforward. Yet the underlying tone of the ballad was less rigid, and the moral was defined in utilitarian rather than religious terms:

> What we drink in excess
> makes the appetite dull,
> and empties the bags be they never so full;
> It shortens our lives and deprives us of health.
> Then young men beware
> and make much of your wealth.

The ballad ended by expressing a flexible and less rigorous attitude to youthful sins:

> Yet with a true friend
> to be merry and jolly
> with a bottle or two
> I do count it no folly.[54]

Didactic texts and writings not infrequently betrayed the sentiments held by the people to whom they were addressed, which did not quite square with the suspicion and hostility of the preachers. Daniel Williams warned young people against boasting of their youthful lives. 'You are apt to boast of these years, as most conductive to happiness; . . . now your spirits are vigorous, your bodies healthy and strong, your senses quick, the cares and maladies of old age are far from you . . .'. Thomas Brooks reproached young men for being 'very apt to lean on their own wit, wisdom, arts, Parts, as old men are to lean on a staff to support them'.[55] Daniel Williams took pains to explain to his readers that strength, vigour and sharpness were but 'vanity', 'a poor thing, a short and empty matter', and to Brooks they signified the loss and ruin of the young.[56] The attempt of these preachers to uproot and condemn such sentiments suggests that many among the audiences were captured by very different images of youth, images which aroused admiration rather than indignation. Williams warned his audiences that the vigour of youth would eventually leave 'its admirers deceived'.[57]

Hope, Vigour, Wit

Juxtaposed with the deficiencies of old age, the period of youth could also be portrayed in a more favourable light. Learned authorities would agree that reason and wisdom were the assets of old age; but they could also evoke the notion, which goes back to Aristotle, that a man reached perfection in middle life rather than in old age, and that in old age he became decadent and degraded rather than wise and dignified. Between 14 and 18 a man 'commeth to his full ripeness', but in old age he 'waxes heavy'; adolescents also represented 'great wit and perceverance', and between 14 and 18 was depicted as a period when a youngster was 'most sensible, full of strength, courage, and activeness'.[58] Adolescence and youth were associated with strength, beauty and blossoming, compared with old age, which in some form or another represented decay. Henry Cuffe spoke about the span of years from childhood to 25 years of age as representing the period of generation, when 'growth is perfected', and within it, the years between 9 and 18 were the period of 'our budding and blossoming age'. He associated youth with hotness and 'strength of body and mind', and with Venus, which generated 'blossoming'. By contrast, old age for him was analogous to 'cold and troublesome winter' and represented dryness and death.[59] In his *History of the World*, Sir Walter Raleigh likewise gave a version of the astrological scheme of life, in which adolescence, the third age, was governed by Venus and was associated with love, desire and vanity, but the fourth age, governed by the sun, was 'the strong, flourishing, and beautiful age of man's life'. In old age, governed by Saturn, 'all our vain passions and affections past, the sorrow only abideth'.[60]

So youth represented the very contrast to old age, an antidote to inevitable death, and a hope – unrealistic as it was, given the high mortality rates in this period – for a long and healthy life. Most people were aware that their life expectancy did not extend beyond the age of 30 or 40; when Gervase Disney was about 13 years old and became very ill, his older brother comforted him by saying that young Gervase 'might live 20 or 30 years [more]', which probably reflected the time-span – between thirty-five and forty-five years – he expected to live.[61] Many popular chapbooks, especially the godly ones, reflected and even manipulated the reality of death in pre-industrial times. Such literature, if not deliberately intending to arouse terror of death and final judgment, reflected a deep horror at the prospect of dying.[62] Yet while death was a real presence for most people, many still sustained a hope for a long and promising future, a hope embedded in images of the young and of youthful lives. The presentation in popular literature of fictional heroes as youths who had a long and promising life ahead – 'a youth forward, and apt for any good impression or matter', as Thomas Deloney described his hero John Hawkwood in the opening lines of *The Honourable*

Prentice[63] – must have reflected widespread sentiments regarding young age. It was because such hopes for a long future prevailed that the deaths of young people could be considered 'sudden' and 'untimely' even when they were already in their mid-twenties. James Fretwell lamented the death of his cousin, who died when he was 26 years old, and referred to him as 'still a hopeful young man'.[64] For most people, youth symbolised the hope that life could be long and that, despite the heavy toll death normally took of people in all seasons of their life, old age was still something to look forward to. Such sentiments, which belied the dreadful reality of death, were also powerfully conveyed in popular songs and ballads, in which love and death were recurrent themes. Here we encounter the tragedies of separations, 'the untimely death of two faithful lovers', and the premature death of young lovers, soldiers or young seamen. The young sailor, who is separated from his beloved, lives under the constant threat of death and has few prospects of returning safely to shore, was a popular theme in ballads which conveyed a sense of the futility of life, but at the same time lamented the opportunities for long and happy lives of which these tragic lovers were deprived. A ballad entitled 'The mortality of mankind: being a dialogue between Death and a young Man' best illustrates the hope youth symbolised. In the ballad, Death encounters youth and informs him: 'I come for thee . . . thy glass is run'. While evoking the sense that death eventually summons both old men and 'youthful buds', the ballad also portrays the youth as 'amazed at the sudden sight' of Death, as pleading with Death to 'let [me] be old before I go', for a 'worldly wealth', his beloved girl, and the 'world's delight' that still awaited him.[65]

Youth could represent hope rather than a threat, even in religious contexts. In the end, despite the strong convictions of the sin and insubordination of youth, any educator, however grim the view of the young he took, was bound to admit that youth also represented hope. For if all human beings were equally sinful, and all seasons of life, including youth, were tainted with deficiency and wrongdoing, why devote special attention to, and write sermons for, the young? as Daniel Williams in a sermon frankly admitted. 'We ministers preach to you young ones as well as to the old,' he claimed. 'Nay, we preach to you with more hopes, expecting that you are not hardened as old persons are.'[66] Unexposed to the disillusionment that more advanced years could bring, young people were thought to possess vigour, affection, enthusiasm, and a mind receptive to new things and ideas. Richard Baxter described himself, when young, as having had 'a quick understanding', while in old age he had a slower understanding 'by that *praematura senectus* which weakness and excessive bleedings brought me to'. As a young preacher, he possessed certain youthful gifts which he lost later in life. 'The temper of my mind hath somewhat altered with the temper of my body,' he said of his transformation since his early years as a preacher. 'When I was young I was more vigorous, affectionate and fervent in preaching. . . . My style was more extemporate and lax, but by the advantage of affection, and a very familiar moving voice and utterance, my preaching then did more affect the auditory than many of the last years before I gave over preaching'.[67] While many Protestants associated youth with the tendency to subversion of the established religious order, others saw this age as the epitome of hope for change and reform, for young men could 'one day be the overthrow of the bishops'.[68]

In ceremonies and celebrations, young people could also be represented in ways which symbolised hope and stability rather than sin and subversion. In medieval times, children were customarily placed at the head of religious processions, where they symbolised faith in the innocence of the child and its atoning power.[69] More secular in their setting than these medieval processions, Elizabethan pageants used the conventions of medieval drama, with its moral theme and allegorical characters. Among the actors were schoolchildren from St Paul's or Westminster, as for example in the Royal Entry of Queen Elizabeth in 1559, when children were present on nearly every scaffold erected at locations on the route along which the Queen and her retinue proceeded. At Fenchurch she was offered two gifts by a child; at Gracechurch, children were seated on an arch with one of them representing, at the top, the Queen herself; at Cornhill, a child representing the Queen was carried by four citizens; and on Sopers Lane eight children represented the eight beatitudes which a poem had ascribed to the Queen.[70]

Royal entries such as this symbolised the continuity and unity of the English nation in a manner perhaps not altogether different from the medieval Corpus Christi play cycles, which expressed the sense of identity of the medieval urban community.[71] Thus, at various points in the procession the Queen confronted paintings of English kings in chronological order down to herself, while Henry VII and Henry VIII were represented by children enclosed in an arch with red and white roses representing the unity of the houses of Lancaster and York. The children in these historical scenes expressed the continuity of the English nation through its past, as well as its aspirations for the future good under the governance of the new Queen, who embodied the True Protestant Religion, Chastity, Wisdom, and so on. That is, they stood for unity rather than subversion; the hopes of the community rather than its perceived threats. So the students offered the Queen gifts to welcome her rule, and gave orations to express her virtues, legitimised by her continuing link to the English past, as well as the hope that these virtues would preserve her throne throughout her reign. To one of these orations the Queen is supposed to have replied: 'I have taken notice of your good meaning toward mee, and will endeavour to answere your several expectations.'[72]

In some types of popular literature, fictional youths were presented as members of bands fighting to protect the honour of their town, and the values and prestige of their community.[73] In her reply to an attack on 'Lewd, Idle, Forward and Unconstant Women' (1615), Ester Sowernam appealed to the London apprentices for protection, asserting that they were 'worthy youth', 'the hope of Manhoode', which called them to 'defend the just reputation of a woman'. In the satirical comedy *Eastward Hoe*, the good apprentice Golding was presented as a youth to be admired not only for his virtues, but for what he represented for future city life: a moral and charitable urban society which would replace the one based on material aspirations of the kind represented by a Dick Whittington.[74] At the same time, the period of youth could symbolise hopes for a better material life. Popular literature had heroes and heroines who rose from low parentage and upbringing to achieve material success, worldly comfort and fame aplenty, from the famous Dick Whittington – the poor country lad who is bound as an apprentice, becomes rich while serving as a factor overseas, and eventually becomes 'Lord' Mayor of London – to heroes such as Jack of Newbery, Tom Thumb and Thomas Hickathrift.[75] The very notion of such a social transformation required that the hero be a youth with a future still ahead of him, to whom the rewards of worldly success could still be of benefit.

It is indeed to popular literature that we must turn if we are to glimpse a set of images encapsulating the beauty, strength, vigour and wit of youth, rather than its follies and sins. Early modern popular literature abounds in young heroes and heroines, maidens and gallant youths, young virgins and lovers, youthful courtiers and country lasses, amorous and courageous youths, servants and apprentices. They figure in the ballad literature which proliferated between 1550 and 1600, and in popular tales and chapbooks the market for which expanded enormously between 1620 and 1700.[76] Traditional heroes such as Guy of Warwick and St George, and newly invented heroes like Tom-a-Lincoln who were based on the chivalric model, were all youths who went on adventures while still in their teens and early twenties. Among the heroes of popular novels in which urban life and trade provided the setting, craftsmen and their apprentices loomed large, as they did in the more sophisticated forms of Jacobean drama and city comedy. Jack of Newbery and John Hawkwood, both apprentices who began their adventures while still young, were famous heroes of Thomas Deloney's novels, many of which were turned into short chapbook versions. Heroic apprentices appeared on the stage, in stories, in songs, and in pamphlets which extolled their noble history and courageous deeds.[77]

It must at once be stated that popular literature in which young heroes predominated did not form what we would refer to today as literature designed to emulate the cult of youth as such. Little in early modern popular fiction resembles modern literature in which youth is presented as an eternal culture with political and social value, which becomes an ideal of regeneration of the individual as well as of society as a whole.[78] Young heroes in early modern popular fiction were not necessarily intended to represent the age group to which they belonged, nor did they present an ideal of life to be emulated by society at large. To some extent, the heroes' qualities were not strictly youthful, and the plots did not always highlight their biological age. In chivalric romances, the presentation of young heroes served to stimulate the fantasy and imagination of the reader, and the hero's adventures unfolded as a corollary less of his age than of his social background, fortune, sheer luck and individual disposition, which transcended not only his biological age but human nature altogether. So in the *History of the Famous and Valiant London Prentice*, the young hero Aurelius performs tremendous deeds and great actions which bring him fame and glory, in the best tradition of the medieval knight, translocated to an urban, commercial setting. Yet his superhuman strength defies nature and his age rather than exhibiting them in an exemplary way. Aurelius's strength is manifest from his very infancy, when he is able to strike a huge snake while still in his cradle, an action that would 'have feared another infant into fits'. When he embarks on a career as his master's factor overseas, his bravery is so extraordinary that it is attributed, again, to his supernatural qualities rather than his age. When he fights the Turks on his ship, he is able to use 'such violent force' that according to the Turks 'he was a Devil, and no Man'. Throughout the tale the hero's disposition is unaffected by age, character or, for that matter, the development of plot. Dreadful animals such as dragons and lions, as well as pirates and enemies, among them Turks, Saxons and Danes, enter into the plots of *The Famous History of Guy Earle of Warwick* or *The Most Pleasant History of Tom-a-Lincoln*, where the young heroes likewise perform tremendous actions of bravery with little regard to their specific ages.[79]

If chapbook romances were not meant to represent a cult of youth or an ideal life style for the young, they nonetheless embodied ideas about what constituted the age of youth, and the descriptions in these stories would have led readers to identify the heroes' qualities with the age of youth. The strength and vigour of Aurelius, although already evident when he was in his cradle, were most manifest when he reached his late teens, and much of the following plot depended on him being in his youthful years, as an apprentice first on land and then at sea, then as a soldier. At times there is an explicit reference to biological age. Aurelius has strong arms 'being not eighteen years of age', he performs 'youthful exercises' at which he excels, and he is surrounded by 'young maidens' who all fall in love with the 'gallant youth'. And then there are his activities as a soldier, when he exhibits a 'love of arms', having failed to gain the love of his master's daughter. There are also his 'flames of love', 'love tortured', his courtship, love letters, and the 'unparallel'd beauty' of his beloved, all inextricably linked with feats of arms and bravery. Aurelius exemplifies passion and physical strength, which are directly and indirectly associated in the plot with youthful years.

The youth as passionate lover was also the hero of many ballads and chapbooks revolving around courtship, marriage, and relations between the sexes. Again, emotions and love were not presented as exclusive qualities of the young; in some stories, for example, older widows displayed sensuous, passionate love as well. In ballads and songs there were adult lovers, among them kings, princes, courtiers and landlords, who were implicated in romance and courtship. Yet by and large, love songs and courtship chapbooks were inhabited by fair and lovely maids, and by sweet, pretty lasses; by passionate young lovers, and by unfaithful lads; by free and independent bachelors, and by many a poor man's son or daughter who married and lived happily ever after.[80] In chapbook tales the heroes were nearly always young, frequently servants or apprentices. While the merchant's daughter in the story of Aurelius refused Aurelius's love because she was still too young to appreciate it – 'she not exceeding fourteen,' as the author was careful to explain – most of the ballads and chapbooks involved young people in their late teens and early or mid-twenties, and the plots concerned marriage. Most young heroes displayed a 'burning desire' and passion, and their behaviour was portrayed as relatively free of subjugation to strict religious codes. Gendered stereotypes were quite pronounced. So young women were passionate but also pretty and docile, while young men's passion was accompanied at times by arrogance and unfaithfulness. Margaret Spufford has shown that in the chapbooks the conventional characterisation of young women was as shy virgins who eagerly wanted to get married. Overall, passion and affection take precedence in these love stories over material considerations, and courtship involves passionate declarations, uninhibited meetings in an ale-house or a dancing place, as well as visits and meetings at home, with the approval of parents and kin. Indeed, many chapbooks and ballads evoked the power of a young man's love and passion, rather than his material and social interests: 'Were thou the richest in worldly treasures in this City, my love could not be more firm to thee than now it is,' declares an apprentice to a serving-maid.[81]

Some young females were portrayed as brave and resolute rather than docile, faithful or kind; that is, they exhibited qualities associated more with their age than with their sex. Long Meg of Westminster has been singled out by Spufford for her unfeminine qualities. Meg is a London servant who arrives from Lancashire, and she performs acts of bravery which would have more befitted male servants and apprentices. She protects with force her female companions on the way to London, as well as poor men, women and children in London itself. She even leads an army of laundresses against the Dauphin of France.[82] If not exhibiting physical strength, many young females in the ballads and popular stories were presented as vibrant, witty and resolute in their actions. So a ballad could represent a Scottish lass as a proud and determined young woman, who refuses many rich and pretty suitors, and eventually finds the husband she fancies.[83] Such a heroine presented an alternative to the desperately in love and eager to marry young maid of many chapbooks. Other 'bonny lasses' in ballads are portrayed as 'brave, lovely, and free', rather than pretty and loving; and some maids are depicted as charitable, courageously saving the lives of their beloved, and poverty-stricken, lads. Still other young ballad heroines are not deceived by unfaithful lovers, and with their wit and resolution are determined not to succumb to the flattery of young men.[84] In some chapbooks the attitude of young females to premarital intercourse shows similar marks of determination and resolution.[85]

Some popular stories presented males as sharp-minded, calculating and manipulative, rather than merely forceful and brave. Many youths in such stories are outlaws and criminals, con men and tricksters who outwit their elders and superiors. The best example of this type of hero is in Francis Kirkman's *The English Rogue*, in which con men and rogues learn their tricks during their apprenticeship, and then plot to outdo their own masters. In *Eastward Hoe*, Quicksilver mocks his master's charitable values and exposes the hypocrisy, greed and material values of the urban classes. In Jacobean plays, apprentices are likewise portrayed as outwitting their dull masters, marrying their daughters, and getting what they want by running away.[86] Even in chivalric romance, where the young hero's physical strength was his single most admirable quality, youths could display sharpness of mind and good judgement which surpassed that of their superiors. John Hawkwood's promotion to commander and then captain is attributed not only to his courage, but also to his 'excellent, sharp, and deep judgement', his 'good counsell' and his capacity to surpass in 'spede and forwardness his fellow captains' who were 'esteemed much more worthy'.[87]

These literary images of youths as sharp, witty and vigorous must have reflected widespread views of young age. Popular stories and ballads, although subject to literary conventions and genres, did not display the skills and values of exceptionally gifted or educated writers, but for the most part were written by, and catered for, ordinary folk. As historians have recently shown, the cost of popular stories and ballads, their authorship, their wide distribution throughout the country, and the themes that figure in them all indicate a wide and non-gentle readership. Consumers of cheap print included urban and rural inhabitants, from merchants and artisans to yeomen, husbandmen and agricultural labourers. Many chapbooks were also written with an eye to a young readership – the serving-maid, the apprentice and the schoolboy – and young people, both men and women, must have been among the most ardent consumers of cheap literature, especially histories, chivalric romances and courtship manuals.[88] The social diffusion of chivalric romances, which in their medieval forms catered mostly to youthful aristocratic audiences, is already evident in the sixteenth century.[89] Once printing allowed wider readership, the ideals of chivalric romance were seized and transmitted with ease, which suggests that images of youth as adventurous, courageous, vigorous and witty were familiar and found a receptive audience among gentle and non-gentle people alike. Unlike devotional and didactic literature, chivalric romance was not designed to explain what youth ought to be. Whether to entertain, inform or inspire, popular literature reflected the public's tastes, preferences, and occasionally their attitudes as well. It therefore reveals what must have been latent, but widespread, images of biological age.

Such sentiments stood in sharp contrast to the images of youth conveyed in didactic and religious literature; in fact, the two sets of images were sometimes diametrically opposed. So the activities the moralist deemed 'youthful vanities' (i.e. sports and games, recreations, physical activities) were precisely the ones described in the story of Aurelius as activities which gained for him admiration and praise; and his amorous undertakings, which would have been anathema to the preacher, were the driving force of his heroic adventures. Even the young hero's display of revenge, something moralists condemned as sinful and reckless, was an underlying motive for his actions, and it was depicted as a normal, if not admirable, trait. This antithetical treatment was to some extent a reflection of the respective biases of the genres. In devotional literature, as in the medieval preaching tradition, youths were chastised and addressed moralistically; in some types of popular literature, as in medieval chivalric romance, young heroes were idolised, satirised or scolded leniently. Both genres presented their points of view in a magnified and overly-dramatised manner to suit the needs and intentions of the authors, and the opposition of the two sets of images of youth must to some extent be considered the outcome of such magnification. At the same time, the contrast in treatment suggests that there was tension between two sets of values which conflicted, rather than simply coexisted.

Inexperience

Aristotle's judgement that young people's lives were 'regulated more by feeling than by reasoning' derived from his understanding of human rationality and its organic evolution in three phases, from a period of growth in childhood and youth, through the attainment of ripeness and the peak of rational powers in middle life, to eventual decline into old age and decay. Closely associated with this understanding of human biological and mental growth was the conviction that growing older also brought a gradual accumulation of experience, which enhanced the human capacity to reason and judge. Human reason, according to Aristotle, reached perfection as a result of organic evolution, but also as a result of social experience. Young people had 'exalted notions' of themselves and of what they could achieve, for 'they have not yet been humbled by life or learnt its necessary limitations'. Men in the prime of their lives, on the other hand, 'neither trust everybody nor distrust everybody, but judge people correctly'.[90] Many life-cycle models, especially those involving six or seven ages, allowed for a distinction between childhood and boyhood on the one hand, and adolescence, youth and maturity on the other, so that the relative maturity of youth alongside its more childish qualities was acknowledged. This was recognised by Augustine, who emphasised not only the growing sins of young people, but also their greater rationality and wider experience. In adolescence, 'action and knowledge are added to the five bodily senses' which had governed the early years of infancy and childhood (sight, hearing, smell, taste and touch).[91]

As Burrow has shown, this close link between age, reason and experience can also be found in medieval poetry, in discussions of the qualities of the ideal ruler, and in hagiographical writings of Anglo-Saxon monks. In the biographies of saints, the child was referred to as the *puer senex*: the exceptional child who acquired great wisdom and power to judge, and, like the biblical figure of Samuel, was young in age but old in wisdom.[92] The idea that life's meanings and limitations could only be fully appreciated by those who suffered losses and experienced the gravity of life was expressed in poetry and sermons; and the belief that true knowledge and wisdom came only with advancing years was common to monks, preachers, poets and educators.[93] The educational theories of the humanists did not radically depart from this view of the evolution from childhood to adulthood as both a biological and a social process. The difference between these two aspects of human growth – organic development and social influence through experience – was not clear-cut, however, and they were described by Thomas Elyot, for example, as mutually affecting a child as he grew up.[94]

These views were not only held by humanists and other learned authorities. Ordinary people associated young years with lack of reason and understanding, characteristics first and foremost evident in small children. In his autobiography, Thomas Melhuish recorded his early conversion, when at the age of eight he had powerful visitations and was fully convinced of the truth, but when he wrote his autobiography in older age he regarded this early enthusiasm with some suspicion, and added: 'as far as my capacity at that age could rightly distinguish'. Even the most pious children were at the age of eight suspected of a lack of seriousness and childishness.[95] As children grew up, they were credited with enhanced capacities to understand, reason and judge, and contemporaries would have referred to them as approaching the years of understanding, or the age of discretion and consent. Although the age of discretion was not strictly a legal term, it was nonetheless given some acknowledgement in the law, especially in some of the rights accorded to a child as he or she grew up. These rights included disposing of goods, consenting to marry, and choosing a guardian. In the Anglican church, adolescents from age 12 were also thought capable of assuming the responsibilities involved in confirmation and taking first communion.[96] These formulations of rights and responsibilities implied some notion of the differences between younger children – up to somewhere around the early and mid-teens; the age boundaries were not clear cut – and adolescents. Older children acquired rational powers and the capacity to make choices based on informed judgement, and hence they could make moral judgements and have some discretion to govern themselves.[97] This relative maturity was understood as the outcome not only of biological development, but also of greater experience in the world. 'At 14 the son is become a stripling,' as one writer explained. 'His courage tendeth to manliness, and his wits are quick and piercing; therefore his nature and experience call upon the parent to sit downe and take counsel and to weigh with himself his child's natural disposition.'[98]

But accumulation of experience was believed to be a long process, which could continue well after a child reached the age of discretion, his twentieth birthday, the legal age of 21, and even beyond. Samuel Bownas was singled out as an exceptionally sensible youth when he reached his mid-teens, and George Brysson thought that he was 'but young' when, at the age of 20, he was apparently quite capable of confronting his father with a reasoned argument. Many people believed that some aspects of politics were beyond the grasp of the young, not because they lacked the capacity to reason, but because they 'knew not what [they] might come to,' as Elizabeth Stirredge recalled; and other youths were confronted with the argument that they could not grasp the reason of measures taken against their nonconforming parents 'before they grew up more to man's estate'.[99] Mary Pennington referred to herself as 'young' when she was 20 years old, although evidently she thought of herself as quite serious and spiritually mature at the time; and she referred to her husband, who was about the same age, in similar terms.[100] Other spiritual autobiographers depicted themselves in their youthful years as being young in age but quite mature in their spiritual lives, and the very contrast they made between age and religion, while serving to enhance their reputation for godliness, could only have been made on the basis of more common assumptions about the limitations of young years until well into the early twenties.

This belief in the long experience required before an adolescent and a youth could become fully mature had many other expressions. It was demonstrated in fables and moral tales which appeared in books of advice and guides for young apprentices,[101] in autobiographies which described the conflicts between young people and their parents in terms of the inexperience of the youth, rather than his indiscipline and insubordination,[102] and in popular fiction. In *The Honourable Prentice*, the hero John Hawkwood is portrayed as courageous and sharp-minded from his early life, making him the 'only absolute and best soldier'; but these qualities were also related to what he had learned 'by long experience in the warres'.[103] Long experience was also thought essential in many professions and crafts, and the justification for the Elizabethan Statute of Artificers, which made a seven-year apprenticeship mandatory, was couched in terms of the experience necessary to obtain perfection in a craft. Only at the age of 24 did a young man acquire judgement, sufficient experience, and the 'full or perfect knowledge of the art or occupation that he professes'.[104] Business failures and bankruptcies were also explained in terms of the youthfulness of the traders and merchants involved.[105] Perhaps the best illustration of the importance placed on long experience, and consequently on the extension of the period of youth, is the autobiography of Richard Baxter. Using various images, Baxter conveyed his belief in the long years of experience required to bring a person to maturation, which meant acquiring the capacity to distinguish between truth and mere appearances, to realise the intricacies of human nature and of people's tendency to 'stir up all their powers to defend what they have once said', and to comprehend the value of 'reconciling principles'. He likened his life to a tree which grew 'downwards and upwards both at once', and said that 'the roots increase as the bulk and branches do'; it was also like a long road on which 'he hath often gone', an account which he 'hath often cast up', and an instrument 'which he hath often played on'. Only these repeated experiences enabled him to acquire competent judgement of, and a greater acquaintance with, 'a multitude of particular mistakes of the world, which [in my youth] I was the more in danger of because I had only the *faculty* of knowing them but did not *actually* know them'.[106]

Among less educated people, an important signpost in this process of maturation, if not the most important, was marriage. As is by now well known, the mean age at marriage in early modern England was late, and most young people could not expect to marry and begin a family of their own before they reached their late twenties. Trends in marriage ages show that between 1550 and 1700 the mean age at marriage for men fluctuated between 27.6 and 29.3, while that for women was between 26 and 26.8.[107] Beliefs about the inexperience of youth were tied in with attitudes towards marriage, for early modern Englishmen not only married late, but expressed a pronounced preference for late marriage. 'Do not marry till you find that you can stand on your own legs,' was the advice of a father to his apprenticed son,[108] and the prohibition on the marriage of apprentices was also partly justified in economic terms.

But marriage was judged not only in terms of possession of financial resources. Among the upper classes, where resources were more than sufficient, and consequently where age at marriage was lower than in the population at large, the marriage ceremony did not necessarily signal the beginning of adult life.[109] Education and experience in the form of travel, as was normal among the upper classes, were considered a prerequisite for full independence to be granted, even after the marriage ceremony took place. The Countess of Warwick recalled in her autobiography that her brother, who married in his late teens, 'being then judged to be too young to live with his wife', was sent shortly after the marriage ceremony to France, while his wife was brought to their house. Her own son, who was married at about the age of 19, was likewise sent abroad while his new bride was taken to live with the Countess of Warwick. They were both judged 'too young to live together'.[110]

Lower down in the social scale, early marriages were treated with suspicion and outright disapproval, even when material resources were sufficient to start a new family. Sometimes this was a matter of the age difference between prospective spouses. William Lilly recalled his hesitations before he offered his widowed mistress marriage, 'the disproportion of years, and fortune being so great betwixt us'; his mistress correspondingly reacted with reluctance, arguing that 'he was too young for her'.[111] Lilly was 25 years old, approaching the standard age of marriage of most young people at the time. But even when there was no age difference, when resources were sufficient to start a new family, and when the two people expressed the wish to get married, they could still be considered too young. In his autobiography, William Stout recalled that his niece, whom he had brought up in her early childhood, married against his advice and without his consent. She was 19 years old, and her husband, a grocer and ironmonger in Cartmel, Lancashire, was about her age. Stout himself had resources enough to enable them to start on their own, but nevertheless decided to withhold financial assistance. 'They being both so young,' Stout later reasoned, 'I had noe hopes they would do well.' He decided to wait 'till they knew themselves better and [could] make good use of it'.[112] When George Fox returned to his parents after his service as an apprentice away from home, he was pressed by them to think about getting married, but refused. 'I told them I was but a lad,' he later recalled, explaining not that he lacked the financial means, but rather that he 'must get wisdom'.[113] He was about 20 years old, certainly no longer a boy, even by most uses of the term at the time. The prohibition on the marriage of apprentices was also justified not only on the grounds of lack of material means, but because an 'apprentice may come to have a family of children while he himself is but a boy'.[114]

So it was not only the possession of sufficient financial resources but also the experience thought necessary to handle them which counted. The ability to manage resources sensibly, to act diligently and industriously, to make calculations and decisions regarding economic life were considered things that required long years of experience. And if a young person was thought fit to govern his own actions when he reached the age of discretion (i.e. his mid-teens), he was not deemed capable of governing and taking care of the lives of others before he reached his early and even mid-twenties. That even a married man in his mid-twenties could be considered as lacking experience in the affairs of the world is made clear in the autobiography of Walter Pringle, who at 24 years old decided to get married; but soon afterwards his father died, and he was obliged to take care of his own kinsfolk. 'Thus I was left,' he commented, 'being 24 years of age, and having little experience in the affairs of the world, with the oversight of eight of my dear brother's children, and sister's son.'[115] Pringle clearly considered himself mature enough to marry and perhaps take care of his first child, but he did not think he was experienced enough to suddenly handle the affairs of many more children and dependants – an experience he would have assumed he would acquire gradually, well after his marriage took place. He might well have recognised as his own Baxter's vision of his life as a long road along which he had to pass many times before he became fully capable and mature.

Conclusion

Notions of youth in early modern English society were in many ways conventional, if by that word one means following existing traditions and models of thinking about the age of youth. Images of the sinful and the pious youth, the disorderly and insubordinate, the vigorous, sharp and healthy, but also the inexperienced and lacking wisdom, were all rooted in traditions which were not only well defined, rich and powerful, but also socially diffuse. Contemporaries did not have to be fully acquainted with astrological theories in order to associate youth with Venus and with love, with sun or fire; nor was an understanding of Galenic physiology necessary in order to refer to youthful humours or to youth as a summer and a hot season. Nor did Englishmen during this period necessarily have to be versed in Aristotelian biology to think of human life in terms of the organic world, analogous to plants, trees and flowers. There was also medieval chivalric romance, which was transmitted, translated and reinvented to suit English audiences in the sixteenth century, in which conceptions about the passions and strength of youth were encapsulated in the twin ideals of the lover and the soldier. Above all, there was Christian morality, deriving from Augustinian theology, with its emphases on the deficiencies and limitations, as well as growing capacities, of young age. And although humanists and Protestants introduced, in the sixteenth century, a particularly vigorous discussion of the young and a powerful assault on their prodigality, subversion and sinful habits – overall their portrayal of young age derived from well-established traditions of thinking on the young.

These traditions were full of images and metaphors which could be utilised to express different views of young age, and they could mean different things to different people. For ideas and notions about youth and youthful lives had to do with religious taboos and injunctions, with visions of the social order, and with human – and what can be loosely defined as secular – hopes, and they did not combine to express a single vision based on shared assumptions about young age. Some people's attitudes towards youth were first and foremost a matter of a rigid outlook on the social order, so the 'fire' of youth was interpreted as dangerous and threatening, and images of youth deriving from the natural world were interpreted as 'poisonous fruits' or seen as a 'fruit growing wild'. For others, advancement in the world, the achievement of material wealth, health, and the future of their offspring were of the utmost concern, so youthful lives were seen as 'buds' and 'blossoming flowers'. This could lead to the attribution to youth not only of a variety of characteristics, but also to conflicting and wholly opposite ones. Boldness, irritability, and inconsiderateness; but also softness, compassion and forgiveness; rashness and vanity, but also deep affections and a capacity to absorb knowledge and learning; inactivity and idleness, but also excessive energy and vigour.

These conflicting notions were a product of the conflicting interests and preferences of different people, although they did not always correspond to distinct social groups. Clearly theologians and pedagogues, magistrates and other men in authority placed great emphasis on the social order, on patriarchal authority, religious morality and, as a consequence, on youth's wild, insolent and sinful practices. But these attributes of young age were not only prevalent among the upper classes. Among writers of autobiographies there were people of gentle origins, but also those of the middle and lower classes, and their vision of youthful sins was very similar to – often an exact duplication of – that expounded in religious manuals. Among writers and readers of popular stories and ballads there were many from among the middle and even lower classes and also some of gentle origins, and they must all have associated youth with health, social opportunity, mental vigour and so on.

Some people must have clung to both conflicting images, for there were different contexts in which a person could think, imagine or describe youthful lives. When a preacher or a layman spoke of his vision of the social order, of the role of the young, of education, or religious Truth, youth could imply threat to the social order, danger, irrationality, inexperience, not to speak of sin. When one spoke about illness, death and bereavement, when one imagined, through stories and romance, healthy and exciting lives, youth could mean a wholly different thing. Religious attitudes themselves provided conflicting ways to interpret the period of youth. So Gervase Disney could discuss in detail his youthful sins, but he could also speak of his brother and sister as pure angels. When he spoke of his own sins, it was in the context of his spiritual journey from sin to Truth; when he spoke of his brother and sister it was in the context of death and dying, and the sorrows these entailed. Richard Baxter also gave a list of his youthful sins, which he thought were natural in youth; but when he juxtaposed his young years with his old age, when he had grown into 'infirmity and decay',[116] he was bound to acknowledge and reflect on his younger years as full of vigour, provocativeness, self-confidence and affection, as well as inexperience and lack of judgement and wisdom.

This is also why the boundaries between childhood and youth on the one hand and between youth and adulthood on the other could become extremely imprecise. Even in scientific theories which aimed at explaining the passage from childhood to old age, and which abounded in numeric divisions and categories, there was no universally accepted division between childhood, adolescence, youth and so on. For there were different contexts for discussing the transition from young to adult life, and the boundaries between the ages could shift accordingly. If a Puritan spoke about his spiritual life, he could refer to himself as old in sins already at the age of 15; alternatively he could think of himself as still young in piety at the age of 20, 30 and well above. And there were varying meanings that could be attributed to youth and to the process of growing up: physical, spiritual, mental, social. So a person might be considered mentally and emotionally mature for specific rights and obligations at different times during his teens, as well as legally mature at 21; but in terms of social experience, the requirements of some professions, or responsibility for a family, he could be considered, at 18, 20, or even 25, as still quite young.

There were then sets of images, rather than a shared view, of the period of youth, and they embodied opposing values regarding young age. But even more, there were two different ways of depicting the relations between the ages: one which highlighted the contrast between the ages, and one which placed emphasis on the continuity between them. Among writers who discussed the Ages of Man, there were those who emphasised the contrast, and therefore irreconcilability, of young and old age, and they provided men and women with a whole range of equally irreconcilable images of the relations between the ages: summer and winter, hot and cold, blossoming and decay. For those Puritans and sectarians who experienced conversion during their lives, this contrast could be utilised to delineate their experience before and after their conversion. Above all, the contrasting qualities of young and old age were highlighted in popular romance and in stories which stressed the physical qualities and mental vigour of youth. Medieval chivalric romance made an explicit distinction between the knight-errant (i.e. the adventurous and irresponsible youth) and the knight-householder (i.e. the mature, responsible head of a family and household), a distinction that fitted aristocratic tastes and life styles.[117] To early modern English readers, such contrasting qualities of young and old age were more an expression of hopes and fears, and of apprehensions about growing old, about life and its vicissitudes, about health, illness and death.

The second way of depicting the relations between the ages placed greater emphasis on continuity. Here one might include Protestant writers and educational theorists who, although signalling youth as particularly prone to sin, fundamentally placed young and old age on a par: an apprentice could be reproached together with his master for excessive drinking; family manuals could criticise both young and old for negligence of their respective duties. Such continuity was recognised in various subtle ways; young people were described as gradually developing from a state of irrationality and total lack of experience in the world towards maturity and ever-expanding knowledge and wisdom, judgement and greater responsibility. In so far as physical maturation occurred in the teenage years and did not take long, such an understanding was bound to express some kind of a prolongation of youth, a prolongation reinforced by the pattern of late marriage and household formation prevalent in England during this period. But this was based on the fundamental belief in young age as preparation for, rather than diversion from, adult life. 'A maid at twelve and a boy at 14 enter into that age wherein body and mind are prepared and preparing to that state of life wherein they themselves may be governours of others,'[118] as it was formulated in a domestic guide of the period. Rather than emphasise generational contrasts, as was often the case in chivalric romance and other types of popular tales and ballads, such an understanding placed greater stress on the gradual transition from childhood to youth, and thence to adult life; from infancy to the age of discretion, when adolescents had acquired some reason and experience to make judgements concerning their own actions, and to marriage, when they were more experienced and could become responsible for other people's lives.

One might argue that both ways of depicting the relations between the ages had to do with real lives: in some ways youths in early modern English society contrasted and even conflicted with adults, and in others the period of youth was a preparation for adult life. But in the end one is bound to observe how little of the concrete lives of young people these contrasting images reflected. In his autobiography, Edward Barlow described his early life as a son of a poor husbandman in Lancashire, and referred to himself at about 11 or 12 years as 'being grown up', and said that he and his brothers 'must provide for ourselves, or else want our bread'.[119] Such an allusion to a 12-year-old adolescent is extremely rare in the sources we have described, not only because Barlow referred to himself as grown up at that age (some Puritans who discussed their sins regarded themselves as quite mature in their early teens), but because, for Barlow, being grown up at 12 years had an economic meaning. For all their versatility and richness, ideas about the sin or piety of youths, their insubordination or exceptional vigour and beauty, even notions about the inexperience of the young, reflected very little of the lives of youth and of what growing up was like during this period. Little in these images reflected the working lives and sometimes deprivations of young people, and the autonomy and independence which many a youth had already acquired in his mid- and late teens. Nor did they reflect the process of social maturation involved in separations from parents, in the moving away from home, and in many other circumstances of life we shall describe in the following chapters.

2 Early Lives: Separations and Work

It is difficult to examine the life of youth in early modern English society without first looking at their early childhood, for there was no single event which marked the transition from childhood to adolescence and youth. Although in the course of their teens most young people left their parental home – mainly to enter some form of service elsewhere – there was continuity between childhood and adolescence, between the children's upbringing before they entered service, and their lives as servants later on. That continuity had to do with their working lives, for by the time they entered service, whether in agriculture, in a craft apprenticeship, in domestic service, or in some form of apprenticeship in the distributive trades, most young people had already been accustomed to work, sometimes for as long as three, four or even six or seven years of their lives. So entry into service did not signal their entry into the workforce. Nor did the departure for service mark the first time children were separated from their parents, for intermittent periods away from home were the lot of many children of this time. So entry into service did not mark as sharp a break in their lives as might first appear.

Historians have so far paid little direct attention to the working lives of young children, partly, as in the case of the working lives of women, because of lack of adequate evidence, but partly also because of the overwhelming presence of the historiography on child labour during industrialisation.[1] More attention has been directed to the separation of children from their parents. As historical demography has shown, service away from the parental home was prevalent, but, contrary to the assumptions that some historians have made, the majority of English children during this period did not leave home before they reached their mid-teens, and the majority of servants were in the age group 15–24, rather than younger.[2] Yet the importance of the departure into service in the lives of children and their families notwithstanding, many children did separate from their parents at earlier points in their childhood at any time between the ages of five and their early teens, for periods of weeks, months, a year or longer. These separations are less amenable to quantification, and the evidence on them comes mostly from autobiographies of the period.[3] As we shall see, these early separations were common, occurred in a wide variety of circumstances, and, together with the experience of work, were formative in the upbringing of many young people.

The Labouring Child

In 1700, as in 1500, the basis of the English economy was still agricultural, and most boys and girls were reared in a rural environment. Two factors influenced the recruitment and integration of children to work. On the one hand, children were bound to be drawn into the workforce early in their lives, since about one-third of the early modern English population was under the age of 15, and labour was the most important factor of production.[4] On the other hand, the economy was also characterised by chronic under-employment, and children, not to speak of those of tender years, were physically limited and less skilled than adults. So their work was also bound to have been irregular and characterised by a great deal of unemployment.[5] All this meant that children were employed to carry out single tasks as they grew up, according to the needs and types of skill required by their families.

Some of the most common tasks allocated by families to children involved animal husbandry; most authors of autobiographies who made any reference to work they had performed in their childhood years mentioned some form of work with animals – for example, sheep, geese or draught animals.[6] Sheep growing, rearing of cattle and horses, and dairy farming predominated in the western and the northern parts of the country, but enclaves of pastoral farming also existed in the south and the east, as well as in the less fertile soils of parts of Yorkshire, Lincolnshire, Norfolk and Suffolk. Many yeomen in these regions kept large flocks of sheep to manure the soil, and children assisted in bringing sheep to the unploughed hill pasture during the day, and returning them to arable fields at night.[7] Moreover, until well into the sixteenth century, many households in the south and the east were self-sufficient and kept some animals to provide for their basic needs. In the midland plains, for example, households relied on cereal production, but also on animals; a few cows, pigs, or small flocks of sheep which children could tend to were kept to provide cheese, butter and clothing. In other regions within the mixed farming zone there were still large enclaves of pastoral farming, as in Cambridgeshire and the forests of Suffolk, Kent, Essex and the Midlands, where wood pasture predominated and shepherding by young children must also have been common.[8]

Where crop farming predominated in the south and the east, children assisted in a host of other agricultural tasks. Although the work was more seasonal than in the pastoral areas, some tasks were allocated to children nearly every season of the year. One major job was ploughing, especially in the autumn season, but sometimes also in the winter and the spring, depending on the crop schedules adopted by individual farmers.[9] Thomas Carleton, William Stout, Simon Forman and Josiah Langdale all remembered working at the plough in their young years.[10] In other seasons, children assisted in harrowing,[11] scaring birds once the corn was sown,[12] weeding, picking fruit, and spreading dried dung to manure the soil in the spring and summer.[13] During the harvest, children also contributed their share by bringing food to those working in the field, leading horses, and helping to bind the corn into sheaves.[14] Older children also participated in haymaking and shearing.[15] Among the very poor, children assisted during the harvest weeks by gleaning alongside their mothers.[16] Even in winter, children provided some assistance: threshing, stacking sheaves, cleaning the barn and, in places and soils that required it in the winter, ploughing as well.[17]

Children carried out household tasks throughout the year: fetching water and gathering sticks for fuel,[18] going on errands,[19] assisting mothers in milking, preparing food, cleaning, washing and mending. In some rural industries, which expanded in the north and the west, children were also taught to spin and card, and girls were trained in hand-knitting, lacemaking and stocking-knitting; the latter became, by the late seventeenth century, a large industry.[20] In some towns, domestic industries such as clothmaking and pinmaking also provided work for children.[21] The pinmaking industry could employ younger boys and girls to put knobs on pins by hand, and from the 1570s, when pinmaking with brass wire became more widespread, in London it was a source of living for many poor adults and their children.[22]

Gender differences in the tasks allocated to children were to some extent already apparent at young ages. William Stout remembered that while he and his brothers were required to assist in husbandry, his sister was 'early taught to read, knit and spin, and also needle work'. When she grew up, she continued to work alongside her mother, assisting in waiting on her younger brothers, and in preparing food and clothing.[23] Girls also provided assistance in housework: in washing, preparing food and marketing. In an estate near Bolton, payments paid by the bailiff to labourers included those for washing to 'wife Turner and her folks'. Some of these folks were probably young daughters.[24] But the division of tasks between boys and girls, especially among the very poor, was anything but clear-cut. In a petition of the inhabitants of Hertfordshire to King James I it was claimed that young girls in that region were employed in 'picking wheat a great time of the year'.[25] In some estates in the north of the country, there are records of payments for 'divers women' for turf-gathering and for weeding; and tasks such as fetching water and milk, gathering sticks, picking and spreading dung, and doing errands were performed by young brothers and sisters alike. The account of Henry Best, a yeoman in Yorkshire, shows that his 'spreaders of muck and molehills' were for the most part women, boys and girls.[26]

The pace of entry of children to work was gradual. While younger children could assist in various jobs – fetching water and milk, gathering sticks for fuel, bringing food to those working in the fields, or picking dung – the more demanding agricultural tasks were normally not given to children before they reached their early teens. Thomas Shepard remembered that he was put to keep geese when he was no more than three years old; but tending flocks of sheep normally did not start until around the age of 10. Thomas Tryon, Samuel Bownas and William Stout all looked after sheep when they were 10, 11 and 14 respectively.[27] Ploughing, which required physical strength and an ability to direct the animals properly, was not normally given to youngsters before 11 or 12 years of age.[28] In the harvest, children under 10 or 12 years of age carried food and assisted the binders; but only at about 12 years and upwards did they begin to drive loaded wagons and lead horses, while participation in haymaking was probably delayed until the mid-teens.[29]

If they were strong enough for their age, and the family was poor and in great need, a child could be recruited to plough or join the older shepherds as early as the age of nine rather than at ten.[30] But overall, training in the more skilled and demanding tasks normally began when children reached about 10 years. 'I believe I was not older then 10 when my father took me to seek the scanty rewards of industry,' was how John Clare remembered the beginning of his going out to the fields in the early 1800s alongside his father, a Northamptonshire agricultural labourer. A century and a half earlier, Edward Barlow, the son of a poor Lancashire husbandman, was sent out to work as a farm labourer at around 11 or 12 years old, 'being [then] grown up', as he wrote later in his autobiography. And William Stout and his brothers, sons of a far wealthier yeoman, began to contribute their share on their father's estate in a variety of agricultural tasks 'as we attained to the age of ten or twelve years'.[31] It is doubtful that a very young child worked full days or very long hours in weeding or threshing.[32] Nor was it likely that spinning would become a normal routine at the age of seven. Evidence from autobiographies written in the nineteenth century by people who grew up in families who relied on handloom weaving for their living suggests that their entry to work was gradual. At seven they spread cotton to help an older brother who spinned; then they began to wind, and at the age of 10 or 11, to spin. Nor was the winding of bobbins done full-time; it began with assistance to mothers, and alternated with going on errands, fetching water, and taking some time off.[33] This was probably how a Lancashire 10-year-old boy, who testified in the 1630s that his mother had brought him up to spin wool, learnt his craft.[34] The pace of entry into most tasks, in agriculture as well as industry, was bound to be adjusted to the physical and mental limitations of the youngsters;[35] so that while child labour was widespread, it did not begin 'as soon as children could walk,' as J.H. Plumb put it many years ago.[36] Nor did it start at a standard age of seven or eight years old.[37]

By their mid-teens many children had acquired some agricultural proficiency. In his autobiography, Thomas Tryon claimed that when he was 14, after two or three years of working as a shepherd, he 'was accounted one of the best shepherds in the country', and shortly afterwards he became responsible for a small flock of sheep on his own.[38] In his diary, the 14-year-old Thomas Isham recorded the day when he and his father went out into the fields to 'decide where new ditches should be dug and hedges set'. Young Isham was the son of a Northampton gentleman, and he was probably never required to actually work in hedging or ditching; but his comment makes it quite clear that by the age of 14 children could become knowledgeable in some agricultural skills and specialisations, for laying a hedge and digging a watercourse required great skill and professionalism.[39] Josiah Langdale, who began to learn to plough at the age of nine, could conduct four horses and 'plow alone' by the time he was 13; two years later he became an agricultural servant. That the skills he had obtained in childhood could be advantageous when he entered service is clear from Henry Best's account of the customs governing the hiring of servants in Yorkshire. Best claimed that it was normal to offer 30sh. per year for a youth who had been 'brought up at the plough'.[40] Women must also have acquired a great deal of proficiency and agricultural skill by the time they left their homes for service. Thomas Hardy's *Tess of the D'Urbervilles*, written more than two centuries after the accounts we are examining here had been recorded, vividly portrays the type of skill the heroine, reared as the daughter of a 'professed poulterer', had acquired by the time she left home and applied for a job as a farm servant:

> While the old lady had been speaking Tess . . . had placed the fowls severally in her lap, and she had felt them over from head to tail, examining their beaks, their combs, the manes of the cocks, their wings, and their claws. Her touch enabled her to recognize them in a moment, and to discover if a single feather were crippled or draggled. She handled their crops, and knew what they had eaten, and if too little or too much.[41]

In small shops and some crafts, older boys and girls could also assist more skilfully as they reached around 10 years. Oliver Sansom was employed by his father in his small shop when he was 10 years old;[42] and in large estates there were carpenters, joiners, tilers and plasterers who were hired with trainees who were often their sons, and the sons were no more than 13 and 14 years old.[43] In some small towns, too, a substantial minority of youngsters never left their homes and were integrated into their parental occupations and small businesses when they were 10 years old or in their early teens, as the research of Graham Mayhew makes clear.[44] In early seventeenth-century Bristol there was a marked tendency among craftsmen, particularly in the building, textile, wood and metal trades, to hire apprentices whose fathers had the same occupation, or one belonging to the same industry. Of the twenty Bristol soapmakers who sent their sons to become apprentices in the early seventeenth century, twelve bound their sons to other Bristol soapmakers.[45] Some of these apprentices may have begun to assist their fathers in their shops in their early or mid-teens, so that by the time they entered an apprenticeship at 16 or 17 they had already acquired some understanding of the soap-boiling business, or, for example, of coopering. In mid-eighteenth-century London Thomas Holcroft assisted his father in hawking various wares between the ages of 6 and 11, and five years later he became apprentice to a shoemaker. Since his father was also a shoemaker, it is not unlikely that young Thomas also assisted him in his shop during his early teens, before he was formally bound as an apprentice.[46]

The Changing Environment of Work

The physical and mental limitations of children under the age of 10 were nowhere more evident than in their overwhelming presence among the growing numbers of poor and those relying on parish relief. In the course of the sixteenth century and the first half of the seventeenth, the English population more than doubled – by 1630 it had reached about 5 million[47] – and one of the consquences of this growth, and of the inflation that accompanied it, was aggravation of poverty. Studies have shown that the majority of the poor were children and old people, but also that among children the relative numbers of those under 10 were greater than those in their early teens.[48] So children who had not yet reached that age worked less but were also particularly vulnerable to poverty, and liable to become a burden on their families.

As they grew up, children became less vulnerable economically, but the demands placed on them were greater. Some relatively simple agricultural tasks, such as weeding or threshing, were arduous and very demanding, even for a child of 10 or 12 years. Edward Barlow referred to all types of country work he did in his teens as drudgery which he grew up to detest; and when he was put to keep geese at a very tender age, Thomas Shepard felt neglected, and only afterwards, when he was relieved of that duty, did he become 'more content'.[49] Some spiritual autobiographers looked back on their experience as shepherds in childhood with longing if not delight; they saw it as 'innocent and contemplative, as also most healthful because of the constant motion in the open air', in the words of Thomas Tryon.[50] But such descriptions were written at a great distance in time, and most writers of autobiographies were people who idealised contemplation and self-reflection. Most children must have found shepherding toilsome, and at times a very lonely employment. William Dewsbury commented that when he was put to keep the sheep he 'was retired from company, so my mind was kept in my mournful estate'.[51] John Clare's description also betrays some of the hardship and loneliness involved in other agricultural employments.[52] Even simple tasks such as errands could – 'in the short days of winter its often been dark' – become threatening.[53] A century and a half earlier, Richard Norwood also remembered that as a child he acquired the habit of praying every Lord's Day, 'that I might not lose my way', when performing his duty in going on errands on the remaining days of the week. Although in mentioning this Norwood wanted to stress his habit of praying regularly when he was a child, the enduring effect on his memory of the fears of a child sent alone to do errands appears quite obvious. Above all, work in corn-growing areas, in ploughing the land, especially in fallow years or in places where the soil demanded ploughing three and even four times a year rather than once or twice,[54] was anything but light, even for a child who had already reached the age of 10 or 12. Working during the harvest was also strenuous and involved long hours, day after day, intensive work which hardly compensated for other more relaxed agricultural seasons. Gleaning, too, was physically strenuous and required long days of work for several weeks during the harvest. As John Clare recalled, his father took him at the age of 10 to work in the field, 'learing me betimes the hardship which Adam and Eve inflicted on their children by their inexperienced misdeeds, incuring the perpetual curse from god of labouring for a livelihood'.[55]

Children of wealthier yeomen were relieved of some of these duties. Given the profits which could in the course of this period be accumulated from large-scale farming, a greater number of children of yeomen were free to continue their education and schooling well into their teens, with the view of obtaining higher education or entering one of the professions.[56] Many were not required to assist in any form of labour before they were 11 or 12 years old; and then they worked only during harvest time or when they were free from school, if at all.[57] On the other hand, many children of poorer families entered a more intensified routine of work once they reached 10 or 11 years. In the course of the sixteenth century some husbandmen reduced the amount of land lying fallow each year, or adopted a more intensive crop rotation.[58] The seasonality of employment was therefore smoothed, and once children began to assist in the fields they would have been required to work more regularly around the year, in harrowing, ploughing, weeding twice or three times during the agricultural year.

Some children brought up by small husbandmen and labourers

also became wage earners. Among small husbandmen, many families combined their livelihood from smallholdings with a variety of other jobs; and among the labouring poor, most could not survive solely on the wages of the head of the family.[59] In the south, where large-scale farming and specialised production emerged, young sons of poorer cottagers and husbandmen found employment on large estates as ploughboys, harrowboys, spreaders of marl, and as labourers in other tasks.[60] From the late sixteenth century, and especially from the mid-seventeenth, poorer children could also find employment among yeomen who specialised in the cultivation of new crops, such as turnip, flax, hemp, woad, tobacco, and a variety of vegetables and fruits.[61] Without exception, these crops were labour intensive, and they provided work, on an unprecedented scale, for poorer people of both sexes and of all ages.[62] In rural industries, such as textiles, glove-making, or pin-making, there were also jobs for children.[63] And the expansion in the exploitation of local minerals in parts of Northumberland and Durham, as well as in the Midlands, south Lancashire and Somerset,[64] could provide work for children, especially in the hauling of coal in the mines.[65] The extraction of other minerals likewise involved work children could do. On the Essex coast, for example, women and children regularly gathered copper and sold it to the local copperas boilers.[66]

Some of this work was probably done by boys and girls alongside their mothers or fathers. But often wage labour involved some separation from the family. The memoir of Edward Barlow, son of a poor husbandman, shows what was probably a typical course of the working life of a child in a growing number of poor families subsisting on a small piece of land that could not provide for them all. The Barlows lived in Lancashire in the mid-seventeenth century, and their annual income was no more than £8 or £9; they were 'but poor people with six children to provide for,' as Barlow later described them. Since his father had work 'which he could do himself for it was not much', Barlow was forced to look for outside employment when he turned 10 or 11 years old. The work he found was irregular – he also mentioned that when out of work he was 'troublesom' to his parents – but it included a variety of jobs. In some neighbouring farms he used to work during the harvest, haymaking and doing other tasks; at other times he went to a nearby coal pit, where he hauled coal for wages he considered 'but small'. It was not until a year or two later – when he was about 13 years old – that Edward Barlow left for Manchester, where he became an apprentice in the textile trade.[67]

Parental Loss

Many children of this period were likely to face the death of a parent in the course of their childhood. Peter Laslett estimated that with life expectancy in pre-industrial England varying between the late twenties and the late forties, between half and two-thirds of young women would have lost their fathers by the time they married; 17 per cent of children aged 10, and 27 per cent aged 15 would have been fatherless.[68] Lists of apprentice registrations in Bristol on which the deaths of the apprentices' fathers were recorded show that up to a third of those apprenticed had lost their fathers before their apprenticeship began. The proportions were particularly high among sons of seamen – 40 (56.3 per cent) out of 71 registered; and among Bristol natives – 260 (42.7 per cent) out of 609; and they also rose following a plague.[69] In Southampton, the proportion of apprentices throughout the seventeenth century whose fathers were deceased likewise varied between a third in the early decades of the century, and a fifth from the 1670s until the 1710s.[70] If we add apprentices who had been bereaved of a mother – apprentice registers recorded only the death of the father – the proportions of orphans among apprentices must have reached well over 40 per cent, and in some decades over a half. Some confirmation of this can be obtained from autobiographies. Out of 74 autobiographies written between the sixteenth and early eighteenth centuries, in 35 (47.3 per cent), the death of a father or a mother, or both parents, occurred before the writer reached the age of 20. In their experience of parental loss during childhood and youth, writers of autobiographies were anything but unique.

There is no doubting the emotional effect and sense of deprivation caused by the death of a mother or a father in the early life of a child. All autobiographers, including those who eschewed detailed descriptions of their childhood years, make a point of the year and circumstances of the death of one or both of their parents – a small proportion had lost both parents by the time they reached their late teens[71] – making it clear that these were events of great importance, if not the most important events, in their early lives.[72] Some autobiographers, whose father or mother had died when the writer was an infant or a very small child, had dim recollections of the event, but its emotional impact was nonetheless evident as the child grew up. Elias Osborn, whose mother died when he was two years old, still made a point of the fact that he had been raised to remember her as a 'very tender, conscientious woman', whose memory was carried by all members of the family. Samuel Bownas, whose father died when he was a small infant, remembered that his father's conduct became a model for his upbringing, for his mother 'would frequently in winter evenings take opportunities to tell the sundry passages of my dear father's sufferings'. And Robert Blair recalled that he received 'certain information' about the piety of his father when he 'came to some years'. Some autobiographies suggest that even when the memory of the father himself was dim, his death could have long-lasting effects. Benjamin Bangs admitted that his father died when he was 'so young that I can remember little of him', but he still remembered that his mother was left 'a very sorrowful widow'.[73] Perhaps above all there was the insecurity of being brought up by one parent. The prospect of losing both parents before adolescence – 'and so I was left fatherless and motherless, when I was about ten years old,' as Thomas Shepard briskly put it – although not very high, still loomed large over families, and especially over those where one parent had already died. Samuel Bownas was brought up by a mother who not only elevated the qualities of her dead husband, but 'frequently [put] me in mind, that if she should be taken away, I should greatly miss her, both for advice and other ways to assist me'. The mother urged him to 'fear the Lord' while still young so he might be 'favoured with his blessing'. And so young Samuel endorsed her suggestions, 'being afraid that she would die before I was capable to live in the world'.[74]

For children who lost a parent at an older age, the rupture in their lives and its emotional effects were harder still. Some spiritual autobiographers described the death of a parent as an event which had an important religious meaning. Robert Blair attributed the first steps in his religious education to his father's death, when he was six years old. 'And so being the youngest of six left upon the hands of a widow not well furnished,' he wrote, '. . . the Lord early owned me, and began to catechise me.' William Bowcock also remembered that his father's death when he was eleven years old 'produced some serious thoughts', which eventually led him to embrace the Baptist faith. For Arise Evans, whose father had died when he was seven years old, the event was a major turning point in his spiritual life, for it was shortly afterwards that he became aware of the power of God, and resolved 'to make it my whole work, to think on God continually'.[75]

There is a sense in which these recollections cannot be trusted as evidence of the true effects of parental death on children. Such accounts were written years after the event, and while the description of some details concerning the material consequences of parental death, to which we shall soon turn, was probably more or less accurate, the evocation of the emotional reaction of the writer is likely to have been moulded by the experience and understanding acquired in the time that had elapsed. Most autobiographers tried to elevate the spiritual qualities of a dead parent – 'My father . . . was addicted to prayer . . . and how tenderly he walked,' commented Robert Blair[76] – not only because they had a natural respect for the deceased, but also because they desired to emphasise the parental contribution to their spiritual lives. For example, Blair's autobiography conveys the impression that his father's death hastened his religious education; but there was in fact nothing unusual for a child to be catechised at the age of seven, when Blair began his religious training. Major events such as diseases, plagues, natural disasters, accidents, misfortunes of a variety of sorts, played an important role in spiritual autobiographies, and they were all given religious significance as signs of Providence and as turning points in the authors' journey in search of the Truth. The death of close kin, especially a parent, was quite naturally described and utilised in similar terms.

But underneath some of these accounts there still lurks the sheer sense of deprivation and loss experienced by the author. Thomas Sheppard remembered that before the death of his father – he was then 10 years old and living with a stepmother – he prayed 'very strongly and heartily' for his father's life.[77] Arise Evans was somewhat younger when his father died, and the effect was no less marked. 'But in the midst of my jollity,' so he described it, 'a cloud comes over me, death takes away my father before I was seven years old.' As with nearly all other autobiographies, it is difficult to capture the emotional atmosphere in which young Arise had been reared, but it seems that his attachment to his father was deep, and he also attributed to his brothers his misfortune in being left out of his father's will. Overall, the sense of pain and anger is unmistakable in his description of the material consequences of his father's death, as well as in his evocation of his religious awakening soon afterwards. To a serving-maid who watched him 'sit solitary alone' and enquired: 'art thou Sorry for thy fathers death?', he replied that he was contemplating 'to go to [his] father at any time' by committing suicide; and with her reply, 'O childe, no; thy father is gone to Heaven, but if thou make away thy self thou wilt go to Hell', he began to be able to overcome his grief and took consolation in thinking upon God 'continually'.[78]

A few autobiographers make even more explicit references to

the emotional consequences of the death of one of their parents in their childhood. Thus Adam Martindale wrote an account of the death of his mother and its effect on his family, which he clearly bore in his heart for many years to come. 'But these things were onely the beginning of sorrowes, which in a short time after, came thicke and threefold,' he began the account of the diseases which afflicted his family when he was about nine years old. His mother died 'to the unspeakable griefe and losse of us all', and to the 'inexpressible sorrow' of his sister, who herself fell sick later on. It is also clear that young Martindale was affected by the emotional reaction of his father, who appears to have been stricken by grief. He summoned Adam's sister and her husband to stay with them all so 'my father and she might be comforts and assistants one to another', but this did not heal his wounds. When he was forced to confront, shortly afterwards, the death of his daughter and a little grandchild, he was so 'overwhelmed with griefe for the losse of his dearly beloved wife and daughter, and . . . of his sweet grand-child', that he 'fell againe to be much disordered in his head'.[79] Simonds D'Ewes described the effect that the death of his grandfather had on his mother, who 'almost drowned in tears for the loss of so dear and loving a father'. Simonds had been brought up by his grandparents. He was eight years old when his grandfather died, and, upon hearing about his death, 'I would in no case believe it; for now my afflictions came so thick upon me, as I even feared to make myself further miserable by believing this'. His own mother died when he was 16 years old and already in Cambridge, and he devoted a special section in his autobiography to describing her illness and death. '"Ah child," said she, "thou hast a sick mother;" to which I answered her with silent tears', was his recollection of his final moments with her.[80]

Above all, the death of a parent called for immediate decisions which affected the lives of some or all children in the family. The sense of urgency that the death of the head of a family could create was powerfully conveyed in the autobiography of William Stout, who described in detail the circumstances surrounding the death of his father in 1679. As soon as his father died – a death the family had anticipated, for he was ill for quite some time – the family appears to have reoriented itself to life without him. The mother took charge of the family affairs and hired an experienced servant in husbandry to manage the estate 'till her sons were capable to manage the same'. Next came Josiah, the eldest brother, who at the age of 18 was recruited to work in the fields. Leonard, a younger brother, who was about 14 years old, was taken from school and was likewise brought to work regularly, in ploughing and carting. William himself, then 16 years old, was bound as an apprentice immediately following the death of his father. Elin, the sister, and Richard and Thomas, the younger brothers, were less affected in their routines. Elin was already 20 years old, but very infirm and tending to chronic illness, and she continued in household work as she had done before. As for the younger brothers, aged 5 and 10 at the death of their father, the account gives the impression that they were left to continue whatever it was they had done before.[81]

The Stouts were relatively prosperous Lancashire yeomen, and the death of the father did not radically alter their economic fortunes. Although Elizabeth Stout, the mother, took on the management of the estate with the assistance of a mature servant, the autobiography makes it clear that she had been quite accustomed to working in the fields alongside her husband and servants well before her husband's death, so she was quite prepared to continue to hold the farm on her own. All her children were well provided for by their father's will, and while taking on the supervision of the family estate with the assistance of two elder sons and arranging the apprenticeship of another, she also continued to provide for the needs of a family of six children, including William's somewhat feeble and sick sister and two younger brothers. So although William Stout's account leaves no doubt as to the new responsibilities placed on the mother and the older brothers, it also suggests that, on the whole, the affairs of the family were not seriously disrupted. The only brother whose course took on a new turn was Leonard, who was taken away from school following the death of his father. Even William was not forced to change what had already been planned for his career, for it is clear that the father had been making arrangements for William's apprenticeship well before his death; it was the timing of his going out to service, rather than the actual decision about his future course, which was affected by the father's death.[82] The Stouts then held on to their estate, under the supervision and care of a mother who continued to manage it on her own. There is nothing in the autobiography to suggest that Elizabeth Stout ever contemplated a second marriage.

In other cases, things worked out less smoothly. Benjamin Bangs, whose mother was left a widow in the 1650s, remembered that she was able to hold on to her Norfolk farm 'for some years', but evidently this was a difficult undertaking, and after some years she decided, on the advice of some friends, to sell the estate.[83] For poorer widows, the responsibility of looking after their children alone was harder still. Samuel Bownas remembered that his mother was left a widow with 'a scanty subsistence' and Thomas Chubb's mother 'laboured hard, in order to get a maintenance for herself and family'; he was obliged to do some work and therefore had 'neither time nor means for further instruction'.[84] Although none of these writers experienced complete impoverishment following the death of their fathers, they appear to have appreciated, and quite early in their lives, the difficulties imposed on a widowed mother left to care for a family of even two children – as in the case of Samuel Bownas – on her own.

Quite a few widowed parents remarried. The evidence available indicates that about 30 per cent of all those marrying in the sixteenth and seventeenth centuries were widows and widowers. Remarriage was common, and not before the mid-eighteenth century does the proportion of those who had been widows and widowers before marriage appear to have dropped.[85] From the few autobiographers who recorded their memories of the remarriage of their parents it is quite clear that the consequences were, for the children, less than desirable. John Wallis, whose father died when he was six years old, made a point of the fact that his widowed mother 'had fair opportunities of marrying well, if she had been so disposed', but she nonetheless remained single 'for the good of her children'.[86] His mother was in her early forties when she became a widow, but her son's appreciation of her choice, whatever the causes, would have been well taken by other autobiographers, who tended to portray the consequences of a parent's remarriage as difficult if not altogether disastrous. Thomas Shepard, whose mother died in 1608 when he was four years old, wrote that [his] father remarried, 'to another woman, who did let me see the difference between my own mother and a stepmother'. Lodowick Muggleton, whose mother died in the 1610s, avowed that he 'was a stranger to [his] father's house' following his father's remarriage. And Arise Evans claimed that following the death of his father he lived with his mother and stepfather 'a short time, and then put away from all, and tossed from place to place'.[87]

It is somewhat difficult to evaluate on the basis of these recollections the conduct of step-parents, for their attitude towards their stepchildren must have varied greatly depending on temperament, character, economic resources, age, and whether they had children of their own. All that can be suggested, with the evidence available to us today, is that while some step-parents were careless, unloving, and even callous,[88] others were more cooperative and did their best to bring up their spouse's children properly. Thomas Shepard, who thought that his stepmother did not love him and 'incited my father often against me', nonetheless admitted that his stepmother's attitude may not have been altogether wrong, and that 'it may be that it [the mother's turning the father against him] was justly also, for my childishness'. What these accounts convey more truly is that, however step-parents conducted themselves, the situation following remarriage was strained and in a child of tender years it aroused feelings of suspicion and estrangement.[89]

Separations from Parents

In the course of their early lives, many children were placed outside their parental home and thus forced to part from their parents. The duration of these separations could vary between a couple of days or weeks and a number of years. About a quarter of the autobiographers mention some form of boarding out during their early and late childhood before they departed for service or the university. The experience of Simonds D'Ewes, who, until the age of 16, was separated from his parents five times for periods totalling no less than twelve years, was to some extent unusual but not altogether unique, both among children of a similar social background – D'Ewes's father was a wealthy lawyer – as well as among those less well off. Thomas Shepard, the son of a small grocer in Towcester, Northamptonshire, was sent away to live with his grandparents when he was three years old, and after a couple of weeks he was placed with his uncle. Following his return to his parents, he was again boarded out for three years, between the ages of six and nine. Oliver Sansom, the son of a trader, was placed with his aunt between the ages of seven and ten, while Mary Rich, a gentleman's daughter, boarded with a gentlewoman from the age of three until she was eleven years old.[90] John Whitting, Anthony Wood, Frances Dodshon, James Fretwell, Edward Coxere, Edward Terril, Simon Forman, Joseph Oxley, Phineas Pett, George Bewley and William Johnson all spent one, two, three or four years away from their parental homes, at least once, in their childhood, before they reached their mid-teens and, in the case of males, before they began a career as university students or apprentices.

The reasons for these early separations between children and their parents varied greatly. Among autobiographers, the most common reason given was the schooling of children. As is by now well known, the sixteenth and seventeenth centuries witnessed a substantial increase in the number of schools available for elementary and higher education.[91] Some schools, such as Eton and Winchester, were well-established institutions designed for the preparation of sons of the aristocracy for a career at Oxford or Cambridge; others among the great endowed grammar schools which had also gained in reputation became more fashionable among gentry and yeomen families. In most cases, sending a son to a prestigious school dictated boarding him away.[92] The practice of 'tabling out' in towns was already well established in the sixteenth century, and the few dozens of major endowed grammar schools must have included substantial numbers of students who came from far away and who were tabled out during their studies, at times for quite substantial amounts of money.[93]

But even when a child was not sent to a particularly prestigious school, he was often boarded away from home for the purpose of schooling, and at times at a very young age. The most common reason for boarding one's son during his school years was the sheer distance of schools, any school, from one's home. The increase in the number of schools spread such institutions geographically, so that most market towns and many rural parishes had a school and only a small proportion of the rural population had no access to any kind of schooling.[94] Nonetheless, even if this meant that there was a school approximately every twelve miles,[95] many parents would still have found this distance too great, and would have boarded their children nearer to school.[96] In large towns, and especially in the rapidly expanding capital, going to school might still require boarding out if the school was not located within walking distance of home.[97] Some autobiographers were quite explicit about the difficulties caused by the distance of schools. Adam Martindale recalled when he first began to attend school. The year was 1630, and Martindale, by then seven years old, was sent to the free school of St Helens, in his own parish of Prescot. As he later described it, the school was 'almost two miles from my father's house, a great way for a little fat short legged lad (as I was) to travel twice a day'.[98] Young Martindale went to school 'cheerfully' owing to his 'innate love of learning', but others found a long journey to school more daunting. James Fretwell, who was only five years old when he began to attend school, found it hard to make the journey between Sandal in Yorkshire, where his school was, and his home. 'At my first going to Sandal,' he wrote, 'I walked it every day, but was not able to hold it long, it being too far for such a child to go daily, for I was not quite 5 years of age.' From his account, it is clear that older children were required to make such a long journey, for he recalled how 'some boys who went with me being much older, hurried me too fast, and sometimes left me behind'. But young Fretwell returned home 'weeping', so his father decided to place him with a widow in Sandal, from where he 'usually came home every Saturday'.[99]

Sandal was not the only place where James Fretwell was boarded during his childhood. In the following years he moved three more times: at the age of nine he moved to Stoney Stainton where he boarded with the schoolmaster; when he was 13 he began to attend the Doncaster free school where he was placed with a widow; and after about a year he was transferred to Pontefract where he boarded with a mercer, who taught him some account-keeping and arithmetic.[100] While some parents desired a prestigious school and a reputed schoolmaster who could be relied on to prepare their son for the university, others, like James Fretwell's parents, removed their son to a teacher who was qualified to prepare him for entry into apprenticeship. Young Fretwell left the Doncaster free school in order to learn accounts, arithmetic, and geometry with a linen-draper.[101] Even when the nearest local school suited parental aspirations, there were children who failed to make the necessary progress and found the demands of the local schoolmaster too high.[102] Finally, since the single largest category of schools was that of the fee-paying unendowed schools,[103] some parents found the local school simply too expensive and were forced to seek an alternative arrangement. Scattered around the country were women and schooldames who taught, without licence, reading and basic literacy,[104] and as some autobiogrpahies suggest, these women could offer boarding to sons of relatives and kin. Oliver Sansom was sent to the nearest school to learn reading at the age of six, and a year later his father sent him to board with his sister and learn Latin and writing; he remained there until he was 10 years of age.[105] His autobiography does not say what made Oliver's father send him to be taught by his sister, but it is not altogether unlikely that the costs required by her were low, if they were required at all.

Outbreaks of plague could also bring parents to send their children away. In 1610 a plague broke out in Towcester, where Thomas Sheppard's parents lived, and young Thomas, who was three years old, was sent away the same day the plague broke out to live with his grandfather and grandmother in a remote place in the countryside. Later on he was placed with his uncle, and returned home only when the plague disappeared from Towcester.[106] Anthony Wood and his brother were also sent by their mother to the countryside for a fortnight when infection spread at Oxford, during the siege of the Parliamentary army in 1644, and then they were removed to Thame to board with the vicar and his wife, who were relatives of the Woods. Soon afterwards the two brothers began to attend the free school in Thame.[107] While wealthier families could afford to travel and escape the disaster together,[108] among poorer families separations of parents and children during times of plague must have been common. Plague occurred frequently,[109] and its impact was often random, striking one community disastrously and avoiding another. Since most people recognised this randomness,[110] sending one's child away, even only a few miles to another village, might have been a reasonable strategy; it could save a child from being infected. Moreover, the disease spread slowly and over a long period, so parents could be aware of the approaching danger the moment it arrived in a nearby parish or town, and react to protect their children. Since the mortality of infants and children under 10 years was exceptionally high throughout the period, and since contemporaries were fully aware that children were the most likely victims of plague,[111] sending them away to relatives and to neigbouring villages, if parents could not afford to move themselves, must have been a common response.

Parental death could also cause the departure of a child from his home. At the age of three, following the death of her mother, Mary Rich was sent away 'by the tender care of my indulgent father, that I might be carefully and piously educated', to 'a prudent and vertuous lady', with whom she lived until she was eleven.[112] The three writers of autobiographies whose parents remarried – Shepard, Muggleton and Evans – were also forced to leave their homes while they were still in their childhood. Thomas Shepard lost his mother when he was 4 years old and his father when he was 10, and he was soon taken from his stepmother to live with his elder brother. There is some indication that children did not tend to remain with a step-parent when left parentless,[113] and that tenuous relations with step-parents could also lead to the departure of children. When the father of Lodowick Muggleton remarried in London, where young Lodowick had been born and reared, he was 'expos'ed to live with strangers in the Country, at a distance from all my kindred'.[114] His account gives no hint of the circumstances that led to his being boarded away from his father and stepmother; it only leaves the impression that this episode in his life appeared to him, in retrospect, particularly harsh, since he was 'but young' when his mother died. He must have been in his early teens, for his account states that it was not until he turned 15 or 16 that he was placed as an apprentice with a London tailor.

The account of Arise Evans likewise does not specify the precise reasons why he was obliged to depart from his mother and stepfather, but he has left more details of his whereabouts following the death of his father, and his description suggests that there was some connection between his mother's remarriage and his departure from home, for the space of four years, at a very young age. Following the death of his father young Arise, then about seven years old, was taken from school and later he moved with his mother and her new husband to a place not far from their native village in Merionethshire. Shortly afterwards Arise left his mother and stepfather, and was forced to look for some employment – doing 'any drugery' – in neighbouring villages. Precisely what he did is unclear, but possibly some arrangement for boarding with neighbours was found for him, perhaps by his mother. He was evidently too young to be placed as a servant or an apprentice, for it was not until two years later that he was able to find more regular employment with a tailor in Westchester in Cheshire. Even this arrangement does not appear to have been an apprenticeship based on a formal seven-year contract, for young Arise provided the tailor with some form of service 'at free cost', while obtaining food and lodging 'from good people'. After two years the tailor became insolvent and sent young Arise home to his mother, who, being a widow again, received him back and employed him in her business. After three years, when Arise was 14, his mother married a third time and went to live in Denbighshire. Arise went with her, and shortly afterwards became an apprentice to Hugh Jones, this time on the basis of a formal agreement. 'I served him untill my master was satisfied, and I had my indenters,' as he put it later.[115]

All these cases suggest that in some circumstances following the death of a parent, children were placed in a boarding arrangement which did not amount to a normal service or apprenticeship term. A child aged 6, 7 or even 10 was not considered old enough to be placed as an apprentice, and was unlikely to be able to find a master craftsman or employment on the basis of a long-term contract. Examples of this in autobiographical material abound. Joseph Oxley, who was born and reared in Yorkshire, lost both of his parents by the time he was eight years old. He was then taken with his brothers to live under the care and supervision of his grandparents. Only five years later, when he was 13, his grandfather then being dead, did he make a first, and unsuccessful, attempt at becoming an apprentice with a clockmaker at Scarborough. The master who examined him at that time thought that he was 'very low of stature', and it was only a year later that he was able to apprentice himself to another clockmaker.[116] Thomas Hardy, born and reared in the mid-eighteenth century, lost his father when he was about eight years old and was taken in by his grandfather, who provided his maintenance and education. Only when he 'arrived at a proper age' did his grandfather begin to teach him his trade of shoemaking.[117] In the 1630s, when William Edmundson was eight years old, he was taken to live with his uncle after the death of both his parents. He stayed there 'several years, being young', and only then was he bound as an apprentice in York.[118]

None of these examples relates to families who were completely impoverished following the death of a father, and children of the very destitute and poor were sometimes placed as apprentices at a relatively young age, especially in the rural countryside, where they could be placed as apprentices in husbandry at the age of 10 and occasionally even younger, as was the case among poor children in the parish of Colyton in the seventeenth and eighteenth centuries.[119] But even among the very poor, many became apprentices only when they reached the age of 12 or 13.[120] Unlike earlier legislation regarding the poor, the Poor Laws of 1598 and 1601 did not specify a lower age limit at which children could be apprenticed,[121] no doubt to enable parish authorities to bind poor children even when very young. But such attempts were bound to confront difficulties, and not only because some parents objected to the forcing of their children into undesirable apprenticeships or labour in workhouses.[122] Parish authorities recognised that children had to reach an age when they were 'fit to be placed forth' – as the churchwardens of the parish of St James in Bristol put it – before they were apprenticed.[123] So in cases of destitute brothers and sisters, parish authorities could order only that the 'eldest of them to be bound apprentice'.[124] In the Southampton Poor-child Register, the overwhelming majority of children were 10 years old and above.[125]

The result of this all was that quite a few, even among the orphaned and very poor, were boarded out for their maintenance and upbringing rather than placed as apprentices or agricultural and domestic servants. The distinction is clear in the case of John Wilson, of Temple parish in Bristol, who, in May 1630, received £2, 'for which he and his wife is to discharge the parish and to keep [the child of Christopher Horner] . . . to be taught to get her living until she be able to go unto service'.[126] There are other examples of children who were boarded out and their maintenance regularly paid for. For example, from the 1620s on in the parishes of St James and St John Baptist in Bristol, various people were paid annually, 'for keeping a poor child', for 'clothing' and 'stocking' and 'shoes for the poor children' who would then be 'placed forth'. It is also clear that the authorities in these parishes allocated monies for the 'placing forth' of children together with the money they allocated for the care of sick and other disabled persons.[127] Similar cases of children who were too young to be apprenticed and who were boarded out by parish authorities can be found elsewhere. According to Tim Wales, in Norfolk it was a common practice for parish officers to pay neighbours, who were often themselves very poor, for keeping paupers, among them orphaned children.[128]

It is difficult to estimate the frequency with which the practice of boarding out in childhood occurred. For example, Laslett's findings on patterns of residence of orphaned children between 1599 and 1811 shows that 46 (3.3 per cent) of 1,383 orphans were living with 'persons other than parents or step-parents'. But this is likely to be a very low estimate, for many resident orphans, as Laslett also points out, were probably not identified in the variety of household listings available; they may have been disguised as resident relatives or as lodgers, who together could constitute nearly a tenth of the population in household listings.[129] There is also a possibility that a very young child who was reared by a widow or a neighbour would still be disguised as a 'son', or 'daughter'. Above all, the temporary nature of many of these arrangements meant that many children – like James Fretwell, who boarded with a widow only during weekdays, or those who were sent away in times of plague – would have escaped being recorded altogether.[130]

What we have shown is neither that all children were placed out at a young age, nor that placing children outside home at a young age was a desirable thing for either children, or their parents, if they were still alive.[131] On the contrary, sending children to board outside the home appears to have been, in most cases, a last resort.[132] A wide range of circumstances could arise in families of a variety of social and economic standings, that would force parents to send their young children away, often for the benefit of the children themselves. The schooling system, which was largely dependent on the needs and financial resources of individual parents, as well as on an inadequate system of communication, forced many parents to board their children away from home, and not only when they desired a particularly prestigious school for their children. High rates of mortality also forced orphaned children to spend periods of their childhood away from home; and plagues and other diseases, poverty, or the sheer lack of adequate employment for children could all lead to their being sent away from home. Elin Stout, who was inflicted with 'bodily infirmities' from a very young age, was sent at some point in her youth to her relatives in order to 'benefit in her health'.[133] Given the limited capacity of very young children to work, their greater vulnerability to plagues and other diseases, and the fact that underemployment was prevalent, many children were likely to have been sent away for shorter or longer durations during their early childhood lives.

How did such separations affect children? One would think that a lot depended on the specific circumstances of the removal from home, on how poor and unable to provide in the home parents were, on the length of time spent away, and on the kinds of arrangements found for children. Simonds D'Ewes, who spent so much of his childhood away from his parents, nonetheless appears to have been quite content with his upbringing, and it is obvious that he formed deep bonds of affection with both of his grandparents who reared and provided for him as a child. When he returned home – he was then already eight years old – he was gradually able to become very attached to his mother as well. As we shall also see in Chapter 7, there were relatives, neighbours, teachers and other people who could well provide for the needs of a small child. George Bewley, who was transferred to a school about twenty miles from his home village in Cumberland, remembered that he was then boarded, for the space of a year, with his uncle, and an aunt, 'who was kind to me and careful over me'.

Nevertheless Bewley's account does convey the sense of apprehension of a 12-year-old child about to part from his parents. He appears to have been quite attached to his 'dear mother', who gave him 'good advice' when he was leaving home; like some other writers of autobiographies, the very point he made of the fact that his uncle and aunt treated him with kindness suggests that this was not something he could fully anticipate when he left his parents. William Edmundson, whose mother died when he was four years old and his father when he was eight, was left under the care of an uncle who 'used [him and his brothers] harshly'. His brothers and sisters scattered soon afterwards, and William, the youngest of them all, left as soon as he grew older and was able to find an apprenticeship in York.[134]

Leaving Home

Some time in the course of their teens, most young people departed from their homes and entered careers as varied as higher education, the mercantile trade and urban crafts, domestic service, and service in husbandry. There was no standard age for leaving home, for the timing of the departure depended on family circumstances, social standing, the type of career involved, the place of destination, and so on. Among writers of early modern autobiographies who mentioned the date or age at which they left their homes, the mean age of those departing for university was 16, and of those who became apprentices 14.7.[135] Other evidence available for age at departure for service and apprenticeship shows considerable variation, but it also suggests that most people left home in their teens and not earlier. In sixteenth-century London the majority of young men did not begin their apprenticeships before their late teens, or even their early twenties: the age among migrant apprentices was particularly high, and Londoners apprenticed themselves at an average age of 17.7. Lower down the social scale, in the rural countryside, age of entry into agricultural service was lower, but normally not below 13 years. Among agricultural servants examined in the late seventeenth century, a few entered service as pre-teens – aged 10–12 – but a fifth were between 13 and 14 years old, and nearly a half were between 13 and 15. Some variation in the speed of exit from home was also related to the occupation of the father, to types of communities and their economies, and to the child's sex; and the average age of entering farm service appears to have dropped a little in the course of the seventeenth century.[136]

Writers of autobiographies in the seventeenth century usually made some reference to their departure from home, making it quite clear that this was a major turning point in their youth, if not in their lives as a whole. We have already referred to the vivid description of Edward Barlow, who left his Lancashire village and migrated to London in the mid-seventeenth century.[137] The sense of drama evoked in Barlow's unique account was partly the result of his attempt to highlight his adventurous youth. But there is no reason to doubt the authenticity of the emotions surrounding his departure, especially since the family realised that Barlow was about to travel a long distance from home. Benjamin Bangs's description of his parting from his mother suggests similar attitudes, despite the fact that his autobiography was a spiritual one and hardly touched by the spirit of adventure so characteristic of Barlow. Bangs was sent away to become an apprentice near his home when he was 13, but later decided to join his master in his migration to another town. 'My parting with [my mother] was with great Reluctance,' he stated, 'and she said to me, child, it will not be long before I shall see thee again; so with an Heart very full I returned [to my master].' It was several years before Bangs saw his mother again, having by then finished his apprenticeship in London.[138]

Leaving home for a period of service elsewhere required evaluation of the alternative courses open to a child, and a choice of which course suited him or her best. Most autobiographies show that in one way or another most young people had some say in this. For example, Richard Davies was born and reared in North Wales in the 1630s. When he was 14 years old his father, who owned a small farm, decided to apprentice him in the shopkeeping trade. As he described it later on, he was accordingly sent to a shopkeeper for a period of trial to see whether the master and the trade suited him. In the course of the trial period, young Davies became convinced that 'the conversation of [his] intended master was not right, and that the fear of the Lord was not there', so he decided to return home to his parents. After some time he heard about a man 'who was very zealous' and performed all 'that which we call family duties'. He travelled to see the man, a feltmaker, offered to become his apprentice, discussed the matter with his parents, and, as he later put it, 'there, with the consent of my parents, I bound myself an apprentice to him'. Instead of entering the shopkeeping business, he became an apprentice with a feltmaker in Llanfair, about forty miles from his parents' home in Welshpool, Montgomeryshire.[139]

Richard Davies's account shows that while the father initiated his son's going into the shopkeeping trade, the son took an active part in the final arrangement of his apprenticeship. That parents – both father and mother – were prime movers in the decision to send a son or a daughter into some form of service, but that the child's approval, inclination and individual judgement were all taken into account, is quite evident in many autobiographies. George Trosse, the son of a wealthy lawyer from Exeter who died when George was still a child, was taught that his father had desired that he continue in his footsteps. When the time came, young Trosse was more inclined to enter the mercantile trades, and he so informed his mother. The mother 'comply'd with my Inclinations, as knowing the Profitableness of Trading', and so young Trosse was sent to France and later became an apprentice to a Portuguese merchant. Gervase Disney also reported that 'my father therefore perceiving me to decline learning, gave me my choice of any Trade', and so Gervase was sent to London, where he became an apprentice to his cousin, a silk-merchant. Other young people preferred an academic career. John Shaw, from the West Riding in Yorkshire, claimed that he had 'a great mind and earnest desire of learning' from early in his life; and so when the time came, he wanted to enter the university. His parents had other plans, for 'having no other child but me, were very loath to have me depart from them'; they also wanted to make sure their son would be trained and prepared to take charge of the family estate when the time came. 'But they observing my eager desire ... after knowledge,' he later recalled, 'and seeing me to have no genius to anything but learning', they decided to agree to his going to Cambridge. Adam Martindale also reported that he was inclined to learning, while his father aspired that he follow him in his business – probably the building trade. 'But he [i.e. the father] guessed right which way my mind still went ... he frankely put it to my choice, whether I would go on as I did at present [helping him in his business], or returne to schoole againe.' Adam Martindale returned to school and eventually became a schoolmaster.[140] William Stout, who brought up two orphaned children of his neighbour John Johnson, reported that when the elder reached 15 years old he wanted him to enter the shopkeeping trade. 'But he inclined to nothing but the sea,' Stout recalled, so Stout helped him become an apprentice on a ship.[141]

From the little evidence we have on young women, it appears that they, too, were sometimes given autonomy in deciding if and where they would like to go.[142] Nor is there evidence that among poorer families children's preferences, however limited, were not taken into account. Edward Barlow, who was forced to leave home and search for employment on his own when he was about 11 years old, recalled that after some time his father made contact with a textile craftsman in Manchester who agreed to take young Edward as an apprentice. Barlow's account of the circumstances leading to his binding makes it clear that the father thought it was the best thing he could do for his son, as long as young Barlow would comply – 'if I was willing,' as he put it. So the father, 'inquiring of me he found me willing to it', placed Barlow as an apprentice in Manchester. There was something rhetorical about the father's enquiry whether young Barlow 'was willing', for Barlow had no other choice, and his account makes it clear that the arrangement was hardly what he had desired. Nonetheless, given that Barlow had so few prospects, the fact that his father still needed his approval suggests that to obtain the consent of a child was something parents were expected to do when their son or daughter was about to leave home.[143] Moreover, as soon as young Barlow entered his apprenticeship he began to plan his next move, and after his trial period with his master was over, he returned home for the Christmas holiday, determined never to return to him. After some time, his parents instructed him to go back to his master, 'to which [Barlow] refused', justifying this by arguing that it would amount to wasting time – 'I was sure I could never stay my time out'. So his parents 'asked [him] the reason'; and young Barlow proceeded to provide all the information he had obtained from fellow apprentices on his master's faults. Barlow's account stops short of his parents' response, but it appears that following some argument and discussion the father 'was forced to go to my master and make peace, and certified him of the matter and what my reasons were'. Before long, Barlow decided to depart for London, since he remained adamant in his decision despite his parents' arguments.[144]

Among more prosperous families, the choice of a career was not unlimited either, and most families were to some degree or another constrained in their choice for a son or a daughter. Gervase Disney, a gentleman's son who was given the choice between higher education and some trade, and who was 'inclined most to a herauld painter', was forced to change his choice several times before he finally became an apprentice. First his family received the information that his chosen occupation was judged to be too burdensome, so Gervase decided he would like to be bound to a bookseller. His father then was told by a friend that bookselling was a declining trade, so young Gervase, already in his late teens, had to change his plans again. Finally 'it was concluded, with the approbation of all concerned for me' that he would be bound to a London merchant. This type of cooperation between parents and children, in which all the relevant considerations were taken into account, is also apparent in Benjamin Bangs's account. When he turned 13 years old Benjamin was prepared to go into service. His mother, although not very poor, explained to him that she could not provide him with a prestigious apprenticeship in one of the lucrative trades – the 'higher business', as Bangs called it. What was at stake, as she explained it to Benjamin, was not simply the costs of training in the mercantile trades, but that it would be imprudent to apprentice him to a trade in which 'a stock would be wanted to set me up when I came out of my time'. She also made him aware of the fact that although he had been well provided for in his childhood, there were eight other children besides him who expected her help. The mother then advised young Benjamin that his choice 'must be to some handicraft', and next she enquired of him 'what trade I most inclined to?' Benjamin Bangs apparently had no strong opinion in this regard and so discussion ensued – 'several things pass'd upon this subject' – in which the advantages and disadvantages of crafts were perhaps evaluated. In the end, Bangs made the decision to become a shoemaker. His description also makes it clear that he took full account of what his mother had told him: 'I thought it would take but little to put me out'. 'She commended my Thought,' he concluded, 'and there being one [shoemaker] about a Mile from our House, who had then a pretty fair Character, we applied to him.'[145]

So parents provided information, explained to their children what was at stake, and, as these accounts suggest, attempted to arrive at some form of joint decision about their future careers. The modern sociologist would find nothing unusual in such behaviour. The parents of Gervase Disney, Benjamin Bangs, Edward Barlow and others were using, in sociological terminology, some sort of support and control techniques in the socialisation of their children. Such techniques could include a variety of attitudes: from encouragement, praise, approval, assistance, cooperation and expression of affection, to giving directions, instructions, commands, suggestions, making requests, providing information and explanations, reasoning, and pointing out consequences of actions. In other words, these parents were trying to both guide and control their children through assistance, encouragement, cooperation, and a good deal of persuasion. None of these examples includes what some sociologists would term 'unqualified power assertion', or coercion; i.e. the use of physical punishment, deprivation of material objects or privileges, direct application of force or the threat of any of these, all of which imply an open conflict or contest of wills between parents and children.[146] In autobiographical accounts, there is one example of a parent using such techniques to avert the decision of his son, and that is the case of Richard Norwood, whose father, a gentleman, disinherited him when he decided to leave his apprenticeship in London and embark on a ship as an apprentice. But Richard Norwood's account also makes it clear that his parents made every effort at using reason and argument, trying to provide information and point to the consequences – '[My father] and my mother had often laboured to discourage me by showing me some seafaring men in the city, how raggedly and slovenly they went' – before they fell back on coercion.[147]

What is evident in these accounts is that parents were acting on the basis of assumptions about the physical and mental development of their children, and, to use the phrasing of the sociologist again, they recognised that 'control attempts might influence younger children differently than older children'.[148] In their actions and attitudes, parents appear to have taken for granted that their sons and daughters had reached the age of discretion, which implied that their opinion and consent was required before a decision on matters regarding their lives was made.[149] That some children found it too demanding a procedure, especially those of poorer families, where sons tended to leave home in their early teens and occasionally before, is betrayed by some autobiographers. Edward Barlow commented that when his father enquired whether he was willing to become an apprentice in Manchester, he agreed, 'being I was young and did not know what was good for myself'. And when Edward Coxere was about to go out to service and could not decide whether to become a seaman's apprentice or not, 'the old tiresome tone sounded in my ears again: "what trade now?" . . . I could never settle my mind to any particular trade, so that I was like one that was neither at sea nor ashore. . . . My life began then to be uncomfortable.'[150] Edward Coxere was then about 15 years old, and soon afterwards he became an apprentice with a master on board the *Saint George*.

Conclusion

By the time they reached their early teens and were about to leave home for a period of service, children had already become grown up in some respects. Most of them had been quite accustomed to work; although the more demanding agricultural tasks were not normally given to children before they were 10 or 11, and although the work was irregular, by their early teens children had learnt to work long hours and to do hard jobs. The skills they had acquired often helped them in finding employment and in entering agricultural service. Many children of poorer families had been accustomed to earn a wage, sometimes outside their homes, and so they already contributed to their maintenance. Edward Barlow remembered that with the money he earned when he was 12 years old he was able to make 'shift to buy me some clothes'.[151]

Many children experienced the difficulties and limitations imposed by the death of a parent. One need only take note of a single remark made in an autobiography in order to envisage the type of responsibility involved. John Whitting, who lost both parents before he turned 10 years old, said that his sister 'was very helpful in bringing up her younger brothers, which were three besides [himself]; being diligent and serviceable... denying herself the diversions that others delighted in'.[152] Other children confronted the difficulties imposed by the break-up of the family or by separations from it for shorter or longer durations – all of which must have encouraged a measure of independence as well. James Fretwell's account of his abortive apprenticeship in London is perhaps the most indicative of the degree of maturation children could acquire by the time they left the parental home for a period of service elsewhere. In his childhood James had experienced neither parental loss nor any other deprivation of the sort we have here described. He was the son of a timber-merchant, and in his autobiography there is no indication that he was required to work before he reached his mid-teens. Nevertheless when James turned 16 years old he had already been placed away from his parents no less than seven times: four times for the purpose of schooling and preparation for apprenticeship; twice with masters for a trial period; and once more when he began to work and learn his father's business, which was located away from where his family lived. During all these periods he had been boarded out with teachers, relatives and strangers. Then his father and mother offered him the opportunity to go to London to become an apprentice to his uncle. From his account we can tell that, although his father thought this suited James as well as the family's financial circumstances at the time, he 'only proposed for me to tarry the following winter', as James put it later. Moreover, once James left for London and began his apprenticeship, his father left it 'entirely to my choice' whether to continue it or not. At this point, all the father could do was put some pressure by writing letters making it clear he thought James ought to stay in London. For his part, James 'had no desire for it', but first he yielded to his father's requests. Then he changed his mind. 'I acquainted my parents with it,' as he described it later on, 'and, after some time, [I] concluded for me to leave'. Shortly afterwards James left London and returned to Yorkshire, where he remained for the rest of his life.[153]

3 The Mobility of Rural Youth

Young servants, both men and women, were an integral part of the rural scene. In parish listings from 1599 to the mid-nineteenth century, almost half of the households contained servants; and in communities in the sixteenth and seventeenth centuries, between a quarter and over a third of the households had one or more servants. Some 20 per cent of village populations could consist of unmarried people living in households other than their own.[1] While the number of servants hired at any one time by gentlemen, yeomen and wealthier village craftsmen was greater than that hired by people in the lower sections of the rural population, the servants themselves, males and females, came from a wide range of middling and lower-class groups. Among them were many sons and daughters of labourers, but there were also the offspring of traders and craftsmen, husbandmen and yeomen.[2] Most of these young people were living with their masters as farm servants, domestic servants or apprentices.

Perhaps the single most surprising fact which has been established with regard to rural servants is their frequent mobility. Marjorie K. McIntosh has observed that even within a period of employment some youths were mobile, being sent to work and live with another employer for a while. Usually the mobility occurred between periods of service; some youths stayed with their masters for a number of years, but most of them moved at the end of their annual term. Most of this mobility was within short distances, normally not further than 15 kilometres.[3] The frequency of moves can be seen in individual biographies. Ann Kussmaul has shown that Joseph Mayett, a farm servant in Buckinghamshire in the late eighteenth century, moved no less than eleven times during his teens. In late sixteenth-century Essex frequent moves following annual terms were also not unusual.[4]

This mobility was one of the most distinct features of the lives of most young people, and throughout the sixteenth and first half of the seventeenth centuries it also involved long-distance migration away from small parishes to the larger towns and to London. These movements were affected by various motives and circumstances, some of which forced themselves on young people; but others, as we shall see in subsequent chapters, involved the initiative of the young themselves. High rates of mobility also had many ramifications in terms of the experiences of the young, their social relations, and their aspirations.[5] In this chapter we will bring into sharper focus some aspects of the mobility of rural youth, especially its effects on the working lives of the young and the acquisition of a wide range of skills.

Service and Labour

On most agricultural holdings, the labour force consisted of two distinct groups: servants and labourers. Kussmaul defined the servant as a person who was hired by the year, lived with his or her master, and was unmarried. A labourer, by contrast, was hired for a shorter period of time, had his own residence, and was for the most part married.[6] Other historians have suggested that this distinction is somewhat rigid, and that patterns of recruitment of servants, especially in the sixteenth and first half of the seventeenth centuries, were less formal than in the century that followed. There is little evidence of hiring sessions during the sixteenth century, and many servants were hired for short periods of months and weeks rather than for a whole year. On the estate of a gentleman farmer in Stiffkey, Norfolk, servants were rarely hired for twelve months or more. In Romford, Essex, servants were also hired, on occasion, for periods of months rather than a year.[7] A. Hassell Smith suggested a classification of the workforce on the Stiffkey estate into 'resident farm servants', who were hired for weeks, months and above; and 'labourers', who were hired by the day, and were divided into specialist and non-specialist labourers, according to level of skill and type of work they did.[8]

These distinctions between service and labour did not reflect separate age categories. Some farm servants were married adults, and many labourers were youngsters in their teens and early twenties; that is, in the course of their adolescence and youth, young people were likely to move not only from one annual service term to the next, but between different types of labour arrangement; their work as annual servants was interspersed with periods, lasting sometimes many months, during which they were hired for the season or worked as daily labourers. The detailed research by A. Hassell Smith on Stiffkey families who were employed on the estate of Nathaniel Bacon is illuminating in that it provides evidence on the ages and marital status of many of the employees. Smith has identified a total of 55 Stiffkey sons and daughters employed on the estate between 1582 and 1597. Two were farm servants on the estate, 4 more were employed as a kitchen boy, a cook, and household servants, and the majority (45) were day labourers employed in agriculture and in various crafts, especially woodwork and the building crafts. The agricultural labourers were nearly all unmarried women, aged 18 years and upwards. The labourers in the building and wood crafts were adolescent males who worked alongside their fathers (carpenters, coopers, painters, masons, tilers, and so on). As Smith suggested, the women might well have been resident servants when they were younger; that is, they were employed as domestics or dairymaids in adjacent parishes when they were in their mid-teens, and returned home to become labourers when they were in their late teens. The males, on the other hand, probably moved on to some form of service or apprenticeship elsewhere after having worked alongside their fathers as day labourers for some time.[9] In addition, there were resident servants on Bacon's estate who were hired for the season, and they, too, were young and unmarried for the most part. They travelled longer distances, and were hired as mowers, to do the hardest and most skilled job in harvesting.

Wage labour was likely to be widespread in the corn-growing areas, where demand for seasonal labour, especially during the harvest, was high. By contrast, annual farm service was more suitable to pastoral farming and areas where livestock husbandry predominated, and where work in tending sheep, horses and other animals was required throughout the year.[10] Moreover, throughout the sixteenth and first half of the seventeenth centuries, annual farm service was in decline, and hiring by the day, the week or the season became common. Population growth, the surplus of adult labourers, rising prices and lower wages, were more conducive to daily labour or short-term service than to annual farm service. Abundance of labour ensured the farmer a continuing supply of workers, rising prices secured the flow of cash to pay daily and weekly wages, and lower wages also made daily labour a more attractive option.[11] Overall, the incidence of service began to rise only in the century following the 1650s.

Contemporaries sometimes made quite clear the advantages of hired labour over the resident servant. When Robert Loder calculated the annual costs of his servants, he remarked in his account book that 'it were best course to keep none'. This was in 1613, in Berkshire, and Loder's farming was based largely on wheat and barley malt.[12]

All this had a number of implications for the working lives of the young. First, young people living with parents and working on the basis of day and week wages, or going out for short terms of a few weeks of residence elsewhere and then returning home with their earnings, were anything but a rarity. In contrast to annual service, where nearly half the wages were paid in kind and the money wage was paid at the end of the annual term or after long intervals of three to six months, short-term hirings and daily labour provided a daily or weekly wage.[13] When they worked as daily labourers or seasonal servants, young people either lived at home or returned to their families at the end of the harvest, and they were likely to contribute to their families at least part of their wage. Once they passed their mid-teens, their contribution could increase substantially. On the Stiffkey estate, boys working alongside their fathers were paid 2d. and 4d. a day; but adolescents above 15 years old already received 9d., 8d. and 10d. a day, only slightly less than their fathers. This wage was the equivalent of the 8d. standard daily wage earned by the non-specialist labourer who worked in the fields.[14]

In the late nineteenth century, wage-earning youth were believed to be independent, self-supporting, and half grown up; their parents were often described as fearful of exercising their authority 'lest the lad should take his earnings and go elsewhere'.[15] There is no reason to doubt that, given the variation in individual temperaments and families, earning a wage in the sixteenth and seventeenth centuries gave young people a similar independence. We have already referred to Edward Barlow who, as a boy, bought clothes for himself with wages he was already earning on his own. When he decided, against his parents' wishes and plans, to leave his village and travel to London, he had already been saving part of his wages from work as a labourer. Although his father eventually accepted his decision, and even gave him some money, this only complemented the money young Barlow had saved towards his long journey to the capital.[16] Working intermittently as labourers and moving between different types of service arrangement also confronted the adolescent with the burdens involved in having to subsist on irregular work and a variety of makeshifts, and, among the poorer sections of society, having to survive near or on the verge of subsistence. Joseph Mayett was forced to trick his master into taking him back as a resident servant, having been released from service and forced to subsist, during three months in the famine winter of 1800, on work as a labourer and on a very poor diet.[17] Such an existence fostered flexibility in adjusting to several types of work, in eking out a living by alternating between assistance to parents at home, casual day labouring, and farm service. It also necessitated the acquistion of a wide range of skills, some of them quite specialised. Often it involved migration into areas and villages where opportunties for industrial employment and craft apprenticeships were available as well.

Agricultural Skills

In the course of their teens, most young people gained a range of skills through working as annual servants, seasonal servants and labourers. Annual servants were normally hired to do the least seasonable tasks, mostly in animal husbandry – shepherding, carting – but also ploughing.[18] So the agricultural servants hired between the years 1702 and 1711 by Nicholas Blundell, a landowner in Lancashire, worked as dairy maids, plough-drivers, cowmen and shepherds.[19] When hired as servants for short periods, young people did such seasonal jobs as mowing; and when employed as daily labourers, they did a wide range of mainly seasonal jobs: weeding, threshing, planting and gathering, haymaking, hedging and ditching.

The range of skills required in these employments was diverse, demanding physical strength as well as manual skill, some agricultural knowledge and understanding, and a great deal of responsibility. Some jobs, like threshing, were relatively simple and were done indoors, but they still required skill in handling tools, and the work itself was monotonous and straining. To properly use the flail, for example, took some time to learn.[20] Ploughing required strength, skill in directing the animals properly, in repairing, sharpening and taking care of the plough, and in horse-keeping.[21] Mowing, shepherding, cattle-herding, hedging and ditching each required its own range of skills. The long-handled scythe demanded both stature and the expertise to swing the scythe in steady movements so as to leave the corn in the least possible disorder. On some large estates, skilled mowers were brought from farther afield, and there were yeomen and gentlemen who were ready to look for good mowers 15 miles and more away.[22]

Some tasks involved in annual service were quite specialised and demanded daily attendance of animals: watering and foddering cattle and horses several times a day, making sure animals were well and safely tied, keeping them in good condition, detecting ailments, applying cures and medications, setting broken legs or bones, bathing and oiling wounds properly.[23] Shepherding entailed a great deal of responsibility in going great distances, making sure no sheep were lost, and guarding the sheep against other animals.[24] It was lonely work, and demanded independence and endurance; a shepherd had to protect the sheep in winter snows, assist the ewes in lambing, change damaged fold hurdles, wash, grease, and do the dusty and itchy work of shearing.[25] In the late nineteenth century the older shepherd was still considered one of the most skilled and independent persons in a village community.[26]

It is extremely difficult to know when these different skills were obtained by adolescents and youths. There were great variations in individual physique and strength, the regularity with which young people were employed, and the experience they had already obtained in childhood. Wage assessments in Quarter Sessions analysed by Kussmaul show that male servants could begin to obtain small wages when they were as young as 10 years old, and female servants when they were 12. Once they entered service, their wages could increase quite substantially with each year. In the late eighteenth century, the wages of males in one hiring session increased by nearly a fifth every year. Lowest ages at which adult wages were finally obtained also varied greatly, ranging between 15 and the early to mid-twenties.[27]

Other evidence shows that some time between 16 and 18 years old, young people would have been recruited to do all the jobs done by mature men and women. Adolescents of 13 or 14 were already employed in carting and harrowing, but in haymaking and shearing their productivity was still considered only half that of adults; 'two of us at 13 or 14 being equal to one man shearer,' as William Stout recalled.[28] By mid-teens, however, adolescents could already be considered 'three-quarter-men', as they were referred to in nineteenth-century Suffolk. A description of harvest work at that late date suggests the types of skill adolescents could acquire as they grew up in earlier centuries as well. At 10 and 12 years old, boys and girls assisted only in bringing the food to the fields and in tying the sheaves. Then they turned 'lads', adolescents between 12 and 17, who began with lighter jobs, such as carting, and by about 16 years old were already considered 'three-quarter-men', doing all the jobs the 'full men' did except lifting the sheaves from the ground to the wagon, the heaviest job of all. A year or two later they were no longer considered 'lads'.[29]

Ploughing, too, was normally mastered at 16 or 17 years of age. As we have seen, some adolescents could plough alone by their mid-teens. A year or two later, having worked as servants, they acquired a great deal of experience in driving two- and four-horse teams properly, and could obtain the reputation of being 'a good plowman', and a 'happen ladde', as Henry Best referred to them. Their wages could then rise substantially.[30] Some time in their late teens servants also learnt to sow and mow, as well as hedge and ditch. In early eighteenth-century Westmorland the magistrates made a distinction between 'inferior servants only fit for husbandry', and older more experienced servants who could 'mow and reap corn, hold the plough, hedge and ditch'.[31] Henry Wise, a servant on the estate of Henry Best, received 36sh. in his first year with his master, the next year he received 50sh., and by the third he was paid 4 marks and 2sh., and was then one 'that could both sowe and mowe indifferently well'.[32] It is difficult to know his age, but his case does suggest that three years of employment as a servant could well equip a youth in the skills of mowing and sowing. Among the jobs Best's servants boasted of doing, the first mentioned were sowing and mowing.[33]

There must also have been variations depending on the size of agricultural holdings and the responsibilities demanded in them. Large landowners and prosperous graziers had hundreds of cattle and sheep and specialised in products such as mutton and beef for a wide market. On such estates, shepherding involved large-scale marketing and management, and the job was given to adults rather than to younger servants. The shepherds of Nathaniel Bacon in Stiffkey, Norfolk, were four mature married men.[34] Yet on medium-sized and small holdings of husbandmen, clergymen, and rural craftsmen or traders, young unmarried servants could be hired as shepherds, and they were then given charge of small flocks of sheep on their own. In addition to the husbandman or craftsman and his wife, such holdings could include a servant in husbandry, one maidservant in charge of the dairy, and another servant-shepherd.[35] Henry Best also had his servants tend the sheep as part of their routine work.[36] And if evidence from late nineteenth-century Suffolk is a reflection of earlier practice, it is probable that a youth of 16 or 17 years could already be hired as a shepherd in sole charge of a flock. Robert Savage, who grew up in the village of Blaxhall at the end of the nineteenth century, was hired as a kitchen boy in a large farm when he was 12 years old; two years later, he began to assist an older shepherd, and when he was 16 years old he was offered the charge of the flock with full adult wages.[37]

In adolescence as in childhood there was a gradual acquisition of skills and a transition from lighter to harder and more skilled jobs, the speed of this progress depending on individual stature as well as the experience acquired by the mid-teens. But scattered evidence also suggests that rough, onerous and demanding work could sometimes turn an adolescent into a young man or woman quite abruptly. Robert Savage remembered that during the first few days that he took full responsibility for the flock in Blaxhall, a nineteenth-century Suffolk village, he felt that he was 'not man enough' and dreaded the long dark night he had to spend with the sheep away from the farm. Because of his fears, his father came to stay the night with him, but very soon afterwards the youth was left on his own, and 'got used to it by myself'.[38] There is no reason to doubt that two centuries earlier young people would have encountered and overcome similar experiences when they were 16 or 17 years old, if not younger.[39]

Earlier autobiographies also give an occasional glimpse of the sense of masculinity and competition these hard jobs could induce in the adolescent male. William Johnson remembered an accident that occurred to his mother while she was working in the fields trying to catch up with 'the young men and lasses [who] were each more anxious to excel another in forking up the hay'.[40] The division of labour by gender could accentuate this sense of masculinity. Few women servants were shepherds or horsekeepers, nor were they normally involved in carting. Few also learnt to mow with the scythe, whose size and weight required strength and whose use was confined to the strongest males.[41] Women tended to perform more feminine and less skilled tasks, and they were often hired as domestic servants who also did various agricultural jobs. On the Stiffkey estate, for example, female servants were hired as dairymaids, and they also did the laundry, spinning, weaving, and stocking-knitting. Best's servant maids did the washing, milking, brewing and baking, as well as sweeping and cleaning in the house. When hired as agricultural labourers, they were employed in less skilled jobs. The thirty-four young women employed on Bacon's estate as daily labourers – fifteen of whom were unmarried and aged 18 and above – did the least skilled agricultual tasks, and their wages were correspondingly lower than those of the males. Wage assessments from the late seventeenth and eighteenth centuries also show that female servants systematically received only a fraction of the wages earned by men.[42]

But these divisions were not always rigid. Some young women, for instance, participated in reaping during the harvest in places where the sickle rather than the scythe was used. Michael Roberts quoted the case of the old woman who in the 1680s boasted that in her youth 'she was able to have reaped as much in a day as any man, and had as much wages'. He has also shown that the demand for women reapers was greater in the mid-seventeenth century than a century later.[43] Many young women were hired as haymakers, and although the jobs they did differed from those of adolescent males, they still acquired a range of invaluable skills. On the Stiffkey estate, women did not mow or cart, but they participated in weeding, haymaking, shearing, and tying sheaves, planting, picking and gathering. Domestic servants were also sometimes employed in the hardest and more skilled agricultural tasks. When William Stout's father died, in 1680, his mother hired a female servant to do the hardest house service, and to harrow, hay and shear during the harvest.[44] Women servants did specialised work involving poultry and cows; like their male counterparts, unmarried dairymaids must have gained a great deal of understanding and some responsibilities in animal husbandry.

Rural Apprenticeships

Between 1500 and 1700 there were some 600 small market towns with from several hundred to 1,500 inhabitants. These small towns, which were at the lowest level of the urban hierarchy of the times, were unevenly distributed in the countryside, with the greatest concentration in the south and east. Nevertheless, in every county, including the north and the west, there were at least half a dozen market towns that provided services for a small area of about five or six square miles.[45] Many of the inhabitants in these towns were still farming the land, but there was also a concentration of workmen in a wide range of industries, crafts and trades. In most market towns in Gloucestershire, for example, between a third and a half of the inhabitants were primarily employed on the land, but the rest were employed in crafts and trades. In a market town like Tewkesbury, Gloucetershire, which was situated on the Severn river and served as the local market for cattle, wool, yarn and grains, the inhabitants included watermen, mariners, trowmen, carriers, carpenters and coopers who were involved in boatbuilding. In addition there were butchers, bakers, brewers, innkeepers and vintners, a few drapers and merchants. There were also representatives from all major industries, such as clothing and textiles (tailors and hosiers, cardmakers, dyers), leather crafts (tanners, skinners, glovers, saddlers), metalworks (goldsmiths, pinners), as well as painters, chandlers, and a bookbinder.[46] Such a market town could therefore provide opportunities for learning a craft or trade to youths in surrounding villages, as scattered evidence from some larger market towns in the north and in the east suggests. In Kendal, a textile town in Westmorland, there were 325 craftsmen and traders and 162 apprentices and journeymen by the late seventeenth century; and in Ipswich, Suffolk, apprentices came to the town throughout the period from local villages and towns, mostly from the eastern part of Suffolk.[47] Apprenticeship in such small towns often involved employment in a craft as well as in agriculture. Edward Barlow, who was apprenticed to a textile worker in Manchester in the mid-seventeenth century, worked in the fields and at threshing as soon as he began his apprenticeship.[48]

In smaller villages there was sometimes a considerable range of crafts, and even small trades, which could provide employment and opportunities for the young. In pastoral and cloth-manufacturing areas in the West Country and East Anglia, and in the metalworking areas of the west Midlands, many villages had craftsmen who relied on manufacturing as a by-employment, and in some places they became entirely reliant upon spinning and weaving, as was the case in Kingswood, in Gloucestershire, in the late 1590s.[49] But the industries and trades which infiltrated small villages were not confined solely to the textile industry – the typical rural industry of the time. In some villages there were husbandmen and yeomen who combined husbandry with milling, tanning or scythesmithing.[50] In some wealthier villages and those adjacent to large towns, the diversification of occupations could be quite marked. In the village of Romford, lying on the main London–Colchester road, craftsmen in the late sixteenth century included fletchers, innkeepers, brewers, bakers, vintners, leatherworkers, clothworkers and a clerk.[51] In Bedminster, situated to the south of Bristol, the inhabitants in the first half of the seventeenth century included husbandmen, but also bakers, a carpenter, a smith, a weaver, a shoemaker, a seaman, a chapman and a barber surgeon.[52] Not a few of these craftsmen and traders had young trainees and apprentices in addition to one or more servants.[53]

A more precise picture of the range of occupations in villages and small market towns can be obtained from an examination of the occupations of the fathers of rural youths who migrated to major provincial towns to become apprentices. In Bristol during the sixteenth and first half of the seventeenth centuries, young people mainly came from market towns and villages in a large hinterland which included Gloucestershire, Somerset, Wiltshire, Monmouth, Herefordshire, Wales, and the south-west, with some also coming from the Midlands and the north.[54] In a group of 180 migrant youths who were apprenticed in Bristol in the year when the registration of apprentices in the town began, 1532–33, the majority (two-thirds) were sons of craftsmen and traders who were involved in all major crafts, industries and trades of the time. Half of the youths came from market towns, but the remainder were from the small villages surrounding them.[55] By the first half of the seventeenth century, representation of the agricultural sector among the fathers of migrant youths in Bristol was larger, but the range of crafts and trades among both village

Table 3.1 *Parental occupations of Bristol migrant apprentices, 1600–45**

	Villages		*Market towns*	
	no.	%	no.	%
Gentlemen	58	8.5	18	6.7
Agriculture	377	55.9	71	26.5
Distributive	15	2.2	28	10.4
Food & drink	25	3.7	27	10.1
Clothing & textiles	64	9.5	52	19.4
Building & wood	37	5.4	8	3.0
Leather	18	2.7	36	13.4
Metal	22	3.3	11	4.1
Transport	18	2.7	9	3.4
Professions	30	4.4	7	2.6
Misc.	11	1.6	–	
Labourers	1	0.1	1	0.4
Total	676	100.0	268	100.0

* The numbers include all migrant apprentices in a sample of 1,512 Bristol apprentices whose parental occupations were recorded between 1600 and 1645.

Source: BRO, *Register of Apprentices*, 04352(1)–04352(6).

youths and those from market towns was diverse. The distribution of occupations of the fathers of migrant apprentices who came from a total of 456 market towns and villages between 1600 and 1645 is shown in Table 3.1. About a fifth of these towns were in the vicinity of Bristol (between 10 and 12 miles), half were from a distance of up to 50 miles, and the remainder were located farther afield.

This evidence suggests that the diversity of occupations in the area surrounding a town like Bristol was not much narrower than that of Bristol itself, for all leading categories of occupation found in the town were present in these small towns and villages as well. The variations that can be observed in the distribution of occupations between the market towns and the villages are predictable: a larger agricultural sector in the villages and greater numbers of traders in foodstuffs and goods in the market towns. But overall, both types of settlements included a diversity of crafts as well as small trade. Certain craftsmen, such as tilers, joiners, carpenters and painters, were in fact more heavily concentrated in the villages. The professions, which largely included clerks and barber surgeons, were also relatively more numerous in the villages. Otherwise all categories of occupation or industry that existed in small towns were present in some village or another one next to it: textiles, metalworking, and the leather industry, along with occupations involved in the distribution of foodstuffs, such as baking, brewing, innkeeping and butchering, as well as apothecaries, grocers, ironmongers and so on. This distribution of occupations among the fathers of migrant apprentices probably underestimates one sector in the rural population – that of labourers. But otherwise it is unlikely to grossly misrepresent the agricultural, industrial and small trading occupations that existed in the rural countryside of a large area in the western part of the country during this period.

Not a few youths must have found some form of apprenticeship among these numerous craftsmen and traders. Settlement records from the first half of the eighteenth century, examined by Snell, show substantial numbers of youths placed as apprentices with craftsmen and traders in many parishes in the south-eastern counties. They were placed privately or through the parish relief system, paid premiums for apprenticeships in a wide range of skills, and throughout the first half of the century they served their masters for between six and seven years.[56] There is no comparable evidence for earlier decades, but what there is suggests various forms of apprenticeship for youths in small towns as well as villages. Benjamin Bangs was apprenticed by a village shoemaker in the parish of Longham in Norfolk. He paid £5 for his apprenticeship, and his contract was for a five-year period. Samuel Bownas was likewise apprenticed with a village blacksmith, in Yorkshire.[57] Overall, parish listings did not normally distinguish between servants and apprentices, but it is clear that not a few youngsters were hired as apprentices in many small parishes. Some of those hired as servants by rural craftsmen were probably also serving as assistants in something comparable to an apprenticeship; others were hired as apprentices, but were also employed in agriculture, like Edward Barlow, a textile apprentice in Manchester who was also employed threshing in the barn.[58] Evidence from wills in late sixteenth-century Romford also shows youths being hired as apprentices by parish craftsmen and traders, for a seven-year term.[59]

Compared with their counterparts in large towns, these young people could begin their apprenticeship at a relatively young age. As we shall see, most apprentices in large towns were in their late teens, but autobiographies suggest that in small towns and parishes in the countryside apprenticeships could sometimes begin earlier. Edward Barlow was apprenticed in Manchester when he was no older than 13; Samuel Bownas was apprenticed with a blacksmith in a Yorkshire village at the age of 13, Richard Davies with a village feltmaker in Montgomeryshire at the age of 14; and Arise Evans was 14 years old when he was apprenticed in Cheshire.[60] Sometimes youths became apprentices after they had already worked as agricultural servants or labourers, at home or elsewhere. On the Stiffkey estate in late sixteenth-century Norfolk, craftsmen such as bricklayers, carpenters, coopers, plumbers, masons, fishermen and embroiderers were on occasion joined by their sons and other trainees. These sons were sometimes trained by their fathers until they were 15 years old, and then probably moved on to some form of apprenticeship in a nearby village or a town. Agricultural servants, too, occasionally moved on to become apprentices in small parishes and towns, as was the case of Arise Evans, who was a servant in his early teens and then became an apprentice about eight miles from where his mother still lived, in Wales.[61]

A few of those who were apprenticed in a rural craft were women, although the evidence on this is by far the least easy to detect, especially for the early part of the period. Snell's evidence on apprenticeships in parishes in southern counties during the late seventeenth and eighteenth centuries shows differentiation along sexual lines, but also lack of complete occupational segregation between men and women. Half of the women were apprenticed in housewifery rather than in a craft apprenticeship; another fifth were in agriculture; and a fifth were apprenticed in industries and skills that absorbed large numbers of women rather than men: clothing, especially knitting, spinning and needlework. The remaining 10 per cent, however, were apprenticed to brewers, a grocer, a turner, a locksmith – the kinds of occupation normally learnt by young males. Among apprentices placed by parish authorities, the proportions of women were particularly high.[62] And as we shall also see in Chapter 6, women acquired a narrower range of skills than men, but those they learnt without formal apprenticeships were far more diverse, even in the large towns.

Conclusion

Most rural youths, both men and women, were at one time or another hired as annual farm and domestic servants. Yet focusing on annual forms of hiring of servants tends to conceal the dynamics involved in moving between different types of service arrangements, the range of skills that could be learnt by the young in the course of their teens, and the individual circumstances that could be encountered by adolescents and youths during many years of labour in the countryside. The case of William Huntington, of very poor origins, illustrates the haphazard course some youngsters might be forced to follow, especially during periods when there were greater pressures on the labour market in the countryside. Huntington was born in 1745 near Cranbrook, in Kent, the illegitimate son of a large farmer, whose reputed father, an agricultural labourer, had been employed by his actual father. Between the ages of seven and eight he was sent to collect bundles of wood, and he then began to work in gleaning during the summer months. He had been an errand boy, a domestic servant, a gunmaker's apprentice and a pitman by the time he was 19 years old. Afterwards he was a coachman, a driver and an agricultural labourer. At the age of 22 he was forced into begging, but then he became a gardener, and worked as this for several years.[63]

There must have been many variations in individual circumstances, depending on local employment opportunities and the socioeconomic background of the young: among the wealthier middling sections, mobility from one type of employment to another was probably less haphazard. But seventeenth-century autobiographies occasionally reveal a diversity of employments and a great deal of physical mobility not only among the very poor. Thomas Tryon was a spinning boy, a shepherd, and then a merchant's apprentice; Arise Evans was a servant and an errand boy, an assistant to his mother in her small farm, and an apprentice, before he migrated to London. Benjamin Bangs was an apprentice in a small Norfolk village, then worked as a labourer in Edmundsbury in Suffolk, and finally migrated to London, where, after a short period when he was unemployed, he became a shoemaker's apprentice. Edward Barlow had even more different jobs, and his experience was probably quite typical of the sons of the labouring poor, as well as those of husbandmen and small craftsmen. Barlow had some rudimentary schooling between the ages of seven and nine; then during his early teens he was a daily agricultural labourer, a hauling boy in the local mine, and a textile worker who also did threshing and other agricultural tasks for his master. He then migrated to London, where he was an errand boy, a post boy, a vintner's apprentice, and finally, after more than a year, he settled as a seaman's apprentice for a seven-year term.

Periods of unemployment must have punctuated these moves, especially while the population continued to grow during the sixteenth and first half of the seventeenth centuries. It was during these decades that pressures on local labour markets drove many youngsters farther away from their home villages and small market towns towards more urbanised parishes, larger provincial towns, and the fast-growing capital, London.

4 Urban Apprentices: Travel and Adjustments

About 1,400 youths began apprenticeship terms every year in mid-sixteenth-century London, comprising, together with those already apprenticed in the town, about one-tenth of the capital's population within the walls at this time. By the early years of the seventeenth century their numbers had more than doubled, and a century later, when their proportion in London's population fell, the overall numbers were of the order of 30,000. Throughout the period, apprentices were a sizeable and visible sector of London's inhabitants, within and outside the walls. In other large provincial centres, the number of apprentices registered every year was counted in hundreds rather than thousands, but their proportion in urban populations was at times as high as in London. In early seventeenth-century Bristol, apprentices enrolled at a rate of between 200 and 230 every year, and their proportion of Bristol's population remained, throughout the century, about 10 per cent. In York and Norwich, the numbers of apprentices registered every year and their proportions in the towns' respective populations must have been similar, if not higher, and in smaller country towns it could reach about 5 per cent of the overall population. In all of these towns, apprentices would have comprised a much higher proportion among adult male citizens, and higher still in the urban servant sector; that is, all urban youths, males and females, who spent their teens and early twenties as domestic servants or apprentices.[1]

What is known to us today about the lives of early modern apprentices is still owing to O. Jocelyn Dunlop and Richard D. Denman's older account of the history of apprenticeship from medieval to modern times.[2] In their view, apprenticeship was characterised by three features: the term of the contract between the master and his trainee was for a fixed number of years, normally seven; the master was subject to the supervision of the 'local community', i.e. the urban guild; and the apprentice was subject to the authority of the master who 'stood to him *in loco parentis*'.[3] This understanding of a hierarchy of roles, especially the paternal authority of the master over his apprentice, has continued to loom large in a long historiography which viewed the relationship between an apprentice and his master first and foremost in terms of family relationship. Such a view also fitted well with historians' understanding of early modern society and the early modern family as hierarchical and paternal, if not patriarchal.[4] Apprenticeship was seen as a type of family relationship rather than labour relationship, and the apprentice was viewed as a child, rather than a trainee, an assistant in a shop, or a skilled worker. In these accounts, the various obligations imposed on an apprentice and his childlike subjection were highlighted: the duty to obey his master, to avoid drinking, to refrain from marrying. The behaviour of apprentices themselves has sometimes been described as childlike and passive: their apprenticeship was arranged by parents who transferred them to masters, who in turn assumed the role of parents and teachers rather than simply instructors in a craft. More recently, historians have shown that at least in London apprentices began their training in their late, rather than early, teens. Nevertheless, the view of apprentices as childlike has persisted.[5]

This description of the childlike apprentice, and of apprenticeship as a form of family relationship, is not altogether untrue. It fits well with early modern contemporary understanding of the apprenticeship arrangement as integral to family life and the domestic order, as well as to the order of society as a whole. Such a description also to some extent matches the social reality of apprenticeship. The apprentice was subordinate to his master by guild rules and town regulations, by the conditions of his indenture, by what can loosely be described as the family morality to which he was subject, and by his dependence on his master for provision of his basic needs for a long period of seven and more years. Nevertheless, as we shall see in the following chapters, the description of the childlike apprentice does not quite fit with the experience, skills and independence most apprentices acquired in the course of their training in large towns. In their actions before and during their migration to a town, in their adaptation to urban life and especially to life in a new household, in the skills they learnt and the initiatives they took once they mastered their craft, most young men were quite mature well before they finished their apprenticeship terms.

Social Composition

The single largest group among apprentices in larger early modern towns consisted of migrants from smaller towns and rural areas. London by far outnumbered all provincial centres and large towns in the number of migrant apprentices it attracted. Behind it, with fewer absolute numbers but with equally large proportions of migrants among apprentices, was Bristol, the second major port and a large provincial centre, which drew on the whole western part of the country, from Lancashire and Ireland in the north, to the Midlands, Wales and Devon in the south. In mid-sixteenth-century London and Bristol, 90 and 80 per cent of the apprentice populations, respectively, were migrants, and by the early seventeenth century about 85 per cent of London apprentices, and nearly 75 per cent of Bristol's were from the countryside. In other provincial towns, such as Norwich and York, the proportion of migrant apprentices in the late sixteenth and early seventeenth centuries varied between a third and a half, but in some other towns, like Shrewsbury and Southampton, their proportion among all apprentices in the town was also in the order of two-thirds and even more.[6] Only in the late seventeenth century did the number of migrants among apprentices fall; but in London, as in Bristol and other towns, they still comprised about half of all the youths apprenticed in the towns.[7]

While a great deal is known about the migration and distances travelled by early modern apprentices, less is clear about their motives and their economic background. Some historians have referred to migrant apprentices in large towns as 'betterment' migrants, distinguishing them from 'subsistence' migrants. At the heart of this distinction was the assumption that, although apprentices were not necessarily an exclusive elite, they were a select group, and their migration to large towns was motivated by aspirations to social advancement. By contrast, subsistence migrants included the poorest sections in society at large, victims of overpopulation who were seeking employment or charity rather than a respectable apprenticeship, and their move to towns was the product of necessity rather than a deliberate, voluntary, choice.[8]

As evidence on the occupational background of apprentices in many towns suggests, the predominance of the better-off among apprentices bound in the mercantile and more lucrative distributive trades was indeed evident throughout the period. The overwhelming majority of sons of gentlemen and yeomen who were apprenticed in mid-sixteenth-century London were placed in companies such as the drapers, grocers, mercers and merchant tailors, as well as in companies which dominated the export trade, especially of cloth. In the seventeenth century between a fifth and a third of those entering the grocery, drapery and haberdashery trades were sons of knights, esquires and gentlemen. In Bristol in the early seventeenth century, two-thirds of those apprenticed in the distributive trades were sons of gentlemen, yeomen, merchants and other large-scale traders, as well as a few from among the professions. In the early seventeenth century, the proportions of sons of gentlemen, yeomen and drapers among Shrewsbury drapers rose to near 90 per cent.[9]

The reasons for the predominance in these lucrative occupations and businesses of apprentices from among the higher ranks of society are not difficult to find. These mercantile trades and businesses, especially those connected with London's export of cloth, required formidable resources for the launching of successful careers, as well as for the initial fees (premiums) demanded from those being apprenticed in them. Already in the fifteenth century, premiums in these large-scale businesses were well established, but in the course of the sixteenth and seventeenth centuries the amounts required as premiums from the families of aspiring apprentices soared from hundreds to as high as £1,000. The retail trades in provincial towns required lower sums, but still the premiums paid for entry into them could be from dozens to hundreds of pounds.[10] Bonds of security in these businesses to protect the master were also quite high; by the seventeenth century bonds for the value of £100 and even more were given to masters, and about a quarter of the bonds paid in a sample of Bristol apprenticeships between 1600 and 1645 were on the order of £200, £300, and even £500.[11] Entry into these trades, therefore, required a great deal of money as well as sureties willing and able to sign bonds, and repay them, in case something went wrong in the course of the apprenticeship.

It should be noted, however, that even in these lucrative trades premiums were not fixed, and there was a great variability between types of business, the social prestige of various merchants and traders, and their scale of dealings, and premiums appear to have varied accordingly. In some provincial towns premiums were much lower than in London, and were in the order of £20 and £30.[12] Even in London itself there were merchant tailors and haberdashers who received no more than £12 or even less.[13] In Bristol in 1623, Iles Godwin, a haberdasher, received £15 for apprenticing Francis Reade, and in 1622, another

Bristol haberdasher received no more than £10.[14] The value of bonds of security also varied greatly, and, overall, only about a fifth of all those apprenticed in Bristol's distributive trades, for example, had to provide bonds of security.[15]

More importantly, the vast majority of urban apprentices, both migrants and natives of a town, were not those whose parents signed bonds of high amounts or paid hundreds of pounds as premiums, and they were not sons of gentlemen, yeomen, merchants or other large-scale dealers and entrepreneurs. In some London companies in the sixteenth century, the predominance of sons of husbandmen was marked, and to judge by the records of freemen admitted to London companies in the period 1551–53, the fathers of no less than two-thirds were craftsmen engaged in small-scale production, as well as husbandmen, and even a few labourers. Sons of husbandmen alone comprised a third of all those admitted free. In other towns, the presence of youths whose fathers were craftsmen, husbandmen and labourers among the apprentices was no less evident. In Southampton in the first half of the seventeenth century, sons of craftsmen, husbandmen, and labourers formed 44.4 per cent of the total number of youths bound as apprentices. In the later decades of the century their proportions rose to two-thirds of all those apprenticed. In Bristol throughout the sixteenth and first half of the seventeenth centuries, these occupational groups comprised nearly two-thirds of all those apprenticed in the town.[16] By the late seventeenth century, sons of husbandmen, leatherworkers, textile workers, carpenters, and various other craftsmen still comprised a little over 40 per cent of all those bound as apprentices in the town.

Moreover, the occupations into which these apprentices entered were small crafts, rather than the large mercantile and distributive trades or the most lucrative crafts, such as goldsmithing or shipbuilding. Most urban apprentices filled the shops of numerous craftsmen and small-scale manufacturers: coopers and hosiers, feltmakers and weavers, cardmakers, shoemakers, carpenters, smiths, farriers, pinmakers, and turners, to name but a few. Early modern towns had diversified economies, and small industries, rather than the entrepreneurial, large-scale businesses and trades, predominated. As indicated by the occupational distribution of freemen in many towns (e.g. Norwich, York, Nottingham, Chester, Hull) in the late sixteenth century, between a half and two-thirds of the citizens were employed in manufacturing and processing a variety of goods and raw materials, rather than in any kind of large-scale trade.[17] Even in the largest commercial centres, small craftsmen and manufacturers formed the bulk of those sworn citizens. In London, workers engaged in manufacturing metal, leather and wood products, and in the building industry, comprised nearly half of all sworn citizens in 1551–53.[18] In the ensuing decades, during which London witnessed a great increase in population, the proliferation of small trades and crafts involved in leather production, metal-work and construction was still evident, both within and outside the walls.[19] In Bristol the distribution of occupations of freemen, and of the apprentices taken by them, present a similar picture: that of the dominant role of small crafts throughout the sixteenth and seventeenth centuries.[20] In addition, from what is known about the sizes of the shops of the majority of these craftsmen (at least up to the second half of the seventeenth century and in many places well beyond), the scale of production of these craftsmen could not have been anything like that of the merchants, mercers, and many of those involved in the distribution of foodstuffs and goods. Most shops comprised a master and a handful of assistants, apprentices or journeymen.[21]

What, if any, were the barriers to entry into apprenticeship in these various crafts and small shops? Unlike the distributive trades, where some qualifications for entry were specified by the law,[22] in many occupations there were no such barriers, for the Statute of Artificers included a clause which allowed the entry of 'the sonne of any person' into a whole range of small manual crafts.[23] On the other hand, premiums were still required by masters in these small crafts. In London, examples of premiums which were paid for apprenticeships, not only in the distributive trades but also in tailoring, metalwork, leather or the silk industries, as well as loans and lands given to masters in a variety of crafts, go back to the fifteenth century at least.[24] Payments in kind must also have been given occasionally to craftsmen in London and in other towns, at least throughout the sixteenth and early seventeenth centuries.[25] The difficulty is that we lack systematic evidence on these types of payment in the smaller crafts, for the costs masters charged were a matter normally agreed upon privately and without formal records.[26] Records of premiums appear very infrequently on indentures, in some court cases which involved disputes between masters and their apprentices, and, very rarely, also in some memoranda attached to the entry in the register of apprenticeship, as was the case in Bristol. I have collected 44 cases of apprenticeships in Bristol in which some record of the premiums paid to the master remained, about half of which (21) were from the period 1615–30, and the remaining 23 from the period 1653–83. These cases do not represent a sample of the large body of apprenticeship records left during these decades. Nevertheless, they involve apprenticeships in a whole range of crafts and small industries, rather than in mercantile businesses or large-scale trade, and together represent all major trades and industries of Bristol at the time, from bakers, butchers and barber-surgeons, to textile workers, saddlers and shoemakers, goldsmiths, tilers, glaziers and coopers. Since so little is known about apprentice premiums paid during this period to craftsmen in these types of occupation, these cases are still valuable for what they tell us about the sums given to masters in a few specific crafts in a large urban community such as Bristol.

The most expensive premiums in the 44 cases involved apprenticeships to a mercer who in the 1650s received £70, and a goldsmith and two barber-surgeons, who received £30 each. Lesser premiums of £20 each were given to a merchant and a saddler in the 1620s. At the other end of the scale were apprenticeships in which no more than £1, £2 or £4 were paid. These small amounts were given to a shoemaker, a buttonmaker, a tiler, a ropemaker and a mariner, all in the period 1615–30, and to one cardmaker in the 1650s. There were also a few cases in which masters in the same craft were paid the same amounts. So in the 1650s, two coopers received £12, and two tailors about £10 each. All this suggests that there was some kind of hierarchy of occupations which depended on the scale of business involved (mercers' apprenticeships were more expensive than those in small-scale trade), as well as on the degree of expertise and time required to learn a craft (goldsmiths and barber-surgeons charged more than buttonmakers, cardmakers or tilers),[27] the type of raw material handled by the craftsman and the trainee (e.g. goldsmiths dealing with precious metal, compared with coopers dealing with wood), and the perceived prestige of the occupation. But this hierarchy was by no means rigid, for differences within crafts were evident as well. In the 1620s one baker received £10, another £2, and a third charged no premium at all.[28] One barber-surgeon, in the 1650s, received only £14; and a mercer received a premium much lower than £70 and probably no more than around £20. Much depended on the economic circumstances and social prestige of the individual himself. As Adam Smith still observed in the late eighteenth century, the 'credit which [a craftsman or trader] gets from other people, depends, not upon the nature of his trade, but upon their opinion of his fortune, probity, and prudence'.[29]

The most striking thing about these payments is that the

amounts invested in most of these apprenticeships were quite modest. None reached anything like the level required in the large distributive trades in London or elsewhere. The lowest payments were in fact similar to the type of payment given by charity donors and allocated by parish authorities for the apprenticeship of poor boys. Overall, in the 21 cases between 1615 and 1630, all but 3 apprenticeships cost £10 or less; and in the period between 1653 and 1670, all but 4 of 23 cases were still £12 or less. Premiums of £5, £6, £9 and £10 were the norm. There were a grocer and a haberdasher who received no more than £10, not to speak of a leatherworker, an upholster, a glazier, and a shoemaker who received less. Such amounts could still present a social barrier to entry into urban crafts. This was particularly so in London, where craftsmen probably charged a little more than their counterparts in provincial towns,[30] and where apprenticeships may well have required even higher amounts. Any family whose income was near subsistence, with, say, only £10–15 annual income, or labourers who made even less and who had no steady employment throughout the year,[31] would find it hard to invest the few pounds necessary for an apprenticeship of a son, not to mention two sons or more.

On the other hand, premiums ranging between £5 and £15 or even £20 were not an insurmountable barrier, and it is evident that youths of poor background not infrequently managed to enter a wide variety of small trades and crafts. In Chancery Court records there are examples of cases of apprenticeships in which premiums of £10 were paid, and the fathers of the apprentices were described as labourers and very poor.[32] It is difficult to know how these poor people raised the amounts necessary for the premiums, but other sources suggest that young people from poor families could themselves accumulate the fee necessary for an apprenticeship. In some places this could be done with the assistance of friends and neighbours, as was the case of William Dubler, an orphan who, in 1635, placed himself with a Bristol merchant and paid nearly £20, a sum mostly raised by his neighbours, the parishioners of St Stevens.[33] Migrant apprentices from poor backgrounds could also find ways to save and raise the money necessary for an apprenticeship, as autobiographical accounts suggest. Edward Barlow arrived in London with some money he had earned in agricultural labour in his native county of Lancashire. During his first year in London he was employed in doing errands, and was able to make some money which he saved in 'an old rag in a mortice of one of the posts of my chamber where I lay'. By the end of the year he apprenticed himself on a ship. And Benjamin Bangs apprenticed himself in London having before lived for a while in Edmundsbury, where he and his older master worked. Some of the money he had earned probably helped him in his first weeks in the capital, when he was still unemployed.[34]

Many migrant apprentices who had worked in smaller places in the countryside before their arrival in a large town could also save towards their apprenticeship. The research of Ann Kussmaul and Marjorie K. McIntosh has shown that agricultural servants were often able to save some of their wages.[35] That those who entered the lesser crafts in the large towns had previously been agricultural servants is suggested by a comparison of the social background and ages of rural servants and urban apprentices. The vast majority of agricultural servants had come from households headed by husbandmen, craftsmen and traders.[36] Although among urban apprentices there were sons of gentlemen and merchants and only a few sons of labourers, the majority, as we have seen, also came from among the ranks of husbandmen, craftsmen and small traders. In other words, some distinctive features of each group notwithstanding, in both there was a large group of young people who were sons of craftsmen and husbandmen. The difference in the ages of the two groups confirms this point. While most youths entered agricultural service when they were 13, 14 or 15 years old, urban apprentices were normally 16, 17 or 18, and in London, even older.[37] So in many instances, adolescents must have gone from one type of service in agriculture to another type of service in an urban craft, with the former providing, as in the case of Edward Barlow, at least part of the money necessary for the latter.

Savings from work as agricultural servants, day labourers and other types of service in villages and towns as well as in a large town where a youth would eventually bind himself as an apprentice, small loans and gifts, legacies of a few shillings left by relatives and kin, could all contribute towards the savings of a few pounds for an apprenticeship. If this was not sufficient, a youth who arrived in a large town could agree to serve a master with whom he wanted to learn a trade or craft for a longer term of service in order to lower the costs of his apprenticeship. As we shall see in the next chapter, the labour of an apprentice in his final years was quite valuable, so that by working one or two years in addition to the required seven-year term, a young man could repay his master £12, if not much more. In mid-sixteenth-century London, the mean length of term served in various companies varied between 7.4 and 7.9, and in a sample of 1,945 Bristol apprenticeships in the first half of the seventeenth century, the mean length was 7.9; more than half the Bristol apprenticeships were for terms varying between 8, 9 and more years.[38] Nor were longer contracts confined to the poorer apprentices. In mid-sixteenth-century London, sons of gentlemen and yeomen signed on longer contracts than sons of husbandmen, and in the sample of Bristol apprenticeships in the early seventeenth century, the mean number of years contracted by sons of gentlemen was 7.8, the same as that of all other apprentices.[39]

Steve Rappaport produced evidence on the correlation between length of apprenticeships and age of apprentices in mid-sixteenth-century London companies; the younger the apprentice, the longer the contract he signed. So youths who began apprenticeships at the age of 18 were somewhat more likely to serve eight years, and those who began when they were 19 tended to sign shorter contracts of seven years.[40] But this still leaves unanswered the question why a youth aged 18 would agree to serve longer than necessary; for by the time he finished his term he would have turned 26 years old, well past the minimum age of entry into the guilds. There must have been some benefits involved. To some youths a longer contract probably guaranteed the right to trade on their own in the final years of their term.[41] To others, a longer contract could lower the costs of apprenticeship. Such bargaining must have been widespread in the less costly occupations, allowing a youth with only slim resources to reduce the costs of an apprenticeship from, say, £15 to £7, or even less, by promising to provide his master with steady labour for a longer period than that required by law. In his autobiographical novel, Francis Kirkman wrote that his master in London demanded 'thirty pounds in money and eight years in service, or forty pounds and seven years service'. In other places, longer service might allow a youth to begin his apprenticeship with no premium at all, as the testimony of Edward Barlow suggests. In his autobiography he claimed that craftsmen and tradesmen required premiums, 'unless we would serve eight or nine years, which is usual with tradesmen in this country'. Barlow first became an apprentice in the mid-1650s, and there is no indication that he thought the custom had declined by the time he began to write his diary several years later.[42]

So there were ways that allowed youths of poor background and with few resources to enter a variety of small crafts and trades in large towns. Such an undertaking was not easy, and in the large commercial centres, such as London and Bristol, it became harder in the course of the period.[43] Yet even by the late seventeenth century, sons of husbandmen continued to infiltrate the apprentice population in towns like Bristol, and, together with sons of rural craftsmen, they were still a substantial segment of the apprentices living in the town. Some paid no more than a few pounds for their apprenticeship, occasionally even in the distributive trades,[44] and throughout the seventeenth century it was still possible to enter an apprenticeship without paying a premium at all. So in April 1627, John Morgan, the son of a husbandman from Monmouth, was apprenticed in Bristol to John Goodman, a baker. According to a petition presented about a year later in Quarter Sessions, he paid no premium and agreed to serve no more than the minimum seven-year term.[45]

Throughout most of the period, apprentices in towns were a large, heterogeneous group which came from all segments of society, including the poor. Their motives for entering a craft apprenticeship must likewise have been diverse: compensation for loss of a gentle status, social advancement, and also the sheer necessity to earn a livelihood and prepare for the future. In a small book of moral advice, *The Pious Apprentice*, Abraham Jackson summarised what was probably an obvious reality to all. He dedicated his book, 'To all such as intend to be servants or apprentices, whosoever you are that in the purpose of your parents and friends, or by the bent of your own inclination, or urged by necessity, or by the occurrence of all these motives, or by any other incentive are to undergoe the condition of a servant or prentice'.[46] Although Jackson made a clear distinction between those who entered apprenticeship voluntarily and those who entered through force of circumstance and necessity – something similar to the distinction historians have made between betterment and subsistence migrants – he assumed that both types were among London's apprentices.

Abraham Jackson also assumed that while some apprenticeships were the making of parents, others involved the inclinations and undertakings of young people themselves. Indeed, if some of the youths who arrived in towns, as was also true of natives of towns themselves, paid for their apprenticeships with money they had themselves saved; and if others raised the money through a combination of parental help and their own labour; and if many more contributed to the costs of their apprenticeship by agreeing to serve longer; then it is hard to think of these young people as passive observers of an arrangement which shaped their lives for several years at the least.

Travel to a Large Town

In the sixteenth century, a youth who was to begin an apprenticeship in a large town sometimes had to travel great distances across the country. In London, a third of the migrant apprentices in the years 1552–53 came from the far north, from Yorkshire and Lancashire, Cumberland and Westmorland, and, together with youths arriving from the western counties, as well as from Scotland, Ireland and Wales, they formed more than half of all arrivals in the capital. The average distance travelled by all migrant apprentices in these years was no less than 115 miles. In other large towns, such as Norwich and York, the journeys most migrant apprentices made were shorter – about 20 miles – and the proportions of those arriving from farther afield were much lower than in the capital. In the first half of the sixteenth century only Bristol had something of the magnetism exerted by the capital. Between 1532 and 1552 a fifth of the migrants were arriving from as far away as Cheshire, Lancashire, Yorkshire and Cumberland, as well as from Ireland and from counties in the east, and about half of all apprentices who came from the countryside travelled 50 miles at the least in order to arrive in Bristol. Overall, 20, 30, or up to 100 miles were covered by youths who travelled to large towns throughout most of the sixteenth century.[47]

Means of communication in the early decades of the sixteenth century were still limited, but by no means absent. Some young people must have travelled on boats and ships carrying grain, timber and coal along the coast. In Norfolk, for example, the migration of apprentices to a town like Great Yarmouth was influenced by the coastal routes along Norfolk and Suffolk, and relatively great numbers of apprentices came from the north and north-eastern fishing towns and small ports such as Cley and Cromer. The longest journeys apprentices made to Great Yarmouth were from settlements on the eastern coasts of Yorkshire in the north to as far south as Dorset.[48] In the western part of the country, travel by vessels along the northern and Welsh coasts and the Bristol Channel must have been common, too. The town of Bristol was already a busy commercial centre in the Middle Ages, and its reputation, symbolised by a ship on the city's seal and on its bells, stemmed from its geographical position and commercial links with Wales, Ireland, the southern counties and the Iberian peninsula.[49] In the period 1532–42, when registration of apprentices in the town began, a group of Welsh migrants were recorded as apprentices, most of them from villages and small towns along the coasts of Glamorgan and Pembrokeshire. Among migrants from the far north during these years were many from Lancashire, and from small market towns like Lancaster, Preston and Liverpool, all located on the coast.[50] In the early seventeenth century some of the apprentices arriving in Bristol from Devon and Cornwall also came from towns and villages, such as Bideford and St Ives, situated along the southern coasts.

Many more apprentices would have made use of the network of rivers and roads, which served for the transportation of a variety of goods and grains. London and most provincial ports were located on major rivers, and in pastoral districts there were few urban areas which were not within easy access of the sea or rivers on which cargoes of grains could travel.[51] In Bristol, relatively large numbers of apprentices arrived from settlements lying along the Severn and Avon rivers, on which goods such as wool, wheat, barley, groceries and imports to and from Bristol travelled.[52] In a sample of 37 Midland villages and towns from which apprentices migrated to Bristol between 1532 and 1542, 25 settlements were located on or within a few miles of the Severn. In the early seventeenth century the Severn continued to exert an influence on migrant apprentices in Bristol and many arrived from towns and villages on or in proximity to it. Other youths also used an extensive system of roads on which cargoes of goods, as well as travellers, were carried by carts and pack-horses.[53] Some towns were served by well-established roads; Bristol, for example, was connected with the south and east by the medieval King's Highway, which led from Temple Gate on the Avon towards Bath and then to the south. By the late sixteenth century there were roads leading to Bristol from Oxford, Cambridge, Shrewsbury and Chester.[54]

Travel on waterways was cheaper than on roads,[55] but it was also quite hazardous, especially on small vessels loaded with goods sailing along the coast.[56] But long-distance journeys on the roads were also rather difficult, and they were well remembered by some writers of autobiographies. James Fretwell devoted a small chapter in his autobiography to a description of his journey from Yorkshire to London, in November 1717; he recalled not only the precise date and time of his departure, but also the people who escorted him, and the inns and posting houses where he lodged on the way. William Lilly and Edward Barlow also recorded their journeys in some detail. Lilly travelled in 1620 from Leicester to London, and his journey of six days on 'a very stormy week' was 'cold and uncomfortable'. Edward Barlow likewise remembered the hardship of his seven-day journey from Manchester to London in 1657.[57]

Improvements in land transportation in the course of the years between 1500 and 1700 probably made travel by land somewhat less perilous. In 1500 apprentices who travelled on roads would have taken long journeys by carts and pack-horses, but by the 1560s the long-wheeled wagon, and from the 1650s the large stage wagon, were in use and carriers regularly went to London from places all over the country. Scheduled services to London more than doubled in the final decades of the seventeenth century, and there was also a substantial expansion of road services to provincial towns, as well as to smaller towns and villages, hitherto without direct links with the capital or other large towns.[58] Journeys also became rather shorter; in 1500, journeys of merchants with pack-horses from the far north to the south could take weeks,[59] but by 1700, young people from northern England could hope to arrive in London within a week and even less. Overall, the distances most apprentices travelled by 1700 were shorter, as studies of apprentice migration in early modern England have shown. In London the average distance travelled fell from 115 miles in the 1550s to 60 miles in the 1710s. In Bristol the contraction in distances travelled by apprentices was already clear in the early seventeenth century; whereas in the 1530s about half the apprentices travelled at least 50 miles, between 1600 and 1645 only a third travelled similar distances. By the mid-decades of the century, the vast majority travelled no more than 20 miles, and by the period 1670–1700 only a handful of apprentices were from Lancashire, Yorkshire, the Midlands or Pembrokeshire.[60]

Nevertheless, even by 1700 travel by land was a difficult and costly undertaking. In London there was still a large minority, about a quarter of the apprentices, who travelled 90 miles or over, as was the case of James Fretwell, who arrived from Sandal in Yorkshire. Fretwell travelled in relative comfort, and his journey appears to have been well arranged and paid for by his father, a timber-merchant. But other youngsters were much less fortunate. William Lilly paid the carrier and his servants the costs of his journey all by himself. These costs amounted to 2sh. 6d., a fifth of all the money he had had by the time he left Leicester. And Edward Barlow remembered paying the carrier in Manchester 6sh., which included charges along the road up to London. Although he thought this a reasonable price, it amounted to what Barlow had been earning in day labour for a month or more, and was nearly all he had saved.

Above all, what Lilly and Barlow recalled with clarity were the hardship and fatigue caused by walking alongside the cart. Lilly mentioned that he 'footed it all along', and Barlow remembered that somewhere on the fifth day of his journey he 'began to tire and my legs began to fail me by reason of my long journey and going afoot all the way, for I was not used to go so long a journey'. Near the end, 'I began to be faint and exceeding weary, though it was our last day's journey and not above ten short miles from London: and taking heart and cheering up myself as well as I could, at the last we came to London'.[61] If a large proportion of migrant apprentices were sons of husbandmen and craftsmen who travelled 20 or 30 miles and more even by 1700, then the experience of many youths on the road must have been similar. Whatever the type of transportation available and however improved the roads were by 1700, for many youths the most toilsome thing about long-distance travel throughout the period was the sheer necessity of taking the road leading to the capital and to other towns by foot.

Encounters with the Urban Scene

Some writers of autobiographies remembered with clarity the moment of their arrival in London. Elias Ashmole left Lichfield, in Staffordshire, in 1633, and although he did not describe the journey itself, he still noted that on 2 July 1633 'I began my journey from Litchfield', and that on 5 July 'about 11 a clock before noon, I entered London'. Benjamin Bangs came to London 'after the great fire in 1666', and Edward Barlow recalled that his first days in London were spent wandering in the streets and looking around; when he reached London Bridge, on his way to Southwark, he looked towards the Thames, and saw 'many things . . . with long poles standing up in them and a great deal of ropes about them'. Barlow had never before seen a ship. Thomas Raymond described some of the things he first encountered on his arrival in London, aged 15, as 'a very dreadful sight to a young country boy'.[62] George Bewley also observed the great contrast between the 'country place' where he had lived, and the 'large populous city' at which he arrived. Bewley was born and reared in a smal village in Cumberland, and was sent to Dublin in 1696 at the age of 14. By then Dublin was a leading port and trading centre, with a population of 60,000, and in its size second only to London.[63]

The physical landscape and social scene of London and other

large towns were undoubtedly strange and unfamiliar to youth, especially if they came from small towns and villages. In early sixteenth-century Bristol about half the migrant apprentices came from provincial towns and smaller market towns, but the remaining half were from villages scattered throughout the regions surrounding the town, as well as from more remote places in Herefordshire, Monmouth and Wales. By the early seventeenth century the porportion of those coming from villages in the countryside rose to more than two-thirds. In London, the predominance of rural youth who had been born in villages rather than in the larger provincial towns was even more marked throughout the sixteenth and seventeenth centuries. Vivien Brodsky Elliott calculated that, between 1574 and 1641, the proportion of apprentices arriving in London from villages in four separate counties ranged between 73.8 and 83.5 per cent.[64]

But perhaps the effect that the contrasting physical environments had on a youth just arriving in a large town need not be pushed too far. Not all youths travelled directly from their villages of origin to a town where they would be bound as apprentices; not a few, especially those in large provincial centres, came from villages nearby, and they must have had some contact with the town before. Accounts in autobiographies regarding early encounters with a large town, scant as they are, also indicate that, while some youths were intimidated by the urban scene, others were quite inspired by the sights and opportunities offered there. Edward Barlow's older brother, who migrated to London before him, did not like his stay in London, and all the time wished he could return to the countryside. His own attitude was rather different. He described himself as a youth whose 'mind [was] given to see places more remote', and who was determined to leave his master in Manchester and migrate to London. Despite the difficulties he encountered on the road and in his first days in the capital, when he did not know 'what was my best course to take, nor which way to go', the whole enterprise was something to which he looked forward and was willing to confront. The two brothers grew up in the same poor family in a small village in Lancashire, but Edward Barlow thought that his brother's difficulties in London had less to do with his upbringing and more with the fact that 'he had not such a wandering mind as I had, and loved the country better than the city'.[65] The contrast between the two brothers could not have been more plain.

Barlow's account of his first weeks in the capital shows that his greatest concern was not the populous city or the new and unfamiliar sights, but rather the need to find a place to live and a master who would take him on as an apprentice. At first he became a servant and an assistant to his uncle, and afterwards he secured an apprenticeship with a Kentish vintner from Dartford. But all along he wanted to go to sea. So he left the vintner, returned to London, and became an apprentice on a ship without even spending a period of trial with his master 'to see whether I would like it'. His uncle's friend made the arrangements and his mistress was present at the time of the binding; only a day later did Barlow meet his future master and embark on his first voyage overseas.[66]

Adjustments

A few young people had known their masters before their apprenticeships began. Lodowick Muggleton, who was born and reared in London, was about 15 years old when apprenticed to a tailor who lived in the same 'walnut-tree-yard' as he. The tailor knew his parents well, and Lodowick also wrote that the tailor 'liked me very well'.[67] In every town there were a few young people who were apprenticed to their own fathers, as well as to cousins, brothers, uncles and grandparents.[68] But overall, the evidence suggests that most apprentices barely knew the people to whom they were apprenticed, and that the masters, their wives and children (if there were any) were strangers to the young apprentice, even when his apprenticeship had been arranged well in advance. For example, Richard Oxinden, the son of a Kentish gentleman, was placed as an apprentice in London with the assistance of one of his kin, Valentine Pettit. Yet there is no indication that Pettit had been acquainted with the master at all. As for the Oxinden parents, it is clear that they had never met the master, Mr Newman, while Richard was introduced to him only after arriving in London, when part of the premium had already been paid and when Richard began a trial period to see what his master and his profession were like. George Bewley was also sent to Dublin on the basis of an arrangement his parents had made; the master was a linen-draper neither young Bewley – who was then 14 years old – nor his parents had known or even met.[69]

Even when parents were acquainted with the master in some way or another – a business associate, a friend they had known[70] – this did not mean that their son had known or met the master prior to the signing of the indenture. For example, the parents of

John Croker from Plymouth arranged an apprenticeship for their son with a sergemaker who lived in the colonies, whence young John was sent in the company of his parents' friends. The parents themselves may have known the master before his migration – the parents, their friends and the master were bound by ties of religion and mutual friendship – but clearly young Croker himself had never seen his master.[71] Even when the master was related to the youth by ties of kinship, this did not necessarily mean that the master would have been an acquaintance or a person with whom the youth had been in any kind of contact before. James Fretwell had, on occasion during his childhood, met his uncle, a London attorney. Nevertheless he appears to have known little about his character, or his business and dealings, before he came to London for a trial period as his apprentice. To some migrant apprentices, especially those arriving from great distances, uncles or cousins in the large town were complete strangers. Edward Barlow had probably never even seen his uncle before he arrived in London at about the age of 14.[72] It is when we realise how strange nearly all masters were to youngsters who came to learn and live under their roofs that we can begin to appreciate the difficulty involved in adapting to apprenticeship.

That difficulty was compounded by the necessity to adjust to life as a young apprentice. During the early part of their training, and sometimes well after, apprentices were required to do a wide range of demeaning tasks: cleaning, carrying, dusting, washing, sweeping, fetching coal, making up fires, and going errands of a variety of sorts. Complaints to the effect that apprentices were required to do household tasks instead of being properly trained in their trade reached the local courts, in London as well as in Bristol.[73] Some youngsters, who were bound at a relatively young age, were employed in going errands for one or two years, and only then began their proper instruction.[74] Overall, meaner tasks were particularly likely to be imposed on the newly arrived youth, whatever his precise age. Simon Forman remembered that 'being the youngest apprentice of four' in his master's shop in Salisbury, he was put to do 'all the worst', and that 'everyone did triumph over me' – fellow apprentices, and also the kitchen maid, Mary Roberts. That sense of humiliation involved in the age hierarchy of the small shop was also conveyed in Francis Kirkman's account of his life as a London scrivener's apprentice, who was not only required to do the dirtiest and most burdensome tasks, but 'being the youngest apprentice was to be commanded by everyone'.[75]

In some shops there were no fellow apprentices or even journeymen, and the youngster confronted only his master. In every town there was a large group of such craftsmen who did not have more than a single trainee or apprentice in their shop. In London in 1566, 13 out of 42 cloth finishers had a single assistant – apprentice or a journeyman – in their shop. And in Bristol in the first decade of the seventeenth century, more than half of the masters who hired apprentices took only one apprentice in the space of eight years. In some occupations this was even more pronounced. Among Bristol woodworkers – coopers, joiners, carpenters, turners, shipwrights and so on – who took apprentices in the years between 1532 and 1658, nearly two-thirds employed no more than a single apprentice in their entire career as masters in the town.[76] In addition, not a few employed two apprentices, and they hired the second apprentice only after seven years, that is, after the previous one had left. Some of these carpenters and joiners probably died relatively young, and others possibly left Bristol after a few years of working there; but not a few among these many woodworkers had only one apprentice in their shop, and so the youngster entered a small shop with only a single master, a stranger with whom he was to begin an intimate routine of hard work.

Some smoothing of the process of adjustment to a master and to the routine of the shop could be obtained through a period of trial during which a youngster could evaluate the character of his master and what life as an apprentice entailed. Edward Coxere, an apprentice on a ship, Richard Davies, apprenticed in Welshpool in Wales, William Stout, apprenticed in Lancaster, and John Coggs, apprenticed to a London printer, all began their apprenticeship with a trial period – to be 'upon liking,' as some called it – of a few weeks.[77] Some youths were able to withdraw from their contracts following a trial period, as the case of Adam Martindale, who returned home to his parents, suggests.[78] But a period of trial was too short to reveal the full extent to which an apprentice could accommodate to his master and the new demands of assistance and work in the shop and the house; a proper alternative, especially for poorer apprentices, was not always available. There was something impractical about this procedure of a trial period, for when the apprenticeship had taken long to arrange, a youth could well find it hard to change his mind. This is clear in the case of Richard Oxinden, who, at the end of his trial period in London, decided to leave his master. Although Valentine Pettit, the kinsman who had arranged his apprenticeship, complied with his feelings and reasoning, and tried to look for another master, the whole process was not without difficulties. Although the apprenticeship was not as yet registered, part of the premium had already been paid to the master and the indentures had been signed, so there was the question of how to make sure the master would return the money. It is clear from Pettit's letter to the Oxinden parents that he and others were of the opinion that even if the master would let his apprentice depart, he would keep at least part of the money paid as a premium. Some time later, after young Oxinden had gone back to the country when he became ill, he decided to return to London. Another kinsman now informed his mother that he would try to persuade his old master to take him back, because to find a new master 'will cost a good summe of mony and a longe time of treatinge, both with his old master to gett in his Indentures and to settle him with the new'.[79]

There were also formal ways to ensure reasonable behaviour of masters, by demanding that they signed on bonds of security. When Richard Risby, a Bristol shoemaker, took Robert White as an apprentice in 1616, he agreed 'that if he put away the boy within two years or cause him to run away through his default', then he would pay back the full £3 he had received as premium. John Davis, a tiler, also signed a bond of the value of £4: 'that if he shall put him away or misuse him whereby he shall run away' then he would repay the premium of £2; and Anthony Bazar, a metalworker, was bound to repay 40sh. 'if the boy departe through his master's default'. Similar bonds were signed by Richard Coulston, a wiredrawer, John Spratt, a haberdasher, Roger Stevens, a lighterman, John Allin, a weaver, Thomas Taylor, a pinmaker, and John Room, a mason.[80] In other cases two bonds were signed: one for the apprentice's 'service and truth', and a counter-bond for the youth's safety and well-being.[81] Still other masters promised, without signing a bond but putting it in writing along with the record of the apprenticeship, that if apprentices or their parents were dissatisfied, the contract would be annulled.[82]

Whatever the safeguards, many youths found the adjustment to apprenticeship quite difficult, as the case of John Nutt, a Bristol cooper apprentice in the 1650s, shows. A year after his apprenticeship had been enrolled, his mistress, Ann Nutt, appeared in Quarter Sessions to ask for the release of her apprentice, because of his 'weakness of body'. Ann Nutt was a widow and probably related by kinship ties to John. There is no indication that she was unable to continue to employ the youth, for she was immediately allowed to take another apprentice for a period of trial; in fact she appears to have been diligent in teaching the youth her art, for the court also ordered that a bond of no less than £100 be signed, to ensure that John would not 'exercise the trade of a cooper'. This order also casts some doubt on the description of young Nutt as being weak and unable to work, for obviously the mistress, the apprentice and his parents, who appeared on his behalf, all agreed that there was a real possibility that he would soon begin to practise the trade of a cooper on his own. The youth also consented to depart from his mistress, even though the departure cost his parents a great deal of money in compensation to his mistress. What remains from the whole episode is that, as it was plainly put by the justices, 'he [the apprentice] having served the space of a year [is] praying that hee might bee released of his apprenticeship'.[83]

Some youths reacted to their masters and the new circumstances they encountered quite violently. In April 1627 John Morgan, a migrant from Wales, was apprenticed to John Godman, a Bristol baker, and after several months the master complained at court that young Morgan had 'behaved himself in very insolent sort' and threatened him with a knife. Unlike other cases in which an unruly apprentice was sent to Bridewell, the court only discharged John Morgan, with his own consent. And Thomas Watkins, apprenticed in the early 1660s to Abraham Edward, a Bristol mercer, was said to have been 'very disorderly', to have assaulted and beaten his master and mistress, absented himself from work and committed several other misdemeanours. Again the court only discharged the apprentice, and it even ordered that he be compensated: the master had to return part of the premium (£10) paid to him before the apprenticeship had begun. The court also ordered that the master should take care of his apprentice and find someone else in his place. In both of these cases the court appears to have acknowledged, probably after some sort of investigation, that the fault was not only in the behaviour of youths like Morgan and Watkins, that John Godman and Abraham Edward and their apprentices were in some way incompatible, and that different masters might well prove more suitable and successful.[84]

Other youths were less violent, but still failed to adjust to their apprenticeship, as is suggested by the appearance in Bristol's Register of Apprentices of many entries that have been crossed out. Most of these were apprenticeships which ended in some sort of informal agreement between the apprentice and his master rather than by an order of a court. For example, Thomas Brown, the son of a husbandman in Gloucestershire, was bound in Bristol with a house carpenter called Robert Price, in June 1615. Five months later, on 15 November, his indentures were cancelled, his record of apprenticeship in the apprentice register crossed out, and in the margin it was written that he was released with the consent of his master.[85] Examples like these are scattered throughout the volumes of the Register of Apprentices. Between five and ten indentures were cancelled every year, and in a sample of apprenticeships in the period between 1600 and 1645, 5.1 per cent were crossed out, a proportion which fluctuated only slightly from year to year. In none of these cases was there any indication of a serious dispute – of the kind recorded in some detail in Quarter Sessions and other courts – which involved some sort of breach of the conditions of the contract on the part of the master or his apprentice. The more or less even distribution of these cases over time also suggests that these dismissals were not affected by conditions that might force masters to dismiss their apprentices, such as an economic depression.[86] Occasionally the clerk recorded in the margin of the entry that the master or mistress had died, and this led to the annulment of the contract. But in most cases all the clerk wrote down was that the apprentice was 'released' or 'exonerated', and that this was done with the consent of his master, or with the consent of the apprentice and other parties involved. By far the largest number of these cases were crossed out within the first months or within two years following the beginning of the apprenticeship.[87]

Getting on with a new, unfamiliar master, in what immediately became an intimate routine of hard, sometimes humiliating, labour and life, was not devoid of strain and tension. Some masters turned out to be exceptionally brutal,[88] but many more were probably simply difficult, stubborn or hard to please. Still others had burdens and responsibilities of their own, and a few were quite young, not altogether experienced in handling apprentices not much younger than themselves. To all of this, an apprentice, a youth in his mid- or late teens and not infrequently with definite ideas about his apprenticeship,[89] had to adjust. Some youngsters were frustrated in their expectations, like James Fretwell, who in the course of the first weeks of his apprenticeship found out that his master was 'not unkind', but he was still apprehensive about not being 'so thoroughly instructed in my business as I could wish,' as he put it later.[90] And John Nashe, a young apprentice, obtained a bond of security from his master, a Bristol pinmaker, to repay 'if his boy goe away through [the master's] default'. John's father, Thomas Nashe, was himself a Bristol pinmaker who was probably acquainted with the future master of his son; but this did not prevent them both from agreeing to sign a bond in which they took it for granted that Thomas Tayler, the master, might fail to fulfil his obligations, and that young Nashe might become dissatisfied.[91] In the case of the apprentice William Middleton, a Bristol native bound to a saddler, his master signed a bond promising to repay the premium in the course of the first three years of the apprenticeship if 'any complaint . . . or dislike . . . shall be between them'.[92] Apprehension about the misunderstandings, complaints and dislike that might arise in the course of the early stage of an apprenticeship must have been prevalent, among young trainees no less than among those acting on their behalf.

There was also the mistress of the house. In some towns, such as in Bristol, the wife was an equal party to the contract and her name was entered along with that of her husband in the Register of Apprentices. Even in places where this was not the custom, a mistress would have been in charge of the apprentice as soon as he entered the household. Some autobiographies convey a sense of strain, if not outright animosity, between male apprentices and their mistresses. Richard Oxinden and his fellow apprentices attributed everything that went wrong with their master to his new wife. 'Hee always telld mee that hee liked his master well,' his kinsman wrote in a letter to his parents, 'but his Mistris was somthinge a strange kynde of wooman.' His kinsman also thought that 'moste of London mistrisses ar strange kynde of woomen'. Edward Barlow also appears to have had greater difficulties with his mistresses than with his masters. When he first came to London he was a servant in the house of his uncle and aunt. While he had little to say about his uncle's character in his autobiography, he recalled that he was displeased with his aunt, for she 'was a woman very hard to please and very mistrustful'. Later on he became apprenticed on a ship, and his recollections also convey the differences between his relations with his master and those with the mistress, with whom he lived in between voyages to the sea. From the start, his master appeared to him a 'very loving and honest person', and so he remained 'for the most part'. His relations with his mistress, by contrast, were more sour. They scolded each other, had many disputes and 'fallings out' whenever he came back on shore and was required to do household tasks.[93] These accounts remind us that there was someone else besides the master to whom the apprentice had to adjust, and that the relationship with new mistresses could be tenuous. If the master himself was a stranger to the new apprentice, the mistress was not only that, but also a woman, sometimes not much older than the apprentice himself.

Some accounts also suggest that it was not simply the mistress but the strain in the relationship between the master and his wife which aggravated the situation. William Lilly remembered that when he began his service in London his life was 'more uncomfortable, it being very difficult to please two such opposite natures' as those of his master and mistress. Simon Forman, who had been apprenticed in the late 1560s in Salisbury, recalled many controversies he had with his mistress, who often turned to his master and incited him to 'beat Simon for it'. But Simon was of the opinion that the master did this 'against his will', and that he 'knew his wife to be a wicked, headstrong, and proud fantastical woman, a consumer and spender of his wealth'. In fact most of the controversies in the house were between the master and his wife; 'oftentimes they two were also at square – insomuch that twice he had like to have killed her by casting a pair of tailor's shears at her'. Forman's account suggests not only that he was exposed to the strain in the relationship, but that he somehow became part of it, for often he and his master used to walk outside the shop and complain to one another about her, and his master would say to him, 'Simon, thou must suffer as well as I myself. Thou seest we cannot remedy it as yet; but God will send a remedy one day.'[94]

Some apprentices failed to adjust to their masters and so they left, but most others persevered, hoping for a remedy for whatever it was that continued to cause them unease or dissatisfaction. Some adjusted with greater ease than others, and became satisfied with their masters and their new home. Some were quite fortunate in finding exceptionally suitable masters to whom they took an immediate liking. Strange and unfamiliar as most masters were, some did show genuine kindness to their apprentices from the outset. We have already mentioned that the master of Edward Barlow commanded his trust from the moment he saw him. Barlow deposited whatever monies he had saved with his master, who turned out to be generous, even though he was a total stranger, an officer on a ship with some 500 men and youths, amongst whom young Barlow felt 'a stranger'.[95]

Individual circumstances and fortunes apart, the adjustment to a new master and mistress was quite demanding, above all because a young apprentice was on his own in confronting his new circumstances. We have discussed the cases that were crossed out in Bristol's Register of Apprentices – some 5 per cent of all apprenticeships – which apparently ended in agreement between the master and his apprentice to part ways. Some time in the early 1620s these entries begin to include the marks or signatures of those involved in the decision to dissolve the contract and who were present when the record of apprenticeship was crossed out. Often there was the signature or mark of the master, the clerk or some other magistrate present, the father or someone else on behalf of the apprentice, the new master in case it was decided an apprentice would be bound again, as well as the apprentice himself. But often it is clear that the only people present were the master and his apprentice. In February 1622 Thomas Elliott was released with the consent of his master, a gunmaker to whom he had been bound only three months earlier. Elliott had come to Bristol from a village in Gloucestershire, and the record of his apprenticeship suggests that his father was still alive. Nevertheless, the only people who appeared when the apprenticeship was crossed out were the gunmaker and young Elliott; the master left his mark, and Thomas Elliott left his signature. In 1634 Edward Gill, apprenticed to a Bristol pewterer, was discharged; only the mark of the master and the signature of the apprentice appear in the margin.[96]

Not all those who left their masters were completely on their own, as we shall see in Chapter 7; but the consequences of the poor adjustment of some youths to their masters and their apprenticeships may perhaps be captured from a case which appeared in Bristol's Quarter Sessions in 1672. From the description of the justices, we learn that Thomas Burgess was the apprentice of John Bryant, a Bristol pinmaker, and that he departed from his service several times without his master's permission. It is uncertain what led to Burgess's decision to leave; there is no mention of exceptionally harsh treatment, and it is clear that the master wanted his apprentice to come back, for he 'had made enquiry after him [and] could not hear any news of him'. The case also indicates that the magistrates, having heard the complaint of the master, made some enquiries regarding his whereabouts and notified the mother about her son. Thomas's mother was aware of the previous times when her son had run away, but she 'did confess . . . that she did not then know what was become of him'. Young Thomas Burgess, who took 'all his clothes' when he left his master, probably with the intention never to return, was quite evidently on his own.[97]

5 Urban Apprentices: Skills and Initiatives

Expectations

When looking for a master, a youth and his family were attentive to the master's reputation in treating his apprentices. Valentine Pettit, a relative of the Kentish gentry family of Henry Oxinden, made careful arrangements for the apprenticeship of their son, Richard, and bound him to a cloth-merchant in London in 1628. When some time later he found out that Richard's master had 'much alterd since hee hath beene marryed' and had begun to beat his apprentices 'for any small occasion', he wrote a letter to the Oxinden parents admitting that 'if I had knowne that hee would have provd soe it should have been farre from mee from wishinge of your sonn unto him'. All in all he thought that he had been 'soe unfortunate in placeing him'.[1]

There was a range of benefits that youths could expect to obtain through an apprenticeship in various trades and crafts: steady provision and maintenance, occupational contacts and business connections, and the privileges which a long apprenticeship guaranteed in entering an urban guild.[2] As various court cases suggest, any one of these benefits was considered part of the arrangement: the return youths could expect for the money they had paid as a premium for their apprenticeship. For example, Benony Claye, a merchant apprentice in Exeter, requested in Chancery Court that his master repay all his premium of 20 marks; this was after five years of the apprenticeship had elapsed, and Claye argued that he was by now convinced that his master was not 'free of the company of merchants, but is only a petty chapman by selling by retail . . . so there is no hope at all of any preferment and advancement as a merchant'.[3]

A central expectation in any apprenticeship arrangement was

the acquisition of skills. As explained in a memorandum attached to the registration of an apprenticeship in Bristol in 1607, the master received 20sh. 'in consideration [he and his wife] covenant and promise to teach the art of knit silk stocking [and] make [the apprentice] a perfect workman'.[4] Some cases make it clear that parents and youths considered the acquisition of skills and the necessary experience no less important than the privilege of entering a guild, and the employment of an apprentice in types of work not directly related to his craft, even if the master was a freeman whose status would allow the youth to become a guild member, could be considered a breach of the contract. For example, Walter Escott, who was bound to a Bristol mercer, John Wells, complained in Quarter Sessions in 1664 that his master had for a year and a half abandoned his trade of a mercer and was 'living privately not using any calling', while his apprentice was employed only in 'household business'. There is no reason to doubt that had Walter Escott remained with his master he would have been able to obtain the freedom of Bristol and of the Company of Mercers, but clearly this was not the only thing he and his father thought they had paid for. As they explained in their petition, the refusal of Wells to release his apprentice meant that the 'said apprentice was likely to lose the whole benefit [of] trade', and the magistrates, who ordered Wells to release and compensate his apprentice, agreed.[5] In other cases, too, apprentices complained that their masters employed them in 'drawing and making fire', in 'household work', or simply failed to employ them in their trade; they were therefore given permission to depart and their masters were ordered to compensate them.[6] In one case it was alleged that the apprentice was instructed only as a gunsmith, whereas his master had promised to teach him clockmaking as well, and the apprentice was given permission to depart.[7] In other cases parents and their sons believed that failing to begin to teach the apprentice his skills in the first year of his training was an obvious ground for his release. Nor was their argument denied in court.[8]

The master, too, had expectations regarding his apprentice, for he relied on his skilled labour as a return on the initial investment while the apprentice was still unskilled, and as a source of cheap labour thereafter. In most indentures that have survived, the major obligation of the master in maintaining his apprentice was made clear. So when Thomas Weldon, a yeoman's son, was apprenticed in Bristol in 1605, his master, a soapboiler, promised to provide him 'meate, drink, lynen, wollen, hose, shooes, beddinge, and washings, and all other things necessary during the said terme, according to custom and order of the Cyty of Bristol'.[9] Precisely how much food and clothing the master was to give his apprentice was unspecified, and the standard of maintenance of apprentices must have varied considerably. Some appreciation of the minimal costs involved in this can be gained from evidence on the allocation of monies for the maintenance of apprentices who were disabled from work. In August 1658 a Bristol joiner requested in Quarter Sessions to be permitted to release his apprentice because he was unable to work. From the description of the justices it appears that the apprentice was mentally ill, and consequently it was ordered that he be released and transferred to the charge of the church-wardens and overseers of the parish of St Nicholas 'until such time that it shall please God to restore unto the apprentice his senses that he be capable of gaining his own livelihood'. The court ordered that the apprentice be paid 18d. a week, a sum not infrequently given to the poor by parish authorities in Bristol during this period.[10] So in early seventeenth-century Bristol about £4 yearly income was considered some sort of minimum requirement for subsistence for a single person in his youth. Some examples of cash sums allocated by parents in their wills for the provision of their children suggest that many would have considered such amounts a bare minimum. In 1612 William Mercer, a Bristol dyer, left a will in which he allocated £20 for the keep and upbringing of his three sons, and five years later three Bristol mercers signed as sureties on a recognizance for the payment of £15 a year for the sons. The sum was by now lower because the eldest son, John, had been apprenticed three years earlier.[11]

So somewhere around £6 or £7 was considered adequate for the maintenance of one child in Bristol in the first decades of the seventeenth century. This would have included clothing, for which some Bristol masters appear to have been expected to pay £2 every year.[12] Maintaining the apprentice could also include small monies at the beginning of a term, as was the custom in Bristol,[13] and pocket money or even small wages later. Nehemiah Wallington, a London turner in the mid-seventeenth century, paid all his apprentices some sort of wages, although on a very casual basis.[14] It is extremely difficult to find evidence for wages given to apprentices, probably because of the informal and casual nature of the arrangements. But sometimes more fixed arrangements were agreed upon at the outset. So Luse Jenkins, the wife of a Bristol merchant who took Elianor Collens as an apprentice in silk knitting, agreed to pay her wages on a regular basis from the fourth to the seventh year of her apprenticeship, a few shillings for each pair of stockings she produced.[15]

Sometimes masters promised to pay for the schooling of their apprentices. In August 1617, Henry Elliot, a Bristol innholder, took Richard Williams, son of a Bristol tanner, as an apprentice for a long term of twelve years. Elliot received a small premium of £5 10sh., but he also agreed to send the boy to school till he became 'serviceable for his trade'. Simon Forman wrote that when he became an apprentice in Salisbury in 1567 he signed a contract that contained the proviso that he would be sent to the grammar school for no less than three years. Such arrangements must have been quite common. An ordinance of the guild of the cordwainers in Bristol, dating from the mid-seventeenth century, expressly condemned the abuse of this system, ordering that no craftsman should take a youth by pretending that he was sending him to school, for in this way some shoemakers had more apprentices then they were permitted to 'lawfully keep'.[16]

There were other costs involved in the training of apprentices, caused by waste and damage to goods and raw material by a new and inexperienced apprentice, and by the time invested in instructing an unskilled trainee. In many shops, masters could rely on older apprentices or journeymen for the supervision and instruction of new apprentices; but quite a few craftsmen were alone in their shops.[17] So there was an investment in time and money spent on materials and perhaps tools, especially in the early part of the training. There were also risks in the commitment masters took upon themselves to train and employ an apprentice for a long period of seven and more years. Some apprentices could turn out unreliable and cause losses through damage and sometimes theft. The reliability of an apprentice was a constant worry, especially in the distributive trades, where apprentices were often entrusted with the conduct of businesses or small shops. But in many other workshops apprentices were also left alone to take care of a small shop and to attend customers when the master was away. Some masters required bonds of security 'for the service and truth' of the apprentice. The evidence on Bristol apprentices shows that bonds were taken by merchants, grocers and mercers as well as bakers and clothiers, shoemakers and smiths, coopers, mariners and barber-surgeons. But overall these arrangements, which gave the master some form of security against possible losses caused by an apprentice's negligence, dishonesty or incapacity, applied to only a small minority of apprenticeship contracts (6.1 per cent of all apprenticeships recorded between 1600 and 1645). Even among traders such as merchants, grocers and mercers, who more frequently insured themselves with bonds, sometimes of high amounts, the vast majority (80 per cent) took apprentices without bonds.

Nor was there anything to insure a master against periods of unemployment, or the sudden departure, illness or death of an apprentice. Trade fluctuated, and the work of many craftsmen was semi-permanent; some industries, such as construction, were subject to weather conditions, and others were vulnerable to fluctuations in demand, periodic depressions, and the sheer irregularity of customers and incomes of small shops.[18] Some masters had no alternative but to send their apprentices away when they could no longer employ them, but many continued to support their apprentices even when their incomes dropped or they were periodically unemployed.[19] Apprentices who ran away from their masters could cause losses by withdrawing their labour; in some court cases it was claimed that apprentices who had gone away caused 'great damage . . . for want of service'.[20] Some apprentices became ill in the course of their apprenticeship. Court cases make it quite clear that masters were responsible for their apprentices during illness or injury, and that, for some, the maintenance of an apprentice during a prolonged illness could become a severe burden. John Veale, a joiner in Bristol, had tried 'all possible meanes' to help his sick apprentice, but then was brought to 'great poverty' and 'almost utter ruin'. His description of his state of poverty, to which the illness of his apprentice probably contributed, rings true.[21] The court appears to have trusted his testimony and allowed him to release his apprentice without any charge; but in other cases masters who requested the release of apprentices who became ill were required to pay for their maintenance until they recovered, and sometimes to repay all or a part of the money that had been received as a premium.[22] And there was always the risk of an apprentice dying in the course of his term. Some masters insured themselves with bonds against losses in case an apprentice died;[23] but there is no evidence that this was in any way a normal routine, despite the fact that the chances that a youth would die in the course of an apprenticeship were quite high, given what we know of mortality rates of apprentices during this period.

It would be quite reasonable to assume that in apprenticeships in the most expensive mercantile trades the premium that was paid in advance more than covered the master's initial investment in his apprentice and the costs of maintaining him for several years. If premiums in these occupations were in the range of several dozens, or even hundreds, of pounds, they could guarantee the master against the risks involved in employing an apprentice as a factor overseas, and provide substantial profits. In small trade and crafts, premiums of £10 or £15 would have covered the adequate maintenance – food and clothing – of a youth for about a year, as well as costs involved in damages and losses caused during initial training. For the remaining costs of maintaining an apprentice in the years that ensued, in guaranteeing oneself against a variety of losses and insecurities, and in ensuring oneself cheap labour and possible profit, small masters would have relied on the skilled labour of their apprentices. To this extent, it was in their interest not only to keep their apprentices the full length of their terms, but to transmit their skills well so that they could rely on the skilled and efficient labour of their apprentices for the greater part of their terms.

Learning Skills

Most writers of autobiographies during this period who had been apprentices in their youth make few allusions to the way they had learnt their skills. Partly this was because, as in many other mundane matters of their lives, the authors gave only few details, many of them tending to focus on their spiritual lives. A rare glimpse of process involved in the acquisition of skills is found in the autobiography of Phineas Pett, a shipwright, who in the early decades of the seventeenth century built some of the largest ships of the Navy. During the early part of his apprenticeship Pett spent three or four years assisting two masters in repairing one ship, and in building another 'from the beginning . . . till she was wholly finished, launched and set sail'. Then his master began to teach him how to design ships, which involved 'cyphering, drawing, and practising to attain the knowledge of my profession'. This was done through some form of exercises, under the active instruction of his master, 'from whose help I must acknowledge I received my greatest lights'. A year later Pett was employed 'upon a small model' of a house for Lord Burghley, probably under some supervision, and then he proceeded to work in the Essex woods as an overseer. The next year he was employed in repairing a Flemish ship, and this was followed by his work as a principal overseer in the repair of another ship in Her Majesty's dock at Woolwich. Both jobs were still under the supervision of other shipwrights. In December 1599, nine years after he began as an apprentice in shipbuilding, Pett began to build a ship's model of his own design, 'being perfected and very exquisitely set out and rigged'. His first employment as a shipwright on his own followed, when he succeeded another craftsman at the timber yard in the Navy.[24]

Shipbuilding was one of the crafts which demanded 'extraordinary dexterity and skill', and much 'labour and time' to learn, as Adam Smith described such professions in the late eighteenth century. It required a great deal of knowledge of timber and its proper uses, the construction of ships and navigation, and drawing and building models.[25] Although Phineas Pett's account leaves unspecified how and what he learnt at each stage of his apprenticeship, it does suggest the importance of sheer labour in his long training. He was an ordinary workman for about four years during the early part of his apprenticeship, and he continued to work on ships well after he began to learn to draft and build models. Pett learnt to design in 1596 from Mathew Baker, master shipwright in the Queen's Navy, in the winter evenings, while during the day he continued to do various carpentry jobs on a ship. Watching and assisting carpenters, sawyers, smiths and numerous others working in different woods or on the construction, rigging and gunning of a ship was the most important part of his apprenticeship, while designing and copying well-known models came much later, about six years after his apprenticeship had begun.

Spending a long part of their early training on practical work as an introduction to their craft must have been common for youths in other lucrative trades, including the distributive trades. James Fretwell, whose father was a timber-merchant in Yorkshire, began his apprenticeship with his father by working two years 'amongst the workmen', making laths and tree nails. Working under the instruction of common labourers was taken by him and his father as a matter of course, as an essential part of training in the timber business.[26] Some apprentices who were bound to ironmongers, soapboilers and other specialised merchants must also have spent the first years of their apprenticeship working alongside labourers and doing unskilled work. By the late seventeenth century a number of great ironmongers owned furnaces, forges, slitting mills and wire stores which were spread over a wide geographical area.[27] In large brewhouses and soaphouses, apprentices would have begun doing work with labourers, in setting soaps to cool, preparing the lye, packing soaps, weighing and carrying casks and barrels, and splitting wood for heating and boiling. In a few of the large sixteenth-century brewhouses that clustered on the Thames there were a score of labourers and sometimes more, amongst whom apprentices would have begun their training before they moved on to learn how to deal with customers, collect money, attend markets, and supervise the actual process of brewing.[28]

Gradually a youngster learnt to master complicated techniques and competences, which varied greatly between trades and crafts, but which often required a great deal of physical and mental maturation. Many occupations required, first and foremost, learning to handle tools and materials with confidence, and with a great deal of precision. Some occupations, such as bell-founding, instrument-making,[29] wood and foundry works, required immense accuracy in designing and preparing moulds, casting metals and cutting and shaping a wide range of metal and wood. The making of knives and cutting tools required great care in forging, hardening and tempering; hardening a forged blade, for example, required care in reducing the hot temperature of the blade in oil without distorting the metal. And the making of such relatively simple and widely used products as casks and barrels also required great exactitude, especially in the case of watertight casks for the storage and transport of liquids such as beer and wine. In order to avoid leakage and to ensure that the cask was able to withstand fermenting liquids, the staves had to be fitted very precisely. Such precision was also needed to avoid wastage of material, as in tailoring or the cutting of leather and finishing shoes.[30] There were crafts which also required the acquisition of the habit of working with a great deal of concentration. In weaving, for example, a youth had to gain sureness of hand in grasping the shuttle, alertness in controlling the warp and the weft, and a careful eye to keep the tension of the warp constant.[31] Craftsmanship as well as small trade often involved elaborate measurement and learning to estimate quantities and length of chemical processes. In weaving, the most difficult stage was preparing the warp, which needed complicated calculation; and in shoemaking and tailoring a youth had to learn to estimate how to cut the leather to fit the precise needs of individual customers. Other occupations, such as leathermaking, soapmaking, dying, and winemaking, also involved long and elaborate processes, in which good judgement of the different stages of the process was critical for the successful application of the technique. The making of tanned leather, for example, was a particularly lengthy operation which required learning, in removing the hair from the rawhide, to estimate how long the leather needed to be soaked in lime without being damaged, and then, in preparing the hides, to judge when to move them from one solution to the next.[32] Soapmaking required learning to know precisely when the mixture of lime and ashes was strong enough and ready for the next stage, when the oil or fat was ready for boiling, when the curd became compact and homogeneous and boiling had to be stopped.[33] In the making of many cutting tools, such as chisels, scythes and knives, a youth had to learn to control a series of colour changes which were not apparent to the untrained eye; overall, working with heated metal required learning to judge different levels of heat and different levels of softness of the metal, for 'if the temper . . . was too strong . . . with the vehement blow of the hammer it flew in pieces; but if it was soft, it bowed, and would not touch the stone'.[34]

In all, most crafts and occupations required a great deal of understanding of raw materials and various wares and parts, as well as their qualities and proper uses. A cooper had to know about kinds of timber and their different characteristics and uses in the making of casks (some were good for storing liquid, others for the storing of solid materials), as well as the precise part of the wood best fitted for the making of his staves. A leatherworker had to know a great deal about skins and hides, to understand the quality of the leather he bought, to instruct the currier to finish the leather to the thickness he needed, and to detect defective leather.[35] In the metal industry, too, knowledge of varieties of metals and their different qualities was necessary. With the introduction of the blast furnace in the sixteenth century, the qualities of the iron produced in forges and foundries became more diverse. Wrought iron, hammered and refined after being completely liquefied in the blast furnace, now came in various grades: high-quality, coarser, and lower-grade iron, the last of which was brittle and unfit for many uses.[36] Knowledge of quality was also needed in the buying of tools and such different wares as threads, pins, buckles, wires, barrels, locks and triggers. In some crafts, such as gunmaking, buying parts was in itself an important aspect of craftsmanship. Detecting faulty wares (silk threads might be mixed with linen, gold and silver threads with wire and so on) was something all young trainees had to learn through a great deal of watching and working in their craft.

Some occupations involved relatively little skill. Shearing, or the cropping of woollen cloths after the nap had been raised, was a slow and laborious operation, and until the end of the seventeenth century it was done by holding a massive pair of iron shears, which required, for the most part, strong arms.[37] Bricklaying,[38] baking, nail- and pinmaking, basketmaking and buttonmaking all demanded less skill, and were therefore easier to learn. In some large towns there was a marked increase in these semi-skilled occupations and others that were relatively easy to learn. There was a growing number of clothworkers and semi-skilled textile workers in London and Bristol in the sixteenth century,[39] a greater number of youths apprenticed as bakers,[40] and growing numbers trained in crafts which specialised in the making of relatively simple parts and wares, like buttons and pins, pots and plates, lanterns, baskets and trunks of various sorts.[41] This diversification of occupations specialising in single products was a mark of the expansion of the market for goods for local consumption. As the populations of towns grew between the early sixteenth and mid-seventeenth centuries, so the goods bought and sold in them were more numerous and varied. The expansion in the market for cloth and linen for domestic and personal ware, for furniture, kitchen utensils and tools of a wide range and variety was evident in the larger towns, as well as in the villages and the smaller towns surrounding them.[42] This diversification was evident in Bristol, in Norwich, and above all in London, where the numbers of such occupations and trades had grown enormously by the mid- and late seventeenth century.[43]

Along with these semi-skilled occupations there was an expanding market for more refined goods and luxury products, which often required great skill in the making. Tailoring and shoemaking, catering to the needs of courtiers and the mercantile classes for high-quality clothing and shoes, in London and other towns, absorbed higher numbers of apprentices.[44] In seventeenth-century Bristol, shoemakers represented the third-largest occupational group among apprentices.[45] Fast-growing towns also encouraged the expansion of brewing, winemaking, dyeing, and even cutlery, the production of which all required considerable skill; all of these industries absorbed greater numbers of apprentices.[46] Soapmaking, centred in towns like London and Bristol, now involved managing larger holdings and heavy equipment, as well as distribution on a relatively large scale.[47] By the early seventeenth century many more apprentices were trained as carpenters, joiners, coopers and shipwrights, all occupations which catered to the needs of a growing population, and which involved a high level of skill.[48] Even in the textile industry some highly skilled occupations expanded alongside those involving simpler skills. In some towns there were greater numbers of dyers,[49] and in others, especially Norwich, the spread of the new draperies ecouraged the diffusion of more complicate techniques. Overall, the manufacturing of the new draperies did not demand new techniques, but combinations of traditional ones. Nevertheless the weaving of some of these draperies required greater refinement, precision and expertise: new methods of warp-sizing, handling many more fine warp threads, planning more complicated designs, and dyeing more colourful and elaborate cloth.[50]

Length of the Learning Period

Given the variation in the types of skills and competences involved, the length of time during which a youth could master a craft was likely to vary greatly. Economic and human factors which had less to do with the specific techniques of various crafts could also affect the length of training. For example, some writers of autobiographies claimed that their masters were quite incompetent in the transmission of their skills. Joseph Oxley was bound to a clockmaker in Yorkshire in 1729, and, according to his autobiography, he was kept 'backward' in his trade because he was employed in cleaning boots and shoes, and looking after his master's horses. When he finished a long seven-year apprenticeship, he still felt that he was not qualified to set up on his own, 'being altogether ignorant in the watch making branch'.

But the autobiography of Joseph Oxley also shows the importance of his age in prolonging the time it took him to learn the art of clockmaking. Orphaned before he was 10 years old, young Oxley was brought up by his grandparents, and at 13, when he applied for an apprenticeship with a clockmaker, he was still considered physically immature and was refused. A year later, in the summer of 1729, he was bound with another clockmaker. By then he was barely 14 years old, and, by his own account, found working in watchmaking 'hard and laborious'. When, after six years, he left his master, travelled to London and apprenticed himself with another clockmaker, he was about 20 years old and within a year acquired what he had failed to obtain in his early and mid-teens.

Differences in individual talents and abilities must have enabled some youths to proceed with greater speed than others. Autobiographical evidence suggests that the initiative, and perhaps even ambition, of individual apprentices could have an effect on the length of their training. Since so much of the acquisition of skills had to do with observing others do more expert tasks, some responsibility was placed on the youth himself in determining how fast he would proceed. Phineas Pett thought that his first two years, when he worked on a ship as an apprentice to a shipwright, were a waste, 'where I spent all that time, God he knoweth, to very little purpose'. Edward Barlow also reproached himself for not having taken the fullest advantage in learning navigation when he could, 'for I minded the things which I should not have minded'. Although his master did not teach him a great deal about navigation, the master was willing to pay someone else for it, 'if [Barlow] had given [his] mind to learn it from another,' as he put it later.[52] In small shops, a new apprentice was left on his own to watch other workers – an older apprentice or a journeyman – and the speed with which he learnt to imitate them must to some extent have been the result of his own initiative and desire to master his craft.

Most important were constraints placed by the irregularity of employment in many crafts and trades. Phineas Pett's account shows that his training was prolonged by two years at the very least because of periods in which he was unemployed. In 1592, two years after he had begun his apprenticeship, he left and went to serve on a ship going overseas. Two years later he resumed his apprenticeship, worked steadily for another two years, and then became unemployed: 'from midsummer, all the ensuing year, till Christmas I lay still and idle without any manner of employment or comings in'.[53] Shipbuilding, house carpentry and other jobs in the construction industry were subject to seasonal employment, and other industries and shops were also subject to periodic unemployment and depended on the 'occasional calls of customers', as Adam Smith referred to it in the eighteenth century.[54] So, if a shoemaker had few customers and little work, the training of his apprentice could well have been prolonged.

It would be hazardous to generalise about the length of time required to acquire and master skills. Phineas Pett became a proficient shipwright after nine years of an apprenticeship; by contrast, as one case in Bristol shows, a year of an apprenticeship with a cooper could turn a youth into a worker who could make casks and barrels on his own. After a year of his apprenticeship, the youth John Nutt desired to depart from his mistress, and his parents were obliged to sign a bond of £100 to ensure that he would not practise his trade independently.[55] In weaving and shoemaking, something like three or four years appears to have been sufficient. Benjamin Bangs spent one year with a shoemaker in Norfolk and then three more with another shoemaker in London, 'in which time I understood my business pretty well, and was a little ambitious in my mind to become master of it'. John Mayes, who was apprenticed to a Bristol weaver called Hill in 1619, argued that, following three years of his apprenticeship, he was able to practise his craft in the countryside.[56]

The length of time it took Bangs and Mayes to master their crafts of shoemaker and weaver was probably quite typical, and three or four years were regarded by contemporaries as the length of time required to obtain a wide array of skills. In 1674 an apprentice called Samuel Weare and his master John Pigott, a Bristol butcher, appeared before the local court to demand the resolution of disputes that had arisen between them. Apparently the master and his apprentice decided to part ways, but they differed in their version as to who was at fault: Pigott claimed that it was Weare who wanted to depart, and Weare argued that it was his master's behaviour that forced him to leave. Deciding who was at fault was critical, for sometimes it involved the compensation of the injured party. If an apprentice desired to depart after a year of his apprenticeship had elapsed, he risked having to compensate his master for his losses in maintaining and training an unskilled worker. Often some agreement on compensation to the master was arrived at in private, as is evident in occasional cases in Bristol which were crossed out in the Register of Apprentices. The clerk recorded in the margin the details of such an agreement, as in the case of William Smith, whose apprenticeship with Richard Sweete was cancelled in 1617. In the margin it was noted that the father paid the master 20sh., 'notwithstanding the 5 pounds given his master' (as a premium).[57]

But as one might suspect, disagreements on who was to be compensated and for how much arose quite often. To return to the case of Pigott and Weare, the court conducted some investigation, and after considering the 'proof and allegations' of both, it accepted the version presented by the apprentice. The verdict was that Pigott had been too harsh in the correction of his apprentice, and that he did 'immoderately beate him for petty offences, and sometimes without cause'. The court was also of the opinion that Pigott wanted his apprentice to depart, but did not want to return the premium he had received. The decision was that Weare had to be compensated, and that 'whereas Samuel Weare was bound two and a half years since, and 5 pounds had been given with him, that John Pigott should pay back . . . 3 pounds of lawful money', and then let his apprentice depart.[58]

This ruling indicates that, while Weare could legitimately claim part of his premium back after two or three years of apprenticeship, at some time after four years the court would no longer order his master to compensate him – that after four years of apprenticeship the court would have considered that Pigott had fulfilled his part in transmitting his skills, and so the return on the premium given to him would have been complete. In other cases involving the skills of a cooper, it appears that after about three years the apprentice was unlikely to succeed in his claim for repayment of a part of his premium. When Henry Sturggs, a cooper, and Edward Hall, his apprentice since August 1624, appeared in court to ask for the cancellation of their contractual agreement, the court ordered that Hall be released, and that his master repay him £3 of the £5 he had received as a premium. This was in February, about a year and a half after his apprenticeship had begun. In another case involving the skills of a cooper, after one year of training the master was ordered to repay £10, which must have been more than half of the premium originally paid.[59] Although, as we have seen, the basic technique of coopering could be transmitted within a year,[60] these cases suggest that the court nevertheless assumed that after a year a cooper apprentice deserved a great deal of his premium back, presumably because he still lacked the working experience and proficiency necessary to conduct a small shop on his own.

In other cases, involving the skills of tailors, haberdashers and leatherworkers, the ruling of the court was quite similar, and based on similar calculations of about four years as the length required to teach an apprentice skills. Thomas Cadle was apprenticed in 1656 to Samuel Weare, a tailor who died about two and a half years later, and in discharging him the court ordered the mistress to repay him a third of the original premium (£3 out of £10). Henry Long, the son of a gentleman from Trowbridge in Wiltshire, was apprenticed in April 1626 to Thomas Davis, a grocer, who was given a premium of £10. Two years later, in April 1628, the youth was discharged from his service by the court, with an order that the master should repay the sum of £5, 'for and in respect that the apprentice dwelt but about two years with his said master'. Another case involving an apprentice in haberdashery was that of Walter Marchant and his master, William Phelps, who received, upon taking him as an apprentice in September 1622, £10 as a premium. After four years, Marchant was dismissed, but was still compensated with about a third of the premium (£3 6sh. 8d. of the £10 he had paid). Again the same calculation was evident, for the court considered that only in the first two years did the apprentice learn haberdashery, and afterwards the master 'left his trade of a haberdasher'.[61] And in the case of Charles Ivy, a Welsh migrant apprenticed in 1617 with a Bristol saddler, the court also appears to have ordered compensations for a period of training of about three or four years.[62]

One case concerned the skills of a goldsmith, and it, too, shows a similar view of the length needed to learn the metal trades. On 19 June 1676 a woman called Sarah Day appeared in Bristol's Quarter Sessions and asked for the release of her son, then apprenticed to Elisha Kelson, a Bristol goldsmith. According to her complaint, her son had been bound two and a half years earlier, but for the last six months his master had no longer been able to instruct him in his trade. The reason was that he had been ill for some time, and he was also imprisoned for reasons which were not made clear. So the apprentice appears to have been trained in goldsmithing for about two years, and the court ordered that his mother be repaid £30 (which had been given in the form of two bonds, now ordered to be cancelled). The only reference to the original premium was that it was a 'considerable' sum paid in addition to the two 'small bonds' of £30, so the £30 given in compensation was probably about half the original sum agreed as a premium.[63]

Three or four years, then, was assumed to be the duration of training necessary in many crafts and trades. That is, contemporaries assumed that a year or two was hardly sufficient to master crafts as varied as coopering, tailoring, haberdashery and goldsmithing. On the other hand, they also believed that the seven and more years to which all apprentices had agreed in their contracts were more than enough to enable a youth to fully master a trade or craft. This also suggests something about the level of skills of an apprentice who applied for membership of his guild after having served the full term of seven or more years. In some companies, a 'proof piece' had to be provided as a test of the young man's skills. There is some evidence of piece works such as shears and stools which were presented at company courts in London during this period. Steve Rappaport has suggested, however, that 'the test was not widely used in Tudor London, for there are but a handful of references to it in the records of only five companies'. He has also argued that there is no evidence that such tests were presented to prevent the journeymen from becoming company members and setting up shops.[64] If guild members were indeed somewhat lenient in their demands, the reason may have had less to do with their benevolence, neglect of duty or lack of interest, and more with the fact that, having themselves trained apprentices in their shops, they took it for granted that those who completed the full length of their terms of seven years were more than equipped to handle such tests with skill.

Responsibilities and Initiatives

In some distributive trades, merchants who conducted their businesses overseas entrusted a great deal of their affairs to young factors. As a small and popular guidebook written by a Bristol merchant, *The Marchants Avizo* (1589), shows, the reponsibilities entrusted to these factors were immense. The book contains a handful of business letters written by a young factor, and it was probably based on material and letters sent in the early 1580s by Robert Aldworth to Thomas Aldworth, a Bristol merchant and one of the city's leading magistrates at the time. The letters pertain to one voyage which 'R.A.' – probably Robert Aldworth – made on a ship called the *Joseph*, which sailed from Bristol to Portugal and then to Spain with the goods belonging to his master. The factor travelled to Lisbon, where he contacted other merchants, made a survey of the various goods available there and their prices, sold some of his master's cloth, wax and lead, and then bought pepper, cloves, mace and cinnamon. At the same time, he also acted as a factor for another merchant, and sold his broadcloth, bought pepper and cloves which he marked properly and sent separately on another ship back to Bristol, as well as collected debts owed to this merchant by local traders. From Portugal he travelled to Spain. Here he sold the remainder of his cloth and lead, and was responsible for buying and shipping home oil, cochineal and sack; when he met with some difficulties in completing the transactions for his master, he borrowed some money, bargained on the rate of interest, and issued a bill of exchange. In all the journey lasted about four months.[65]

The Marchants Avizo was addressed to 'sonnes and servants, when [merchants] first send them beyond the seas, as to Spaine and Portingale or other countreys', and, as Patrick McGrath, the book's editor, suggested, these servants were apprentices serving their terms. It is difficult to know at what point in his apprenticeship a youth began to act as his master's factor, but some evidence suggests that this would have occurred well before the final year of his term. In 1616, Andrew Barker, the son of John Barker, was bound apprentice with his brother, John. Their father, a wealthy Bristol merchant who had been mayor in 1606, had by then died, and young Andrew was covenanted to serve his brother in their family business for seven years. Six years later, Andrew Barker wrote a will in which he bequeathed his money and possessions to a wide circle of kin and friends. He was by then 23 years old, 'in perfect health and memory', and still formally an apprentice. Nevertheless he referred to himself in the opening lines of the will as 'I Andrew Barker of the city of Bristol, merchant'.[66]

By the time he wrote his will, young Andrew Barker must have been conducting business as a factor for some years.[67] Other evidence suggests that apprentices were entrusted with a great deal of business dealings for their masters, and well before the end of their terms of service. Thomas Morgan was an apprentice to Edward Cooke, a Bristol mariner, and when he appeared in 1674 at the Bristol sessions he told the court that he had been on a voyage for his master in Ireland for nearly a year. When he came to court to ask for his release, he still wanted to be transferred to another seaman in order to serve the remainder of his term. Bristol mariners were involved with a variety of mercantile businesses, mostly in internal trade along the Severn Valley and the western coasts.[68] Even if Morgan had only a year or two more to serve, he would have been engaged on his own in businesses far away from Bristol from the fourth year of his term at the very least. In another case involving the dealings of a Bristol soapboiler, the length of time the apprentice served his master as a factor on his own was much longer. John Doggett was the apprentice of Tobias Culme, a Bristol soapboiler, who some time after the apprenticeship began left Bristol for Barbados – Culme's businesses probably involved more than the distribution of soaps – to where he took young Thomas, and where he employed him in his business. He trained his apprentice for some time, and then departed, leaving Doggett behind to look after his business there. Some time later, Culme died, and young Doggett continued to act on his mistress's behalf for three more years. When he returned to Bristol at her request, his apprenticeship was not yet over. Overall, he must have acted on behalf of his master overseas, with no apparent difficulties, from at least the third year of his term.[69]

In such circumstances, many apprentices began to conduct business on their own behalf. Some youths were given special permission to trade. In the case of Andreas Charlton, a merchant whose apprentice was bonded for £100 for his honesty, it was agreed that the apprentice would not conduct trade 'for himself or for any other' without special order from his master or mistress. And in the case Henry Kedgwin, a Bristol grocer who took John Nelme as an apprentice in October 1611, it was also agreed that Nelme would trade only with the 'consent of his master or mistress'.[70] Such practices must have been quite common, whether the permission of masters was given in writing or not. Robert Tyndale, an apprentice with John Smythe, one of Bristol's wealthiest merchants, was acting as his master's factor in Bordeaux in 1537, only two years after his apprenticeship had begun, and he continued to act as Smythe's factor throughout his apprenticeship, and well after. Yet by 1544, before his apprenticeship came to its formal end, he was already in partnership with his brother, William Tyndale. His fellow apprentice, Thomas Shipman, was sending wine from Bordeaux not only to their master but to three other merchants, and there is no reason to doubt that the two apprentices were conducting a great deal of business, for their master as well as for themselves, well before the end of their terms. In sixteenth-century London there were also young men who were conducting business in the wool trade on a large scale while they were still quite young.[71]

In small shops, too, a great deal was entrusted to apprentices. The diary of Roger Lowe, written between 1663 and 1665, shows the transactions of an apprentice to a grocer in a small market town in Lancashire. Lowe's master dealt with a variety of commodities and owned two shops, one of which he entrusted to Lowe. In 1663, when he began to write the diary, Lowe was already well on his own in managing the shop, fetching the commodities supplied by his master, buying goods – honey, wax, scythes – on his own, selling goods on credit and collecting debts, and keeping some accounts. There is no evidence that he actually engaged in trade for his own benefit, but he was given a commission on goods he bought, and was also quite active as a sort of public scribe, writing letters and drawing up indentures and bonds for a fee, as well as lending money.[72] Thomas Alford, an apprentice to a Bristol public notary, was also lending money, but without the knowledge of his master, and probably by embezzling him. Thomas was an assistant to his master in his capacity as clerk of Bristol's Tolzey court, but he also managed his master's shop, received money from customers, wrote bonds, bills and accounts; some time in the course of his apprenticeship he already had a desk outside the shop, where he kept the bills and bonds he handled for his own profit and use.[73]

Many masters relied quite extensively on their apprentices in their shops. Simon Forman, who was the apprentice of a Salisbury grocer and apothecary during the 1560s, began his apprenticeship while there were still three other apprentices in his master's shop. Gradually they all left, and towards the end of his fifth year 'all things for the shop was committed to his charge'. In addition to the shop in Salisbury, his master had a small farm in the countryside, and Forman often managed the shop when his master was away. The account of William Stout, who was apprenticed in the 1680s to Henry Cowarde, a grocer in Lancashire, makes quite clear the fact that apprentices were relied upon as supervisors of shops even at a much earlier stage in their apprenticeship. His master's former apprentice kept a shop for him at Cockerham for a couple of years, and young Stout himself was appointed, about two years after he began his apprenticeship, to tend a new shop his master took in Bolton. This he did two days a week, and in the remainder of the time he was employed in the other shop, preparing sugar, tobacco, nails and other goods for market day. Some of this work he did alongside his master, but in tending the shop he was on his own, while his master was 'often out . . . [in] bargaining, and supporting persons in declining circumstance'. Once he became a shopkeeper himself, Stout took an apprentice with the obvious intention that he would replace him in the shop. His apprentice was boarded with him and began to tend the shop, 'so I had now more time to divert my selfe'.[74]

In craftsmen's shops, apprentices worked more closely alongside their masters, but the evidence suggests that here, too, their skills could be of great value to their masters. In 1615 Edmund Jordaine, a Surrey man who worked as a shipwright in London and who belonged to the London company of ship carpenters and shipwrights, hired two apprentices, Daniel Jordaine and Edward West, for a term of seven years. As it was later argued in Chancery Court, Edmund Jordaine instructed his apprentices quite well, and after three years of training they were skilful in their craft.[75] Then, in 1618, he died, and the two youths continued to work on behalf of his widow for a while. When she remarried, they were earning weekly wages for the benefit of Elizabeth, the widow, and her new husband. Suddenly, in February 1619, the two apprentices 'secretly departed from [their] dwelling house' and went to live with another shipwright. According to Elizabeth and Robert Barlow, the plaintiffs in a petition against the Company of Shipwrights, their apprentices were enticed by five members of that company – among whom were three high-ranking members (a master and two wardens) – to get hold of their indentures and then leave the service of the Barlows and work for some of them. The shipwrights had been receiving the apprentices' weekly wages since that time, which, the Barlows claimed, 'in all right and equity' were theirs.

After three years of their apprenticeship, Jordaine's and West's skilled labour was so valuable that they were enticed by no less than five members of the shipwrights' company to leave the service of their widowed mistress. This is not surprising, given that the Barlows claimed that the two apprentices were then earning 18sh. a week (the wages of the two together), a sum which the shipwrights were allegedly dividing between them. This meant an annual income, for each of them, of no less than £22 10sh., which was higher than wages paid to adult workers in the building industry. According to Rappaport, around 1600 a skilled construction craftsman in London could earn a maximum of £19 a year.[76] Wage ceilings for Bristol shipwrights ordered at the Easter Session in 1654 made distinctions between three wage levels: labourers, apprentices 'who had served two years', and masters and able workmen. To judge by the wages of Daniel Jordaine and Edmund West, the work they performed clearly belonged to the third category of able workmen.[77] Moreover, if in early seventeenth-century Bristol the maintenance of an apprentice cost about £7 a year, and even if we allow for higher costs of maintenance in London, the profits to the masters could hardly be marginal: in the range of up to £15 a year.

Apprentices were obviously serious competition to older journeymen, who normally received wages in addition to the room and board given to apprentices. For example, Rappaport has shown that the complaints in the final decades of the sixteenth century of journeymen in companies involved in London's clothing trade, that apprentices were depriving them of work, were not groundless. By the 1580s, master clothworkers were taking apprentices at a higher rate than in the three previous decades, presumably at the expense of the journeymen.[78] Masters preferred to take a new apprentice, train him, and benefit from his work when he became skilled, rather than hire a journeyman who had to be paid annual wages as well as maintenance. If the trade of clothworking involved some semi-skilled and even unskilled work, such as shearing or packing, then the time necessary for training was particularly short, and the gains from the labour of apprentices could be obtained sooner than in some other crafts.

Use of apprentices' skills as waged labour, equal to that of journeymen, must have been widespread not only in the building of ships and in the construction industry, where wage labour was common. Some masters responded to the difficulties arising from the obligation to maintain their apprentices, even during periods when there was little employment in their shops, by sending them out to work. When this occurred, apprentices were paid, as a normal routine, in journeymen's wages. In 1607 the Company of Coopers in Bristol issued an ordinance which forbade coopers 'to set any apprentice to work journeywork above 1 day without consent of the masters', and they ordered a 3sh. 4d. fine for its violation. The ordinance indicates that the company was only placing under some supervision what had previously been, and continued to be, a common practice. Among shoemakers this must also have been common. In 1672 some members of the Bristol shoemakers' company complained in Quarter Sessions that their craftsmen allowed their apprentices to work as journeymen and obtain their wages 'contrary to an ancient ordinance' which was passed in 1635.[79] Shoemaking and coopering were among the most numerous occupations in Bristol in the first half of the seventeenth century; together, their apprentices formed well over a tenth of the entire apprentice population in the town.[80] These were scattered among many small shops, often with only a single apprentice in each.[81] After about three years, many of them were quite skilled. Sometimes when their masters had little work in their shops, they were sent out to work in a neighbouring shop, and their masters bargained for wages which did not fall behind those of journeymen, and which were legally theirs.

Apprentices also used the skills they had acquired to their own benefit rather than to that of their masters. Some apprentices were discharged after two or three years of their term, but as some cases in court suggest, they were then able to use their 'profession', as one Bristol apprentice referred to it, elsewhere.[82] Some evidence on pilfering and frauds committed by apprentices suggests that such actions were a prelude to the departure of an apprentice who had decided to begin to work on his own. In one such case, which was appealed in Chancery, it was claimed that the apprentice, one Thomas Meacock, had stolen leather, tools and implements, and other goods from his master, a tanner, and carried them to his father's house, 'counting them to his own proper use'. Some runaway apprentices were youths who had departed from their masters and begun to practise their craft on their own somewhere else. In one such complaint in Bristol it was claimed that a carpenter's apprentice, Thomas Phelps, deserted his master and went 'to work in the country'.[83]

By far the most suggestive piece of evidence that, once they were sufficiently trained, apprentices used their skills to their own ends rather than to those of their masters, is the completion rates among apprentices in large towns. The vast majority of them, in nearly every town where abundant evidence has survived and in a wide range of trades and crafts, left their masters some time during the course of their apprenticeship without finishing the term of seven or more years on which they had signed. In London, the drop-out rate of apprentices was so large that complaints to the effect that 'there is not one in twenty that serves his time out' were not unusual.[84] Throughout the sixteenth century, as many as 60 per cent of London apprentices never finished their terms, with little variation between decades or between companies. Among London brewers the rate of attrition was even higher, reaching two-thirds of all apprentices.[85] In provincial towns the situation was no different, and at some points in the course of the period the proportions of those who completed their terms were even lower. In Norwich about 6,000 apprenticeship records have survived for the whole period; less than a fifth of these (17 per cent) 'can definitely be said to have remained in the city at the end of their terms'.[86] In Bristol throughout most of the sixteenth century, the proportions of those who stayed for their entire terms, and then proceeded to become town citizens, did not rise above a quarter of all those apprenticed. In some decades, as in the 1570s and the 1590s, they were not above a fifth of all those who had registered earlier as apprentices.

Some 10 per cent of these apprentices died in the course of their apprenticeship;[87] and a few of them remained in the town and turned to vagrancy and petty crime, risking being sent to Bridewell.[88] Most of these youngsters left the town and returned to their home town or village, or turned elsewhere. The motives inducing them to depart from the town were many,[89] but what was common to all was a reluctance to continue to work for their masters when they could use their skills to pursue their own ends. Some aspects of the Statute of Artificers (1563), which made a minimum of a seven-year apprenticeship mandatory throughout England, therefore remained largely ineffective. Even by the late seventeenth century the drop-out rate among apprentices in London and Bristol, for example, continued to be in the order of 50 per cent.[90] Most apprenticeships then lasted three, four or five years; this was by no means a symptom of disintegration or decline of the system of training in the large towns but a normal feature of the course taken by most apprentices throughout the period. Whatever the economic and other circumstances affecting individuals who abandoned their service before it came to its formal end, most urban apprentices never served the full length of terms required by law and specified in the indentures they had themselves signed.

Conclusion

When Benjamin Bangs arrived in London, soon after the great fire in 1666, he first had difficulty in finding employment. But with the assistance of his previous master, a Norfolk shoemaker who came to London along with him, he was eventually able to find another shoemaker who took him as his apprentice. He worked with this shoemaker for about three years. Soon afterwards he left his master and became a foreman in another shoemaker's shop. He was by then no more than 17 or 18 years old, and quite literally on his own.[91]

But for the fact that Bangs embraced Quakerism while he was an apprentice in London, there was little in his migration and experience in the capital that was unique. His gradual move to London – from a small village to a market town and then to the capital – the change of masters, the short period during which he was unemployed, the departure from his second master after three years' apprenticeship, all reflected the more widespread pattern and experience of those who ended up as apprentices in the large towns. Steve Rappaport has shown that in mid-sixteenth-century London the average age of apprentices when they began their apprenticeship was 19.5, so that an apprentice would have been quite skilled by the time he was 22 years old. But this average conceals the wide range of ages of entrance to apprenticeship in London: from as early as 12 up to 25 and 26 years. There is some evidence that towards the late sixteenth century the average age of London apprentices at the beginning of their terms dropped;[92] any glimpse into scattered evidence on apprentices placed privately and by parish authorities in the ensuing decades suggests that most began their apprenticeships in the mid- rather than late teens. In provincial towns the age of entry into apprenticeship may well have been somewhat lower than in London's largest companies. Among writers of autobiographies who had been apprentices in various towns during the seventeenth century, there were a few who started at 17, 18 or 19, but others who began at the age of 14 or 15. George Bewley was sent to Dublin and bound to a draper there when he turned 14 years old; and Thomas Chubb was apprenticed to a Salisbury glover at the age of 15.[93] By the time they had acquired their skills and could make up their minds whether to leave their masters or stay on, most of these youths had hardly turned 18 years old.

The training of an apprentice in the early part of his apprenticeship transformed him from a youth with few skills to a young man who could master complicated techniques, perform responsible tasks, tend small shops and, in a few select cases, conduct large-scale businesses, in England and abroad, on his own. Most crafts involved more than technical skill; they also needed concentration and endurance, measurement and calculation, knowledge of raw materials, the understanding of tools and parts, and management of small-scale trade. By the time some four or five years of apprenticeship had elapsed, these young men had acquired not only an understanding and a capacity to judge in their craft and trade, but shrewdness and independence in handling their affairs and using their skills to advance their careers by whatever means they saw fit. As we shall see in subsequent chapters, such independence was bound to affect their handling of masters and other social relations, the demands they could make on masters and other adults, and the ways they pursued leisure activities and whatever else they thought best for themselves and their future.

6 Women's Youth: The Autonomous Phase

Social expectations regarding the roles and skills of young women were manifestly different from those of young males. While men were expected to make choices between various occupations during their teens, women were allocated a more restricted set of opportunities and skills. The lack of vocational choice for women was evident in contemporary advice literature for the upbringing and promotion of children in their mid- and late teens. It was assumed that diverse professions and careers were appropriate for sons: higher learning, the church, law, medicine, business and crafts, military service, the Navy and husbandry. Daughters, on the other hand, were thought fit to learn cookery and laundry, and their parents were recommended to place them out as servants where they could learn sewing, confectionery and 'all requisites of housewifery'.[1] Such divergent attitudes were also evident in the skills girls and boys were expected to learn in schools. The period witnessed an expansion in the number of schoolgirls and the rise of the girls' boarding-school, which attracted mostly daughters of the upper and well-to-do families. By the mid-seventeenth century, most larger and smaller towns had some kind of educational institution for girls and adolescent women. But the education in such schools was for the most part based on domestic subjects such as cookery and needlework, and the inculcation of social graces through the teaching of music and dancing.[2] In Bristol's Red Maids Boarding School, founded in 1634, the widows in charge were instructed to teach the girls to read, to employ them in things that might contribute to their 'preferment' afterwards, and to employ the girls in household affairs. By contrast, the masters of Queen Elizabeth Hospital, a school for boys founded in 1586, were instructed to teach not only reading, but writing and book-keeping, 'so that they may be capable and fit of being apprentices when they come out of the Hospital'.[3]

Memoirs and other records that indicate the actions and expectations of some parents show that these injunctions were by no means solely the reflection of the norms of a minority elite for adolescent children. The father of James Fretwell, a tradesman in Yorkshire, sent James and his younger brother to be apprenticed, while their sister remained at home until she was 22 years old, when she went to keep house for her brother. And when Jane Martindale, the daughter of a Lancashire yeoman, desired to go to London to become a servant, her parents objected on the grounds that she lacked nothing at home, and that if she desired to marry, her father could well take care of it nearer home. By contrast, Adam, her younger brother, was sent to school at an early age, and when he was 14 years old he was given the choice between higher learning and an apprenticeship in a trade.[4] Clearly his parents believed that he should be guided towards a career, while their daughter was destined to stay at home and marry, as was often the case among affluent urban families as well.[5] Moreover, when women did leave home in the course of their teens, as most of them did, the opportunities for learning and training open to them were less diversified than those open to the adolescent male. In late sixteenth-century London, migrant women in their teens and early twenties generally lived with their kin or served as domestic servants; hardly any were formally apprenticed, and the chances of obtaining a livelihood in ways other than through domestic service were extremely low in the period 1580–1640.[6] So caution is required in placing too strong an emphasis on the equality of skills and tasks obtained by women and men in the period before industrialisation. Early modern contemporaries' prejudices regarding the inferiority and subjection of women already placed women of various social classes in a disadvantageous position when they were in their teens, and this was particularly evident in the case of long-distance migrants to large towns and the opportunities offered to them there.[7]

Arguably, however, young women still acquired a range of skills even in the towns, and, no less important, in the course of their teens they exercised a measure of autonomy and independence in their decisions and actions. We have already seen that in the countryside women in their teens learnt and performed a host of agricultural tasks and skills.[8] In what follows, attention will be focused on a range of skills and competences acquired through formal and informal apprenticeships, and through domestic service in the large towns. Three factors which fostered the mastery of skills and the assumption of autonomy during the youthful phase in women's lives are examined: variations in the market for male labour, especially in the skilled crafts; the centrality of the family shop as a unit of production; and the experience gained in long years of service outside the parental home. The combination of these factors, while still placing some limits on young women in comparison with their male counterparts, left considerable scope for independence and initiative during their adolescent and youthful years.

Apprenticeship Skills

The apprenticeship system offered far less opportunities for women than for men. Where systematic evidence is available it shows that women who became apprentices were often a minority; in some places they were a tiny minority, and in others none were apprenticed at all. In London in the period between 1580 and 1640, not a single female apprentice appears in the records of fifteen companies.[9] In Bristol, of about 1,500 apprentices enrolled between 1542 and 1552, only 50 (3.3 per cent) were women, and in the following decade the numbers were similar, 52 (2.8 per cent) out of about 1,800 apprentices registered. In the seventeenth century the proportions of young women among all apprentices in Bristol remained low – only 43 (2.2 per cent) in a sample of 1,945 apprentices registered between 1600 and 1645.

Yet women did become apprentices and were bound by indenture in various crafts, particularly where the market for male labour was less competitive. London was probably the single most attractive town for young men seeking apprenticeship; with a population reaching 200,000 by 1600, young women, as mentioned above, hardly appeared in the records of major companies. Male registrations, by contrast, numbered in the thousands every year. Yet in Bristol, whose population by 1600 was only 12,000, and whose apprentices arrived from a more restricted migration zone, the numbers of female apprentices were somewhat higher and their appearance in the records was more noticeable.[10] Lower down in the urban hierarchy were towns like Southampton, which had a population of 4,200 by 1600. Southampton's migration field was much narrower than Bristol's, and no more than a dozen or two new apprentices were registered each year. The proportions of women were already higher – about 10 per cent of all apprentices in the town. In smaller towns and villages female indentures could reach even higher proportions, as evidence produced by Snell on the southern counties throughout the seventeenth and eighteenth centuries suggests.[11]

No less importantly, there were also variations in the market for male apprenticeships over time, and these had effects on the rate of entry of women into apprenticeships, as well as on the patterns of their recruitment and training. In fifteenth-century London, when population pressures were relatively low, young women found their way into formal apprenticeships with pursers, broiderers, mercers, tailors and silkworkers.[12] In the following century, when the population began to grow and London itself expanded at an unparalleled rate, no women were registered in a wide range of companies. But in the late seventeenth century a few women reappeared in company records: in the cordwainers company between 1657 and 1700 38 women were registered as apprentices; 14 women appeared as bakers' apprentices; and the turners company bound 9 women between 1671 and 1700 while none had been bound throughout the period from 1604 to 1671.[13] This suggests that in the decades up to the mid-seventeenth century, when the population was growing and London absorbed thousands of male apprentices from all over the country, women were seldom considered for apprenticeships. However, by the second half of the seventeenth century, when migration pressures eased and the overall numbers of apprentices formally bound dropped, the competition for training in the skilled crafts was less fierce.[14] In addition, the plague of 1665 may well have contributed to a labour shortage – all of which allowed a few women to enter the apprenticed crafts.

Evidence on early sixteenth-century Bristol likewise shows the limited, but by no means wholly restricted, nature of opportunities for apprenticeships for women, and the effects of changes in the availability of male labour in the ensuing decades.[15] Of the small group of women apprenticed in the 1530s, two-thirds were bound in occupations associated with the female role, i.e. in housewifery and sewing (Table 6.1).

'Housewifery' was not a craft apprenticeship in the strict sense of the word; it was akin to domestic service, although involving perhaps the less arduous tasks, such as household management, care of small children, sewing and other similar work. The women bound as housewives were apprenticed with masters involved in a variety of crafts and trades – for example merchants, innkeepers, brewers, grocers, cappers, glovers or weavers – and in the entry recording the details of the apprenticeship it was added that the woman was to be brought up in the occupa-

Table 6.1 *Occupations to which women apprentices were bound, Bristol, 1532–52; 1617–28* (%)

	1532–52	1617–28
Housewife and sempstress	41	
Sempstress and tailor	31	2
Distributive and foodstuffs	18	1
Manual crafts	8	
Servant-maid		35
Textiles* and service		50
Textiles** without service		8
Shopkeeping and service		1
Sempstry and service		3
Total	98	100

* Knitting and spinning.
** Knitting, spinning, lacemaking and stocking-knitting.

Sources: D. Hollis (ed.), *Calendar of the Bristol Apprentice Book, 1532–1565* (Bristol Record Society Publications, Vol. XIV, 1948); Ralph and Hardwick (eds), *Calendar of the Bristol Apprentice Book, 1542–52* (Bristol Record Society Publications, Vol. XXXIII, 1980); BRO, Register of Apprentices, 04352(4)–(5)a.

tion of a housewife. Like all apprentices, these women were bound to the master as well as his wife for a period of seven or more years. But unlike apprentices, they were trained by the wife, who in a few cases was herself designated a 'housewife'. Women apprenticed as sempstresses were likewise trained by the master's wife, for most of them were bound to a master and his wife, whose occupation was recorded separately as a 'shepster' (dressmaker).

Yet the women apprenticed in the 1530s were not altogether a distinct group. While many were bound as housewives and sempstresses, about a third were bound in a host of other occupations and trades. About a fifth were in trading occupations, shopkeeping, and the distribution of foodstuffs: as drapers, grocers, haberdashers, apothecaries, fishmongers, brewers and vintners. Eleanor Morgan, the daughter of a Bristol wiredrawer, was apprenticed to Robert Jeoffreys, a mercer, and his wife Johanna, a shepster. It was specifically stated that Eleanor would be taught the occupation of a mercer.[16] Other women were recorded in such crafts as joiner, pinner, cofferer, and even bell-founder.

Nor did women altogether differ in their social background from their male counterparts: nearly half of the women apprenticed in Bristol were daughters of craftsmen and artisans engaged in a variety of industries and crafts, from the textile and clothing trades to leather or metal industries.[17] Daughters of merchants, grocers, mercers, barbers, clerks and ship's carpenters could all be found among the women apprenticed in the town. A little less than a fifth were daughters of men involved in mercantile and retail trades, or in some profession; while about a third originated, as did male apprentices, from the landed and agricultural classes. Daughters of gentlemen were particularly prominent, comprising 7 per cent of the women. Among male apprentices, the proportion of gentlemen's sons, in the 1530s, was 3.6 per cent. Daughters of yeomen also figured more distinctly among women apprentices than among the apprentice population as a whole, comprising 10 per cent of the women, compared with 5.5 per cent among men. On the other hand, daughters of husbandmen were somewhat less prominent among the women than were sons of husbandmen among the young men.[18] Finally, a few daughters of labourers could be found among the young women, as was the case among men apprenticed in the town during the 1530s.[19]

While nearly half of the women apprentices were Bristol natives, the majority came from the countryside: about two-thirds of these from the surrounding regions of Somerset, Gloucestershire and Wiltshire, and the remainder from areas farther afield, such as Shropshire, Worcestershire and Staffordshire towards the north, Devon and London, and from Glamorgan and as far as Pembrokeshire in South Wales. Although none of the girls arrived from the far north or from Ireland – as was occasionally the case among male apprentices – and although Bristol natives were more prominent among women apprentices than among men, migrants who arrived from as far as the Midlands, Wales, and the south-west were no less prominent among the women than among the men apprenticed in the town.[20]

By the early seventeenth century, the proportion of apprenticed women in Bristol remained similar to the 1530s: between 2 and 3 per cent of all apprenticeship bindings in the town. In absolute terms, their numbers rose with the growth of the apprentice population as a whole. While in the 1530s about 5 female indentures per year were recorded, between 1617 and 1625 a total of 70, or 9 apprenticeships per year, were recorded; and between 1625 and 1635, 100 indentures were recorded, or 10 per year. Overall apprentice registrations in Bristol in the course of this period – both male and female – rose from about 150 per year in the 1530s to between 200 and 250 from the 1600s on.

Nevertheless, some of the features characteristic of the recruitment and occupational distribution of women apprenticed in the town changed. In the first place, women apprentices now included those who were placed by urban or parish authorities; that is, they were bound through the charity system and the administration of poor relief which was established in the preceding decade. Whereas the women apprenticed during the 1530s and 1540s were bound privately, parish and charity apprenticeships comprised about a fifth of the women recorded between 1600 and 1645 (8 in a sample of 41), and about a quarter of all female apprenticeships between 1617 and 1627 (28 out of 100). The social composition of these women also changed, the proportion of daughters of gentlemen and yeomen decreasing from 17.2 in the 1530s and 1540s, to 10.5 per cent in the decades following 1600 (Table 6.2).

About a fifth of the women were still daughters of merchants and traders, but daughters of mariners became particularly dominant, rising to 16.8 per cent from only 1.1 per cent of women apprentices in the 1530s to 1550s. Fewer women also came from the countryside, and they were far less likely to have migrated from great distances. Over two-thirds of the women apprenticed in Bristol in the 1600s were natives of the town, and the remaining came almost exclusively from Somerset and Gloucestershire. None arrived from farther north – Shropshire, Staffordshire

Table 6.2 *Social origins of women apprentices Bristol, 1532–52; 1617–28*

	1532–52		1617–28	
	nos	%	nos	%
Gentry and yeomen	16	17.2	8	8.4
Merchants, traders, professions	15	16.1	21	21.1
Craftsmen	44	47.3	36	40.0
Mariners	1	1.1	16	16.8
Husbandmen	14	15.1	12	12.6
Labourers	3	3.2	2	1.1
Total	93	100.0	95	100.0

Sources: as for Table 6.1.

or Cheshire – as was the case a century earlier. Moreover, the proportions of women whose fathers had died by the time they were bound as apprentices rose dramatically from less than a fifth in the 1530s to nearly two-thirds in the 1600s, at a time when the proportions of orphans among male apprentices remained around 30 per cent.[21] Orphanage was no less frequent among females apprenticed privately than among those apprenticed by the parish; of 76 women apprenticed privately between 1617 and 1628, 46 (60.5 per cent) were orphans, and of 19 apprenticed by the parishes, 13 (68.4 per cent) were women whose father was dead by the time they were bound. Orphanage of female apprentices was also more frequent among daughters of gentlemen, merchants, traders and mariners than among daughters of husbandmen and craftsmen.[22] Women apprenticed in Bristol in the seventeenth century, therefore, were most likely to be natives of the town and orphans, regardless of social standing.

Most of the occupations in which all of the women bound in the 1600s were apprenticed were clearly different from those of men. Domestic service now replaced what was earlier described as 'housewifery', and it became the major training occupation for women. Almost all the women apprenticed in the seventeenth century were apprenticed as domestic servants, or in a combination of a craft and domestic service (see Table 6.1). In some cases it was specifically agreed that the master and mistress would maintain another maidservant to do the housework, so that the woman apprenticed to them 'may the better apply her needle work'.[23] Yet such an agreement was unusual, and by the seventeenth century household service became not simply an additional duty which, like their male counterparts, women might on occasion be required to perform, but a formal and major obligation of their apprenticeships. Women apprenticeships, therefore, became more distinct from those of men.

The crafts in which women were trained also became segregated, and opportunities for entry into some crafts, which had existed on a limited scale in the 1530s, were eliminated altogether. Virtually all the women who entered the clothing and textile trades were trained in knitting and sewing, and in spinning, hosiery, bone-lacemaking, buttonmaking, or some combination of these occupations. In all, of 100 women apprenticed between 1617 and 1628, 35 were bound as maidservants; 50 in the clothing and textile trades and as maidservants as well; and ten were apprenticed in the textile industry. Only one woman entered an occupation in which men were commonly bound:

shopkeeping. This women, Dorothy White, the daughter of a deceased gentleman in Dorset, was apprenticed to Lawrence Swetnam, a haberdasher, and Elizabeth his wife, 'to be brought up in shopkeeping, selling and buying these things that belong to the profession and trade which the said Lawrence and his wife do and now use'.[24] The cost of Dorothy's apprenticeship was £24, but this amount was quite exceptional, being a relatively high premium compared with the average cost of male apprenticeships at that time. Most other women paid far less for their apprenticeship, normally about £2–£3. Parish apprenticeships were the cheapest, generally not exceeding 30sh. or 40sh., although a few recorded cases were £3 and £4.[25] Even private apprenticeships for women hardly ever cost more than £4, substantially lower than premiums normally paid for males.[26]

An understanding of the changes that occurred in the patterns of recruitment and occupational training of women can be gained by placing them in the context of changes in the training and recruitment of male apprentices. In mid-sixteenth-century Bristol, the number of men registered as apprentices stagnated, but by the late sixteenth century it began a sustained growth, reaching unprecedented levels in the 1660s. The reasons for this had to do with Bristol's economy during this period. Throughout the sixteenth century, Bristol's economy experienced difficulties: its trade in textiles was particularly hard hit, and the trade with Ireland and France declined.[27] With the gradual recovery of Bristol's trade at the end of the sixteenth century, the town now offered better prospects for advancement for young aspiring males. In all, the number of apprentices registered per year in the late sixteenth century was in the order of 150–200, reaching 270–300 registrations a year by the 1660s. Bristol's population itself nearly doubled from around 12,000 in 1600 to around 20,000 in 1670.[28] Moreover, by the early seventeenth century the proportion of apprentices who came from among the gentry and the yeomanry rose at the expense of those who came from among craftsmen, husbandmen and labourers. Sons of labourers – a small minority among the apprentices registered in the 1530s – disappeared altogether. Even in the smaller trades, and in a variety of manual crafts, the presence of sons of gentlemen and yeomen became more marked.[29] In such circumstances, when male demand for urban employment and skills was greater, women appear to have been pushed away from the retail trades and the crafts into which they had occasionally entered in earlier decades. Most of them now entered either domestic service or the textile trades, in which opportunities for well-paid employment must have dwindled as a result of the decline of Bristol's textile industry in the course of the previous century.[30] Within the textile industry, the clustering of some low-paid occupations, organised around the putting-out system, appears to have emerged. Between 1532 and 1552 no clothier or clothworker appeared among the numerous masters taking apprentices, and all young men in the textile industry were bound with independent craftsmen: weavers, fullers, shearmen and dyers. By the early seventeenth century, about a fifth of the apprentices entering the textile industry were absorbed by clothworkers, who were themselves probably employed by a few wealthier clothiers now operating in the town.[31]

The women who were apprenticed in the textile and clothing trades from the 1600s on now tended to form a segregated sector. Most were trained in knitting, sewing and button- and lacemaking, which, while providing them with some skills, could only prepare them for particularly low-paid crafts. Knitting was a part of the regular upbringing of many girls. It could be taught by mothers, and for women apprentices in Bristol, was often accompanied by domestic service. Lacemaking, buttonmaking and knitting were the kind of training commonly provided in the workhouses that had been set up under the Elizabethan Poor Law. When the Common Council in Bristol decreed, in 1652, that a workhouse be established, its aim was to put 'the poor on work within this city in spinning of yarn, knitting of stocking and other manufacturers'. The council also ordered that a few women be employed to train the children in these occupations.[32] Adolescent women who were apprenticed in these occupations were taught by women, and in households in which the master, and perhaps other apprentices or journeymen, were often engaged in a separate craft or employment. Most of the women were now bound with masters whose occupation clearly differed from the training for which the girl was apprenticed. Of the 100 indentures recorded between 1617 and 1628, only about a third were with masters in the textile and clothing trades: dyers, feltmakers, shearmen, weavers, or clothworkers. For example, Ann Jurden, bound with a shearman and his wife, agreed to serve as a maidservant as well as an apprentice in the knitting of silk stockings, for 'which the said Thomas and Joan shall employ her'. She was probably integrated into a workshop in which both her master and mistress worked. But Joan Pendock, apprenticed to a gunmaker and his wife to be taught knitting and household service, was probably trained by her mistress alone, with her work largely confined to housework.[33] Many girls were likewise bound with masters engaged in such crafts as soapmaking, shoemaking, wiredrawing, smithing, butchering, brewing and the like. A large segment (12 per cent) were now also bound with mariners. Some of these women were probably engaged primarily in domestic service, with knitting or sewing as supplementary or rudimentary work. Others may have been producing on a slightly larger scale for the market under the supervision of their mistresses. Often it was the mistress alone who appeared at the local court to record the indenture, and her sign or signature appeared, alongside her apprentice's, in the register.

A loss in the prestige of female apprenticeships accompanied these changes. Perhaps the most distinctive feature of women apprentices in early sixteenth-century Bristol was the predominance of daughters of gentlemen and yeomen, who arrived in Bristol from great distances and whose fathers were still alive at the time of their binding. By the seventeenth century, however, there were fewer migrants from substantial origins, and many more orphaned daughters; women apprenticeships in the town became distinctly associated with parish apprentices and with orphanage – with women who were more likely to be forced into apprenticeship rather than to choose it. Unlike male apprenticeships, in which the indentures were drawn up and signed privately with copies kept by the master as well as his apprentice, women's indentures by the seventeenth century were recorded in the apprentice register itself, in a manner more akin to the recording of parish apprentices bound for their relief. From the 1610s, long indentures pertaining solely to women were interspersed quite distinctively among the many short entries in the register for male bindings, and, unlike private male apprenticeships, they included the full agreement, its conditions, and, as in the case of parish indentures, the sums paid as a premium as well as the signatures of all those concerned. Like the poorer among male apprentices, women were the first to fall victim to competition for better employment and careers, and female apprenticeships became more directly associated with the parish relief system rather than with private and more prestigious apprenticeships. As in Southampton, where women apprentices were bound almost exclusively through the parish,[34] in Bristol more women were placed by parish authorities. By the late seventeenth century, women apprentices appear quite regularly in collections of indentures kept by separate Bristol parishes.[35]

Finally, it should be noted that in the 1530s and 1540s a few of the women apprenticed in the town were guaranteed, at the time of their binding, the sum of 4sh. 6d. towards eventually obtaining the freedom of the town, a privilege to which women in Bristol were entitled by borough custom.[36] It is difficult to know whether these women ever proceeded to become burgesses, for records of freemen admitted in the mid-sixteenth century are incomplete. But by the seventeenth century, not only are women absent from the Burgess Books, but among women apprentices there is not one single case in which money towards freedom was obtained. Among male apprentices, payments towards freedom were by now provided almost as a rule to all apprentices in the town.[37]

Pressures on the market for skilled labour affected, then, the lot of women apprenticed in a single community. While this meant that in some places and during specific decades opportunities for entry into skilled and more prestigious crafts diminished altogether, in other smaller places and towns, and in periods of slow population growth and greater demand for labour, such opportunities could, within certain limits, open up. By far the greatest body of evidence on female apprenticeships in a variety of crafts comes from smaller towns and parishes rather than the large towns, and in the century between 1650 and 1750, when the population ceased to grow, and the demand for labour was greater. Snell's evidence on apprenticeships in the south and the east during the seventeenth and eighteenth centuries shows relatively large numbers of women, especially among youths apprenticed through the parish, but also among those apprenticed privately by their parents. These included a large group of women apprenticed in women's trades: housewifery among parish apprentices, and mantua-makers, milliners and tailors among private apprenticeships. But there were also women apprenticed in a host of other trades and crafts into which young men were habitually bound. In the first half of the eighteenth century women were apprenticed privately as carpenters, cordwainers, blacksmiths, ironmongers, butchers, bricklayers and sawyers. Some 10 per cent of the women apprenticed by the parish were bound with butchers, grocers, brewers and fishermen. Overall, by comparison to males, women were under-represented, especially among youths apprenticed privately rather than through the parish relief system. Yet by comparison with their proportions in the largest towns, their presence in smaller urban settlements and parishes was much more marked. Private apprenticeships in the counties of Sussex, Surrey, Bedfordshire, Warwickshire and Wiltshire in the decades between 1700 and 1760 comprised some 5, 6 and even 10 per cent women, compared with only 2 and 3 per cent, or less, female apprenticeships in London or a large provincial centre like Bristol throughout the sixteenth and first decades of the seventeenth centuries. Parish listings in various places in the south and the east included even more young women, whose proportion among all apprentices reached as much as 30–40 per cent of all parish bindings.[38]

Informal Training

To judge from the range of occupations held by independent widows who operated workshops in a town like Bristol, the scope for women to obtain informal training in a variety of crafts and trades must have been wide. In fact, a brief examination of the evidence reveals that informal training encompassed a much wider range of occupations than that provided by formal apprenticeships. Between 1600 and 1645 widows in Bristol were engaged in almost all the major occupations in which men could be found as apprentices or masters. The only category of occupation from which widows were consistently absent was that of merchants and mariners. Widows were more likely than men to participate in textile trades (about a third in a sample of 103 widows taking apprentices between 1600 and 1645 were in the textile industry), while about a fifth were engaged in occupations in retail trades and trades involved in the distribution of foodstuffs – in occupations such as haberdasher, grocer, merchant tailor, baker, innkeeper, butcher and vintner. In the textile industry they appeared not only as clothworkers but as weavers, shermen, feltmakers, tuckers, dyers and cardmakers, i.e. all the major occupations involved in the industry. About a quarter of the widows were engaged in a wide variety of manual crafts, particularly, though by no means exclusively, in woodworking. Widows worked and supervised workshops as coopers, joiners, plasterers, wiredrawers, smiths, cutlers, ironmongers, platemakers, shoemakers and leatherworkers. On the whole, despite some variations, to which we shall return, the occupational distribution of widows did not radically differ from that of craftsmen and traders who were citizens of the town.

Some women appear in the apprenticeship register as independent craftsmen or traders rather than as widows, but their number is extremely small. In the 1530s and 1540s there were only two women, a goldsmith and a roper, who took apprentices on their own, and in a sample of 1,945 indentures registered between 1600 and 1645, there was only one woman who was not described as a widow, and who took an apprentice on her own. Widows showed up more frequently, since, following the death of her husband, a widow assumed the responsibilities for the workshop as well as the husband's rights and privileges, among them the right to take apprentices. The proportion of widows among masters taking apprentices remained low throughout the period: in the 1540s, 15 (1.6 per cent) apprentices out of 930 were bound with widows, and between 1600 and 1645, 75 (3.9 per cent) in a sample of 1,945. Yet the fact that the number of widows among all masters in the town was small need not obscure the wide range of skills to which they had been introduced without a formal apprenticeship. For by the early seventeenth century no girl was apprenticed in any of the occupations held by widows; few were apprenticed in grocery and clothing trades, and none in crafts like the building, leather, wood and metal trades, to which men were apprenticed routinely.

The evidence on these widows indicates a range of skills with which many a married woman must have been at least partly familiar. Many women did not remain widows for long; they remarried, whether because of the difficulties they encountered in managing a shop and a household alone, or because they desired to start a new family.[39] In other words, remarriage was not necessarily the consequence of lack of skills required to continue running a shop. Married women in Bristol were normally considered formal parties to apprenticeship contracts, and in the Register of Apprentices their names appeared almost as a rule alongside those of their husbands, indicating that the apprentice was subject to their discipline and supervision as well. In guild ordinances it was assumed that women were proficient in their husbands' crafts or trades, and an apprentice was expected to continue his training with the widow 'so long as she doth . . . use the same trade after her husband's death, and doth keep and retaine [the apprentice] . . . in the trade aforesaid'. For young men, an apprenticeship with a trader or craftsman who did not have a wife could be considered somewhat risky. Francis Reade, apprenticed to an unmarried Bristol haberdasher, was guaranteed with a bond of £5 to be repaid if his master died during the apprenticeship 'not leaving a wife that shall keep on his trade'.[40] The evidence on apprentices who petitioned in Quarter Sessions in Bristol for release of their apprenticeships following the death of their masters appears to confirm the same point. Some petitions were the result of the remarriage of a widow and her consequent removal to another household; others were presented when a mistress decided to change her occupation; but none of these apprentices appears to have claimed that the mistress lacked the skills necessary for their training. For example,

Thomas Cadle appealed to the court three months after his master died, requesting his release, and arguing that his mistress kept her apprentice to do household work for she 'hath given over her said trade [of a tailor]'.[41] Although the workshop closed down following the death of the master, the widow was not unskilled in her trade.

When and how did women obtain this wide range of skills? Some women probably learnt a trade or a craft in the early part of their marriage, as assistants in the workshops their husbands operated.[42] But many must have obtained skills not only from their husbands or during widowhood, but earlier in their lives and before they married. Evidence suggests that in Bristol young unmarried women were employed in some skilled crafts, although they were never formally apprenticed in them. When in 1652 the tobacco-pipe makers were incorporated as a guild, the employment of 'women or maids or any women stranger' was prohibited.[43] From the 1620s, when tobacco-pipe making first appeared on the urban scene, some women must have been trained and employed in the new craft. There are indications that, as early as the 1620s, women tobacco-pipe makers were working in their own right, occasionally taking on young men as apprentices in the trade.[44] Although no woman was apprenticed formally, women comprised about a fifth of the members admitted to the new guild. A few were widows, but others were described in the record simply as 'freeburgesses' of the city. While it is possible that, as a new craft, tobacco-pipe making provided exceptional opportunities for women, the eventual prohibition on the employment of maids suggests that young women could be employed and trained in shops or crafts without a formal apprenticeship.

The informal nature of such learning makes it difficult to gauge its precise dimensions, but domestic industries provided a setting for the informal training of many women during the early part of their marriage, as well as during their youth. The centrality of home-based industries in the acquisition of skills by women is quite evident in the distribution of occupations among Bristol's widows, as can be seen in Table 6.3.

The occupations in which Bristol widows were least likely to be found were those conducted away from the home: mercantile trades, seafaring occupations and the building crafts. No widow was involved in the mercantile trades or in the occupation and business of mariners or sailors; but not a few held on to the shops of grocers, haberdashers and apothecaries (the distributive trades). Very few widows were masons, painters or glaziers,

Table 6.3 *Occupations of male and female masters, Bristol 1600–45**

	Male masters		Female masters	
	nos	%	nos	%
Merchants	110	6.0	–	–
Distributive trades	270	14.5	12	11.7
Foodstuffs	157	8.5	12	11.7
Clothing and textiles	451	24.4	40	38.9
Building	150	8.1	2	1.9
Leather	187	10.1	9	8.7
Metal	204	11.0	8	7.8
Wood	141	7.6	15	14.5
Sailors, watermen	95	5.1	–	–
Professions	43	2.3	2	1.9
Misc.	47	2.4	3	2.9
Total	1855	100.0	103	100.0

* The numbers for male and female masters are samples.

Sources: as for Table 6.1.

whose work was frequently outdoors, but quite a number of them continued to manage shops in the leather, textile and even metal industries.

By contrast to seafaring occupations or building crafts, home-based industries were likely to rely on the work of women, whose assistance in certain circumstances could become critical. Small-scale shop production was vulnerable to the ups and downs of the market, and to the sudden death of any worker in the shop. Death, injury, or the prolonged illness of masters or their apprentices and journeymen may all have required the temporary assistance of wives, but also of daughters, sisters, and even domestic servants. Intervals between the hirings of apprentices, especially if an apprentice left abruptly or ran away, could also require some temporary help, and provide learning opportunities for women. As can also be seen in Table 6.3, there were some variations in the proportions of male and female masters in different domestic industries. The proportion of widows engaged in the clothing and textile trades was higher than that of men; and widows also appeared more frequently among woodworkers (mostly coopers) and small craftsmen engaged in miscellaneous crafts (ropemaking, sailmaking and basketmaking). Metalwork, by contrast, was relatively less common among the widows than among male masters. These variations were probably the consequence less of the type of skill involved in each craft, than of the size of the shop and the degree to which it relied on apprenticed labour. Wealthier masters whose shops had a continuous supply of one and two apprentices were less likely to rely on the assistance of women. Among a group of metal masters operating shops in the first decade of the seventeenth century, about half (25 of 47 masters) took one apprentice in the space of eight years; but nearly a third (14 masters) had 3, 4 and even 5 or 6 apprentices bound between 1604 and 1612. Among a group of textile and clothing workers during the same years, the proportion of those who took only a single apprentice in the space of eight years was higher (99 – 60.3 per cent – out of 164 masters); and among coopers, too, as many as 60 per cent (25 masters of 41 who took apprentices between 1604 and 1612) hired only a single apprentice. In addition, none of the textile workers and coopers took five or more apprentices during this time span, as was the case occasionally among metal workers. Overall, coopers throughout the period appear to have worked without the assistance of apprentices for at least part of their mature working lives. As we have already seen, nearly two-thirds of woodworkers operating shops in Bristol in the years between 1532 and 1658 had only a single apprentice during their entire careers as masters there.[45] If we also take into consideration the fact that some of their apprentices served only three or four years rather than the full seven or eight, the possibility that these coopers worked for long periods of time without any apprentice in their shops becomes more evident still.

In such circumstances, women – wives, daughters, sisters – were likely to provide assistance in a shop. William Stout recalled that his sister Elin, a young single woman, frequently helped him in his shop during fairs and on market days, and 'was as ready in serving retaile customers as a young apprentice could have done'.[46] Elin never left the parental home, but her assistance to her brother during the years when he was only beginning to trade and was yet without a single apprentice in his new shop was of great value, and was evidently considered as such by her brother. Such assistance to brothers, fathers and masters could equip young women with the skills necessary for running shops when they grew up and married. The freemen's lists in Bristol in the first half of the seventeenth century show that about a third of 217 young traders and craftsmen who obtained citizenship through marriage to a freeman's daughter married daughters of artisans who practised the same or a similar craft or trade.[47] Daughters of grocers married merchants, drapers or haberdashers; daughters of drapers married tailors, and those of skinners married shoemakers, and so on. Such marriages were probably the result of occupational connections between families. They also reflected a certain hierarchy that existed between different occupations: for example, daughters of gentlemen and merchants were more likely to marry into the more prestigious distributive trades.[48] But such patterns also indicate that young women spent at least part of their teenage years in the type of working environment they eventually entered when they married. During these years they were exposed to the world of business and trade, to the particular demands and expertise required in the retail of some crafts, and occasionally also to the skills required in a shop.

Domestic Service

Many young women did not remain in the parental home during the long years before they married. Margaret Johnson was the daughter of a Lancaster trader, and when her father died she was still a child. Although her stepmother was still alive, Margaret spent most of her teens boarding with neighbours and kin. First she was boarded out through provisions made in her father's will; then when she was 14 years old she went to live with William Stout, a friend and neighbour of her late father. During the two years she lived there she went to school to learn to write, sew, knit, and other 'necessary imploy'. She then decided that she wanted to spend some time with her aunts, who lived near Warrington, about 50 miles away from Lancaster. She travelled on her own, stayed with her aunts for a while, and was introduced to a Presbyterian preacher whose teaching made a great impression on her. Soon afterwards Margaret decided to stay in Warrington. She wrote to William Stout that he 'might not expect her return', and that she had chosen Mr Owen, the preacher, as her tutor. Margaret remained with her aunts for several years, and continued to assist them and obtain her education from her tutor. Eventually she married a young craftsman, a joiner, to whom she bore several children before he died, forcing her 'to industry' – as William Stout described it – in order to continue to maintain her children on her own.[49]

Among the wealthier urban classes, women were more likely

to stay at home than their counterparts lower down on the social scale; and overall there is some evidence to suggest that women in their teens were somewhat more likely than men to remain in their parental homes, especially if their mothers were widowed.[50] Nevertheless, the majority of women did leave home, whether to advance themselves by finding a proper match, or, more frequently, to find suitable employment. Even among the middling and more prosperous classes such moves were hardly unusual. Margaret Johnson lived in relative comfort with William Stout, yet when she was 16 years old she chose to leave her guardian; and Jane Martindale, a yeoman's daughter, decided to leave her home and travel to London to become a servant there despite her parents' objections.[51] Most women probably left home because their parents lacked the means to support them and they had no proper employment at home, or because they were orphaned; among women apprentices in seventeenth-century Bristol, as we have seen, there were many orphans who were compelled to leave home and find suitable employment in the large town.

Often these moves involved long-distance migration to towns, where women became lodgers in the houses of kin or domestic servants. Throughout the sixteenth and seventeenth centuries, most women migrants in London entered domestic service, and in Bristol well over a third of the women registered as apprentices for a long seven-year term were hired as housewives or serving-maids. Many more must have been hired on an annual basis to serve in the houses of merchants, mercers, grocers and numerous other craftsmen. By the late seventeenth century the employment of domestic female servants among London's middling classes was virtually universal,[52] and many provincial towns and smaller urban settlements also had a large sector of female servants. As David Souden has shown, by the later decades of the seventeenth century, when in the country as a whole long-distance migration contracted, migrants to the large towns were disproportionately female. Most of these women were in their late teens and early twenties, and the distances they travelled to towns like Exeter, Salisbury, Oxford, Leicester and others were only slightly shorter than those travelled by men. In general, these young women tended to reside in the wealthier, inner parishes of towns, where the demand for domestic servants was high. From the late seventeenth century and throughout the eighteenth, there was a marked female domination – including many young migrants – of the growing populations of towns.[53]

Life as a domestic servant was strenuous and physically very demanding, especially for those serving in the larger houses of the more affluent urban classes, where great effort went into cleaning, washing and scrubbing kitchens, stairs and floors. Kitchen work and cooking were especially arduous and dirty, and the workload, when families were entertaining guests, could be great.[54] In small urban shops, too, the work of the domestic servant could be demanding, even when the house was small and living standards relatively modest. As we have seen, by the seventeenth century Bristol's women apprentices were often employed in domestic services, as well as in textile work – knitting silk stockings or spinning. The Bristol woman apprentice referred to above, who was specifically promised that she would be employed only in knitting, underlines the fact that in many other households young women were employed in knitting or lace-making as well as in domestic service. The maids employed by a number of tobacco-pipe makers in Bristol might well have begun their work as domestic servants, and those who were hired as domestic servants must also have assisted in the shops of their masters – haberdashers, grocers, cheesemongers, chandlers, shoemakers, tailors and the like. Others helped in the inns, ale-houses and eating houses of their masters or mistresses. Simon Forman, apprenticed in his youth to a Salisbury grocer, remembered that the kitchen maid at his master's house was often asked to 'look into the shop and help, if occasion served'. When his master was away, Simon was in charge of the shop with the maid providing help.[55]

Like their male counterparts, domestic servants left service rather frequently. Marjorie K. McIntosh referred to a domestic servant near Romford, in Essex, who worked for three mistresses and a master, before migrating to London. In none of the households did she spend the full term of her contract.[56] Once in the town, women not infrequently continued their moves. In some apprenticeships, a young woman was provided with a bond of security which allowed her to leave service if she saw fit. For example, Alice Otely, apprenticed in 1626 to a Bristol feltmaker, was provided with a bond for the value of £3, to be repaid 'if the maid departe within the said term by the default of him or his wife'.[57] Most women were not guaranteed with such bonds, but they nonetheless left their masters or mistresses at the end of their terms, and often before. In early seventeenth-century London, domestic servants sometimes spent long periods of service with single masters, but often they stayed in one household no more than a year or two, and occasionally even less. By the late seventeenth and eighteenth centuries, female domestics were notorious for their tendency to change places of employment, and the turnover in some households was quite remarkable.[58]

Movement between different masters necessitated the acquisition of a range of skills to suit the requirements of different households. Among the women who were apprenticed in Bristol in the seventeenth century, and who appear to have found places on their own, there were daughters of husbandmen and craftsmen from the countryside who had probably been employed as cooks, dairymaids or agricultural servants before their arrival in the town. By the time they had lived in the town and changed one or more households, they had acquired a range of household and other skills, and encountered divergent household economies. While domestic service as such hardly prepared them for independent vocations, the experience entailed in living in various households could enhance their understanding of the economic strategies of different rural and urban families, and of the risks that were involved. When William Stout considered selling one of his shops to his former apprentice, he consulted his older sister, but also his maidservant. The maid was quite confident that such a decision was mistaken, and told Stout that he should not 'give over trade'. Stout took her opinion seriously, and eventually decided to withdraw from his plan.[59]

Many domestic servants faced the risk of unemployment, and were forced to use their initiative when they were fired, or when they were unable to secure another employment at the end of an annual term. Migration to a large town involved its own hazards and unexpected hardship. When Jane Martindale arrived in London she had difficulties in finding suitable employment, despite promises for assistance given to her before she left her home. She soon ran out of money, and was obliged to write to her parents to help her out with money and food; later on she 'had thoughts to sell her hair'.[60] When Edward Barlow arrived in London without a proper arrangement for employment or an apprenticeship, he first turned to his sister, then a servant in the city. Lacking any material means to offer, his sister nonetheless gave him some shrewd advice and persuaded him to turn to his uncle, which he reluctantly did. She was obviously well informed and quite familiar with the difficulties entailed in settling to a proper course in the large town.[61] And while many domestics were discharged by their mistresses, often it was the young servant herself who decided to leave, taking the initiative in confronting masters or mistresses, and in deciding where and how to continue and provide for herself.[62]

As they grew older, women who had served in domestic service in various places also gained a range of social competences, cooperating with fellow servants and apprentices, supervising and sometimes instructing younger ones, and, as we shall see in

Chapter 9, negotiating with masters. Francis Kirkman described how as a young apprentice in the house of a London scrivener he was given instructions by serving-maids in his master's house.[63] Other women would have learnt to collaborate and cooperate with their male counterparts. Simon Forman recalled that when he first came to his master's house he had a series of squabbles with Mary, the kitchen maid; but in the course of time, they learned to help each other and Mary routinely assisted Simon in the shop. Eventually they 'agreed so well that they never were at square after, and Mary would do for [Simon] all that she could'.[64]

Such cooperation could continue for several years, and eventually shape the manner with which couples established themselves on their own when they married. Marriages between domestic servants and apprentices, from the same neighbourhood if not the same household, were probably quite common.[65] Women who married after several years in domestic service could offer invaluable household skills such as sewing, knitting, brewing, cooking, washing, and rearing children; they could contribute small dowries they had themselves saved; and they could also provide practical understanding in managing small trade, in supervising apprentices, offering advice, and managing shops when occasion required. Many couples must have begun a joint enterprise on the basis of the divergent skills and experiences obtained before marriage by both husbands and wives. William Stout recorded the marriage of a neighbouring couple and commented that 'they entered upon the chandler or cheesemonger trade in London'.[66] That they should open a small enterprise as a team was recorded by him as a matter of course. Jane Martindale started an inn with her husband soon after she was married. Jane had been a domestic servant in London, and when she made her decision to marry, she and her husband, together, were 'thought very fit to keep an inn, as accordingly they did'.[67]

Perhaps above all, women brought with them into marriage the experience of long years during which they learnt to cope with many tasks, and to switch between different skills, masters and working environments. The ability to pull resources from a variety of jobs, to find new employment, to apply a range of skills when confronting uncertainties and hardship must have been pertinent to the maturation of most women, and not just among the very poor. Elin Godsalves, whose husband went bankrupt in 1707, was capable of managing on her own, 'having before marriage kept a milliner's shop to her profit and reputation,' as William Stout described it.[68] And the mistress of Edward Barlow, a seaman's apprentice in the mid-seventeenth century, was a former widow who managed a cook-shop that served food to country pedlars in London. Between voyages to sea, Barlow was employed by his mistress in her shop, and on his return from voyages he routinely transferred his wages to her. His mistress not only managed an eating house on her own, but also had complete control over the family finances.[69]

Scattered throughout Bristol court cases are examples of women who not only followed in their husband's footsteps in his craft or trade, or simply helped in the management of shops and supervision of apprentices, but who practised something on their own, complementing and adding to the economy of the family in more ways than by doing housework or by their typical feminine skills. In October 1654 Alice Beale was apprehended for drunkenness and was then forbidden 'from keeping an ale-house'; another case involved Susanna, the wife of Francis Bayly, a shipwright. She was engaged in the retail of iron bolts to local smiths, and was suing two apprentices who stole her goods.[70] These examples give only a glimpse of what must have been a much wider diversity of practices and skills acquired by young women independently during many years of labour and service outside the tutelage of parents or husbands. That experience, more than the fluctuations in the demand for male labour and the opportunities it could occasionally offer to young females, was the most formative in the lives of women, whether among the labouring poor or among middling groups, in the countryside and in towns.

7 The Widening Circle: The Social Ties of Youth

Once they left the parental home and became servants and apprentices in the households of others, many youths did not see their parents, brothers, sisters, old playmates, or the neighbours with whom they had grown up, sometimes for years. Some youths were orphaned and quite on their own at an early age; not a few travelled great distances from home. Benjamin Bangs saw his mother in Norfolk several years after he had left there in his early teens; and Edward Barlow did not see his mother for many years, until he was already an adult. Even shorter distances could prove a great obstacle. The Josselins, who appear to have had good contacts with all their sons and daughters after their departure from home, did not see them, on occasion, for periods of months and even more.[1]

Lawrence Stone has interpreted the removal of children from their parents as characteristic of the remote relations that existed between them, a traumatic experience which impaired the lives of children as they grew up. As historians have pointed out, and as we shall also emphasise in what follows, there is much fault in this interpretation, for the parental bond continued to play a vital role in the lives of many youths well into their early adult lives.[2] Nevertheless it remains arguable that once they left their parental homes, adolescents became quite vulnerable. As we saw in Chapter 4, to establish a beneficial and rewarding relationship with a master was not an easy undertaking, and even if masters were not normally as harsh or sadistic as Stone portrayed them, it is still true that the master–servant bond into which many young people entered was not always successful. It was also temporary, obliging the master only for the period when the youth stayed and worked under his roof. If for one reason or another servants were turned away from their masters before the end of their terms, if something went wrong with their service or apprenticeship, if their master died and they could not find another one in his place, or simply if youths were unable to find a new employer when their contract expired, they were likely to need help. Since they were normally in their mid- or late teens, they were unlikely to rely on the parish relief system for aid, for they were no longer considered amongst the 'deserving poor'.[3] Even if they did not find themselves in acute circumstances, they were likely to need some assistance as they moved along from one place to another. Throughout most of the sixteenth and seventeenth centuries, there were few formal institutions – newspapers, clubs, advertising agencies – to regulate and direct the mobility of youths. Even the hiring fairs, which helped young people find masters and work throughout the country, became regular only in the late seventeenth century.[4]

What we know today about social relations in early modern English society underlines the fragility of the situation in which youths might find themselves once they left the parental home. Most historians now accept that social ties beyond the nuclear family were, for the most part, based on the local community, and this was true of the countryside as well as in towns. Kinship ties were weak, and the kinship system was impermanent and lacking rigid and normative rules regarding aid and support to one's kin. By contrast, neighbourly ties provided many forms of aid and services, and even in large towns like London such neighbourly communities provided assistance of a variety of kinds; they were 'islands' of stability in the midst of a great deal of social and geographical mobility.[5] Given, however, that servants and apprentices were by far the most mobile segment in the population, they were the least likely to establish strong relationships with their neighbours or become integrated into the communities and neighbourhoods where they lived.[6]

How then did youths fare, and on whom did they rely? In this chapter we explore a range of social ties and the assistance and support they provided to young people in various circumstances that were likely to be confronted. We begin with an examination of the nuclear bond, the ways it was sustained, and how it assisted youths during their teens and early twenties. We then examine the uses and support of kinship ties, the bonds with masters, neighbourly ties, and the assistance young people obtained from peers and other youths or age groups.[7] I have divided the support young people could expect to obtain into three categories. The first might be termed 'critical' support: financial help, assistance in times of hardship and difficulty, and protection against maltreatment. The second category can be termed 'casual' assistance: social contacts, advice, information, small benefits and gifts. A third type might be termed 'non-practical' support: companionship, comfort and sociability, which could contribute not only to the survival of young people, but to their well-being and their sense of being supported and not being wholly on their own. Overall, although the evidence used to answer these questions is scattered and somewhat weak in comparison with evidence which is more amenable to measurement, the consistency of the picture that emerges appears true in its broad outlines.

The Nuclear Bond

To many youths, the nuclear bond was of immense value in their first steps as servants or apprentices outside the parental home, and this bond continued to provide a great deal of assistance in the course of the period of service. We saw in Chapter 2 that parental guidance and advice in deciding what occupation to choose were important, not least because a youth relied on his parents' financial means in arranging some types of apprenticeship. In the case of youths who desired to become apprentices in major towns in the large distributive trades or one of the more lucrative crafts, entry without the financial assistance of parents was unthinkable; not only was the premium for these trades costly, but bonds of high amounts were sometimes required as well. Even in the smaller crafts and trades, any assistance to cover the costs of at least a part of the premium, or the costs of travel to a large town, could be of critical value. When Edward Barlow became an apprentice in Manchester it was his father who 'made up the bargain'; and about a year later, when he decided to leave for London, he financed his trip partly with his own savings, but partly also with the little money he had been able to obtain from his father.[8]

Parents also provided the social contacts necessary for service and apprenticeship, in the countryside as well as in towns. Although Edward Barlow lived only four miles away from Manchester, where he became an apprentice, and although he had before then been employed outside his home in nearby villages, nevertheless it was his father 'hearing of a man of a reasonably good trade',[9] who provided Edward's initial contacts with his master. Of prime importance in these parental networks were ties based on occupations and on trade. George Bewley's apprenticeship in Dublin was arranged by two people who came from Ireland and lodged at his father's house in Cumberland, and Edward Barlow was also apprenticed, for a short while, with a Kentish vintner who was a guest at his uncle's inn in London.[10] Inns, ale-houses and local markets and fairs were foci of information networks through which parents found or assisted their sons and daughters in finding a master. Among apprentices in large urban centres, the preponderance of youths who had originally come from market towns was marked. In mid-sixteenth-century London about a third of migrant apprentices were from market towns; and in early seventeenth-century Bristol the proportion was even higher, particularly among those who travelled longer distances to the town, among whom nearly half had arrived from market towns.[11] Urban apprentices tended to come from places and areas that had distinct trading connections with an urban centre: industrial regions in which cloth or metal was produced; coastal trade and coal routes which linked the countryside with large towns; or simply agricultural centres from whence the grain consumed in the town came.[12] Patterns of apprenticeship as recorded in registers of apprenticeship reflect these parental occupational ties too, for nearly half the apprentices in all major industries and trades in a town like Bristol chose masters who had an occupation similar or closely related to that of their fathers.[13]

Networks of adult friendships which extended beyond the village or town where they lived also facilitated the arrangement of service or apprenticeships for daughters and sons. Edward Barlow recalled that his uncle, a London innkeeper, had 'a friend, living in the country . . . who had a son which he was willing to send to London for to be prentice'. Soon after, the youth arrived and was bound an apprentice. As Steve Rappaport has suggested, since so many Londoners were themselves migrants, their links with the countryside are likely to have been strong. Jane Martindale left her home in Lancashire to become a servant in London through contacts she made with Londoners who came to stay with their friends in Lancashire during the plague of 1625.[14] In large towns themselves, parental links with fellow craftsmen, guildsmen, neighbours and other friends also helped a youth obtain an apprenticeship or a service placement. Bristol's shoemakers, coopers and other craftsmen often sent their sons to become apprentices with other shoemakers or coopers: friends, neighbours and fellow craftsmen of the same guild with whom the parents probably had more than a fleeting acquaintance.

Next to parents, the assistance of older brothers or sisters in arranging service or an apprenticeship was often quite important. Sometimes brothers and sisters who had already left home and migrated to a large town assisted their younger brothers or sisters to find lodging or employment, or simply provided advice and first connections in and around a new place. When Edward Barlow arrived in London, his sister, then a servant herself, provided advice and cautioned him on his moves.[15] Other youths followed in the footsteps of their brothers as apprentices with the same masters, or, more commonly, with another craftsman who belonged to the same guild. Among 771 Bristol apprentices who were bound between 1605 and 1608, 145 (18.8 per cent) had brothers apprenticed in the town in the course of their apprenticeship or afterwards. Many of these youths were migrants who were probably active in the arrangement of the apprenticeship of their younger brothers. Richard Horte, the son of a husbandman in Congresbury in Somerset, was apprenticed to a Bristol haberdasher in 1603; his brother, Henry, followed him and was apprenticed in 1606 with a Bristol tailor, one John Cole; and a still younger brother, Samuel, was bound in 1614 with another Bristol haberdasher. Since the father of the Horte brothers died in 1603, it is likely that the older brothers were active in finding and arranging the apprenticeships of the younger ones. Of the 145 apprentices who had brothers in the city at one point, more than 40 per cent were orphans, but among those who had no brother there, only a third were orphans.[16]

Contacts with home and parents continued to be vital in the lives of many youths. Edward Terril, a Bristol apprentice, used to go to see his widowed mother every Sunday, 'after sermons'; and Edward Barlow met his father on Saturday, 'being market day' in Manchester. In the Havering manor in Essex, servants met their parents routinely at the local market of Romford.[17] Many youths were able to return home for short visits, on holidays and other occasions,[18] and apprentices in large towns not infrequently went home with the consent of their masters. Some cases which appeared in Quarter Sessions in Bristol suggest that going home to visit parents was anything but unusual, for it was used as an excuse by apprentices when they wanted to go away or simply have some time off.[19] Many servants and apprentices did not reside too far from their parental homes; agricultural servants normally did not move more than a few miles,[20] and even in the large urban centres substantial numbers were natives or came from villages and towns nearby. Among Bristol apprentices, for example, natives and those arriving from villages no further than 10 or 12 miles from the town comprised nearly half of the apprentices in the town.[21]

Sometimes daily contacts were kept up between the youth, the master and mistress, and the youth's parents. So in a case petitioned in Chancery in 1620, regarding an apprenticeship in the town of Hereford, it was claimed that the father was 'hearing from day to day' about his son's whereabouts and the master's neglect in properly employing the youth.[22] Parents often interfered with, or were called upon to mediate and help, a master in his dealings with their sons. Anthony Brewerton, a Bristol upholsterer, argued in Quarter Sessions that his apprentice absented himself for weeks from his shop; yet before resorting to court, Brewerton had turned to his apprentice's parents, and with their mediation succeeded in obtaining from the youth 'large promises of amendment'; these proved of no value. In another case it was the apprentice who asked his father to interfere and beseech the master to amend his ways, to no avail.[23] George Brysson, too, remembered that his master asked his father to come to his house in Edinburgh to try to dissuade young George from going to religious meetings and from following 'men that were not allowed by law to preach'.[24]

Sometimes parents themselves went to visit their daughters or sons. John Gratton mentioned coming back from the field to his grandfather's home where he was apprenticed, 'and finding my father and mother were come over to see us'.[25] Ralph Josselin and his wife both went to see their sons and daughters who served as apprentices and domestics in London, some 40 miles away from where they lived. Even the father of Edward Barlow, who was poor and must have found the trip to London a great financial burden, managed to make the long journey from his home in Lancashire to London, where he met young Barlow, then already an apprentice at sea.[26] When a master went into the countryside, he might go to see his apprentice's or servant's parents;[27] and many parents, through the same social ties that had enabled them to arrange the service in the first place, were well informed about their sons and daughters.[28] Parents themselves sometimes moved nearer to a son or daughter, and so the contacts with them were resumed;[29] and letters were occasionally sent by parents, brothers, sisters, or their neighbours.[30] For their part, some apprentices who had had to go to more distant towns kept their parents informed by writing letters. Not all youths could write, but among London apprentices, who were likely to be the furthest away from their parents, literacy rates were sometimes quite high.[31] This does not mean that they all sent letters home regularly, but it indicates that they could write letters if they so desired, or if they were in some sort of need. Richard Norwood wrote his father a very long letter at least once when he was an apprentice at sea; and John Woodhouse, a London apprentice whose parents were dead, wrote his uncle a long letter in which he asked for assistance. By the eighteenth century, manuals of letter-writing contained a substantial number of model letters which were exchanged between youths who were servants and apprentices, and their parents.[32]

Some parents also provided direct financial assistance to their sons and daughters. The evidence on this is very sparse, but what there is suggests that there was nothing unusual about such financial provision. John Coggs, a London printer's apprentice, recorded in his diary that on 27 April 1703 his mother bought him gloves, shoes, a wig, a hat and some books when she came to visit him. In addition, he had some money that his mother had given him, which was kept for him by his aunt.[33] Gervase Disney recalled that his master was 'pretty penurious' in his supply of food – a very common complaint among apprentices and servants – so he bought things 'out of that money my friends sent me'.[34]

More important was the assistance parents provided when an apprentice became ill or injured during service. As we have already seen in Chapter 4 and will emphasise shortly, masters were both obliged and expected to take care of their servants and apprentices when they became ill. Nevertheless difficulties could arise, and parents were sometimes called upon to assist. Adolescent illnesses and injuries while at work were common, and recovery was a painfully slow process. Some masters were too poor and simply could not continue to provide for a youth until he recovered;[35] sometimes the apprentice was incapacitated – soreness of leg, a limb injury, mental illness are mentioned in a number of petitions presented at the local court in Bristol – and it was decided by mutual consent that parents would take upon themselves the responsibility for the recovery of their child. Sometimes there was little hope of recovery, and parents took their sons back; sometimes it was decided that a youth should go back to the countryside to recover; and at other times parents themselves called their sons back, as when plague broke out in the town where their sons were apprenticed.[36] Occasionally youths themselves appear to have desired to return to the parental home: for example, when they had the smallpox, or when they contracted other diseases which threatened their lives. Benjamin Bangs headed towards his mother's home when he was not well; Ralph Josselin's daughter, Ann, returned home in the midst of her service in London, and shortly afterwards she died and was buried in Earle Colne. Adam Martindale's daughter, Elizabeth, was likewise 'desirous to come home' when she became ill during her service, so she was brought back; but although her parents took great care of her, she died soon afterwards.[37]

The most common circumstances which made youths return to their parental homes were when they encountered difficulties with harsh, dishonest or incompetent masters, when they ran away or were forced out of their apprenticeship, or when they became unemployed. George Trosse returned home to his widowed mother in Exeter after a series of misfortunes with his master, a merchant in Portugal;[38] and John Ricketts, a Bristol apprentice whose master failed to teach him the art of butchery, was sent home by an order of court to 'his father, there to be provided for till the first day of Easter sessions'.[39] Unemployed youths were often driven back to their parents. John Croker returned home from his apprenticeship overseas (in Philadelphia) when his master died and no alternative was found for him, and William Hyett, a Bristol soapmaker's apprentice, argued at the Quarter Sessions that his master sent him 'home to his friends' for he had 'no employment for the said apprentice'.[40] In some cases, youths were sent to their parents when their masters became unemployed: Arise Evans was sent home when his master became insolvent, and Robert Persons was sent to his parents when his master, a merchant, 'lost nearly the whole of his fortune'.[41] In other cases it was youths themselves who decided to go back to their parental homes when they became unemployed.[42] Ralph Josselin helped his daughter when she was unemployed,[43] and Edward Barlow remembered that as a child, when he was 'out of work', he was a 'burden' to his parents. In the late eighteenth century, Joseph Mayett, an agricultural servant who had had no less than eleven masters in the course of his youth, returned home to his parents at least three times, when he was fired or thrown out and was unable to find another master quickly enough.[44]

Returning home was not necessarily the privilege of a minority who had come from wealthy families. Joseph Mayett was the son of an agricultural labourer in Buckinghamshire, and John Ricketts, the Bristol apprentice who was sent back to his father in 1627, was the son of a Gloucestershire husbandman. Among youths who presented petitions in Chancery alleging that they had been abused by their masters and were forced out of their apprenticeship, one who returned home to his parents in Yorkshire was the son of a gentleman, but there was also a Nottinghamshire labourer who took his son back. This labourer, John Gregorie, claimed he was 'a very poor man' who was earning only 2d. 'most days'.[45]

At the end of service and apprenticeship, some youths, especially among the middling classes, could expect to inherit portions of land, houses, stock, money, household goods and tools which had been left to them in their parents' wills.[46] Many also obtained a great deal of advice and information from their families to help them set up. Just as their arrival in a town was directed by parental ties, so they could be drawn away from it by family ties.[47] Parents provided advice, contacts and information about lodging and shops available for rent. Sometimes they suggested that their children come to live near them, so that they could 'be helpful one to another in the best things,' as the father of Gervase Disney put it.[48] There is also evidence that youths who were apprenticed in large towns eventually returned to the countryside to establish themselves near their parents. Among Bristol's apprentices who never became freemen in the town two groups were least likely to establish themselves in the town: apprentices whose fathers had been craftsmen in the countryside, and those who themselves learnt occupations widely practised in the regions surrounding the town, i.e. textile and metal industries. Some of the youths who learnt smithing or weaving must have returned to live near parents who were themselves involved in occupations closely associated with those their sons had learnt in the large town.[49]

Throughout adolescence and youth, the parental bond continued to have material as well as emotional value to youths. There were countless variations in ways of maintaining contacts and providing assistance, and these were to some extent determined by the level of parental resources, the distances travelled by the young people, and the individual temperaments of youths and their parents. Some youths sustained deeper and more intense relations with their parents,[50] and others became more detached as they grew up and moved on. There were those who never needed to return to stay with their parents, but others who returned once, twice, or many times. Some returned home with relief, having forsaken a disagreeable employment or master; others came back much more reluctantly, when all other means failed.

But there was also something less loose and unstructured about the way the nuclear bond functioned when children were dispersed. For throughout their teens and beyond, youths tended to gravitate back to their homes, especially in moments of crisis and hardship. It was this critical support, more than the casual assistance and perhaps even the emotional ties and bonds of affection, which appears to have been the most crucial, and most durable, in the lives of many youths. In this sense, life-cycle service was obviously complementary to, rather than a replacement of, the parental home. Along with its role in preparing children for their future, life-cycle service was a means whereby parents could spread the risks involved in maintaining them during the long phase before they married. Children were sent out to become servants for a wide variety of reasons: when parents had no employment for their adolescent children,[51] when one or both of the parents died,[52] when they encountered economic difficulties or felt threatened by them.[53] But once an arrangement with masters failed for similar reasons – death, poverty, lack of employment, inadequate training, occasionally the illness of the youth – children could return home, and were taken back. In its duration, provision of assistance and security – a sort of a safety net – sometimes in its emotional depth, the parental bond surpassed all other ties. Even if occasionally inactive for quite a long time, the nuclear bond was the core around which all other social ties of youths revolved.

Other Kin

We saw in Chapter 2 that many children were separated from their parents during their early childhood years and were sent away to spend periods of time in the households of other people. Although grandparents, uncles, aunts and various in-laws were prominent among these people, children were also sent to non-kin, sometimes to strangers who resided quite far from the parental home. Overall the evidence regarding the uses of social ties in sending children away appears to agree with some of the major findings regarding the flexibility and lack of 'unambiguous kinship obligations',[54] as Keith Wrightson put it, which characterised the English family and kinship system during this period. For example, James Fretwell was boarded out four times in his childhood, but only once with a kinsman.[55] Among 24 relations and acquaintances to whom parents of writers of autobiographies sent their children, only 14 were kin. To judge by what the writers remembered about the treatment they met outside their parental home, there was no significant difference between kin and non-kin, either. There were relatives who aroused tenderness and affection in the children, and others who did not; and there were also non-kin – widows, schoolteachers and other acquaintances – who took 'good care', as James Fretwell put it, of the children who came to live under their roof.[56]

Evidence regarding the selection of masters and the arrangement of service and apprenticeship appears to confirm the same point, for contemporaries were not inclined to mobilise their relatives to become masters of their children. Only a few urban craftsmen and traders took servants and apprentices from amongst kin. Apprenticeship records in towns such as London, Bristol, Norwich and Salisbury all show only a small minority of youths with identical surnames to their masters, and however one multiplies this to include connections on the maternal side or other in-laws, the numbers of youths apprenticed by their kindred could not have been high.[57] There is much less evidence for agricultural servants, but what there is does not show any marked tendency to become servants amongst one's kin.[58] Autobiographical evidence also suggests that when masters were chosen from among relatives, they could turn harsh, unreliable or disappointing as skilled craftsmen or traders.[59] Such evidence also shows that kin were mobilised only after other masters had been tried, or after other occupational careers had been considered.[60] As a whole, it indicates not only that relatives were not a first and preferable choice, but that youths and their parents sometimes avoided binding themselves with kin, even when such ties were available and relatives were willing to take them as servants or apprentices. Sometimes it was because young people had specific careers in mind,[61] but sometimes because they had reservations regarding the wisdom of such a choice. As John Woodhouse, an apprentice who decided to depart from his master, a cousin of his who lived in London, wrote, 'it were better for so near relations to be at a greater distance'.[62]

Yet Woodhouse's remark also serves to illustrate some of the complexities involved in the kinship system, for it by no means implies that kin ties were unimportant, or without well-defined roles. All it suggests is that there was a widespread sentiment (which Woodhouse used to excuse leaving his master) against mixing relationships based on 'contract' and self-interest with interactions based on kinship ties. Other evidence indicates that where children, adolescents and youths were concerned, kinship ties did involve a great deal of social and moral obligation. Orphaned children were often taken in by kin, especially grandparents, uncles and aunts, and evidence from wills in some communities shows that if testators were already widowed, a relative was commonly their first choice as guardian of their children.[63] Autobiographical evidence also indicates that when non-kin were chosen to board young children, this was normally when children were sent to school, or to prepare for apprenticeships; that is, when one or both parents were still alive. But when they became orphaned, children were more likely to have been taken by kin who also acted as their guardians. This obligation towards the orphaned child continued well into adolescence and youth. In early seventeenth-century London, the vast majority of women migrants who were living with kin were fatherless; according to Vivien Brodsky Elliott, among 226 female migrants who had kin residing in London, 135 (59.7 per cent) were living with them. Moreover, in the majority of these cases, the young women were not there as domestic servants; they came to reside with their kin, whose responsibility it was to assist the young women to establish themselves – and especially to find a suitable husband in the large metropolis.[64]

In service and apprenticeships, the assistance of kin was also much more substantial than first appears. As previously noted, only a minority of urban apprentices had identical surnames to their masters, but relatives sometimes did take kin as servants and apprentices. While the tendency need not be overestimated, it should not be undervalued, either;[65] autobiographical evidence shows that kin and relatives in a large town not only took apprentices, but sometimes instigated a youth's move to town. Nor was it wholly unusual for kin to offer apprenticeships free of any premium and charge.[66] In other words, while kin were not a first and most obvious alternative as masters, their existence could be crucial in decisions on where some youth would go.

Even more important was the assistance kin provided in arranging apprenticeships. Joseph Oxley's uncle, who lived in London, assisted him in finding a master when he came from London to Lancashire for a visit (Joseph had been an orphan since the age of eight). Some seven or eight years later, when Oxley arrived in London, the uncle once again provided a proper placement for his nephew.[67] In Havering, too, many young immigrants had relatives who had already settled in the community and who helped them find employment and service arrangements.[68] Records of apprenticeships in towns are rather scant in the details they provide about all those involved in arranging service, but occasionally such information surfaces. In collections of female indentures, for example, references are made to the parties involved in the arrangement and signature of the contract, and they make abundantly clear that, next to parents, it was normally kinsmen who assisted their female relatives in these arrangements. In 71 indentures recorded in Bristol in the early decades of the seventeenth century, 35 were signed or marked by the apprentice as well as by her father or mother; and in 16 more it was a relative – uncle, aunt, mother-in-law – who gave their consent and became the third party to the contract.[69]

Many of these young women were orphans, which may in part account for the relatively high numbers of kin present at the time of their binding. But evidence from autobiographies suggests that the assistance of kin in the arrangement of apprenticeship for males was hardly an exception, and that it involved more than simple mediation or provision of information about available masters. Relatives invested a great deal of time in looking for, and negotiating with, masters, and they continued to provide assistance in the course of the early part of an apprenticeship.[70] No less important was the assistance kinsmen provided to youths who arrived in towns without a proper arrangement for service or apprenticeship. When Richard Norwood first came to London he stayed with his uncle, a carpenter in Barnsby Street, 'till I might otherwise be settled'.[71] Edward Barlow also stayed with his uncle and aunt for nearly a year until he found an apprenticeship that suited his plans. His uncle first offered him an apprenticeship, but when Barlow explained his desire to go to sea, his uncle helped him to be accepted on a ship: he not only made the proper connections through a friend in the Navy Office, but interviewed prospective masters, dissuaded young Barlow from binding himself with a person he suspected would sell him as an indentured servant overseas, and all the while employed him in his inn. For his part, Edward Barlow, although quite determined to pursue his own plans, and although he grudgingly accepted the terms of his employment at his uncle's house, nevertheless listened to his uncle's advice carefully and did not think of binding himself with any master 'without his [i.e. his uncle's] consent,' as he put it later on.[72]

Kinsmen also appear to have been prominent as sureties on bonds of security which masters in some large-scale trades and crafts required. Again, in lieu of fathers and mothers, it was relatives who were expected to sign on these bonds. In a sample of 113 bonds signed for apprentices in Bristol, 62 signatures were those of parents, and 23 more had identical surnames (many from the same place of origin as the apprentice, and others from Bristol itself). The remaining 28 sureties may also have included relatives. The liability involved in signing these bonds was quite serious, for their value, in a town like Bristol, was as high as £100 and upwards. Even if they did not sign a bond, kin who arranged an apprenticeship were likely to be summoned to court if the apprentice misbehaved or violated the rules of his contract.[73] Other cases suggest that kinsmen took upon themselves to protect the apprentice against his master, and demand redress for 'wrongs done' to him, in a manner not unlike that of parents.[74]

There were other ways in which kin assisted youths: supervising the money intended as a premium to the master; keeping monies saved by an apprentice or sent to him by his parents; providing credit and loans.[75] Kin were expected to provide what we have called critical support: assistance in times of illness, hardship or unemployment. Edward Barlow's uncle in London took him back when his first attempt as an apprentice in Kent failed; and George Blake, apprenticed to John Harris, a Bristol cooper, seems to have relied on a relative when he had an infectious disease which made him 'unfit for his service'.[76] Some court cases also show that, next to parents, it was to kin that apprentices turned when they lost the means to support themselves. John Hiscock was an apprentice with John Jaine, a Bristol cordwainer, who left Bristol in 1667 and went overseas. As described later in the court, since the master 'is still at sea, the said apprentice hath been driven to seek his employment amongst his friends, he being a poor orphan'.[77] Overall, in 13 petitions of apprentices who complained against their masters, and in which some reference to a third party involved on behalf of the apprentice was made, 7 referred to parents and a brother, and the remaining 6 all referred to kin: uncles, fathers-in-law, a grandfather, and in one case a 'friend'.

It may never be possible to trace the precise dimensions of the networks of kin on which youths relied, but the evidence available indicates that the combination of the youthfulness of servants and their mobility tended to awaken kinship ties that may have been dormant, and to reinforce the special social and moral obligations associated with such ties. The mobility of youths made such ties simply indispensable. So kin were mobilised to assist in the careful selection of masters, and to provide temporary assistance or lodging to youths they might never have known or met before and to risk themselves in signing bonds. Furthermore, they were trusted with the money a youth had to keep, and called upon to help and protect him against his master, or when he was in hardship and need. And it is unlikely that kinship was important solely in the case of long-distance migrants to towns.[78] Rural servants and domestics were more mobile than their counterparts who moved to towns; although they moved short distances, they changed masters and communities with an even higher frequency than servants or apprentices in towns. Ann Kussmaul quoted the case of an agricultural servant who found a place for his cousin with the son-in-law of his master, and she has suggested that kin networks had an important role in the hiring of servants.[79] Given that the hiring fairs became regular places where youths could look for new masters only in the late seventeenth century, the role of kinship ties in finding masters throughout most of the sixteenth and first half of the seventeenth centuries may well have been critical.

Arguably, the very need to recruit kin for the sake of children would have strengthened kinship ties in society at large. When Edward Barlow left for London without a proper arrangement, his father sent his uncle a letter notifying him of his arrival, and a few years later, when the father came to visit, it was in the house of his uncle, rather than his master, that they all met. Barlow himself appears to have well remembered, even cherished, the assistance provided to him by his uncle and aunt. When he first arrived in London he felt that he 'would not [have been] willing to have gone to my uncle's if I could anyways have helped it',[80] and later on he grudged the terms of employment in which he was kept. He also found it difficult to adjust to and have warm feelings towards his aunt. But in the end he could hardly dispense with the help his uncle could offer, and that assistance was indeed immense. Some eight years later, when Barlow had already spent a long time at sea, he learnt about the plague that had broken out in London and wrote to a friend to enquire who amongst the people he knew was dead. In his autobiography he later recorded the death, first, of his closest kin, his brother George, but then of his three cousins, sons of his uncle and aunt, all of whom died during the plague. Only after them did he record the death of his mistress and his master's son, followed by the death of 'divers neighbours and acquaintances more'.

It is to these two later categories of masters and diverse neighbours and acquaintances that we must now turn.

Masters

There is some difficulty in capturing the nature of the norms governing the support and assistance of masters to their servants and apprentices, for there was some ambiguity in these norms. That ambiguity had to do with the fact that the interaction involved in any service or apprenticeship arrangement – whether made for a short or long period, in writing or not – was, in addition to being an interaction based on a contract, something akin to the special obligations associated with kin and even parents. The master provided his servant or apprentice with food, lodging, clothing, skills and small wages in return for labour, and sometimes for premium money he had paid. But given the intimacy in which the master and his servant worked and lived, and given the fact that servants were young, special commitments and obligations were attached to these ties as well. This lack of clear boundaries between the contractural and the moral aspects of the arrangement of service could lead to many expectations, but at the same time to frustrations and disappointments. And there were always those who failed to fulfil even their basic contractual obligations, because they were too harsh, incompetent, or simply too poor. So, implied in this arrangement was great scope for variation in types of interaction between masters and their servants, possibly more than the variation one could observe in interactions with kin, or in relationships between parents and their offspring.

Despite ambiguity and variation, there were several types of aid and benefit a youth could reasonably hope to obtain on entering a service contract – aids and benefits which were not made explicit in the terms of employment agreed upon in the contract, whether orally or in writing. The first and most distinct benefit was that an apprentice was guaranteed his basic needs for the whole term of the contract, including periods when his master had little or no work on his farm or shop. Agricultural servants were normally hired to do the least seasonal tasks (especially in animal husbandry); but in corn-growing areas the burden of work during the winter slackened and the wages of a farm servant had to be paid whether or not there was daily work to be done.[81] In small shops and domestic industries, an apprentice was likewise guaranteed his basic needs for the whole term of his contract, including the periods when his master had little or no employment. We have seen in Chapter 5 that some craftsmen sent their apprentices out to work for wages when they could give them no employment themselves; others were forced to send their apprentices away when they became destitute or unemployed. But many more continued to support their servants and apprentices even in difficult circumstances. For example, Benjamin Bangs, whose master, a Norfolk shoemaker, was forced to migrate because of debts he was unable to repay, told him that 'if I would go along with him, he would take as much care of me as of himself', and so the master and his apprentice travelled and found temporary employment together in a nearby town.[82] During periods of depression, bad harvests and other hardship some masters discharged their servants or apprentices, but most did not. For example, while a number of apprentices in Bristol were dismissed from service during the depression of 1622, there is no evidence that any massive firing of apprentices occurred.[83]

Support could also be expected when an apprentice became ill or injured and was unable to work. Evidence from court records in towns like Norwich and Bristol makes abundantly clear that to send an apprentice away when he became ill was considered a violation of the norm. When apprentices were discharged because of illness, the master was legally required to cover the cost of maintaining the disabled youth.[84] This requirement also included the costs of special medical treatment and medications. Lucinda McCray Beier has shown that among the patients treated by Joseph Binn, a seventeenth-century London surgeon, nearly a fifth were servants and apprentices, both male and female. Binn's treatments were quite expensive, but there is some reason to believe that the masters of these servants covered at least part of the costs. A case in Chancery, in which a London apprentice demanded that his master repay the costs of a rather luxurious treatment he took in the natural springs of Bath, suggests that masters were expected to pay the costs of whatever treatment the apprentice, or his parents or kin, felt was necessary.[85]

Other types of assistance were also quite common, although they were more varied and flexible, and were likely to depend on the type of relationship between the master and his servant. These might include small gifts and benefits, casual wages and pocket money,[86] and legacies. Bristol's merchants and traders left legacies to female servants, and to male apprentices and servants, occasionally naming as many as four, five or six servants in their wills. Among wealthier merchants these legacies could sometimes be quite large. In 1571 Alderman William Pepwall left his servant, Mary Roche, £20 towards 'the preferment of her marriage'.[87] Some 10 per cent of kin mentioned in the wills of yeomen and traders in Essex and Wiltshire were servants.[88]

Direct financial benefits and rewards were likely to be gained when a servant stayed with his or her master for a number of years, or when an apprentice remained the full length of his term of seven and more years. Edward Nelson, a Bristol sherman, promised to pay his apprentice 12d. a week 'for half a year service', after six years of his term; and Francis Eaton, a Bristol carpenter, promised to give his apprentice, a Bristol orphaned youth, 25 acres of land in New England, and 15 bushels of wheat, if he served him 'truly' the full term of seven years.[89] In many crafts masters promised to give their apprentices £1, £2, and sometimes £3 at the end of their terms towards buying tools and material or stock to help them start a shop of their own. In Bristol, nearly half the apprentices registered between 1605 and 1609 were promised financial assistance and tools if they stayed the full length of their terms.[90]

Youths who served long enough in the distributive trades could expect exceptional benefits. Bristol's apprentices who acted as their masters' factors, sometimes after three or four years, were given a commission of 2 per cent or more on transactions they handled overseas.[91] Roger Lowe, apprenticed in a grocer's shop, also received commissions on commodities he bought on his own; and some Chancery cases show that merchant apprentices were not only promised that they would be taught the profession but that they would be employed as factors for the master and for 'others in that professon'.[92] Others were allowed to trade on their own. John Prickman, apprenticed in 1601 to Ann Dyes, a Bristol grocer, was permitted to buy and sell his own stock 'to his own profitt and comoditie' in his last year of apprenticeship. Other contracts guaranteed youths special permission to trade on their own in the final year of their long terms of apprenticeship.[93] Apprentices who had served their full terms could hope to be given a great deal of advice and special concessions by their masters: credit, raw materials, various moveable goods in the shop, and occasionally even the shop itself, as was the case with William Stout, who offered his apprentice the opportunity to buy his shop on good terms when the latter finished his term.[94]

Some servants developed particularly strong attachments to their masters, establishing relationships based on emotional support, friendship and companionship. A few examples will serve to illustrate the quality of these bonds and the circumstances in which they could develop. Simon Forman's master had continuous rows with his wife, so he confided in Simon, and the two used to talk together and complain about her. Roger Lowe recorded in his diary that very early one morning, when his master was still in bed, they 'talked of every thing, [and] something about his [i.e. the master's] marige'. Benjamin Bangs, forced to join his master in his migration in search for work, remembered that when they finally arrived in London they 'dwelt together in the name of brothers'.[95] Some masters became companions to their servants, not only in times of hardship, but when the two sought relaxation from work. Joseph Oxley described how his master took him as a 'companion' to places of 'diversion' where he 'learned to sing what they called a good song'. From court evidence it is also apparent that youths sometimes frequented ale-houses under the influence of a master who was inclined to spend a great deal of his time there rather than in his shop.[96]

Some masters and servants referred to each other as 'friends', which implies that at a certain point their relationship had taken on the quality and obligations involved in ties of kin. Benjamin Bangs referred to his master as a 'brother', and John Smythe, a Bristol merchant, left in his will a dowry for an illegitimate daughter in London 'whom my friend Hugh Hammon[d] [his apprentice] do know'. References in wills to servants as 'friends' were not uncommon either.[97] Youths often described their masters as 'friends', but the connotation was less of kin than of friendships based on voluntary support and reciprocity. Joseph Oxley remembered that he and his master parted 'good friends, continuing a correspondence as occasion required'; and Thomas Chubb also preserved with the family of his master, a glover in Salisbury, 'a particular friendship the remainder of his life'.[98] These examples suggest that, when attachments were formed between masters and their servants, they were modelled on the interactions of brothers or friends rather than on those between a father and his son, and that they involved elements of parity and reciprocity rather than hierarchy, authority and control. Given that servants and apprentices were sometimes not much younger than their masters, such references are perhaps not altogether surprising.

Even when no companionship or special commitment between the master and his apprentice formed, and even when an apprentice served his master only a short while, casual assistance could still be hoped for. In the countryside, servants sometimes moved from one master to the next on the basis of information given by their old masters, or of connections formed through them.[99] Apprentices could be given advice and information about lodging and shops to rent, regardless of whether they stayed their full terms. Even when an apprentice left before his contract came to an end and against his master's will, he could still hope to benefit from the master's connections, or obtain a letter of recommendation to assist him with another master. For example,

John Woodhouse had obtained a letter of recommendation from his old master before he left and became an apprentice with another.[100]

It is true that, given the strong contractual element in any arrangement of service, and given that many masters themselves lived quite perilously, a degree of precariousness was built into all types of interaction between masters and their servants. There are examples of apprentices who were discharged not only when their masters were on the verge of total deprivation, but simply when they decided to improve their lot, or migrate elsewhere; and there were also servants and apprentices who were discharged during a depression.[101] In the countryside, too, servants were sometimes turned away or denied treatment when they were ill.[102] In general, servants and apprentices of small craftsmen and husbandmen were less likely to obtain legacies from their masters. In a collection of 103 wills approved by the Consistory Court of Bristol in the period 1546–93, in which the vast majority were those of widows, small craftsmen (farriers, wiredrawers, glovers, weavers, tanners, etc.), there was not a single reference to servants or apprentices.[103] Even among wealthier merchants and craftsmen, the leaving of legacies to servants and apprentices was by no means a normal rule. In addition, the pressures created by a growing population, especially in the late sixteenth and the first half of the seventeenth centuries, reduced the opportunities for annual service; in the countryside many masters preferred to take labour on a seasonal or daily basis rather than for longer periods. In towns, too, such pressures could have an effect on the conditions of apprenticeship and the benefits youths were likely to obtain even if they served the full length of their terms.[104]

Nevertheless, the assistance masters provided their servants was usually quite substantial, first and foremost because it included critical support; that is, support when an apprentice or servant was unemployed or unable to work. Although by comparison with the parental bond the support of masters was less predictable and much less durable, masters could still provide assistance in times of hardship and, especially in services which lasted a long time, they provided a wide range of valuable benefits and supports, both practical and non-practical.

Neighbours and Peers

The frequent mobility of youths hindered the formation of strong ties based on the communities and neighbourhoods where they lived. Because many of those who started an apprenticeship in large towns were already in their late teens and likely to have been removed from their villages of origin some years earlier, their reliance on neighbourly ties in their places of origin was likely to have been less pronounced. Some evidence on the migration of apprentices to London and the arrangement of their apprenticeship suggests that, in comparison to the role of kin, neighbourly ties were weak. Brodsky Elliott has found that, in the early seventeenth century, youths from the same village might be apprenticed successively to different masters in one London company, but she also found that often these were related affinally or through the master's wife.[105] In autobiographies there are many references to the assistance and role of kin, and relatively few to the role of neighbours in the arrangement of service in towns. Signatures on bonds given by Bristol apprentices likewise suggest a much higher incidence of involvement by kin than by neighbours; and evidence from court cases reflects the same level of assistance on behalf of apprentices based on kinship, rather than neighbourly, ties. All this should not be surprising: servants and apprentices came and went from the communities where they lived, but their masters and their neighbours remained, a fact which may have placed limits on the assistance the later were willing to provide to youths who departed, or were expected to depart, some time soon.

It is also possible that such mobility hindered the creation of strong associations based on the solidarity of peers and other youths. In his autobiography, John Clare wrote of two close childhood friends; the first friendship, with a neighbour boy, began in 'playing at feasts by the cottage wall with broken pots', and continued in the 'partnerships of labours toils and Sunday leisures'. But this friend suddenly died. Clare then befriended his friend's brother, but very soon after, the friend's cousin arrived from London and offered to arrange for his kin a placement there, and so Clare and his new friend parted ways.[106] It may well be that the great turnover of youths in villages and towns was partly responsible for the absence of the well-organised youth abbeys or kingdoms. Young people participated in and sometimes organised feasts of fools, charivaris, dancing festivals, games, sports and contests; but there is no evidence for the existence of established organised groups, with permanent hierarchies, jurisdictions and well-defined roles in the community at large, as was the case in France and other countries. London apprentices were notorious for their riotous behaviour, but the evidence does not warrant the supposition that they had formal organisations and institutions of the kind known to have existed in Rouen or other cities in France.[107]

Nevertheless, despite the limitations on the formation of ties based on neighbourhood and formal groupings of youths, neighbourly and friendship ties did play an important role in the lives of young people. Neighbours were present in the daily lives of children: in their leisure and play, at work, in village gatherings and on holidays, festive days, or at church. Scattered references in autobiographies show that neighbours interfered with, and even exerted pressure on, other families and their children in such matters as dressing properly when going to church, obeying parents, going out to work or entering service when children reached their mid-teens and were expected to leave home.[108] To the children themselves, of course, playmates and neighbours of the same age were of special value. Edward Barlow recalled his neighbours' children, with whom he used to play, do small businesses on the side, or just 'discourse'. When he left for London, it was his playmates, besides his parents, to whom he went to take his leave and to say 'that that would be the last time that I should play with them'.[109]

Neighbours could also be quite helpful in arranging service or an apprenticeship away from home. Edward Coxere went as an apprentice with his neighbour on a ship, on which the neighbour's own son, as well as Coxere's brother, were also apprenticed. Although the presence of kin in chains of youths migrating from the same village to London companies was strong, neighbours were often involved, too.[110] In the western part of the country there were small towns and villages who sent scores of apprentices to Bristol, as well as masters who took apprentices from the same village they themselves had originally come from. Occasionally such communities had extensions in the towns themselves in the form of associations based on the province or county of origin, and these sometimes provided assistance, advice and information to a youth just arriving in a large town.[111] Thomas Raymond remembered how he spent the nights out 'with some of his countrymen' when he was in service in London.[112] In the countryside, too, some servants must have obtained information on available masters from neighbouring farmers, in the local market or ale-house. Neighbours sometimes interfered in the affairs between masters and their servants, despite the fact that they were less likely to complain or appear on behalf of an apprentice at court. Neighbours could be called to testify when conflicts between an apprentice and his master or mistress occurred;[113] and perhaps no less important, neighbours helped sustain the master's reputation, and by so doing helped eliminate the likelihood of abuse or severe treatment. Lodowick Muggleton made a point of the fact that his master was a neighbour whom he had known, and that he was a 'quiet peaceable man, not crewel to servants'. Other writers also remembered being informed about a master who was unfair to his apprentices, and with whom 'nobody would stay'.[114] Sometimes neighbours exerted pressure on masters to amend their ways. Edward Barlow's master's neighbours in Manchester were fully aware of what went on in the house of his master, and thought his behaviour towards one of his apprentices unjust. Although they did not interfere, they gossiped, and announced to the youth that they were wholly on his side. Such social pressures on masters who were thought to behave unjustly must have been common, as occasional references in court records make clear. Some complaints made in court indicate that, before turning to the court, pressures might be placed on masters to change their decisions or amend their ways by fathers, apprentices and relatives, as well as by 'several others', 'divers gentlemen and others of [the father's] good friends'. Neighbours were sometimes directly or indirectly involved. In one case in Chancery a Hereford vintner, Walter Davis, told the court that he had long tried to persuade the master of his son to change his ways by warning him that 'the world conceaved ill opinion of him'.[115]

Young people did manage to establish neighbourly ties even if they lived in a place intermittently or for short periods of time. Edward Barlow, who spent so much of his time as an apprentice at sea, established neighbourly ties when he was on shore in his master's house, and he continued to nurture them while he was at sea. Such ties were at times as helpful as the master in eventually establishing one's self. William Stout received information about a shop to rent from his master, but when he began to trade on his own he relied a great deal on connections with neighbouring shopkeepers who frequented 'our market at Lancaster'. When he went to London to obtain goods and raw materials he turned to such tradesmen, 'as . . . recommended to' by his neighbours back home in Lancashire.[116]

Many of these neighbourly ties were with fellow apprentices and fellow servants or local youths. Although there is no evidence for the existence of abbeys of youths, there is much to suggest that youths helped each other in adjusting to new places and households, in providing information and advice, and in offering companionship and friendship. When Edward Barlow first came to his master's house in Manchester it was a fellow servant who helped him the most. Barlow's description of this episode shows that the moment he moved into the house they befriended each other and spent a great deal of their time together. Barlow hardly mentions the master in this context. The youth told him about the terms of his employment, the conditions in the master's house, and the character of his master; he instructed him in 'how to look after the cotton', they ate and drank together, and they also worked outside the shop, threshing in the barn. It was hard and tedious work, and they passed the time together by talking and fantasising about 'what a fine thing it was to travel'.[117]

Many households and shops, in both countryside and town, would have contained such young co-workers with whom a new arrival was likely to make friends. Some agricultural jobs, such as shepherding, were particularly likely to strengthen such bonds, and in small shops strong bonds of attachment could also be formed. When Joseph Oxley left London and returned to the countryside, he left behind in his master's shop his 'friends', with whom he had 'sweet and precious unity'. Joseph Pike also wrote that when he was working in the wool trade for his brother-in-law he became 'intimately acquainted and contracted a particular friendship' with a young man, with whom he later became a partner. Even if not working together, youths from nearby farms or adjacent shops joined each other for company. Edward Terril spent time at a 'neighbour's shop' in Bristol; Benjamin Bangs found a companion in London – a young man with whom he was 'a little jocular in a bantering way', and George Bewley likewise remembered 'divers young people, whose company I loved, and with some of them I was at times too free in discourse and jocularity'.[118] Many of these neighbouring youths met together at the local alehouse, whose prominence in the social lives of servants of both sexes has been well recorded.[119] Sometimes they gathered to drink and talk in homes and more private places. John Clare recalled that he used to spend winter nights and Sundays at a neighbour's house, which was a 'sort of meeting house for the young fellows of the town were the[y] usd to join for ale and tobacco and sing and drink the night away'. The place was not a regular ale-house, for it was owned by 'two bachelors and their cottage was calld bachelors hall'.[120]

Practical assistance and protection was sometimes involved in these friendships. In a will written when he was 23 years old and still a merchant apprentice in Bristol, Andrew Barker left £20 each to two former fellow servants; to another 'loving friend' and a 'present fellow servant' he left £7, and to Margery Alstatt, likewise a 'fellow servant', he bequeathed £3.[121] Servants and apprentices were helpful to each other in finding work, in passing information on available masters and on the character of the master and his treatment of his servants. Some friendships solidified into business partnerships. At times youths collaborated against their masters, and, like neighbours, they could be recruited to put pressure on masters. Roger Lowe recorded in his diary in October 1664 that two friends promised to 'go together to my master and speak my greavances', and some time later he recorded that he 'gat Thomas Smith to go speake my business' with his master. Smith was a friend whom Lowe mentioned many times as a companion with whom he spent a great deal of leisure time, in the evenings and on Sundays.[122]

Young companions offered not only companionship and practical aid but sometimes also emotional support in times of stress and difficulty. Arise Evans recalled the consolation and support he obtained from a fellow serving-maid when the news about his father's death reached him; and Roger Lowe, an orphaned apprentice, recorded in his diary one Sunday that when he went back to Leigh he was 'very sad in spirit by reason of myself and seeing my father's and mother's grave'. He then went to see his old friend John Bradshaw, and the two youngsters walked to the fields and 'talked of former things'. Some spiritual autobiographies also give testimony to the emotional support provided by young companions who consoled and helped each other in their spiritual struggles and their estrangement from an environment increasingly hostile to their new preoccupations and more pious and devotional life styles.[123]

Conclusion

In their movements and employment during the long phase of transition to adult life, young people relied on a matrix of social ties. In this matrix, the parental bond was of prime importance, for it provided a sort of a safety net on which youths could fall back, as long as even one parent was still alive. Beyond this there was a series of social ties which provided support of various types and degrees. Masters had a central role, for however difficult and uneasy the bond with them sometimes was, they provided critical support in times of unemployment or illness. Kinship ties were indispensable, too, for next to parents, and in some ways like them, relatives gave the adolescent or the young person temporary lodging, a place to return to, and protection.

Despite the looseness of the kinship system in society at large, the combination of the age and the frequent mobility of youths reinforced moral obligations associated with kin and kinship ties. The matrix of social ties also included neighbours, fellow servants and other youths. What evidence there is suggests that for critical support youths turned to parents and kin more readily than to neighbours, but neighbourly ties nevertheless furnished a host of valuable kinds of support in arranging service, providing information, and, perhaps most importantly, putting pressure on masters to behave within the accepted norms of proper behaviour. We may never know how many youths were abused by their masters; and in the end, even a small community or neighbourhood was unlikely to fully supervise the actions of masters inside closed rooms or on isolated farms. Yet evidence on the low rates of illegitimacy during this period, for instance, suggests that communal and neighbourly opinion could exert some control on the potential abuse of female servants by their masters.[124] For male youths, as well, neighbourly ties could provide a certain protection by placing checks on serious breaches of what was considered appropriate behaviour of masters towards their servants and apprentices.

The existence of all these social ties around the hard core of the nuclear family explains not only how youths survived, but how they managed to obtain a degree of choice and power in their relations with masters and other adults, including parents. To some youths, exit from home and entry into service with a master allowed some liberation from parental authority and discipline.[125] Once in service, many youths could rely on various social ties in balancing their relationship with their masters. Kin and relatives turned to court to provide protection; neighbours and friends interfered and tacitly cooperated with servants. Whatever the shortcomings of the master–servant bond, these could be offset to some extent by the assistance and pressure of neighbours, and especially by parents and kin. Sometimes masters could be brought into line because they were of lower social status than the parents and kin of their servants. And parents usually collaborated with their sons or daughters, providing shelter, sometimes instigating and enticing them against a bad master. It was by no means without reason that Henry Best advised farmers 'never to hire such [servants] as are too near their friends'.[126]

Of course, these social ties could not always fully guarantee the security and well-being of the young. Against a background of extreme poverty, in periods when employment and long-term service contracts were hard to find, especially at the end of the sixteenth century and the first decades of the seventeenth, in years of bad harvests, plague or depression in trade, the weight of these ties might loosen and occasionally diminish altogether. In these circumstances, and given the strength and importance of the parental bond, youths whose parents both died during their service term were at greater risk than others. So, too, were youths with few or no kinsmen alive. Nevertheless the social ties most youths had, or were likely to establish in the course of their teens, provided a degree of control over a variety of situations, including poverty, hardship and other misfortunes.

By the late seventeenth century the emergence and expansion of a host of public insititutions and agencies enlarged the scope for support young people could hope to obtain in the course of their teens. The expenditure of the parish relief system rose considerably, and with it the numbers of pauper adolescents who were placed as apprentices in their early or mid-teens. Clubs, voluntary associations and regional and philanthropic societies could also widen the scope of services and aids for the young by providing the cost of apprenticeships or the social contacts young people might need.[127] The hiring fair, which facilitated the search for masters in the countryside, became a regular part of the rural scene, and registry offices and newspapers with advertisements for vacancies in domestic service and other jobs also made their first appearance.[128] The growth in the number of provincial attorneys may also have widened the range of services and professional assistance a youth could obtain when turning to the law, or when serious disputes with his master arose.[129] Arguably, however, these institutions and mechanisms could not compete with or replace social networks and ties, which provided a more varied range of help and support, had deeper roots in the lives of the young, and were within the reach of all. As long as life-cycle service continued to play a vital role in the lives of most young people, and as long as mobility and migration continued to dominate the transition of youths to adult life, ties with parents, kin and masters, but also with neighbours and fellow youths, were unlikely to diminish in importance or in the measure of control they gave youths to govern their social lives and pursue their goals.[130]

8 Spirituality, Leisure, Sexuality: Was There a Youth Culture?

It has become commonplace among historians to speak about a 'youth subculture' or 'adolescent culture' in early modern English society. By such formulations, a sense of the separate identity of young people in society at large is evoked – an identity which has been defined in terms of the separate values, associations and life styles of the young. Historians have pointed to youth riots, the receptivity of the young to novel or radical ideas, their recreations, festivities, popular literature and sexual mores, as expressions of their distinct position and culture. London apprentices in particular have been singled out as an age group with a subculture of its own, with separate associations and a sense of solidarity and fraternity which were embodied in fictional heroes like Dick Whittington and Simon Eyre.[1]

London apprentices were indeed notorious for their riotous activities, especially on Shrove Tuesday and to a lesser extent on May Day. On these occasions they organised wrestling matches, football games, cockfights and other sports, but they also harassed prostitutes, attacked brothels, and assaulted foreign traders or gentlemen and their serving-men. In the period between 1604 and 1641, such riots occurred at least twenty-four times, and the Civil War and Restoration era witnessed bawdy-house riots and Shrovetide disorders on an even larger scale.[2] Nevertheless, as some historians have argued, the activities of the apprentices need to be placed in the context of crowd action and social protest, rather than in the context of age relations and conflicts between subcultures or generations. The apprentices' modes of action, their targets and motives (where these can be detected), were all expressions of broader issues and social conflicts rather than of values distinctly characteristic of youth. Often apprentices and their masters joined disturbances together, and even if apprentices were visible in the crowd, they seldom monopolised it, and only rarely were they punished or prosecuted by the law. Overall, their visibility is hardly surprising, given their high proportion in London's population as a whole.[3]

Other forms of youth culture in this period raise similar issues regarding the distinctive character of youth activities or values. No one would deny that there were age-related differences in England during this period, and it is also likely that there were some forms of culture based on what might be called the spontaneous tendency of young people to associate one with the other. But just how significant were these age-related differences, and was there such a marked split between 'youth' and 'adult' cultures? In what follows, we examine three dimensions in the lives of youth, and the extent to which these separated young people from adults and the adult world: religion and spirituality; leisure activities; and relations with the opposite sex.

'The fittest time for [Christ] to come to you'

Early modern contemporaries were quick to blame young people for the reception and spread of new ideas and heresies,[4] and according to some historians these accusations were not wholly without foundation. It has been argued that youths were predominant among the early Protestants, and thereafter among Puritan divines, Presbyterians, Independents, and nonconforming groups or sects. Some of these people left autobiographies in which they described their spiritual experiences during their adolescence and youth. Explanations vary with respect to what drew people in their teens and early twenties to embrace novel ideas, or to become deeply engaged in questions of sin, salvation and damnation. Some historians have adopted a psychological explanation, in which the idea of an adolescent 'identity crisis' is central, while others have focused on the socioeconomic context of specific generations or cohorts of youths, as in the case of the first generation of Protestants.[5] Christopher Hill has also suggested that the experiences of some sectarians during the mid-seventeenth-century revolution need to be understood in the context of family relationship, as a contest between the generations in a period when patriarchal authority in the home was the norm.[6]

That young people had a predilection to join or embrace new heresies is to some extent uncontested. Protestantism in its early phase made headway in university circles, and the audience for lectures by young masters were undergraduates, adolescents aged between 14 and 18. Among London apprentices, new religious ideas were probably disseminated with relative ease as well.[7] But there are difficulties in gauging the precise dimensions and significance of this phenomenon. Conversion to Protestantism was by no means an experience exclusive to the young; some of the leaders and most ardent followers of the early Protestants were in their thirties when they converted to Protestantism.[8] Moreover, it is impossible to know the precise age structure of either the first generation of Protestants, or any other religious group in the sixteenth or seventeenth century. If we include people in their mid- and late twenties among those described by contemporaries as 'young', it is hardly surprising that the young were the most likely converts to any religious doctrine – what appeared to contemporaries as a predominance of youths among these groups may have been no more than a reflection of the fact that the majority of the population in this period was under 30 years old.[9]

There are also great difficulties in interpreting the experiences described by godly and nonconforming people. Again, it is quite evident that early modern contemporaries sometimes saw the act of joining a religious sect as the distinctive mark of youth. For example, when Arise Evans announced his revelations and 'what judgment was a coming' for the first time, his neighbours thought he ought to be shut at home by force, for he was 'in the flower of his age, and his bloud boileth in his veins, and his great strength hath brought him to his Frenzy'.[10] Nevertheless, it is doubtful whether the experiences of conversion recorded in spiritual autobiographies can be understood as the manifestations of a psychological, adolescent crisis of identity. Some autobiographers appear to have modelled their descriptions of their personal repentance and conversion on St Augustine's *Confessions*, and this places limits on a proper assessment of their actual experiences in childhood. Robert Blair remembered that at the age of 23 he was reading 'holy Augustine's Confessions', and what impressed him the most was how 'in his old age' St Augustine discovered his childish sins.[11] It is difficult to know how many of those who wrote their spiritual biographies read or were familiar with the *Confessions*, but they seem to have followed St Augustine in his description of three very long stages: the first stage in which the sins of childhood and youth were described; the second in which repentance began but sin still prevailed; and the third involving full conversion. St Augustine reached the third stage only when he was 29, and even then he still succumbed to sinful habits.[12] This image of the older person who forsakes sins and habits of mind which had become ingrained after many years of bad conduct highlighted both the immense obstacles a young person had to surpass as well as God's powers of salvation; for the older a person, the greater the burden of his sins. Even if others did not have St Augustine in mind when they wrote their autobiographies, they all employed a model in which the sheer length of the process was the most distinctive trait. Richard Baxter was unable to trace precisely the event that began the 'working of the spirit upon my heart', a process which spanned practically all his life.[13] While there was some variation in the specific age the autobiographers identified as the beginning of their conversion, nearly all described the process as being prolonged well into their mid- and late twenties, and sometimes beyond. George Trosse became a nonconformist long after he had abandoned his apprenticeship; Oliver Sansom's conversion became certain only after he married; Gervase Disney did not avoid 'sin' until his mid-twenties and well after his apprenticeship had come to an end; and Richard Norwood thought that at the age of 25 he was 'still marvelously captivated unto sin and Satan'.[14]

If the purpose of all this was to show the great burden of sin and the power of salvation, it is hardly surprising that some descriptions were characterised by deep uncertainties, fears of Satan and Hell, and agonising struggles to obtain Truth and assure one's salvation. Such struggle and self-scrutiny were, after all, at the heart of the piety and theology of the period, and for those who experienced it in an intense way, the experience was ongoing – an integral part of their whole life, rather than confined to a particular, adolescent, phase. The intensity and types of experience also varied, even among the small group of writers of autobiographies. For example, Gervase Disney went through a gradual and long process of abandonment of sin, but he never experienced the sort of inner struggle and insecurity sometimes likened to an adolescent crisis. Page after page in his autobiography provides many details about his sins and a variety of occurrences that showed Providence at work, but there are few signs of a troubled or deeply insecure mind. Moreover, despite the long and elaborate descriptions of sin and salvation which the autobiographers chronicled, the circumstances of their conversion and their motives often remain wholly obscure. Occasionally the autobiographies reveal that joining a radical sect or becoming pious and devoted simply provided comfort and consolation in difficult circumstances which did not necessarily involve deep psychological disturbances. Sadness, a 'mournful and retired way of life', the loss of parents or other close friends, hard and lonely work, and the need for company drew some autobiographers into different modes of godly life or nonconformism.[15] William Kiffin was first attracted to preaching while he was 'wandering up and down the streets' on an early Sunday morning in 1631. And Benjamin Bangs remembered that once he began to attend Quaker meetings in London he had many 'longing desires' to go to these meetings, for there he could sit in the company of Friends, 'in a retired manner, out of the hurries and cares of the things of this world'. Bangs at this point had already finished nearly three years of his apprenticeship, worked as a foreman in a shoemaker's shop, and was involved in a 'multiplicity of business'. With the exception of a short period in which he was somewhat hesitant, there is no trace in his autobiography of serious psychological stress or agonising struggles with dark and threatening forces.[16]

There is also something in the sociology of conversion which defies simple assertions about the distinctiveness of the experience of youth and the generational conflicts that might ensue. If we look at the individuals or groups who were formative in the spiritual experiences of writers of autobiographies, it is difficult to come to the conclusion that peers or young associates were of prime importance. Some writers mentioned the influence of other youths in the decisions involved in starting their repentance and conversion: a young companion, a serving-maid, a journeyman, 'two young men', and just a 'fellow worker'.[17] Some young people also had a serious clash with their parents or their masters when they began to attend the sermons of a nonconforming minister, as was the case of George Brysson, whose master forbade him to go to such meetings and called upon his father to intervene. The father told his son that if he 'followed that course, he would disown [him] from being his son'.[18]

Most autobiographies, however, do not quite fit into this model of either peer influences or conflicts with parents and masters. A distinctive feature of many is the authors' portrayal of the positive influences of his or her parents. Sometimes parents were themselves already members of a sect,[19] and often parents provided a pious environment, although their child grew up to take a different or more radical stance. 'I was born of believing parents in the country, they strove what in them lay to give me good advice,' is typical of the opening of many autobiographies.[20] Some parents themselves went through a process of conversion, and persuaded their children to follow suit.[21] For other youths, their masters were models of piety.[22] Yet other parents were models of defiance of authority. When Charles Doe began to attend the Baptist church in the 1660s and was confronted with his father's opposition, he argued that, 'You deny me that which you fought for yourself, liberty of conscience', referring to his father's participation on the Parliamentary side during the Civil Wars. According to Doe's report, his father 'made no reply', and afterwards did not 'endeavor to make me go anywhere against my conscience'.[23]

Most young people were away from their mothers and fathers by the time they reached their mid-teens, and, as the autobiographies show, by far the most direct effect on them was neither from youth groups nor even their parents or masters, but from a host of other people, mostly adults – a neighbour, a 'poor man' who came to the house, 'many people' and 'godly people' in or around the village or town where the writer lived, travelling preachers, godly ministers, and women and men a youth encountered at the local inn, or in his master's shop.[24] The strong presence of the community and neighbourhood is obvious in all these references, although some writers remembered 'hearing' about people, preachers and other divines in different places or towns. Some of these travelling preachers or neighbours may have been relatively young, but many were adults. Alexander Reid recalled the influence of 'Mr. Robert Hunter' and of 'Mr. Patrick Shiels'; Gervase Disney referred to Mr Flavel as his spiritual father; and George Brysson resolved to follow 'Mr. James Kirton' and his teaching, and to 'impart my mind to him as I could'.[25] Some apprentices were encouraged by their own masters to 'sing a song' against the sacrament of the altar.[26] And despite occasional references to religious meetings designed especially for young people,[27] there is no evidence that there were permanent associations exclusive to the young. Most other accounts of the sermons, preaching and gatherings in which writers of autobiographies took part suggest a lack of age segregation. Piety, religious observation and fraternity based on doctrinal persuasion appear to have transcended age differences and even to have cemented ties with adults rather than with peers and other youths. Benjamin Bangs, George Brysson and Roger Lowe all spent time in 'field meetings' and other forms of association which were not exclusive to the young and which provided instruction and guidance, but also consolation, refreshment from worldly preoccupations, and companionship. Roger Lowe's relations with Mr Woods, a Presbyterian minister, involved visits to each other's shops and in Mr Woods's house, exchange of books, and discussions about theology, but also on more mundane matters and business. Mr Woods may have provided a 'father figure' to Lowe, but it is difficult to overlook the element of companionship, mutuality and the close, informal aspect of the relationship between this young man and his mentor.[28]

Other writers remembered disputes they had with other young people rather than with their parents or other adults, and some also mentioned the assistance adult religious networks provided in forming business contacts and helping them to start out on their own.[29] Above all, in many autobiographies the historian senses the estrangement of a youth who withdrew from the games and sports of his companions and playmates. Some writers may have exaggerated their distinctive behaviour once they began to withdraw from the company of their peers and companions, but, given what we know about contemporary attitudes towards sects like the Quakers,[30] there is no reason to doubt the ridicule to which some of these writers were subjected, especially from fellow youths and playmates.[31] Some of these descriptions suggest that the courage to dissociate oneself from, rather than the inclination to be part of, peer groups and age associations was the most distinct experience of those who took the sectarian or spiritual course.[32]

This only underlines the fact that writers of such autobiographies were a tiny minority among their peers, who appear, in these accounts, as wholly profane. The descriptions of the profanity and sins of the playmates and young companions of these autobiographers accord well with the complaints of moralists, magistrates and clergymen about servants, apprentices and 'idle boys', who 'spen[t] much time in playing', swearing, cursing and disturbing the peace, and who passed their Sundays playing games in the churchyard and disturbing the preachers in their sermons.[33] Patrick Collinson pointed out that preachers also accused ballad-singers of seducing the youth of the parish out of church and into the Sunday dances.[34] And S.J. Wright has shown that attempts to compel the young to practise their religious duties in the post-Reformation period were dilatory: many people escaped confirmation, and the enforcement of the duties to catechise children and of legislation regarding first communion varied considerably from place to place and over time. People over 14 years of age were required by law to attend morning and evening prayers, but this was enforced haphazardly at best.[35] Martin Ingram has also shown that the mobility of servants placed great limits on the ability of the church courts to enforce legislation on major sexual offences, such as fornication and bearing illegitimate children. He has established that those guilty of such offences were for the most part young, unmarried, and often in service, and some of them cared little about spiritual courts, sin, damnation or hell. Youth may well have been the stage in the life cycle when official religion had the least impact.[36]

Yet it is doubtful that this in itself fostered the emergence of a youth culture based on distinct religious sentiments or values. Conduct books and books of advice and instruction for the 'pious prentice', 'youth' and 'young men and maidens' were sometimes purchased by adolescents and youths; and while many youngsters consumed chapbooks of romance and adventure, others must have bought the godly chapbooks and ballads that were sung, and listened to, by the young.[37] Clearly quite a few young men and women, servants and apprentices, did attend church. The evidence on new seating arrangements in parish churches shows some age segregation: young women were separated from their mistresses, and servants stood at the back, but clearly they all did come to church, and the servants stood among adult labourers, rather than being completely separated from the community at large.[38] Some adolescents repeatedly disturbed their fellows at church, but there were apprentices who followed the sermon intently and even took notes.[39] And while many among the young rejected or avoided confirmation, not a few participated in this formal acceptance into the established church. Some were confirmed when they were in their early teens, but others entered church membership during adolescence and afterwards; that is, when they were older and quite capable of making up their own minds on such matters.[40] It is difficult to know what motivated them; there were the social pressures and dictates of adults or preachers, but attachment to religion may have played its part as well. Moreover, many also took their first communion, and, if they were servants and earned wages on their own, they then began gradually to take up their religious duties, especially the obligation to assist in running parish affairs.[41]

As with adults, it is difficult to know how widespread and with what regularly the young attended church. While some adults went to church regularly with their children,[42] other parents themselves failed to attend. In some places, many of those presented at court for failing to take communion were married men and their wives rather than youths;[43] and, like their younger counterparts, adults sometimes went to church for company; nor did they always listen attentively to sermons on Sunday afternoons.[44] Still other adults cared little about their servants' whereabouts on Sundays, or were unable to send their children to church. Edward Barlow's father could not provide him with clothes 'fitting to go to the church', so he and his brothers and sister went very irregularly, if at all.[45] Given what we know today about religious attitudes and practices in society in general, there was bound to have been not only leniency towards the young and their predilections, but shared values and beliefs as well. Although historians differ in their assessment of the degree of piety and religious feeling of the vast majority of the population, the picture that emerges from their analyses is one in which most adults during this period adhered to a range of more or less pious ways, rather than to a strict discipline or deep devotion and religious zeal. A measure of laxity in religious practices, and occasional contempt for or indifference to religion, could be found, too.[46] Despite some differences owing to age or to youthful preference, there was room for basic agreement between young and old in matters touching on religion and the church. Ingram described the details of the prosecution, in 1642, of Thomas Kent, a yeoman who was accused, together with his son and daughter, of absence from church and various types of negligence of religious duties. Ingram showed that Kent was hardly indifferent to, or resentful of, religion, but he did profess a great antipathy to the rector's religious zeal, and he complained about his strict and unreasonable enforcement of communion and church attendance. His daughter appears to have been even more bitter and her complaints were expressed more extremely; she described the rector as the 'great devil'. Moreover, while her father thought that his servants should stay at home and work rather than attend long sermons, she preferred the dancing organised in a neighbouring village. But on the whole, Susan Kent was hardly irreligious. She relied on her father to support her arguments, shared his antipathy for religious zeal, objected, like him, to the frequency with which young and old alike were forced to attend church, but still thought that the rector who served the parish before had been rather 'a good parson'.[47]

Leisure

We saw in Chapter 7 that, despite the absence of formal age groups or abbeys of the kind that existed on the continent, young people during this period provided assistance to one another, and associations with peers had an important role in their lives. Such associations provided companionship for the purposes of play and recreation during holidays, periods between service hirings, and, on a more regular basis, on Sundays and weekdays after work.[48] Everyday diversions occurred most frequently around the house, and often at the nearest ale-house, a place where many servants and apprentices, both male and female, congregated to pass the time in drinking, playing cards, talking, and just 'being merry,' as Roger Lowe referred to it.[49] Lowe spent a great deal of his time with friends and neighbours at ale-houses, drinking, playing and talking. During the month of September 1663, for example, he mentioned in his diary going to the ale-house seven times, mostly on weekdays, but once also on a Sunday, from noon on.[50] Lowe was a devoted Presbyterian who also spent a great deal of his time at prayer and religious meetings, so his experience may underestimate the frequency with which other youngsters attended the local ale-house.

Some holidays and other days in the year were also specifically associated with young people and with servants. Shrovetide and its customs of games, contests and cockfights, May Day with its maypoles, games and revels, were primarily festivals for unmarried young people, and they attracted many youths in both towns and countryside.[51] In Gloucestershire in 1610, a maypole was set up at the parish church of Bisley, with piping and dancing by the 'youth of the parish'.[52] Hiring fairs, especially from the late seventeenth century on, were occasions for the diversion and recreation of farm servants, who spent the day drinking, racing and dancing.[53] There was a variety of competitive, sometimes dangerous, games and sports in which the young men could display their physical prowess and masculinity: football and other ball games, skittles, archery, throwing the sledge, and cudgel and sword play.[54] There are indications of customs involving coronation of lords of misrule: for example the young men who invaded the parish church in 1535 with pipes and minstrels, preparing to choose a lord of misrule to preside over the Christmas holidays.[55] There were also, on occasion, initiation rites involved in becoming journeymen, perhaps apprentices, too.[56] Some types of popular literature, especially romance and heroic stories and ballads, catered mostly for the young; and small, cheap 'merry' books – with jests, old tales, sometimes with woodcuts and pictures – were bought by 'young men laughing', 'maides smiling' and 'pretty lasses feeling in their bosomes for odde parcells of mony wrapt in clouts'.[57] Dancing, organised in the open space, the barn or the ale-house, attracted mostly the young. Patrick Collinson has shown that if there was one youthful activity which aroused the particular anxiety of moralists it was dancing, 'the vilest vice of all'.[58]

Compared with adults, young unmarried people were likely to spend more time in these types of diversion and recreation. William Lilly remembered that during the spring of 1624, dozens of boys would congregate near the house of his master in London, 'some playing, others as if in serious discourse' from about five or six o'clock in the afternoon and until 'it grew dark'.[59] Young people had fewer responsibilities than adults, and once they finished their daily routine of work, in the fields or in shops, they spent their time in leisure, play and talk. Urban apprentices were especially notorious for their habits of drinking, playing dice and cards, and gambling; Gervase Disney described how on Sundays he and other companions, all London apprentices, spent time in 'walking from place to place for pleasure'.[60] Such leisurely excursions could continue throughout the night, as is suggested by ordinances of Bristol's merchant adventurers who forbade their apprentices to walk abroad late at night.[61] Apprentices were sometimes punished by their masters by being forbidden to go out; but normally they were allowed to leave the house, sometimes until late. John Coggs, the London printer apprentice, routinely spent his time in card-playing until one o'clock at night; Roger Lowe often spent his time out 'all night' in the ale-house or at a friend's house; and Thomas Alford, a Bristol apprentice during the 1610s, sometimes spent the entire night drinking and gambling at dice and cards.[62] Youths walking in the streets late at night, sitting in the front of shops during the days, walking in the fields, drinking at the ale-house, chatting, joking, perhaps engaging in some forms of cruising or loitering were a normal part of the urban and rural scene. As one disapproving contemporary summarised it: 'many lazy losels and luskish youths both in towns and villages . . . do nothing all the day long but walk the streets, sit upon the stalls, and frequent taverns and alehouses'.[63]

Youths were also more liable to become unemployed. In between periods of an annual service, when their service contract was broken, when they were dismissed and left service and were unable to find a new master, some youths returned home and worked on an irregular basis, or failed altogether to find some form of work or service arrangement. When George Trosse returned home from France after two years there, he stayed with his mother for 'some months', living 'vainly and foolishly', and only then did he become an apprentice with a London merchant.

Poorer youths sometimes turned to vagrancy, petty crime and theft. As evidence adduced by historians of crime indicates, young unmarried people predominated among the vagrant and criminal population in the countryside and especially in the large towns. In sixteenth-century London, servants and apprentices were the most prone to vagrancy, and runaway apprentices were also found among Bridewell's prisoners. By the late seventeenth century, defendants committed to London's houses of correction included many young people, and it has been suggested that most of them were servants temporarily out of work. Theft or fraud, vagrancy coupled with other offences, disorderly activities, and prostitution were the commonest offences for which they were apprehended.[64]

Special types of recreation, special days on which youthful collective activities reigned, and greater time spent in leisure activities and out of work – all this amounted to cultural forms typical of the young. Nevertheless, the cohesiveness of these forms was undermined by other, no less powerful, forces, and such cultural forms were an integral part of broader patterns of recreation and culture shared by youths and adults. The streets, the fields, the marketplaces and fairs, even the ale-houses, were seldom monopolised by the young. The ale-house catered for the young, but along with them came the craftsmen, the labourers, and other married men, young and middle-aged. Within the ale-house, youths sometimes congregated, but they also intermingled with married men, and at times with their own masters. The small numbers of people who attended the local ale-house on a single evening made the interaction of generations almost inevitable. According to Peter Clark, a typical clientele in a town ale-house included two slaters, a labourer, a butcher, a weaver, a whitawer (leather worker), two servants and an apprentice, as was on one Saturday night in the late autumn of 1607 in Leicester. William Lilly also remembered spending time, when his master was away during the plague of 1625, at the local in with 'Wat the cobler' and 'Dick the blacksmith', and 'such like companions'.[65] The evidence on games and sports likewise suggests that these often attracted older men as both spectators and participants.[66] Ballad-singers and sellers attracted 'boys or countrey fellowes that pass them by',[67] rather than adolescents alone. And the evidence on Shrovetide, the famous day of the apprentice, is far from unambiguous. Contemporary observations on Shrovetide celebrations in towns like Oxford and Bristol show that youths and adults alike participated, the women playing at stoolball, and the men playing football. Bristol's magistrates referred to 'sundry unruly persons' rather than to apprentices, who participated in 'throwing at cocks' and 'tossing of doggs' and unlawfully assembling on Shrove Tuesdays.[68] In London, too, Shrovetide celebrations and riots included apprentices and their masters.[69]

Even dancing was often a community affair from which the middle-aged and the old were not wholly excluded. Sometimes dancing was an event designed specifically for farm servants, milkmaids and domestic servants from several villages in the area. But more often, organised dancing took place as part of festivities in which the whole community took part: parochial ales, which still flourished in some places, fairs, weddings, and a host of other celebrations. Midsummer celebrations frequently included feasting, singing and racing, as well as organised dancing, and harvest dinners and feasts could include masques and masquerading, as well as dancing.[70] On these occasions older people were generally spectators, but sometimes they participated as well.[71] Even May Day dancing was not an event organised exclusively for or by the young. Richard Baxter, a keen observer of 'youthful' follies and young people's predilection for sin, noted how in his Shropshire village 'all the town did meet together' under a maypole, spending a great deal of their day in 'dancing'. His description of the event evokes the strong sense of a community event in which the ages intermingled; the piper, he recalled, was one of his father's tenants, probably an adult.[72]

In towns, too, the location of most leisure activities encouraged a great deal of mingling of the ages. Some civic ceremonies, especially those associated with the guilds, accentuated age divisions and ranking in the community, and so helped to infuse a sense of hierarchy and authority in a tightly organised urban community.[73] But everyday recreations centred on the streets and the local ale-house or tavern, where age demarcations and divisions were unlikely to occur. London Bridge, the streets and the large urban fairs attracted many acrobats, travelling actors, ballad-singers and other entertainers, and their performances catered for all age groups. When the first permanent theatre opened in London in 1576, the audience included craftsmen and shopkeepers, as well as their apprentices.[74] The shops themselves could become sites of recreation and entertainment, which must have attracted neighbouring adults and youths. In instrument-makers' shops and barbershops music was played, and the shop's master and his apprentices, as well as the customers, were likely to join in as both players and audience.[75]

The temporal dimension of many recreations and leisure activities also undermined too rigid a segregation of the ages. The agricultural rhythm of the year, the seasons and patterns of work and non-work they imposed, and the ecclesiastical calendar were shared by all. Moreover, patterns of work and unemployment were too diverse and too entwined with those of adults to allow free time for youths to indulge in leisure activities while their adult superiors were at work. A depression, a slack in demand for goods, or the winter season did not always mean that youths had free time. In the countryside, an apprentice who had little work in his craft or shop was employed in keeping the cattle or horses, and in other household tasks.[76] Roger Lowe, who tended a grocery store, went out to work or help the neighbours during the barley harvest when he had little work in the shop.[77] And Edward Barlow was required to help his mistress in her London inn when he was between voyages at sea; rather than spending his time in the ale-house, he was employed in brewing, making mustard, fetching water, looking after the horses and cleaning the stable, sweeping the yard, scraping the ditches and cleaning the street.[78] On Sundays, too, some apprentices were put to do household chores rather than allowed to go to church, or play.[79] Sometimes an apprentice was sent to work for wages elsewhere if his master had little employment in his shop, as was customary among Bristol's shoemakers and coopers.[80] Variations in the fortunes of individual shops and industries also meant that while a youngster on one corner of the street had little work in his master's shop, another youth at the end of the road worked, on the same day, from morning till dusk. Masters were hardly uniform in their habits regarding the allowance of free time to apprentices; some were more lax, and others less so, as London apprentices themselves admitted.[81] When he was unemployed, a youth might well find himself sitting in front of a shop or drinking in the nearest ale-house alongside his master rather than with the apprentice next door. Simon Forman used to stand 'by his master or mistress at the door' of their shop in Salisbury, where he was an apprentice in the late 1560s.[82]

There were also social, educational and occupational divisions among the large and heterogeneous group of young people scattered around the towns and the rural countryside, and these divisions could place marked barriers among the young. This was true even of urban apprentices, whose age, experience as migrants, and sheer numbers could in some ways enhance the formation of a distinct adolescent subculture. As we saw in Chapter 4, throughout the period apprentices in the large towns were nearly a cross-section of society, including sons of gentlemen and merchants, as well as many sons from the middling and the lower sections of society. Their social backgrounds and the variation in occupations in which they were trained were bound to have a profound effect, if not on the types of recreation in which they took part, then on their life styles and associations. Shrovetide celebrations could momentarily create a sense of cohesion among the young; but on most other daily occasions the divisions among them were unlikely to be blurred. Apprentices in the mercantile and distributive trades embarked on careers that carried them around the country and overseas, in the company of other factors, traders and merchants, both young and old. When they arrived on shore, in England or elsewhere, they often sought the same kind of company. They dressed differently and more luxuriously and spent more money – often money provided as an allowance by their parents, or saved in business transactions they handled – on clothing, hats, stockings, or gloves which distinguished them as merchants, and sometimes even as courtiers and gentlemen. An enormous gulf separated the seaman apprentice, in his old jacket, cap, breeches and a linen shirt with buttons made of hardened cheese or shark-bones,[83] from the merchant apprentice wearing expensive shoes, gloves, gold lace on the sleeves of his doublet, a wig, and gold and silver buttons, as was the case among the apprentices of Bristol's merchant adventurers, who had to specifically forbid their apprentices from dressing like 'courtiers'.[84] When George Trosse decided to become an apprentice in the mercantile trades, he was first sent to France to learn French and to be educated in the manners of a would-be merchant-gentleman: he spent a great deal of money on drinking, but also on learning to dance, becoming accomplished in music, and buying fancy clothes. When he was apprenticed some two years later he used to spend his Sundays overseas in the company of the 'English merchants and factors', in alcoholic revels and in recreations on the river.[85] When he spent time with fellow youths and factors, it was in the tavern rather than the ale-house. And while some of the games, sports, drinking and dancing in which he took part were like the ones in which other London apprentices engaged, the places he went, his companions, and the manner and style attached to his social standing were unmistakable, and placed him much more on a par with his master than with many other apprentices in London or elsewhere.

Other distinctions could cut across the young in the lower sections of society as well. There were different occupations, and these dictated wholly different demands and life styles among the young. The scrivener, shopkeeper or attorney apprentice was living in a world quite apart from a fellow apprentice employed in hard menial labour in the shop of the blacksmith, cooper or weaver. And there were growing variations also in reading and writing skills. As is by now well known, literacy levels rose in the course of the sixteenth and first half of the seventeenth centuries, and they allowed a growing section of the population, especially among the middling groups, access to an expanding print culture, hitherto restricted to a small minority among the elite. By the late seventeenth century the literacy rate reached some two-thirds and even more of adult males in some occupational groups.[86] Apprentices were sometimes highly literate. In some trades, literacy was required on entry into apprenticeship, and most of those entering the distributive trades had some form of schooling before they began their apprenticeship terms. Occasionally, masters promised to send their apprentices to school on certain days of the week.[87] Already in mid-sixteenth-century London, nearly all the apprentices in the ironmongers' company could read and sign their names on an oath of admission, and they could also write the entire text of fifty-eight words.[88]

Yet literacy levels varied greatly between social classes and within communities, cutting across urban and rural dwellers, parishes within counties, and even people in the same parish.[89] These variations were equally marked among the young. Apprentices in some trades were fully literate, but farm servants had a much lower than average literacy rate.[90] Among 64 Bristol apprentices who were discharged in the years between 1625 and 1636 and required to sign in the apprentice register in the presence of the clerk, there were youths trained by merchants, mercers and grocers, but also by weavers, pinmakers, carpenters, coopers, tilers, joiners, sailmakers and skinners. Of these 64, 8 still signed by mark. Of the remaining 56 apprentices, about a quarter wrote only their initials, many in a very unsure hand, which betrays limited, if any, writing skills. Together, the illiterate and semi-literate formed more than a third of the group. Moreover, while there were some sons of husbandmen or weavers among those who could write their full names, the social selectivity of literacy was quite evident. Among the illiterate and semi-literate there were no sons of gentlemen, merchants, drapers and mercers, and only four sons of yeomen. Among those who wrote their full names, sons of gentlemen, yeomen and merchants constituted over a half.

These variations in literacy skills within a community of apprentices in a single town brings into sharper focus the social and occupational divisions among the young. They also had a divisive effect in themselves, for literacy had practical and cultural implications in the lives of the young. The fully literate apprentice could read anything from business letters to the books on medicine, astrology and romance to which he devoted his free time, sometimes late at night.[91] In addition to handling accounts, bills and bonds in his master's shop, he could put his literacy to use elsewhere. Roger Lowe wrote letters to his friends and neighbours, drew up bonds for various people, and on one occasion was required to write a will for a dying man in a nearby parish.[92] His literacy gave him not only material advantages (Lowe obtained money for some of these services), but also a measure of respectability: his services appear to have been quite well known in the parishes around Ashton in Lancashire, where he lived. This would have given him a measure of authority in his relations with other youths, as well as with some adults. Some of Bristol's apprentices who signed their names fully had masters who themselves were illiterate or could barely write their names.[93] Their value to such masters was greater, and their position *vis-à-vis* their masters may have been stronger because they were more valuable and provided more services than the illiterate and less educated apprentice.

By the late seventeenth century these divisions amongst youths were widening, particularly in the towns. The social and cultural scene in many towns was beginning to change in ways that would alter urban life and place new barriers between the patterns of recreation and leisure of 'polite' and 'plebeian' societies.[94] Such a transformation magnified divisions in the life styles and mental horizons of the young. The literate apprentice now had access to a much wider range of publications, and the cultural tastes of the wealthier apprentice were likely to have changed too. He could afford to spend money in the more costly theatres and coffee-houses, at horse races, perhaps even at concerts and balls.[95] High-living apprentices in late seventeenth-century London spent money on dancing schools, drink, gambling, the theatre and late-night suppers; they bought swords and fighting cocks, and some kept a wench in Covent Garden, and paid dozens of pounds for her clothing and other expenses.[96] New patterns of consumption placed a greater barrier between apprentices who could afford luxurious dress and those who could not. During the year 1703, John Coggs, a London printer's apprentice, recorded in his diary buying a silk handkerchief, a wig, a silk cap, a pair of silver buckles, a head for his cane, a clasp knife with a 'tortishall [tortoise-shell] handle', and no less than six pairs of shoes. All this (which is not an exhaustive list of his consumption) cost £7 at the least, all probably paid by his mother. The next year Coggs spent, in a single day, nearly £4 on four yards of cloth, another wig, gloves, and shoes.[97] Coggs's expenses in a single day were nearly as high as the premium required for an entire seven-year apprenticeship in a host of lower crafts in the suburbs of London, the parishes around other towns, or in the countryside.[98]

Sexuality

When George Trosse was about to become an apprentice in the mercantile trades, he first went to London, and from there sailed to Portugal. This was in 1648, and Trosse, then 17 years old, lodged in a London house with his master. The family with whom they lodged had two daughters, one of whom attracted the attention of the young Trosse. She was pretty, well educated and quite pious, and the two young people spent a great deal of time together in places where no 'mortal eye' could see them, and where 'impure flames betray'd themselves in amorous glances, words, and actions'. The relationship continued for three or four months before Trosse had to leave for Portugal. He asked the young woman to accompany him to Gravesend from where his ship was sailing, and the girl came along with her family. Just before leaving the youths managed to retire from the company of the other adults, and so in the 'height of... passions', they parted; there is no evidence that they ever saw each other again.[99]

Much in this description indicates that the relations between the sexes among the young had distinctive features and norms: mutual attraction, time spent together, physical contact and the half-secrecy that surrounded it, and, overall, the relative freedom of interaction of unmarried couples. Recent historical findings on sex and marriage in early modern English society suggest that this episode, or at least the way Trosse recalled and chose to describe it, was not unusual, and could occur among youths in a broad spectrum of middling and lower groups. It has been shown that courtship involved a wide variety of practices, which could include casual companionship during festivities and fairs, but also frequent and more regular meetings, close familiarity, and a great deal of physical contact in private or semi-private places. Sometimes couples stayed the whole night together in the house where the young woman lived, in an alehouse, or in the open air.[100] Servants and youths were prominent among sexual offenders involved in bastardy cases and were prosecuted by the ecclesiastical courts; liaisons between fellow servants were quite common in all sex cases brought before the court and involving single women.[101]

Some young men, especially apprentices in towns, visited bawdy-houses. Existing evidence suggests that this was not altogether unusual. When Richard Norwood absented himself from his service on a ship in the 1610s, his master sent to search for him in the town, 'giving out withal as if I were taken in love with some light woman'. And Gervase Disney recalled going with a fellow apprentice, one John Mildmay, to an ale-house which they later found out was a bawdy-house. He contended that they returned there twice during their apprenticeship – Gervase was an apprentice in London during the 1660s – and remembered being urged to visit a prostitute by friends who pretended that this would 'the better . . . work in us an abhorrence and antipathy against the practices'.[102] As Ian Archer has shown, during the 1570s there were at least 100 bawdy houses operating in London, located mostly outside the walls but often also in the city's commercial heart, where quite a few apprentices lived. Some prostitutes in these establishments were allegedly enticing young men 'to their utter ruyne and decay'.[103] The merchant apprentice who kept a wench in Covent Garden spent some £40 or £50 for her clothes and other expenses.[104]

Young people appear then to have been more promiscuous and less rigid in their morals than married adults. This was true of males and to some extent of females. Married women's reputation was more important than that of unmarried young women, and female plaintiffs in sexual slander cases, as Ingram has shown, were by and large adult and married, rather than young.[105] In the manor of Havering in Essex, the vast majority of women who were brought to the church courts for sexual misbehaviour were accused of sex before marriage.[106] Autobiographies indicate that young women sometimes displayed independence, openness and even initiative in their relationship with young males. Simon Forman tells of how when he was an apprentice in Salisbury, a young woman, a neighbour somewhat younger than Simon, fell in love with him. She used to come to see him in his master's shop nearly every day, 'or else she would be sick,' as he put it.[107] When Simon was standing at the front of the shop, 'she would come and stand by him, and would not go from him till necessity did compel'. There appears to have been little secrecy about her courting and affections; she came to see him when he went with other youths for games and play to a spacious place before the door of the shop, and her visits to the shop occurred when the master and mistress were present. When asked about it, she admitted quite frankly that she was in love. As for Simon, he appears to have been fond of the woman, though he was somewhat less enthusiastic: 'He loved her not but in kindness.' The young woman was not herself a servant, and she dwelt with her parents, people of 'good reputation and wealth', who lived not far away from the shop.[108] Other young women who were migrant servants, and who lived away from their parents, shared the same roof with male servants and apprentices. The openness of their relationship and the freedom of courting among them was unlikely to have been any less common.[109]

Did such attitudes amount to a cohesive, and distinct, adolescent or youth culture? Any discussion of this question cannot fail to point out, first, the pronounced gender divisions among the young themselves. Although young women acted with a measure of independence in their relationships with males, social prejudices and expectations regarding the sexual habits of married women were bound to affect perceptions and attitudes towards female youth as well. Such expectations were based to a large extent on what historians have called the 'double standard', whereby breaches of the moral code, especially in the form of adultery, were more seriously regarded in the female than in the male.[110] In courting practices there were also differences in the norms regarding the roles of the sexes. Young men exercised greater freedom of action than their female counterparts, who were sometimes subject to constraints especially by family and kin and especially if they were still living with them at the time they married. Even when in service and away from home, family pressures on women's choice of partners and their courting were stronger than those placed on young men.[111]

There was also the marked vulnerability of young women. Court cases analysed by Ingram show that some servants entered liaisons with their masters voluntarily and even with a measure of calculation; but often seduction occurred following considerable harassment and even the use of force. Sexual abuse of female domestics by masters, their sons or servants could occur in closed bedchambers, barns or halls.[112] No less importantly, female servants had higher stakes than men in entering a relationship with their male counterparts. A male servant or apprentice who impregnated a female servant and broke his promise to marry her could escape punishment; but the fate of the female youth was harsh. She was likely to be dismissed instantly, prosecuted in court, subjected to public penance, treated with suspicion and hostility by justices, neighbours and midwives, and was forced to move from place to place in search of assistance and support.[113] The discrepancy in the experiences of young males and females was probably nowhere more pronounced than in prostitution. While going to the brothel entailed, for the male apprentice, leisure, costly expenditure and a form of induction into the company of mature, even respectable, males,[114] for women, especially the younger and inexperienced, the reverse was true. It involved earning a living perilously, sometimes in isolation, and under the constant threat of incarceration and punishment. As Robert S. Shoemaker has shown, in late seventeenth-century London women were more than twice as likely as men to be committed to houses of correction, mostly for prostitution or any sign that they were 'loose' or 'lewed', particularly when they were out of work. He also suggested that the majority of these women were unmarried, probably domestic servants temporarily out of work.[115]

It should also be emphasised that the sexual attitudes of the majority of unmarried youths were less sharply delineated from those of adults than might first appear. Youths often acted in concert with adults and against excessive promiscuity or breaches of morality and sexual norms. During Shrovetide celebrations in London, apprentices took aggressive action against bawdy-houses and prostitutes; and in the countryside young people were often involved in various forms of punishment and public ridicule – ridings, rough music and parades, placing horns outside a person's house, the composition of derisive rhymes – of adulterers, fornicators, or husbands beaten by their wives.[116] Ingram has observed that these forms of aggression and ridicule were not simply expressions of condemnation of immorality, but themselves involved some form of latent sexual indulgence if not pornography. But these actions expressed a general hostility, and intolerance towards serious breaches of religious and moral taboos which the young and the old frequently shared. Nor were these actions monopolised by the young. Young people were sometimes prominent in these events, but the evidence available to us today suggests that ridings and charivaris involved the community at large rather than simply its younger inhabitants. Sometimes charivaris were shared or encouraged by the wealthier and more substantial members of the community, and these public acts were an integral part of complex forms of a 'plebeian', rather than a 'youth', culture.[117] In a riding organised in a Wiltshire market town in 1618, a 'young fellow' was present, but there were also 'three or four men', and 'ten or twelve boys' who in the course of the day were joined by 'four hundred men'.[118]

Relatively low levels of illegitimacy and the frequency of bridal pregnancies throughout most of the period underline the extent of the rapport between young and old. Bridal pregnancies were anything but rare – as many as a fifth of all brides throughout most of the period were pregnant by the time they went to church[119] – and sexual intercourse during the months preceding the solemnisation of marriage was common. Nevertheless, sexual intercourse does not appear to have been part of the courting practices of the young, unless a promise of marriage was given. While a rise in bearing bastards was observed in the decades around 1600, the illegitimacy rate generally averaged no more than 3 per cent throughout the sixteenth and seventeenth centuries.[120] This relatively low rate may not have implied chastity or strict moral codes among the young, but, as Keith Wrightson suggested, they could reflect widely held assumptions about marriage within economically independent units, and cautious attitudes towards marriage formation and the begetting of children.[121] Many of those implicated in bastard-bearing were young and in service, and the women not infrequently became pregnant having assumed that marriage would take place some time soon.[122] While failing to adhere to the stern prescriptions of moralists, according to whom sexual intercourse was licit only after marriage, the young nevertheless appear to have subscribed to a strict sexual discipline which discouraged sexual intercourse unless marriage was in sight.

Adults themselves were quite tolerant of the sexual indulgences and leisured activities of the young. McIntosh has pointed out that while the church courts in the manor of Havering opposed having an unmarried man and woman sleep in a single bed, they made no objection when people of both sexes slept within the same room.[123] Even more lenient were ordinary adults, men and women who acted as the masters and mistresses of youngsters employed in their houses and shops. Quite a few of their servants were no longer in their early or even mid-teens, and they seem to have been accorded a measure of freedom in their leisure, play and sexual activities, as long as their daily tasks and duties were performed. Some masters turned a blind eye to youthful playfulness, in an attempt to avoid open confrontation with the young, especially the grown-up youth; others may well have tolerated youthful habits of pastimes fearing that their servants or apprentices might leave service and go away if they were too restricted.[124] But in some adults there also appears to have been sympathy, if not attachment, to the indulgences and privileges of the young that were no longer accorded to the married adult. Simon Forman's master was obviously quite pleased about the relationship between his apprentice and the young woman who frequented his shop. According to Simon, the master was not only 'well perceiving the great affection of the gentlewoman towards Simon', but often, when she came to the shop, he would say to her, 'Mistress Anne, ye love my boy well, methinks'.[125] For her part, Ann approved – 'yea forsooth', as Simon remembered it – and she would soon begin to entreat the master to let Simon leave the shop with her, so that the two might spend more time together. 'Whereupon oftentimes he would give him leave,' Simon recalled many years later.

Conclusion

Young people in early modern England shared some quite distinctive traits: they were often servants, nearly all were unmarried, and they were quite visible – in the streets, the fields, the ale-houses or the local fairs. A minority among them were attracted to new ideas and religious devotion and zeal; many others displayed greater laxity in matters regarding religious practices and moral codes of behaviour. They had fewer responsibilities than adults, sometimes they worked shorter hours and spent more time, at night and on holidays, away from work or from the church, and in the company of each other. They were also more vulnerable than adults; in search of work and on the move, they were more likely to turn to petty crime, theft and vagrancy.

Nevertheless, most youths had few values that truly distinguished them from adults, and they had few, if any, institutions which were wholly theirs, separating them from society at large. That is, few, if any, of the features we tend to associate with a cohesive subculture can be attributed to young people in early modern English society, even to those who lived in the large towns.[126] Recreation and leisure time were shared by adults; while the religious sentiments and attitudes of the young, even if somewhat more pronounced than those of adults, reflected broader attitudes and widely shared assumptions. So did aspects of their sexual mores and practices. Adults in authority not infrequently felt threatened by this more pronounced behaviour and the greater liberty of the young, and many a master in his shop or farm may have been exasperated by them. But there were also those who were more lenient in their attitudes, who accepted the behaviour of the young as the normal and quite legitimate part of the 'ages of man' – expressions of a distinct stage and a season in life which they themselves had once experienced.[127] Most importantly, there were concrete elements in the social life which undermined the formation of a cohesive youth subculture, even in the large towns. Among these were the lack of marked spatial and temporal segregation of the young and old, intricate and growing divisions in the social standing and life styles of the young themselves, divisions along gender and occupational lines, and, finally, the great mobility of the young.

Martin Ingram has suggested that the spatial mobility of young people was itself perhaps the most important feature of an adolescent culture in early modern English society; lacking strong local ties, these young people were the least amenable to church discipline.[128] Arguably, however, while the mobility of the young was of crucial importance in shaping their experience, it also had a dual, and ambivalent, effect on the degree to which they were separated from adults and had values of their own. On the one hand, such mobility induced youngsters to spend time together, to ally with each other for recreation and for support and companionship; the mobility accentuated their capacity to form spontaneous contacts quite distinct from the types of social relations established by adults.[129] Moreover, this mobility was often an expression of freedom from adult authority; sometimes it was true defiance of it. By opening up possibilities for choices and movement initiated and carried out by a youth himself rather than by others,[130] the mobility of servants and apprentices undermined the capacity of the family and the domestic group to keep a strong grip on the young. As we shall see in the final chapter, it allowed, and even encouraged, a measure of manipulation of adult authority, and it could give more freedom to those who tended towards misrule, or, conversely, to those who fell under the rule of a harsh and demanding master, or one who was too strict and authoritative.

But at the same time, the mobility of youths undermined the potential for strong and durable alliances between young people themselves,[131] and it also tended to encourage conduct and habits of mind more closely associated with adults and adult life. Mobility into and out of service or apprenticeship, and frequent changes of employment, forced the young on to the competitive world of labour, with its constraints and its demands. It forced youngsters into hardships of the kind that could lead to violent and abusive acts not only against their masters but also against fellow servants and peers.[132] Mobility did not truly mean the freedom to do what a youth pleased; it required the assumption of adult responsibilities, for it confronted the young with the difficulties involved in finding employment and negotiating for it, and with the hazards and uncertainties of economic life. Such movement enforced a great deal of intermingling, as well as cooperation, with adults and various social networks,[133] and it sometimes required tough decisions and negotiations.[134] If a youth ran away from his master he confronted the risks of punishment, unemployment, or having to move further away from parents and other supporting networks. Running away sometimes involved having to beg, or trick, a master to take him or her back.[135] Hard decisions regarding where and how to go often had to be made.[136] At other times, unpleasant jobs, and masters, had to be submitted to. Moving for the purpose of other employment, a new service arrangement or another apprenticeship involved becoming aware of social disadvantage, the threat of poverty, and the degrading necessity to rely on the parish for relief.[137] But mobility could also encourage the young to attempt to improve their prospects, and to sustain material and social aspirations for advancement – aspirations shared and approved by many in society, young and middle-aged alike. These and related issues are the subject of the final chapter.

9 'Rites of Passage': Transitions to Adult Life

The single most important event in the entry of most young people into adult life was marriage. Marriage in early modern England involved the formation of a separate household which performed a multiplicity of social and economic roles – it was a locus of male authority and rule, and a unit of procreation, consumption and production. The act of marriage, therefore, was an event with enormous implications.[1] It was marked by a series of ceremonies in which the couples, as well as their families and other people in the community, took part. Betrothal and vows, the calling of banns, and eventually the church wedding were perhaps the most important rite of passage to adult life throughout the sixteenth and seventeenth centuries. A minority of couples married by licence, without the publicity of having the banns called, but they still attended church and were likely to celebrate in the company of family and friends.[2]

The transformative power of these rites, however, was much more muted than it might first appear, for the act of marriage was the culmination of a series of transformations rather than a sudden transition to adult life. As previous chapters have demonstrated, some of these transformations (for example those involved in separations from parents) were decisive, demanding and quite abrupt; others (such as the adaptation to households and the acquisition of skills) were more subtle and prolonged. In what follows we examine other facets of this process of maturation: the acquisition of negotiating skills; the evolution of material preoccupations and concerns for betterment; and the assumption of responsibilities for other people, both young and old. The final sections of the chapter examine the process of exit from service, the setting up on the land or in a shop, and marriage.

Negotiating Skills

As a young person grew up, his moves from one employer or master to another were affected by his own decisions and actions. The process is well illustrated in the autobiography of John Croker, who, at the age of 13, left his parental home and travelled overseas to Philadelphia to become apprentice to a sergemaker. This apprenticeship was arranged for him by his parents, and young Croker was only asked to give his consent. Some three years later, his master died and he was forced to make the long trip back to Plymouth, where his parents lived. It was then decided that he should try and look for another master. His father gave him the money for the apprenticeship premium, but John was free to choose the trade and also 'what city or town I pleased'. Moreover, his father was not involved in the arrangement of the apprenticeship, but rather 'bid me try, by looking amongst tradesmen'. Young Croker then left for Exeter, where, with the assistance of a Quaker, he became apprentice to a fuller. He agreed with the fuller to serve six years, paid £30 'at the time of sealing my indenture', promised to pay £50 more if the fuller sent him to Holland in the final two years of his apprenticeship, and then informed his father, 'who seemed to be pleased with it'.[3]

With every change in their circumstances that they made, young people were likely to gain greater experience in arranging their own affairs: in looking for a master and gathering information about him, in choosing where to go, in using various social ties other than parents and in negotiating with a new master. Such negotiations characterised a great deal of the hiring of servants in husbandry. Wages of servants were regulated by statute and were announced every year by the justices of the peace, but some of the evidence evailable suggests that these regulations were not strictly enforced. Excessive wages were sometimes paid to servants,[4] and since the regulation involved the announcement of wage ceilings, there was scope for negotiation. These took place in private, often only in the presence of the master and the youth who was his prospective male or female servant. When this happened at the local church, the master might 'call [the servant] aside, and walk to the back side of the church, and their treate of theire wage'.[5] Servants often put on their best apparel to attract masters; but they also bargained, sometimes with a measure of success. Some would go around the farm to check 'how many sheepe there is' and then negotiate their wages; others bargained to obtain an old suit, an old hat, a pair of shoes or, in the case of female servants, an apron or a smock, or both. Some servants also bargained with their skills, experience or physical strength, for wages varied with age and the experience of servants, and masters questioned a youngster about his employment history, 'in what services hee hath beene, with what labour hee hath beene most exercised'.[6]

In towns, some youths negotiated their contracts on their own. In September 1605, Thomas Weldon, son of a Worcestershire yeoman, signed an indenture to become an apprentice for ten years with a Bristol soapboiler, and the only people present at the time of the sealing of the indentures were his master, another apprentice named Robert Chipp, and a public notary whose name was Roger Harris.[7] When in the course of their apprenticeship youths turned to courts to complain about their masters, they sometimes acted on their own rather than with the assistance of parents or kin. In 1620, Benony Claye, a London apprentice, petitioned the Chancery Court to demand that his master pay him the costs of treatment he had received when he was ill, as well as to return the premium he had paid for his apprenticeship. He was in his early twenties, orphaned, and had no assistance from anyone who could act on his behalf in court.[8] Among Bristol apprentices who appeared at Quarter Sessions to petition against their masters, nearly half, and perhaps more, appear to have approached the court on their own.[9]

Most servants and apprentices did not end up in courts, but in the course of a long period of service, or a series of services, many had acquired the skills necessary to bargain with their masters, assert what they thought were their rights, or simply improve their lot. As we have already seen, servants and apprentices often made use of the assistance of others: parents, kin and neighbours who intervened on their behalf and provided some protection in a wide range of circumstances. Roger Lowe used friends and adults to speak about his grievances to his master; and Joseph Mayett, an agricultural servant who had a series of rows with his alcoholic master, returned home to his father, who promised that if the master refused to take him back he would 'mocke him smart for it'.[10] But sometimes servants themselves resorted to the use of physical force against their masters. When he was no more than 14 years old, Mayett threatened his drunk master with a working tool; and Edward Barlow confronted his mistress and nearly threw her into the fire when she tried to strike him early one morning before he was to leave for a voyage overseas. In 124 petitions presented at the Bristol local court between 1620 and 1682, 9 cases (7.2 per cent) involved apprentices who bit, assaulted or abused their masters. While such offences occasionally earned a remand to Bridewell, more typically the apprentice was discharged from service. In late seventeenth-century London apprentices were sometimes sent to houses of correction for being involved in violent acts against their masters, and for insulting and abusing them.[11]

Most youths did not assault their masters, but instead became more resilient in the face of the difficulties they encountered in their master's house and at work. While provided with their basic needs and a certain amount of security, quite a few servants and apprentices were estranged from their masters and felt disadvantaged, or were simply overworked. The variations in the living and working arrangements of servants and apprentices were great, but hardship and a measure of exploitation were likely to occur in all of these forms of labour relationship. Some servants were fed and lodged poorly, others were given inadequate rewards for the highly skilled work they performed, and many simply worked hard, from morning sometimes until late at night. Bristol's carpenters demanded that their journeymen and apprentices be at work from between five and six o'clock in the morning until seven at night; and London apprentices petitioned to order their masters not to exceed the usual hours of work, from eight in the morning until eight at night. William Stout remembered tending his master's provincial shop until ten o'clock at night during the 'longest and sharpest frost with snow' in the winter of 1683.[12] Household tasks were also a part of the normal routine of most servants: milkmaids were required to do the brewing, baking, and also sweeping and washing; and male apprentices sometimes continued to do the meanest household duties long after they had begun their apprenticeship, when they were already 'grown up to some maturity and understanding', as Francis Kirkman described it.[13] In the face of a particularly harsh environment or master, and especially if they were young and less experienced, some youths could become rather withdrawn.[14] As they grew older, however, many servants became more defiant: insolence, pride, impudence, and contempt for authority and the master's rule were the characteristic attitudes which contemporaries attributed to their servants.[15]

Other youngsters were less provocative and more cautious, using skills of persuasion and manipulation in interactions with their masters. There were obvious limits to the use of persuasion and argumentation by servants. Benony Clay claimed in Chancery Court that when he realised that his master had failed in his promises to train him to be a merchant, he first requested of his master 'in most friendly manner' the 20 marks he had paid as a premium, but to no avail.[16] Adam Martindale's master, a 'high and tyrannical' merchant, used to chide him for every mistake he made, and when young Martindale answered 'for himself', the master told him that 'servants must not answer'.[17] Nevertheless, many other youths did answer for themselves; Simon Forman, for example, 'told his master flat that he had not performed his covenants according to promise'.[18] Simon's boldness derived partly from the closeness of his relationship with his master, who sometimes confided his innermost secrets to him. In other cases the intimacy which existed between a master and his servant allowed a degree of manoeuvring on the part of the young. At one point in his apprenticeship, Roger Lowe was displeased with the provision of clothes his master arranged for him. He went to his master's house early in the morning, when his master was not yet up, sat at the foot of his master's bed, talked to him, and only brought up the matter of his complaints after the master had talked 'somethinge about his marige'. A couple of weeks later his mistress ordered the tailor to take Lowe's measurements for a pair of breeches, a doublet and a coat.[19]

The living-in arrangement gave the youth bargaining power in dealings with his master, if only because few secrets could be kept from servants and apprentices, and their loyalty and cooperation could be quite critical. The cooperation of servants was important for the efficient working of the land and of farms;[20] and in small shops, loyalty was essential, since so much was entrusted to apprentices, especially as they became more expert in their crafts or trades. Numerous opportunities to cheat masters existed; and shoplifting, pilfering, embezzlement or carelessness in taking care of horses or sheep caused continuous worries to masters. One summer day in 1656, James Abbotts and William Mathewes, servants to a Bristol smith, bought ten iron bolts for their master, but instead of returning home with the goods, they went away and sold them to another smith. An upholsterer's apprentice, one Thomas Wheeler, left the windows of his master's shop open and returned to the place to steal goods at night. According to his master, this was something he had been doing for quite a while.[21] Similar cases occurred in many places, and, as Quarter Sessions and other court records suggest, servants could conduct their small businesses for months and sometimes longer without being caught.[22] Women, too, were not infrequently implicated in thefts. Barbara Roberts, a Bristol servant, allegedly managed to obtain three keys with which she opened a chest where her mistress usually kept her money.[23] Other court cases give a glimpse into more subtle ways of invasion of the master's private affairs and their possible uses for the benefit of a youngster. John Lite, the apprentice of a Bristol woollen-draper, was accused of receiving a letter directed to his master, opening it without permission, and then refusing to deliver it or disclose its contents to his master. The apprentice was ordered to find sureties for his good behaviour in the future.[24]

The skills and expertise of an apprentice, and the profits he sometimes made for his master, likewise gave him scope for bargaining. Roger Lowe often expressed his grievances to his master, and the timing he chose was hardly coincidental. On one occasion he chose the time when the annual profits were calculated, which showed that Lowe gained over £20 for his master. So he 'boldly speak [his] greevances', and his master promised to give him a stick, a doublet, a hat and stockings. The next year, when Lowe was near the end of his term, the profits were again calculated and his contribution was even larger; his master promised to sell him the shop and the goods in it on good terms. Edward Barlow wrote that during one of the many brawls he had had with his mistress, she gave up, considering he might 'take [his] wages up in the ship' and fail to return home.[25]

By far the single most effective means youths had at their disposal was to leave and find another master. Some court cases which involved abuse of apprentices by their masters suggest that by the time a petition reached the court, the apprentice was no longer in service; he ran away, or departed for another master, or left the town and returned to his parents.[26] At times the threat to depart could in itself be quite effective. When Richard Norwood decided that his life as an apprentice at sea was too rough and his master negligent in his duties, he 'one morning . . . broke my mind to him'. After 'some debating', the master was content to discharge him, but when he pressed him to reveal his plans, Norwood conceded he might well end up on the ship again, but as a surgeon apprentice rather than a sailor. 'Here upon he [the master] grew jealous that our surgeon had enticed me', and afterwards was able to procure the intervention of the purser, who persuaded Norwood to stay with his former master on the ship, 'having means allowed me and leisure enough for half a year together'.[27]

Youths might leave their masters at the end of an annual term, in its midst, or during an apprenticeship term. Some simply waited until their contract expired, or until the first opportunity arose when they could leave with the consent of their masters, thus ensuring themselves against possible legal action or the forfeiture of a bond, if a master was guaranteed with one.[28] Others were more active in the timing of their departure. Sydenham Poyntz's master was a poor man who allegedly 'almost starved him', so the youth ran away and took service on a ship. Still others were careful and arranged their future employment in advance. When John Woodhouse, a London attorney's apprentice, decided to leave his master, he first found another with whom 'he had thoughts to serve'. He then informed his master that he desired to leave, paid him his debts (partly by borrowing from friends), obtained a letter of character from his old master, went to his new master and 'agreed with him upon terms'.[29]

When asked by his master for the reasons for his decision to depart, Woodhouse argued that he preferred to serve a stranger rather than kin (his master was his cousin). But it is also clear that Woodhouse was careful to arrange better terms with his new master. 'I am to serve my other master . . . easier terms then I did Mr Wilcocks [i.e. his old master], having 20s a term, which I should have had of Mr Wilcocks.' There was nothing unusual about such moves, for other youths, in both towns and countryside, were quite decisive in trying to ensure better terms wherever they moved. Urban apprentices were sometimes enticed by neighbouring craftsmen to leave their masters, probably with promises of better conditions and wages.[30] In the countryside youths sometimes manoeuvred their masters with some skill. In his treatise on the improvement of methods in husbandry, Timothy Nourse complained about the tricks and knaveries of servants who, when their annual terms drew to an end, went around looking for 'fresh service.' When a youth found a place where he could increase his wages, he hired himself by taking 'earnest' money (a token sum). He then went back to his old master and 'discours[ed] [with him] if he cannot make better terms [than those offered by the second master]'. If the master refused, the youth left; but if he agreed, the youth stayed and left the new master 'in the lurch, sending him only his earnest again'.[31]

Nourse made these observations in 1700, when the market for labour provided better opportunities for such bargains: the population had ceased to grow, fewer youths were available to work, and farmers were more willing to take annual servants rather than labourers on a daily or seasonal basis.[32] But the movement of youths from one master to another was a constant feature of the rural and urban scene throughout the sixteenth and the seventeenth centuries. The individual motives underlying these movements were as diverse as the personalities and circumstances of those who made them. Sometimes servants were driven away by dissatisfied masters, and at other times they left simply because they needed a respite and wanted to go home for a while.[33] Apprentices who left their masters in the midst of their term or near its end were motivated by a variety of concerns and aspirations. Some found it hard to adjust to urban life and preferred the countryside; others had exceptionally harsh masters, or found their chosen craft unsuitable. Still others were forced away by contingencies over which they had little control: the death of a parent, which forced them to return home to assist the surviving parent; or plague, which drove them away from the urban scene.[34] There were also those who dedicated their lives to the salvation of their souls and those of others, and material considerations played little, if any, part in their moves.

Nevertheless a powerful, perhaps the most powerful, force which lured young people away from older masters in search of new employment and places was material concern – an attempt to improve their lot, as well as to find a way to ensure their prospects for the future and their setting up thereafter.

Social Advancement

When Edward Barlow was an apprentice at sea, he arrived during one of his voyages in Lisbon, where he was struck by, among other things, what appeared to him as the difference between Portuguese and English parents. The Portuguese children were 'well brought up' by their parents, but were not put to work outside the home; Englishmen, he thought, put their children out to work 'in a higher manner than they can always maintain'.[35] Barlow was not alone in ascribing to the seventeenth-century English attempts to furnish their sons 'not only according to [their] power, but in truth beyond it,' as one contemporary put it. Moralists and writers of autobiographies condemned these practices and the aspirations for preferment that they entailed,[36] but writers of popular literature idealised and manipulated such hopes. Social advancement and spectacular transformations from lowly and poor backgrounds to the status of merchant or gentleman by means of rank, blood, wealth and sheer magical forces were a common staple of popular novels, drama, and the chapbooks which flooded the market from the late sixteenth century on.[37]

Autobiographies of the period show that young people sometimes already harboured hopes of material advancement before they left the parental home, and more often once they began their service or training elsewhere. When he finished his apprenticeship, Lodowick Muggleton had little money with which to begin on his own. He became a workman in a broker's shop, but at the same time continued to hope 'to be rich in the world'. William Edmundson followed his brother at the end of his apprenticeship, 'promising great matters to ourselves'; while Richard Norwood decided to abandon his dangerous and desperate course as an apprentice at sea, believing that 'the Lord had given me occasion to hope for better things'. James Fretwell quit his apprenticeship after only a few months, having begun to fear that his master had 'made no great improvement in the world'.[38] James was the son of a merchant, but his aspirations for improvement were shared by others in the lower ranks of society. Edward Barlow, whose father was a poor Lancashire husbandman, went for a trial period as an apprentice with a Manchester master, but soon discovered that he would like to go to see 'places more remote', as he later told his parents. Working in his master's barn in the company of a fellow apprentice, young Barlow began to think about the advantages of travel, and how 'they that had gone a long time returned very gallant with good store in their pocket'. The year was 1656, and Barlow, then a 14-year-old adolescent, decided that he would 'not tarry long'; he would leave his master and head for the capital.[39]

How realistic were Barlow's hopes? One of the most obvious ways to alter the prospects of poor living in the countryside and advance oneself socially and economically was by migration to and apprenticeship in the large towns. But social transformations of the kind described in stories like that of Dick Whittington and his cat – the poor young country boy who becomes an apprentice, a merchant overseas, and eventually Lord Mayor of London – were extremely rare throughout the sixteenth and seventeenth centuries. Several factors contributed to this, of which the most important was the cost of apprenticeship and of setting up in these lucrative trades. As we have already seen in a previous chapter, premiums in the large distributive trades were far beyond the reach of most youngsters who came from low and modest origins. Already in the 1530s, only 10 per cent of the sons of husbandmen bound as apprentices in Bristol entered the distributive trades, and by the early seventeenth century the proportion remained equally low. The number of those who managed to enter the top few mercantile trades was much smaller, and the number of those who finished their terms and became merchants and citizens smaller still. In early seventeenth-century

London only one of the 140 richest merchants was the son of a husbandman.[40]

The costs of setting up in such businesses once an apprenticeship was over could be equally high, if not higher. In mid-sixteenth-century London, the capital required to enter large-scale trade in Spain, Antwerp or Hamburg must have been hundreds of pounds; and even the cloth finishers in the merchant tailors' company claimed they needed above £100 to establish themselves in 'housing and other implements for their handy occupation'.[41] Large sums were required in industries in which equipment was costly, such as soapmaking and brewing; in those in which raw materials were expensive, such as silkmaking and the production of high-quality metal; and in those in which the production process was particularly long, such as tanning.[42] In mid-seventeenth-century London, Lodowick Muggleton, a tailor apprentice, estimated that £100 was required to set himself up; and by the end of the century William Stout invested some £300 on equipment (boards, chests, boxes) and goods for a grocery shop he opened in a small town in Lancashire. The evidence produced by Peter Earle for late seventeenth-century London shows that well over £100 was by then required in a wide range of shopkeeping businesses, and that in most cases 'those who ended up rich started off rich or at least pretty well off'.[43] Parental resources and inheritance portions were indispensable,[44] and people with only modest resources were unlikely to start on their own. Already in mid-sixteenth-century London, more than a half of the sons of gentlemen and yeomen among London apprentices opened their shops less than a year after the completion of their apprenticeships, compared with only a quarter of the sons of husbandmen.[45]

Population growth and migration pressures in the large towns in the sixteenth century and first half of the seventeenth century aggravated the difficulties entailed in aspirations for social and material betterment. The influx of growing number of sons of gentlemen and yeomen who hoped, or were forced, to enter the distributive trades was particularly marked; in the 1540s there were already sons of yeomen, merchants and traders who entered not only the lucrative and mercantile trades but much less profitable crafts.[46] As the sixteenth century wore on, this infiltration of sons of gentlemen and yeomen into the distributive and artisanal crafts narrowed the opportunities for the sons of husbandmen. By the early seventeenth century, for example, the proportion of sons of gentlemen among Bristol apprentices rose, and that of yeomen more than doubled, while the proportion of sons of husbandmen and craftsmen fell. The few score sons of labourers who were apprenticed in the decade 1542–52 had disappeared from among the apprentice population altogether by the first half of the seventeenth century.[47] The process continued well into the second half of that century, when Bristol entered its golden phase as a centre for overseas trade and a metropolis of the west. Between the early sixteenth and the late seventeenth centuries, the proportion of sons of yeomen among Bristol apprentices rose threefold, and that of sons of husbandmen fell from a fifth to a mere 6.6 per cent.[48]

There were other ways in which the competitive world of large commercial centres affected the prospects for advancement of poorer youths. Evidence on the length of terms for which Bristol's youngsters signed when they entered their apprenticeship indicates that by the seventeenth century only a few apprentices could benefit from agreeing to serve longer terms in lieu of lower premiums; by the mid-seventeenth century most apprenticeships in Bristol were for a standard seven-year term and the number of longer apprenticeships, of eight and nine years, dropped substantially.[49] Benefits at the end of term – cash sums, provision of bedding and tools – which had regularly been guaranteed in the sixteenth century and which could help a young man set up on his own, had been nearly eliminated a century later.[50] Prospects for journeywork, which could allow substantial savings towards setting up,[51] were likely to have become rather bleak as well. When apprentice labour abounded, and when this was coupled with periodic unemployment in some industries, masters preferred apprenticed labour to that of the journeyman, who could command better renumeration.[52] Finally, the costs of housing and shops, especially in London where the population nearly quadrupled in the course of the sixteenth and first half of the seventeenth centuries, also placed greater obstacles in the way of setting up. One of the major complaints of London apprentices in 1641 was that, when they finished their terms and 'should begin to trade in the world', they could 'get neither house or shop for our money'.[53]

At least some of the youths who were able to become apprentices in the large towns were discouraged, and their hopes were frustrated, as the evidence on the high drop-out rate among apprentices in all major towns suggests.[54] Some of these young men left without ever completing their terms or trying to obtain work as journeymen; they returned to the countryside, or settled near the town in the expanding parishes surrounding it, where housing costs are likely to have been lower,[55] and where guild rules regarding a seven-year apprenticeship as a condition for setting up were unlikely to be enforced. It was during the final decades of the sixteenth century that London's suburbs began to expand, and their fast population growth thereafter must have been caused at least partly by the movement of youths who never finished their apprenticeship terms with London's many freemen in the parishes within the walls.[56] In seventeenth-century Bristol, quite a few of those who were frustrated in their hopes to establish themselves in the town eventually found their way as indentured servants to the overseas colonies; other youths may have been forced to turn to agricultural labour in the countryside. Benjamin Lay, a glovemaker's apprentice in Colchester during the 1680s, became an agricultural labourer at the age of 19, having already served an apprenticeship for three or four years. He never settled in his craft of glovemaking at all.[57]

Yet it must also be emphasised that not all those who failed to establish themselves in the town necessarily lost all prospects for improvement; nor was the hard labour as an apprentice, even of those who served only three or four years, always unrewarded. Some people who left the town were able to achieve modest success by using the skills and connections they had obtained in the town elsewhere. Short-term fluctuations in different industries, towns and regions sometimes introduced exceptionally good opportunities; in late sixteenth-century Bristol, as well as in London, some industries were expanding while in others unemployment prevailed, so opportunities for setting up varied.[58] A plague year could also provide new opportunities for cheap housing and shops, as was the situation encountered by William Edmundson when he arrived in Dublin in the mid-1650s, where he therefore decided to set up.[59] More important still, many young people were able to set themselves in the countryside with the assistance of parents and kin, an assistance which sometimes took the form not only of financial support, but of providing information about available shops and lodging, temporary employment, victuals and lodging, and partnerships which could be of benefit to both parents and sons.[60]

In addition there was the immense value of credit, loans and gifts which could help young people to obtain a measure of success even in dire circumstances. In the seventeenth century, masters were still providing cash payments to apprentices who served the full length of their terms. William Dawson, a Bristol orphan, was promised in his indenture £10 if he remained the whole term; and Abraham Gullock, the son of a husbandman from Somerset apprenticed in 1622 with a Bristol brewer, was promised £5 towards his setting up. About a third of all Bristol's apprentices in the period 1600–45 were guaranteed with monies towards setting up at the end of their terms.[61] Loans and gifts from charity donors to help young starters were available in many towns, throughout the period. Bristol's loan book for the years 1644–47 included special loans to 'young men' in ten parishes, in a wide range of crafts and trades: soapmakers, haberdashers, halliers, bakers, joiners and carpenters.[62] Writers of autobiographies make abundantly clear the importance of credit and loans. William Stout, who had been furnished with a substantial inheritance portion, still bought the goods in his shop partly on credit. He paid London traders only half in cash and the rest on credit, 'as was then usual to do by any young man beginning trade'. For poorer people, such assistance could cover the whole cost of setting up. Roger Lowe, an orphaned apprentice, took his master's shop, as well as the commodities he bought, on credit. And Samuel Bownas, who came from a very poor family in Westmorland, eventually managed to open a shop of his own with the assistance of loans from friends. Joseph Oxley likewise furnished everything he needed in his shop with £30, 'and that not my own'.[63]

The costs of setting up also varied enormously. While £100 and upwards was needed in many shopkeeping and more costly trades, lower crafts, such as shoemaking, weaving, coopering and the like, normally required much less.[64] Joseph Oxley managed to open a clockmaker's shop in a Norfolk village with no more than £30, and in late seventeenth-century London, setting up in small artisanal shops – metal- and woodworkers, building trades – required only about £20 or £30. If we focus on the modest transformation involved in the entry into the less costly crafts, the chances of achieving it, though by no means guaranteed, were not altogether slim. Small trades and crafts could still offer some opportunity of improvement for apprentices from modest or poor backgrounds.[65] Even wage-earning occupations, such as the building crafts or seafaring, could entail, for the son of the husbandman, modest success. Edward Barlow greatly belittled the hardship involved in the hazardous and uncertain course of a sailor which he chose,[66] but evidently he still managed to improve his lot. In twenty years of extremely hard labour he rose slowly from the rank of apprentice to ordinary seaman and eventually to chief mate. He became a master navigator just once, when his captain died,[67] but his slow promotion amounted to an increase in his wages from 18sh. a month as an apprentice (which he gave to his master), to the £6 10sh. monthly pay he obtained more than twenty years later. This monthly pay was equal to two-thirds of his father's entire annual income when Barlow was a boy, and it allowed him, among other things, to return to his home village dressed more luxuriously, as he had fancied in his youth.

Such infiltration of poorer young men into the smaller crafts, and occasionally even into more profitable ones, continued throughout the period. By the early seventeenth century, sons of husbandmen still comprised nearly a fifth of the apprentice population in a town like Bristol, only slightly lower than their proportion a century earlier. Together with sons of craftsmen, urban and rural alike, they continued to dominate the apprentice population in the town right through to the mid-seventeenth century. About a fifth of the sons of husbandmen managed to enter, if not the top mercantile trades, then some other businesses involved in the distribution of goods, as well as those dealing in foodstuffs (butchers, vintners, bakers).[68] Some completed their terms and established themselves in the town. In a sample of 32 sons of husbandmen who eventually established themselves as citizens in Bristol between 1600 and 1645, 23 were craftsmen; but nine were in large-scale trade and more lucrative crafts: one was a merchant, five were involved in the distribution of foodstuffs and goods (two drapers, two bakers, one vintner), two became soapmakers, and one, Christopher Cottrell, the son of a Gloucester husbandman, became a shipwright in 1637, nine years after his apprenticeship had begun.[69] By the period 1670–1700, there were still migrants from the countryside, especially from Somerset and Gloucestershire; fewer than ever before were sons of husbandmen, but there were many sons of small rural craftsmen, occasionally even labourers. John Monke, the son of a Somerset coalminer, was apprenticed to a Bristol tailor in 1672; and John Thomas, the son of a labourer from Monmouth, became the apprentice of Thomas Ellis, a merchant.[70] Larger proportions of all the apprentices eventually established themselves in the town as small traders and haberdashers, coopers, glaziers, tailors, and occasionally also as shipwrights or grocers.[71]

While social advancement of the kind described in the Whittington myth remained throughout the period no more than an adolescent fantasy, more modest advancement was much less so. The very mobility of many youngsters, and the success of some of them, could continue to affect the aspirations of younger youths who followed in their footsteps. More than a third of Bristol apprentices, even in the late seventeenth century, never settled in the town but probably returned to the countryside instead.[72]

Whether or not they returned dressed fashionably or more luxuriously, they continued to entice the imaginations of adolescents in the rural countryside; if not to head for the capital or other large towns, then to try to improve their lot by whatever means were available elsewhere.

Assumption of Responsibilities for Others

On 24 January 1622, Andrew Barker, then aged 23, wrote a will in which he bequeathed to various kin and friends cash sums totalling no less than £250, and to his 'well beloved brother', Thomas, the rest of his 'estate, debt, and legacies'. Andrew Barker was the son of one of the richest merchant families in Bristol, an orphan who by the time he wrote his will was unmarried and still formally an apprentice. His will shows not only his wealth and extensive dealings as a 'merchant', as he referred to himself, but his adoption of the ideals of charity extant among the mercantile elite. He left monies to his brothers, in-laws, cousins, an old widowed aunt, a godson, and former and fellow servants. But in addition, he bequeathed £10 to the parish minister, his 'good friend' Mr John Farmer, £5 to the libraries in Bristol and in Oxford, and £5 each to seven of Bristol's poorest parishes, including those of Temple, Redcliff and St James.[73]

Evidence about young people who were servants in the manor of Havering, in Essex, indicates that, lower down in the social scale, young people also occasionally accumulated resources which they bequeathed to kin, friends, and even to their own masters.[74] Others assumed responsibilities involved with assisting other people, both young and old. William Taswell remembered contributing regularly to the poor while he was a student at Oxford, and William Lilly took charge of his master's house and assumed his master's duties of paying weekly pensions to the poor during the plague of 1625 while he was a servant in London.[75] Servants occasionally came back to their parental home to assist parents when they were ill. When Jane Martindale heard about her mother's illness, she left her service in London and 'post[ed] downe with all speed', to help her, and later, when her mother died, to assist and console her father. Richard Baxter likewise left his service in London when his mother became ill, and Edward Coxere, who was an apprentice at sea, decided to leave his ship and return home when he met a Devonshire man who told him his mother was ill. Some youths were called back by their parents and asked to provide help, as was George

Brysson, whose father died and whose mother needed his assistance in the management of her estate and servants. Brysson was by then in his mid-twenties and near the end of his apprenticeship, but he returned home and took full responsibility.[76] By his mid-twenties a young man could be described as 'a great comfort to his poor mother, and a father to the younger children', as was John Wasteneys, who died unmarried at the age of 26.[77]

Many youngsters would have found it difficult to abandon their service in order to help their parents, but they sometimes sent money to their parents. Historians have suggested that servants' earnings were not intended as a form of assistance to parents, but to provide subsistence and savings for their own future. Agricultural servants normally received wages personally, often only at the end of an annual term or when they left their masters, so regular support to parents would have been unlikely.[78] Moreover, young people were not expected to take care of their parents while they were still young and in service. Edward Barlow remembered that when his father came to visit him in London and they met at his uncle's house, he gave his father a little money for his mother and others of his kin, 'it being but small but as much as they could expect from me in the condition I was then in, being only an apprentice'.[79]

Yet Barlow's remark and the small token he sent his mother suggests that, despite the fact that he was apprenticed very far from his home, he saw it as an obligation, now that he was 'grown up to a young man's estate', as he wrote, to help his mother according to his means. Barlow was by then 19 years old, and his apprenticeship wages were already higher than those of a fellow younger servant.[80] His autobiography shows that he could hardly expect to assist his parents as long as he was an apprentice, for he regularly gave his wages to his master and mistress, in spite of his dislike of such practices. Some evidence on apprentices in the building industry would suggest similar practices in other industries, where wages were common and where apprentices were not paid by their own masters. Nevertheless young Barlow did manage to keep some money for himself while still an apprentice; at first by cheating his master and using part of his wages to buy for himself 'pears or apples or cherries', and then occasionally by obtaining pocket money and tokens from his master. Eventually, when he was near the end of his term, he received full pay for his final seven months' service. Soon afterwards, 'considering that my father and mother were ancient and poor people and in debt', and since his brother was a labourer with six children to care for, Barlow thought it 'good' to send his father, his mother, his brother, his brother's children and his sister, 20sh. each.[81]

The evidence on such practices is sparse, but it indicates that Barlow's sense of obligation and responsibility towards his kin was hardly unique. Ann Kussmaul suggested that in the countryside there were sometimes arrangements whereby masters sent their servants' wages to their parents; she also cites cases of servants who remitted their wages to their parents. Joseph Mayett appears to have given all his wages to his father, a poor labourer who lived in a parish nearby, as did Fred Kitchen, who brought his wages to his mother at the age of 14.[82] Servants in husbandry, agricultural labourers, and apprentices who managed to obtain some money or earn it on their own, not infrequently gave at least part of their earnings to their parents. Edward Coxere, unlike Barlow, was able to send wages and goods back to his parents while he was still an apprentice at sea. The first occasion was when he began to participate in the plunder of ships and he got 'some and sent home to England'. Then, when he decided to leave the ship and seek another master, he returned home and 'delivered my money to my father and mother'.[83] His autobiography implies that there was nothing unusual about such practices, that he gave assistance whenever he returned home between service terms or when he quit his service, and that he gave his parents his wages despite the fact that they were not particularly poor or in need of relief. There were probably no hard rules regarding assistance to parents, and children were first and foremost expected to help themselves before they helped their parents. But this by no means excluded assistance to parents, and there appears to have been reciprocity between parents and children who earned wages away from home, and kept contact, however irregular, with their families during many years of service.

Quite a few young men assumed some authority over children younger than themselves. In some shops and trades, older apprentices and journeymen instructed younger ones. If they were well educated, especially in the case of apprenticeships with merchants, drapers, clerks or attorneys, their duties might include teaching the master's children to read and write, as did William Taylor, a trainee in the house of Serjeant John Hoskyns.[84] Adam Martindale, then 16 years old, also taught the children of his master, a Manchester merchant, when he was a servant there. Two years later, when he was forced to leave his master and return home to his father, he became a teacher, first in Holland and then in Rainford, where some of the wealthier inhabitants promised to send their children to him. Some time later, when he was about 21 years old, he became a master in a newly founded school in Cheshire.[85] All we know today about the teaching profession in the early modern period suggests that it was bound to include many relatively young men and even women. Most teachers had no formal licence; many taught before they went into religious orders, but others were not connected with the Church at all.[86] Some obtained their first experience in teaching when they were quite young, with only the equivalent of a grammar school education; and hiring a schoolmaster was sometimes quite informal, depending on contingencies. When his old schoolteacher fell ill, Richard Baxter replaced him in his native Shropshire village for a few months. He was at that time no more than 17 or 18 years old.[87]

More widespread were practices regarding the taking on of servants and apprentices. Phineas Pett, a shipwright's apprentice, hired his first servant, 'a boy', when he was 25 years old: he was himself still an apprentice, unmarried, and employed as an ordinary workman on Woolwich dock; William Edmundson also employed a servant when he was 24 years old, and before he set up as a trader on his own.[88] Guild ordinances in towns show that in some lucrative trades, such as that of the merchant tailors in Bristol, journeymen and even apprentices sometimes hired younger apprentices on their own.[89] Evidence on 157 Bristol woodworkers in the century between 1550 and 1650 shows that nearly a fifth of them took their first apprentice seven or eight years after their apprenticeship had begun, that is, immediately after they finished their own terms, when they were probably in their mid-twenties. Some of these people may have taken their apprentices earlier, for it normally took some time between the actual start of term and the entry in the central Register of Apprentices. In two cases in Bristol, young coopers took their first apprentices when they had themselves been apprentices for only six and two years respectively.[90] Among the two-thirds of apprentices who left Bristol and turned elsewhere – before or soon after their terms – such practices must have been more common. Nor were all of these people married by the time they took their first apprentice. William Stout, who had been apprenticed in Lancaster, took his first apprentice when he was 26 years old. He was single, had no house of his own, and rented a small shop and a room in a house nearby. For his victuals and boarding he paid some £5 a year, but he also frequently lodged in his small shop. Once he took his apprentice, an adolescent named John Troughton, the two boarded together in the house of one

Richard Sterzaker, but they also often spent the night in the shop.[91]

Between Service and Marriage

It is difficult to know the precise age at which men and women left their service or apprenticeship term. Rappaport calculated that, in mid-sixteenth-century London, apprentices who eventually became company members and citizens finished their terms when they were 26 years old.[92] Many others finished somewhat younger. Age of entry into apprenticeship in provincial towns was probably lower than in London's largest companies, and so the end of training would occur earlier. William Stout must have been quite typical. He became an apprentice in Lancaster at the age of 16, and finished when he was 23 years old.[93] Some young people evidently considered themselves 'too old' to begin a seven-year term at the age of 20, which suggests that they considered 27 as too late an age to finish a term.[94] More importantly, since many apprentices, in London and in other towns, did not finish their formal terms, their exit from apprenticeship occurred when they were 23 or 22, and sometimes even younger. We may recall Benjamin Bangs, who quit his shoemaking training in mid-seventeenth-century London when he was no older than 18, feeling quite confident about his skills and expertise in the shoemaking trade.[95]

Evidence on rural servants and youths who never moved to towns is even more sparse, but it shows that many left service in their early and mid-twenties, and sometimes even before. In the eighteenth century, exit from service occurred at about the age of 20, and even if servants spent periods of ten years in service they still left before they reached their mid-twenties (given an entry age in farm service of 13 or 14). Keith Snell calculated a mean age of 20 for leaving rural craft apprenticeships in the first half of the eighteenth century, and some indentures of poor boys and girls in parishes around Bristol in the same period show an expectation of exit from service in husbandry at the age of 24, and occasionally at 21. McIntosh's evidence on servants in the manor of Havering in late sixteenth-century Essex also shows an age in the early and mid-twenties for leaving service.[96]

Kussmaul has argued that young people left service to marry, and that exit from service and marriage were nearly coincident.[97] Some servants had already inherited land and so were able to set up on their own; those who did not expect to inherit land left service, and, by combining their savings with those of their future spouses, were sometimes able to buy a smallholding or cottage of their own. Servants who had already bought land during their service term could also leave service, marry, and set up on their own.[98] The evidence on inheritance practices in villages in Essex, the Midlands and elsewhere shows that the marriage of sons was not dependent on inheritance, and that many heirs were already married and even set up on their own when their fathers were writing their wills.[99] In the manor of Havering in the sixteenth century servants probably remained in service until they married, at the estimated average age of 25 for men and 23 for women.[100] Women servants in London also married as soon as they left service, at an average age of 26.5; and some apprentices married as soon as they finished their terms. Edward Coxere married some seven years after his apprenticeship at sea had begun, when he was 22 years old and probably just out of his apprenticeship.[101]

Yet if most people in early modern English society married only when they reached their late twenties, and if many left service in their early and mid-twenties, there is bound to have been, for many people, a gap between the two events. This was particularly so in the case of men, whose average age at marriage throughout the period was 27–29. Kussmaul's evidence on servants in the late eighteenth century, when the average age at marriage was lower,[102] shows about half of people marrying before or immediately upon leaving service. But some 40 per cent waited up to eight or more years following their service before they married.[103] Two centuries earlier such intervals were likely to occur, too. Even those apprentices who finished their terms in mid-sixteenth-century London at the late age of 26 normally married about two years later. Most other apprentices left their masters at a younger age, before the end of their terms, so an interval between the end of their service and their marriage was even more likely to occur. Richard Norwood finished his apprenticeship at the age of 23 and married four years later; Thomas Chalkley married three years after he finished his term at the age of 21 or 22; and for Gervase Disney, a London apprentice who returned to the countryside, there was a gap of five years between the end of his term and his marriage. Most other autobiographies reveal similar patterns, and in some cases six, seven or even more years elapsed between the end of service and marriage.[104]

What course did young people take in the interim, between the end of service and marriage, and why was their marriage postponed? In the countryside some continued to work as wage earners. Samuel Bownas, the son of a poor widow in Westmorland, left his long apprenticeship with a village craftsman in Yorkshire and was employed as a mower during the harvest season in a village nearby; some time later he headed homeward, where his mother still lived, and he was then hired by a young man who had himself only recently set up on his own. Only five or six years later, when he was 30 years old, did he marry and manage to set himself up in his trade.[105] This was in the early 1700s, but a century earlier, when population pressures were greater and labour more abundant, many former servants took a similar course, leaving service, returning to their parental home if their parents were still alive, and joining the growing mass of adult labourers. As evidence from a late sixteenth-century Norfolk estate shows, there were women who, following their service terms as milkmaids or domestic servants elsewhere, returned home to live with their parents, and became labourers who brought substantial wages to their families, working in the fields in a wide range of other jobs.[106] Kussmaul's analysis of the seasonality of marriages in the south and the east suggests that in the late sixteenth century and first half of the seventeenth there were relatively few celebrations of marriages in October – the time of year when servants' contracts ended – indicating a lower incidence of annual service. Many of those who married were already day labourers rather than servants just out of their terms.[107] Some, like Samuel Bownas, would manage eventually to save and set up on their own. But others would continue to be employed as labourers well after they married, if not for the remainder of their lives.

In towns, young people sometimes became journeymen with their craft, but often they turned to some other form of wage work. In mid-sixteenth-century London, entrants in some companies spent an average of 3.2 years as journeymen following their apprenticeship terms. In Bristol, too, some of the young men who eventually became citizens probably spent a period of journeywork before they set up in their trade.[108] As pointed out above, however, throughout the sixteenth century and first half of the seventeenth, journeywork was not always a viable or attractive option. It was sometimes not well paid, and autobiographical evidence suggests that other forms of wage work could quite frequently be taken up instead. Thomas Chubb, who worked as a journeyman glover in Salisbury, apparently was still forced to complement his earnings with wage work, and he began to tend the shop of a tallow-chandler nearby.[109] Others left their employment as journeymen sooner. Following his apprenticeship in Exeter during the 1680s, John Croker became a journeyman. Finding that his 'stay was not likely to avail [him] much', he decided to leave after a very short while; he returned to Plymouth, where he inherited a room, and became a wage earner.[110] In twenty-eight autobiographies in which details of young people following their apprenticeship were given, only one became a journeyman; others became wage earners in jobs which were sometimes related to their training, and sometimes not. Benjamin Bangs became a foreman in a shoemaker's shop, Lodowick Muggleton assisted in a broker's shop, Richard Norwood began to teach, George Bewley became a clerk, and Benjamin Lay became an agricultural labourer in the countryside. Most of these lived as lodgers in the houses of others, and their marriage occurred three, four or more years afterwards, when they had already left the town and turned elsewhere.[111]

Among the middling groups, some young men moved from apprenticeship directly to small shops and businesses of their own, but their marriage was still delayed. Roger Lowe was offered a position as a journeyman when he was about to finish his apprenticeship in Ashton in the 1660s, but he turned it down, and instead set up in his own business. He married only three years later.[112] Nehemiah Wallington, a mid-seventeenth-century artisan, set up on his own when he was 22 years old, without ever working as a journeyman.[113] A century earlier, a third of the London apprentices who finished their terms and became company members had opened their shops within several months to a year after their apprenticeship had ended, but married only two or three years later. In late seventeenth-century London, wealthy young men married when they were 30 years old and probably quite well established in their trade or craft.[114]

In the countryside, too, marriage was postponed, and not only among the very poor. Some youths returned home to claim land left to them when they were still minors, as was the case of Joseph Oxely who returned to Brigg, in Yorkshire, where his father's estate was. He sold the land, then migrated to London and married only a couple of years later.[115] Others returned to their parental home to take charge of an estate or agricultural holding alongside an ageing mother. Thomas Bond left service when he was 22 years old and returned home to live with his mother, and George Brysson also returned home following his apprenticeship to take charge of the family affairs. He married only when he was 42 years old.[116] Others assumed the management of land inherited or bought on their own, settled down, and took a housekeeper or a female servant to help them on the farm. They married only a few years later, if at all.[117] And there were also many yeomen's sons who, following a service term elsewhere, assumed the management of farms headed by an ageing parent. Richard Wall has shown that sons of yeomen were no less likely than sons of other occupational groups to leave home for a period of service elsewhere; but they tended to marry at an even later age than tradesmen, craftsmen and labourers.[118] Josiah Stout, the eldest son in a family of six children, took over management of the family estate and improved it for the benefit of his younger brothers when he was in his early twenties and still unmarried.[119]

The reasons for the postponement of marriage varied with socioeconomic circumstances, but common to all was a sense of apprehension about married life and its demands. As Edward Coxere described his wariness when he decided to marry, 'care began to creep in, which before I was unacquainted with'.[120] Historians have argued that poorer people waited until they had accumulated the resources necessary to support a new family on their own.[121] In Thomas Deloney's *Jack of Newbery*, young Jack refuses to marry his widowed mistress on the grounds that 'it is not wisdome for a yongue man that can scantly keep himselfe, to take a wife . . . for I have heard say, that many sorrowes follow marriage, especially where want remaines'. Some autobiographies suggest that youngsters with few resources so dreaded the difficulties entailed in entering married life in a state of poverty that they preferred to remain single, 'judging it greatly improper to introduce a family into the world, without a prospect of maintaining them,' as Thomas Chubb said.[122] Among wealthier groups some did not rush to marry, possibly because they enjoyed the freedom that unmarried life still afforded. Many years of service under the tutelage of masters may have produced a sense of liberation which some young people were unlikely to give up all too soon. Lodowick Muggleton could not wait until the moment when he would no longer be 'subject to the humours of people to please them, which I had experience of in my apprenticeship'; and William Stout also commented on how impatient 'too many youths' were to be out of their service terms.[123]

Many others were apprehensive about handling their economic affairs on their own. Some were already taking care of a family farm or an estate and were burdened with obligations towards their widowed mothers, fathers, or younger brothers and sisters. Such responsibilities could place obstacles in the way of finding a suitable match, as is suggested by Lodowick Muggleton, whose mistress preferred him as a husband for her daughter because, among other things, no 'kindred came after me to be any charge or burthen to her daughter'.[124] Those who were on their own had other concerns. Loans had to be repaid, competition with older and more experienced traders had to be confronted, and new occupational connections sometimes had to be established. Roger Lowe, who took his master's shop and commodities on credit, was 'sadly troubled for fear of miscaryinge' during his first year on his own. While some youngsters had to repay debts in one or two instalments, others remained indebted for much longer.[125] There was also the insecurity involved in economic decisions that young starters had to make on their own. Samuel Bownas was not sure whether he should settle in Ireland, 'where he was not known', and George Bewley felt 'fearful of engaging too soon in business for myself'. Some young people had to settle in a wholly new course for which they felt unprepared. Richard Norwood, who left a long and hard apprenticeship at sea, felt 'unacquainted with the world and altogether ignorant how to settle myself into any good course of life', once he decided to abandon ship and settle ashore.[126]

And there were the apprehensions about married life itself. Quite striking was the advice given by Elizabeth Stout to her daughter, Elin, who at the age of 27 was approached by several yeomen in her native county of Lancashire. Elin had suffered from limb injuries since she was a child, and now her mother advised her to remain single, 'considering her infermetys and ill state of health', and 'knowing the care and exercises that always attended a married life, and the hazerd of hapiness in it'.[127] George Bewley appears to have approached marriage with no less caution and care. A native of Cumberland, he finished his apprenticeship in Dublin and returned home, where his father gave him money to set up for himself in Dublin.[128] He was by no means poor, apparently had no kin to support, and he had fairly secure employment, money with which to set up, and social contacts on whom he could rely. Nevertheless he waited some three years before he 'was inclined to marry'. He then 'applied to the Lord' to direct him 'in this great and weighty undertaking', as he referred to his marriage soon afterwards to Blessing Fennell, a woman from the Irish village of Youghal. This was in 1713, and George Bewley was 28 years old, the standard age at marriage for men throughout most of the period.

It would be difficult to establish how many young people married soon after their service, and how many postponed this for several years, but the impression is that a sizeable minority in the countryside, and perhaps a majority in the towns, married only several years after they had left service. Given the greater constraints on independent skilled work for women and the sexual division of labour, women were more likely than men to wait until they decided to marry and then move out of service, as was the case among London servants. Male servants who had no family to rely on, and those whose parents were too poor, might also prefer to remain in service until they could combine their resources with those of a future spouse. But others, even among women and among the poor, did not enter matrimony soon after service. Well before they married, they worked or established themselves as independent adults; as labourers in a variety of jobs in shops, industries and agriculture; as owners and managers of an agricultural holding or an estate, and as independent craftsmen or traders with shops of their own. Journeymen, too, sometimes began small businesses of their own while they were still with their masters. In Bristol, journeymen in the leather industry worked on their own, with the knowledge of their masters, whose guild (the cordwainers) only ordered that 'no journeyman work as a cobbler without license'.[129] In the countryside, too, journeymen sometimes worked on someone else's broad loom, but at the same time they owned their own narrow loom and were earning a living on their own.[130]

'A great and weighty undertaking'

In many ways the decisions regarding marriage and the choice of a marriage partner reflected the past experiences of couples: their family relations and interactions, their material fortunes or disadvantages, their divergent gendered roles, and the independence – in actions and habits of mind – they had already gained. Given the important role of parents and kin in providing security and assistance at critical moments throughout adolescence and beyond, it is hardly surprising if parents interfered with, or tried to exert influence on, matters concerning the marriage of their children. This was of course true of the upper classes and some families of the middling classes, among whom there was considerable parental influence in the choice of marriage partner.[131] But lower down the social scale parents also had a say, and their consent was considered essential to successful marriage. By the time he married in his early twenties, Edward Coxere had already been away from home for many years. Nevertheless, throughout his apprenticeship he continued to preserve contacts with his parents and regularly came home to visit them. When he decided to marry, he 'did nothing without the consent of her friends and my own', as he recorded in his autobiography.[132]

The social and economic standing of prospective spouses were important considerations in the choices people made regarding their marriages. Many recognised the benefit of a good marriage, and social patterns of marriage during this period show many endogamous unions: people tended to marry within their own ranks.[133] This was a consequence partly of the values inculcated in children at an early age – especially among the upper and more prosperous social groups[134] – but also of the experiences they encountered during many years of service and labour outside home. When he decided to marry, Edward Coxere relied on the money 'which he had gathered together through hardship and difficulty'; but, in addition, he hoped to obtain the assistance of his future father-in-law. 'Considering with myself that I had in my father-in-law's hands something considerable to supply our present occasions'.[135] Among more prosperous groups, young men chose women from their own social milieu, even when their parents were deceased and they were relatively free to pursue their own tastes and inclinations. In May 1598, Phineas Pett, whose parents were dead, married Ann Nicholls, who, by his own reckoning, was the daughter of 'a man of good report and honest stock'.[136] In autobiographies there are examples of sons of merchants and yeomen who were recommended to women of 'good yeomanry family' and 'good rank', and who found the matches wholly suitable. 'After some mature consideration,' Gervase Disney described his reaction to his cousin's offer of such a match, 'I returned him thanks, and embraced the motion.'[137]

The independence of mind and the social skills the young had obtained by their mid-twenties were also evident in most of these decisions on marriage. Gender-related roles diverged quite dramatically: while men became heads of households and owners of shops and land, women entered matrimony in a subservient status, and legally lost whatever financial independence they had obtained.[138] Nevertheless, the skills and independence of judgement they had acquired in many years of service and other work were indispensable, and ensured a certain cooperation and mutuality between spouses. Women entered marriage as 'true help-meets . . . both inwardly and outwardly,' as George Bewley put it.[139] Many autobiographies also point out the love and affection that drew two people into married life, and the autonomy with which both made their choice. Gervase Disney, the son of a gentleman, was offered the opportunity to meet a potential future wife, but was also assured that he could choose to decline the offer.[140] Lower down the social scale the independence in choice of spouse was more marked. Edward Coxere, who expected and obtained the permission of all the adults concerned, approached his parents and those of his future wife only after the matter was 'confirmed between us both'. Other autobiographies suggest similar procedures.[141]

Social skills can also be seen in the interaction of youngsters with their parents. Marriage cases dealt with by the ecclesiastical courts show that some children boldly confronted parents who opposed their choice of spouse, and even took legal action against them, although they often lost their cases.[142] Most people, however, used means and tactics other than the law, and these are bound to have been much more effective. The autobiographies give a glimpse of the intricate ways in which children put pressure on their parents to obtain their approval, and so make their marriage economically successful and socially legitimate. Caution in approaching parents and in preparing the ground during the long months of open courting which preceded the marriage,[143] persuasion,[144] arguments and discussions, and negotiations and manoeuvring based on long years of acquaintance with parental tastes and habits of mind, were all involved. Phineas Pett met with resistance from his kindred, but being 'determined resolutely' to marry his chosen woman, was able to persuade them, admittedly 'with great difficulty'. He was then 28 years old and already quite competent in his craft as a shipwright.[145] Elias Osborn's father was opposed to his intention to marry a widow's daughter, who lived nearby, because of her religious persuasions. 'But I believed, and so did not make haste, but would wait Times when he was in a loving Temper, and then speak to him again.' Soon after, Elias's father realised that his son was 'grounded' in his decision, and so he gave in.[146]

Such tactics often met with considerable success, for by the time they were in their mid- and late twenties the relationship between children and their parents had been transformed. People who reached this age – and who for many years had earned their own living, relied on a wide range of social ties, dealt and negotiated with masters and other adults – were likely to use, with a degree of sophistication, a variety of means to counter or circumvent parental opinion and achieve cooperation. And while considerable moral and financial pressure could be exerted by parents, their adult offspring were at times no less likely to use similar pressures. When he was about to marry, Edward Coxere took parental cooperation and assistance for granted, for, as he himself explained it, there were wages and monies he had sent them while he was still an apprentice.[147] By the time most people – men and women – married, they had already achieved a delicate balance of power with their parents, and simple obedience to parental dictates was unlikely to occur. Nor was such blind obedience always expected, even by adults. In his autobiography Gervase Disney recalled 'unhappy differences' between his father and his elder brother, Cornelius, whom Gervase described as having already 'grown a man'. This conflict between father and son reduced the brother 'to great straits' which also became difficult to conceal; family members, friends and neighbours were quite uninhibited in forming an opinion on it. While some thought the brother 'too stubborn and rebellious in his carriage', others asserted that 'my father [was] too strict with him, in his years of manhood'. Cornelius died unmarried two or three years later, when he was 28 years old.[148]

Conclusion

By the time they married in their mid- and late twenties,[1] most people in early modern English society were adults, and sometimes they were described as such. William Stout wrote that his sister, Elin, was offered marriage by 'several country yeomen, men of good repute and substance', all of whom she refused. Elin was 27 years old, and her suitors were probably the same age or somewhat older. Her brother referred to them all as mature adults, 'yeomen' and 'men', rather than 'youths', 'sons', or even 'young men', the normal way in which Englishmen during this period referred to people in their early twenties.[2]

Many people at this age had already assumed a multiplicity of adult roles and a wide range of responsibilities. Some had already become responsible for the care of children, occasionally acting as guardians; others were godfathers, or had written wills in which they bequeathed monies to kin, friends, brothers and fellow servants.[3] Most people, men and women, had been earning wages for many years, sometimes helping out their own parents or other kin. Many of them had experience working in a wide range of skills, supervising and employing servants or apprentices, or caretaking or managing land they had inherited or bought on their own. Mature apprentices acted as factors, conducted extensive dealings of their own together with those of their masters, loaned money on interest, gave services to fellow servants, masters and neighbours; journeymen practised their craft and traded on their own. There were also those in their early and mid-twenties who had shops of their own, or managed farms with their widowed mothers. Many youths would have recognised the ramifications of social status and hierarchy, and of gendered roles; others had already been disillusioned in their initial hopes for improvement in the world. A growing number in the course of the sixteenth and first half of the seventeenth centuries joined the mass of labouring poor during their teens, and they remained labourers well past their wedding day. Long years of experience of labour, unemployment and daily and seasonal work forced them to develop a great deal of ingenuity in combining various types of earnings, and in finding different sources of employment. In autonomy and capacity to decide where and how to turn for their immediate needs, in their experience of how to handle material life and its uncertainties, in the shrewdness that some of them showed in handling their masters and other adults, early modern newlyweds were hardly adolescents or even young. The postponement of marriage was in itself a measure of that maturity and of the recognition of the heavy responsibilities that wedlock involved.

To the extent that the period of adolescence and youth in our modern society involves a series of transformations which extend over a long period between puberty and adulthood, there was something quite modern in the transition to adult life in the early modern past. It was a long transition which extended for twelve, thirteen or more years, and which covered a substantial part of human life. The complexity of the process of transition, the varied social and gendered experiences, and the absence of clear-cut transformations in the form of a single rite of passage which would have endowed the young with a new status and role, all conform to some of the features we normally associate with the period of youth in the modern world. Then as now there was a lack of synchronisation between the various processes of maturation, so that a youth could in some respects be an adult, and in others be in a position more akin to that of a child. In early modern England a servant could be expected, like other mature members of the community, to pay his duties to church, but he was still subject to the orders of his master; he was already highly skilled, but did not have full control of his wages; he could inherit land, but, if an apprentice, still not be allowed to marry. A young person could be considered – by state agents as well as his or her parents – as economically self-sufficient at 16, could act as a supervisor of people younger than himself at 19 or 20, be responsible for complicated business transactions at 22 or 23, yet in all these years he was denied membership of a guild, or a position of authority in a household of his own.

Yet overall, the maturation of the young in the early modern past was an intensive process which forced them to have a great deal of independence, sometimes at a relatively early age. Some youngsters were already on a par with able-bodied adults in their mid-teens, as was made clear in an order of Bristol's magistrates in 1654 for the recruitment of 'two hundred able mariners, seamen and watermen being above the age of 15 years and under sixty'.[4] Even if still living with their parents, many adolescents would have joined them in the fields, the shops, ships, households or estates where they were employed as labourers or skilled craftsmen.[5] Adolescents in their teens were expected not only to work hard, but to stand on their own and prepare for a future in which they would have to fend for themselves. They were expected to be able to make up their own minds regarding work and training, and to cope with the difficulties that might ensue. Social pressures were exerted by parents and neighbours on adolescents who hesitated between jobs and opportunities, or on those who left a service arrangement without securing themselves another master. Youngsters sometimes internalised these social norms and could scoff at a companion whom they found 'mammy-sick'[6] – which was not in keeping with their self-image that demanded self-reliance and independence. Other youths thought it was not fitting to ask for their parents' help once they had left home. Jane Martindale, who migrated from Lancashire to London, wrote her parents a letter in which she asked in 'a gentile way' for their assistance, trying as much as she could to disguise the difficulties she had met in the metropolis.[7]

In this sense, there was incompatibility between two sets of norms prevalent in early modern English society: the one stressed the deference and submission the young owed their parents and masters, and the other encouraged their early independence. The first set of norms stemmed from the patriarchal ideal and the family morality it encompassed; the second was rooted in a family system in which the independent nuclear household was the norm, and in which children were expected to be on their own not only when they formed a new household, but well before. Writers of moral guides sometimes betrayed the ambiguity the two sets of norms might involve. Parents were exhorted to keep their offspring under their direct supervision and avoid sending them away, but it was also recognised that children would inevitably leave the parental home to become servants elsewhere; the young were admonished to remain with a single master and pursue a single course with diligence, but it was also acknowledged that in various circumstances such a prescription was difficult to follow, and that many a youth was bound to use initiative and 'betake [himself] to some other calling or course of life'.[8]

This incompatibility between two sets of norms goes some way towards explaining the great anxiety some adults expressed about the unruliness and disorders of the young. For the independence the young achieved – and were expected to achieve – during their teens worked against social expectations about the submission of the young, and was perceived as threatening to the social fabric. This was especially true during periods, such as that which obtained throughout the sixteenth and first half of the seventeenth centuries, when the population was growing, and when children who left home were likely to face the prospect of unemployment. Some may have roamed the streets with little or nothing to do; many others travelled greater distances, and moved more frequently in search of new masters or temporary employment. Apprehensions about vagrancy, social disorder and the subversiveness of the young consequently mounted.[9]

But such apprehensions were not confined to these more difficult decades. Throughout the period, young people continued to leave home, and life-cycle service, as well as other forms of labour, continued to be their most formative experience, compelling greater autonomy as they grew up and moved along. And although encouraged to leave home, young people were not left wholly vulnerable, nor were they usually dependent on a single master. Most could hope to rely on a variety of social ties which gave them a degree of flexibility and choice, allowing them to change masters and employment not only when they were forced to, but when they wanted to improve their lot. The independence and manoeuvring involved in these constant shifts could hardly escape the notice, and apprehensions, of contemporaries. Servants were considered the 'most disorderly part of the parish' because 'they [were] constantly shifting from place to place', as the rector of Finmere in Oxfordshire explained in the early eighteenth century.[10]

The Oxfordshire rector made another observation. He pointed out that servants avoided attending catechism classes because they were 'thinking themselves . . . too old or too big for this discipline'. His comment aptly underlines the conflicting demands that early modern English society placed on the young, and the tensions that inevitably ensued. As they grew up, young people were expected to be submissive yet autonomous, passive and disciplined but also capable of making decisions and taking the initiative to find service and obtain skills that would equip them to stand on their own. They were brought up to defer to parents and masters, but at the same time to be capable of earning a living, working hard, and establishing themselves on their own in an increasingly competitive world. Tensions between youths and adults were bound to surface, and resentment of masters and preachers, defiance of authority, and boldness in dealing with adults were likely to recur. Complaints about lack of rewards, unfairness of masters, humiliation at being obliged to do the meanest jobs in a new household, were common among the young. 'All the apprentices of our acquaintance came to see me,' as Francis Kirkman said of his return to London after running away from his master, 'they were all of one tune, complaining against the severity of their masters.'[11]

These tensions, however, were kept within limits. There were areas of agreement, cooperation, and shared concerns and aspirations between young and old; and options for improvement and change of masters and employment might also reduce the potential for tension between youth and mature adults. For the independence the young had achieved in the course of their teens involved a measure of freedom: to move between different households, to choose between alternatives, to earn money and save on their own, and to pursue leisure activities and friendships with greater laxity and without the burdens and commitments that adults had. And however dependent and ultimately unequal the position of youth *vis-à-vis* adults remained, the young were not wholly powerless, and could often manipulate and circumvent adult authority and rule. Some adults, themselves burdened with responsibilities, were unable to counter and discipline the young; others relied on their skills and loyalty in tending their shops, guarding their interests, and providing a source of cheap, but well trained, labour. There were also those who recognised the independence the young had assumed, responded to them with greater leniency, and treated them as equals as they grew up and became more skilled and mature. An older servant and apprentice, in his early or mid-twenties, was given relative freedom to pursue leisure activities, social relations, and whatever decisions she or he made regarding employment, setting up, and the starting of a new family of his own.

Given many variations in individual fortunes and experiences, the transition to adulthood in the early modern past was demanding and not devoid of strain. The very expectation that a youngster become independent and capable of standing on his own – perhaps even more than the expectation that he be obedient and subordinate to his adult superiors – placed many burdens on the young. Frequent separations and movements, a certain vulnerability in the face of various life crises, loneliness in new places and households, dealing with, and manoeuvring between, masters – were all part of the adolescent experience of many men and women, and not only among the very poor and those forced out of their homes at a relatively young age. With the slowing down of population growth in the second half of the seventeenth century, some of these difficulties were alleviated: long-term service contracts were easier to obtain, and the migration of the young was on a smaller scale and involved shorter distances. There was also a diversification and expansion in opportunities for learning a skill or entering a small trade in the countryside, an expansion to which young people had contributed greatly in their continuous moves from the large towns to the countryside, throughout the period.[12] The proliferation of crafts and trade in small towns and in the villages surrounding them was already evident in the late sixteenth and early seventeenth centuries; by the end of the seventeenth century, nearly a tenth of the people examined for settlements in the southern parishes, as Keith Snell has shown, had been apprenticed in some craft or trade. In some more urbanised parishes the proportion was much higher. The range of trades and crafts in which these young people were trained was hardly less narrow than that which existed in the large towns and in London, and the premiums paid for apprenticeships also varied greatly, allowing wealthier as well as poorer youths to enter these crafts and trades.[13] Nor were women wholly excluded from these types of apprenticeship, as they often were in the large towns. And to a greater extent than before, poorer youths could hope to rely on the parish relief system for assistance and support when they were unemployed.

Nevertheless, many of the difficulties involved in the transition to adult life, and in the autonomy and responsibilities it enforced on the young, persisted. Throughout the period, women had far fewer opportunities then men for entering a wide range of skills and occupations, in the countryside and especially in towns. In London they could hope, at most, to become domestic servants; and by the late seventeenth century, long-distance migration to many towns was dominated by young women, who likewise became domestics in the households of the wealthier segments of the fast-growing towns. Throughout the period, they were allowed many fewer choices than men, and were given less rewarding employment. In their movements to the large towns they were more vulnerable than men, and were liable to be apprehended for prostitution, not only when they were out of work. Male youths who continued to migrate to London and other large towns still faced the risk of unemployment, and were likely to attract the attention of magistrates searching for vagrants as soon as they became unemployed.[14] Overall, the difficulties involved in separations from parents, encounters and dealings with masters, frequent adjustments to different households, and hard decisions which young people, both women and men, had to make throughout their adolescence and youth, hardly diminished at all.

Most young people adapted, and in the course of their teens they were bound to develop a great deal of flexibility in their actions and habits. But that flexibility was often hard-won. William Stout recorded in some detail his experience in working during his apprenticeship in a grocer's shop during long nights in the winter. Stout came from a relatively well-to-do family in Lancashire and was bound as an apprentice not far away from where his mother and brothers still lived. With the money he was provided with in his father's will, he was able to secure a beneficial apprenticeship that guaranteed relative security later in his life. Nevertheless, as he recalled it, the experience of working alone in the long cold nights of the winter, in his master's shop, made him 'so hardy' that afterwards he could endure the 'couldest season'.[15] Edward Coxere also remembered the moment in his life when he grew 'hardy'. He was an apprentice at sea to a master who was well known to his parents, and who protected him and treated him decently. Still, the master was quite severe and aroused fear in young Coxere; altogether the experience of adjusting to the new faces and many seamen on the ship, and to the routine of waiting on merchants in the captain's cabin, was quite daunting. In later years Coxere recalled that it took him some time before he could begin to 'lay quiet a-nights' and sleep without being disturbed by people asking for his services. Then, gradually, he began 'to grow hardy and did not so much think of home'.[16] Edward Coxere was then in his mid-teens, and a long and laborious, and in this sense by no means exceptional, career still lay ahead of him.

Notes

Introduction

1. *Barlow's Journal*, 20–3. The signal of his mother with her hand cannot be interpreted from the drawing itself, but it is clear from the text of the autobiography that Barlow wanted to portray her as trying to prevent him from leaving.

2. P. Laslett, 'Characteristics of the Western family considered over time', in *Family Life and Illicit Love in Earlier Generations* (Cambridge, 1977), 12–49, esp. 34–5; J. Hajnal, 'Two kinds of pre-industrial household formation systems', in R. Wall, J. Robin and P. Laslett (eds), *Family Forms in Historic Europe* (Cambridge, 1983), 65–104; R. Wall, 'Leaving home and the process of household formation in pre-industrial England', *Continuity and Change*, 2 (1987), 90–7.

3. Kussmaul, *Servants in Husbandry*, 168–89; R.M. Smith, 'Some issues concerning families and their property in rural England 1250–1800', in R.M. Smith (ed.), *Land, Kinship and Life-Cycle*, 33–4; J.M. Bennett, *Women in the Medieval English Countryside* (Oxford, 1987), 62–3.

4. Laslett, 'Characteristics of the Western family', 34; Wall, 'Leaving home', 91; McIntosh, 'Servants and the household unit', 11.

5. For fluctuations in the incidence of service in husbandry and the decline of service and apprenticeship in the eighteenth and nineteenth centuries, see Kussmaul, *Servants in Husbandry*, 97–134; K.D.M. Snell, *Annals of the Labouring Poor: Social Change and Agrarian England, 1660–1900* (Cambridge, 1985), chs 2 and 5. For the decline in numbers of apprentices enrolled by the guilds in various towns, see M.J. Walker, 'The Guild control of trades in England, *c.* 1660–1820', a paper presented at the conference of the Economic History Society (Loughborough, 1981). A copy of the paper is in the library of the Cambridge Group for the History of Population and Social Structure.

6. For an extensive discussion of this literature, see H. Hendrick, *Images of Youth: Age, Class, and the Male Youth Problem, 1880–1920* (Oxford, 1990), esp. chs 3, 4 and 5. For the emphasis, in this literature, on industrialisation and urbanisation and its effects, see ibid., 88–91; 127–8; 144–5.

7. O.J. Dunlop and R.D. Denman, *English Apprenticeship and Child Labour: A History* (New York, 1912), chs 1 and 2, and pp. 17–23. See also Hendrick, *Images of Youth*, 65.

8. For these writers, see ibid., 127–8.

9. F. Pollock and F.W. Maitland, *The History of English Law Before the Time of Edward I* (Cambridge, 1895), Vol. II, 436.

10. P. Kecskemeti (ed.), *Essays on the Sociology of Knowledge, by Karl Mannheim* (Oxford, 1952), 276–321, esp. 288–94, 298. For Mannheim's definition of 'generation' analysed in the context of the intellectual climate of his time, see R. Wohl, *The Generation of 1914* (Cambridge, Mass. 1979), 73–84. For the influence of Mannheim on historical studies of generations and generational differences in the modern world, see A.B. Spitzer, 'The historical problem of generations', *American Historical Review*, 78 (1973), 1353–85.

11. Kecskemeti, *Essays on the Sociology of Knowledge*, 302; see also 295, 303–4.

12. S.N. Eisenstadt, *From Generation to Generation: Age Groups and Social Structure* (1958), esp. 44–6; 87–92; 'Archetypal patterns of youth', in P.K. Manning and M. Truzzi (eds), *Youth and Sociology* (1972), 15–29.

13. Ibid., 24–7.

14. In such societies adolescents who reach the age of 12, 14 or 16 go through a ritual, or series of rituals, which signifies the separation from childhood (through the cutting or mutilation of parts of the body) and integration into adult life. The ceremonies endow the young with new adult status and roles, and they can extend over a period of days, weeks, several months, or occasionally more. Evans-Pritchard, for example, described the transition to adulthood among the African Nuer as consisting of three stages: the first is an operation of six cuts in the brows of the 14- or 16 year-old; the second extends over a short period during which the adolescents live in partial seclusion and are subject to various taboos; and the third is a celebration during which sacrifices are made and licentious horseplay and singing of lewd songs is allowed. E.E. Evans-Pritchard, *The Nuer: A Description of the Modes of Livelihood and Political Institutions of a Nilotic People* (Oxford, 1940; 10th edn, 1978), 249–50. For a description which emphasises the lack of tensions and relatively smooth process of transition involved in these rituals, see M. Mead, *Growing Up in New Guinea: A Study of Adolescence and Sex in Primitive Societies* (1930; Penguin edn, 1963), 134–58. For a discussion of the features of puberty rites in primitive societies, see also R.E. Muuss, 'Puberty rites in primitive and modern societies', *Adolescence*, 5 (1970), 109–28.

15. See, for example, Muuss, 'Puberty rites', 109; K. Keniston, *Youth and Dissent* (New York, 1970), 3–4. For a standard summary of these views, see J.J. Conger and A.C. Petersen, *Adolescence and Youth: Psychological Development in a Changing World* (3rd edn, New York, 1984), 5–11, where it is considered that in the past the usual adult age was 17 or 18.

16. P. Ariès, *Centuries of Childhood: A Social History of Family Life*, trans. from the French by R. Baldick (New York, 1962).

17. Ibid., 329; see also 29–32.

18. For a critical examination of Ariès's methods, see A. Wilson, 'The infancy of the history of childhood: an appraisal of Phillippe Ariès', *History and Theory*, 19 (1980), 132–53. For praise and criticism of historians like L. Stone and N. Davies, see ibid., 132–3. For other criticisms, see S.R. Smith, 'The London apprentices as seventeenth-century adolescents', *Past and Present*, 61 (1973), 149; R. Thompson, 'Adolescent culture in colonial Massachusetts', *Journal of Family History*, 9 (1984), 127–8; S. Shahar, *Childhood in the Middle Ages* (London and New York, 1990). For a more favourable critique of Ariès, see A. Burton, 'Looking forward from Ariès? Pictorial and material evidence for the history of childhood and family life', *Continuity and Change*, 4 (1989), 203–29.

19. J. Demos and V. Demos, 'Adolescence in historical perspective', *Journal of Marriage and the Family*, 31

(1969), 632–8; J.F. Kett, 'Adolescence and youth in nineteenth-century America', in T.K. Rabb and R.I. Rotberg (eds), *The Family in History: Interdisciplinary Essays* (New York and London, 1973), 95–110, esp. 97, 109.

20. J. Springhall, *Coming of Age: Adolescence in Britain 1860–1960* (Dublin, 1986), 8–9.

21. K. Thomas, 'Age and authority in early modern England', *Proceedings of the British Academy* (1977), Vol. LXII, 214; M. Mitterauer and R. Sieder, *The European Family: Patriarchy to Partnership from the Middle Ages to the Present* (Oxford, 1982), 95–7.

22. P. Laslett, 'Mean household size in England since the sixteenth century', in P. Laslett and R. Wall (eds), *Household and Family in Past Times* (Cambridge, 1972), 125–58; Laslett, 'Characteristics of the Western family'; Hajnal, 'Two kinds of pre-industrial household formation systems'; E.A. Wrigley and R.S. Schofield, *The Population History of England 1541–1871: A Reconstruction* (1981).

23. P. Laslett, *The World We Have Lost* (New York, 1965), 2–6; G. Schochet, 'Patriarchalism, politics, and mass attitudes in Stuart England', *Historical Journal*, 12 (1969), 413–41; C. Hill, *Society and Puritanism in Pre-Revolutionary England* (1964); L. Stone, *The Family, Sex and Marriage in England 1500–1800* (New York, 1977, Abrdg. edn, 1979), 109–27; Mitterauer and Sieder, *The European Family*, 93–119.

24. A. Macfarlane, *The Family Life of Ralph Josselin: A Seventeenth-Century Clergyman* (New York, 1970); K. Wrightson, *English Society*, 89–118; L.A. Pollock, *Forgotten Children: Parent–Child Relations from 1500 to 1900* (Cambridge, 1983); Houlbrooke, *The English Family*, 127–56.

25. Kussmaul, *Servants in Husbandry*, 33, 44–7; R. Houlbrooke, 'The making of marriage in mid-Tudor England: evidence from the records of matrimonial contract litigation', *Journal of Family History*, 10 (1985), 339–52, esp. 350–1.

26. Laslett, *Family Life and Illicit Love*, 4; Rappaport, *Worlds Within Worlds*, 232–8.

27. N.Z. Davis, 'The reasons of misrule: youth groups and charivaris in sixteenth-century France', *Past and Present*, 50 (1971), repr. in *Society and Culture in Early Modern France* (Stanford, 1975), 97–123.

28. Smith, 'The London apprentices'; S. Brigden, 'Youth and the English Reformation', *Past and Present*, 95 (1982), 37–51; J.R. Gillis, *For Better, For Worse: British Marriages, 1600 to the Present* (N.Y. and Oxford, 1985), 11–12, 20–30, 34–7. See also Ch. 8.

29. Smith, 'The London apprentices', 149, 157–61; Rappaport, *Worlds Within Worlds*, 236, 326–9. For a reference to apprentices under 21 years old as boys, see, for example, A.L. Merson (ed.), *A Calendar of Southampton Apprenticeship Registers, 1609–1740* (Southampton Record ser., Vol. XII, Southampton, 1968), introduction, xvii.

30. P. Laslett, 'Parental deprivation in the past: a note on orphans and stepparenthood in English history', in *Family Life and Illicit Love*, 163–4; Kussmaul, *Servants in Husbandry*, 69.

31. For references to an 'unusually impressive young man' acting as a merchant, and to a 'young man of only 24' who ran his father's land on his own, see G.D. Ramsay, 'The recruitment and fortunes of some London freemen in the mid-sixteenth century', *Economic History Review*, 2nd ser. 31 (1978), 539; A.H. Smith, 'Labourers in late sixteenth-century England', 372.

32. The book does not deal directly with the theme of formal education, although some aspects of schooling are touched upon, in Chapter 2 and elsewhere. Although formal education was obviously important, it affected the lives of only a minority of adolescents throughout the period. Formal

education has also been covered extensively by other historians. See K. Charlton, *Education in Renaissance England* (1965); J. Simon, *Education and Society in Tudor England* (Cambridge, 1967); R. O'Day, *Education and Society 1500–1800* (1982).

33. For sociological definitions of 'adolescence' as the early teens, followed by 'youth', which is considered to begin somewhere between the ages of 14 and 19 and to continue until about 25 years of age, see R.G. Braungart, 'Youth movements', in J. Adelson (ed.), *Handbook of Adolescent Psychology* (New York, 1980), 561.

1 Images of Youth

1. William Shakespeare, *As You Like It*, II, vii.

2. J.A. Burrow, *The Ages of Man: A Study in Medieval Writing and Thought* (Oxford, 1986), 5–54, esp. 51–3.

3. Ibid. For a discussion of Renaissance astrology and the qualities associated with each planet, see also W. Shumaker, *The Occult Sciences in the Renaissance: A Study in Intellectual Patterns* (Berkeley, 1972), 1–16, esp. 5–6.

4. For the variety and sources of these theories, see Burrow, *Ages of Man*, 1–94. And see also A. Burton, 'Looking forward from Ariès? Pictorial and material evidence for the history of childhood and family life', *Continuity and Change*, 4 (1989), 207–8. For Ariès's discussion of the seven-ages theme, see P. Ariès, *Centuries of Childhood: A Social History of Family Life*, trans. from the French by R. Baldick (New York, 1962), 15–32.

5. Sometimes authors referred quite freely to their sources. Examples are discussed in Burrow, *Ages of Man*, 50–51. Henry Cuffe, in *The Differences of the Ages of Man's Life* (1607), referred to the Pythagorean division of life into four, according to the four seasons; the Aristotelian division of three; and the astrological division of life into seven ages, each corresponding to a planet. An anonymous author referred to Isidore of Seville and his divison of human life into six ages: *The Office of Christian Parents* (Cambridge, 1616), 43. Cuffe's discussion of these various schemes is on pp. 113–21.

6. Cuffe, *Differences of the Ages*, 118–21; *Office of Christian Parents*, 43–4. For definitions of 'adolescentia' and 'juventus' in various medieval texts, see S. Shahar, *Childhood in the Middle Ages* (London and New York, 1990), 22, 27–31, 264–5, note 3.

Most contemporaries probably referred to children at 10 years as still 'children'; at 15 years as already 'youth', and in the early twenties they already thought of them as young adults. 'What hast thou gotten by the ten years thou hast lived, oh child of ten years old?' asked Daniel Williams in his appeal to his young readers, 'what hast thou improved by the fifteen years thou hast lived, oh youth of fifteen years old? yeu may no I as justly ask the young man of twenty, what hast thou done, what hast thou made of thy twenty years?' Daniel Williams, *The Vanity of Childhood and Youth* (1691), 74.

7. In so far as historians have discussed early modern Englishmen's attitudes towards youth, as distinct from family relations or attitudes towards children in general, their discussion has been overshadowed by this insularity in the sources, especially in didactic and theological writings. See S.R. Smith, 'Religion and the conception of youth in seventeenth-century England', *History of Childhood Quarterly*, 4 (1975), 493–516; S. Brigden, 'Youth and the English Reformation', *Past and Present*, 95 (1982), 37–8. For a broader perspective, see K. Thomas, 'Age and authority in early modern England',

Proceedings of the British Academy (1977), Vol. LXII, 205–48, esp. 207–8, 218.

8. Aristotle, *Rhetoric*, Book II, in Burrow, *Ages of Man*, Appendix, 192.

9. Ibid., 198.

10. *St Augustine's Confessions*, Books I and II, esp. Book I, chs X, XVI, XIX, Book II, chs I, II, IV. For medieval and especially Augustinian conceptions of childhood and adolescence, see Shahar, *Childhood in the Middle Ages*, 16–17.

11. For medieval attitudes to adolescent sins, see ibid., 16–17. For pre-Reformation preaching see J.W. Blench, *Preaching in England in the Fifteenth and Sixteenth Centuries* (Oxford, 1964), 232–5.

12. Vives, quoted in J. Simon, *Education and Society in Tudor England* (Cambridge, 1966), 117; S. Ozment, *When Fathers Ruled: Family Life in Reformation Europe* (Cambridge, Mass. 1983), 136–7; Thomas Elyot, *The Boke Named The Governour* (1531; Everyman edn, 1907), 19.

13. 'Daily experience tells us, that there is nothing more common than Drunkness, both among young and old, Masters and Servants': Nathaniel Crouch, *The Apprentice Companion* (1681), 79. See also Thomas Gataker, *Davids Instructor* (1620), 13.

14. William Fleetwood, *The Relative Duties of Parents, Husbands, Masters* (1705), 88.

15. John Dod and Robert Cleaver, *A Godly Forme of Household Government* (1630), V8.

16. Ibid., S8; Elyot, *The Boke Named The Governour*, 20.

17. 'The fittest, best, and safest place for the young bird is her nest, where the old ones will be providing well for it and watching carefully for it'. Thomas Cobbet, *A Fruitful and Usefull Discourse Touching the Honour due from Children to Parents* (1656), 33.

18. Dod and Cleaver, *Godly Form of Household*, Q7. Cobbet, *Fruitful and Usefull Discourse*, 75; A.W. Brink (ed.), *The Life of the Late Reverend Mr George Trosse* (Montreal and London, 1974), 57.

19. E. Morgan, *The Puritan Family* (New York, 1966), 93; Smith, 'Religion and the conception of youth', 498–500; P. Collinson, *The Birthpangs of Protestant England: Religious and Cultural Change in the Sixteenth and Seventeenth Centuries* (New York, 1988), 78.

20. Dod and Cleaver, *Godly Forme of Household*, S8; Williams, *Vanity of Childhood and Youth*, Preface.

21. John Bunyan, *Grace Abounding to the Chief of Sinners* (1688), 2–4. For other examples, see Smith, 'Religion and the conception of youth', 506.

22. Disney, *Some Remarkable Passages* (1692), 33; Trosse, *Life of*, 62–3. And see also Smith, 'Religion and the conception of youth', 499–500.

23. Disney, *Some Remarkable Passages* 16, 32–5; *The Journal of Richard Norwood*, 35–6; Trosse, *Life of*, 52, 59, 63.

24. For references to the vanities of youth see Williams, *Vanity of Childhood and Youth*, 72, and *passim*; Bunyan, *Grace Abounding*, 4; Oliver Heywood, *His Autobiography, Diaries, Anecdote and Event Books* (Brighouse, 1882), ed. J. Horsfall Turner, Vol. I, 153; Trosse, *Life of*, 52. For assumptions about the inconsiderateness of youth, see Mary Rich, Countess of Warwick, *Autobiography* (1848), ed. T.C. Croker (Percy Society, Vol. XXII), 17. For references to tale books and romances, Richard Baxter, *A Breviate of the Life of Margaret Baxter* (1681), A2, 4. See also M. Spufford, *Small Books and Pleasant Histories: Popular Fiction and its Readership in Seventeenth-Century England* (Cambridge, 1981), 233–4.

25. Rich, *Autobiography*, 4; Thomas Powell, *Tom of All Trades* (1631), 47.

26. Morgan, *Puritan Family*, 92–6; Stone, *The Family, Sex and Marriage in England 1500–1800* (New York, 1979), 125–6; Smith, 'Religion and the con-

ception of youth' 493–516, esp. 498–501; Houlbrooke, *English Family*, 140–2.

27. For a critique of the notion that Puritan moral guides expressed a new ideal of family life, see K. Davies, 'The sacred condition of equality – how original were Puritan doctrines of marriage?', *Social History*, 5 (1977), 563–80. For the suggestion that sixteenth-century theologians and pedagogues, Catholic or Reformed alike, spoke on the sins of the young in similar terms, see Brigden, 'Youth and the English Reformation', 38. It is also noteworthy that there was a marked resemblance between the portrayal of youthful sins in puritan autobiographies and in St Augustine's *Confessions*. Although it is difficult to know whether seventeenth-century autobiographers read the *Confessions*, their portrayal of sinful youth in spiritual autobiographies appears to have been modelled, to some extent, on it. For example, Richard Baxter's list of the sins he had committed in his adolescence included lies, games and plays, foolish chat, boldness to parents – all of which appear in the *Confessions* – as well as 'eating apples and pears', and going 'to other men's orchards and [stealing] their fruit', which may have been a reproduction of Chapter 4, Book II, where Augustine described 'how he robbed a Pear tree'. N.H. Keeble (ed.), *The Autobiography of Richard Baxter* (Everyman's Library, 1974), 5. See also Chapter 8, 185–6.

28. Shahar, *Childhood in the Middle Ages*, 18.

29. *Office of Christian Parents*, 43.

30. Walter Pringle, *The Memoirs of Walter Pringle* (Edinburgh, 1847), 2.

31. *Journal of Richard Norwood*, 6, 10; Samuel Burrowes, *Good Instructions for all Young Men and Maids* (1641), 5; Oliver Sansom, *An Account of Many Remarkable Passages of the Life of Oliver Sansom* (1710), 3.

32. For an analysis of the conception underlying the medieval biographies of the saints (the *Vitae Sanctorum* composed by Anglo-Saxon monks), see Burrow, *Ages of Man*, 95–7.

33. Disney, *Some Remarkable Passages*, 12–13.

34. W. Armistead (ed.), *The Journal of George Fox* (7th edn, 1852), Vol. I, 49–51.

35. *Journal of Richard Norwood*, 10. For other autobiographies that emphasise the spirituality of childhood and youth see Samuel Bownas, *An Account of the Life and Travels of Samuel Bownas* (4th edn, 1795), 2–3; William Dewsbury, *The First Birth*, in *The Discovery of the Great Enmity of the Serpent against the Seed of the Woman* (1655), 12–14; Alexander Reid, *Life of Alexander Reid, a Scottish Covenanter* (Manchester, 1822), 1–4.

36. Burrow, *Ages of Man*, 12–13.

37. Cuffe, *Differences of the Ages*, 115–21.

38. Quoted in Burrow, *Ages of Man*, 202.

39. Trosse, *Life of*, 52–3; Edmund Bolton, *The Citie's Advocate . . . whether Apprenticeship Extinguishes Gentry?* (1629), 38–9; N.H., *The Complete Tradesman* (1684), 74; Fleetwood, *Relative Duties of Parents*, 15.

40. Shahar, *Childhood in the Middle Ages*, 16.

41. N.H., *Complete Tradesman*, 74; Bolton, *Citie's Advocate*, 38–9; Williams, *Vanity of Childhood and Youth*, 23–6; Brigden, 'Youth and The English Reformation', 38.

42. Thomas Tryon, *A New Method of Educating Children* (1695), 83.

43. Quoted in Brigden, 'Youth and the English Reformation', 39–40.

44. 'I am much more sensible now how prone many young professors are to the spiritual pride and self-conceitedness, and unruliness and division, and so to prove the grief of their teachers, and firebrands in the Church': Keeble (ed.), *Autobiography of Richard Baxter*, 116.

45. For plays on the prodigal son theme, such as *Disobedient Child* by T. Ingelend (printed *c.* 1569), *Misogonus* (acted between 1568 and 1574

in Cambridge), Gascoigne's *Glasse of Governement* (1575), and others, see F.P. Wilson, *The English Drama 1485–1585* (Oxford, 1969), 96–101. For prodigal son plays in the late sixteenth century, see also L.C. Stevenson, *Praise and Paradox: Merchants and Craftsmen in Elizabethan Popular Literature* (Cambridge, 1984), 103–4.

46. For Protestant plays, see Collinson, *Birthpangs of Protestant England*, 105. For the prodigal son in ballads, woodcuts and story-painting, see T. Watt, *Cheap Print and Popular Piety 1550–1640* (Cambridge, 1991), 120, 202–10.

47. Josiah Woodward, *The Young Man's Monitor* (1706), 11.

48. Bunyan, *Grace Abounding, passim*; John Croker, *Brief Memoir of the Life of John Croker*, in J. Barclay, *A Select Series, Biographical, Narrative, Epistolary and Miscellaneous: Chiefly the Productions of Early Members of the Society of Friends* (1836), Vol. VI, 285–7.

49. *Journal of Richard Norwood*, 30–31. For the use of the prodigal son theme in sermons, see, for example, Woodward, *Young Man's Monitor*, 11.

50. Quoted in Wilson, *The English Drama*, 197, from the *Disobedient Child* (1569).

51. G.J. Schochet, 'Patriarchalism, politics, and mass attitudes in Stuart England', *Historical Journal*, 12 (1969), 413–41; G.J. Schochet, *Patriarchalism in Political Thought* (New York, 1975); Stone, *Family, Sex, and Marriage*, 109–13; K. Thomas, 'Age and authority', 207–10; D. Underdown, *Revel, Riot and Rebellion: Popular Politics and Culture in England 1603–1660* (Oxford, 1985), 9–11.

52. Samuel Clark, *Lives of Sundry Eminent Persons* (1683), 106.

53. Burrow, *Ages of Man*, 147–9.

54. *The Prodigal Son Converted; Or, The Young man return'd from his Rambles*, in W. Chappell (ed.), *The Roxburghe Ballads* (1871), Vol. IV, 48–50.

55. Williams, *Vanity of Childhood and Youth*, 7–8; Thomas Brooks, *Apples of Gold for Young Men and Women* (1657), 179.

56. Williams, *Vanity of Childhood and Youth*; Brooks, *Apples of Gold.*

57. For lenient attitudes towards youthful follies see also Chapter 8, 204–5.

58. *Office of Christian Parents*, 43–4.

59. Cuffe, *Differences of the Ages*, 114–21.

60. Burrow, *Ages of Man*, 51–2.

61. Disney, *Some Remarkable Passages*, 20.

62. Spufford, *Small Books*, 201–4.

63. Thomas Deloney, *The Honourable Prentice . . . The Famous History of Sir John Hawkwood: Sometime Prentice of London* (1616), 1.

64. Fretwell, *A Family History*, 201.

65. Chappell (ed.), *Roxburghe Ballads*, Vol. II, 27–9; Vol. IV, 24.

66. Williams, *Vanity of Childhood and Youth*, 92.

67. Keeble (ed.), *Autobiography of Richard Baxter*, 103–4.

68. Henry Burton, *The Narration of the Life of Henry Burton* (1643), 1. See also Elias Osborn, *A Brief Narrative of the Life, Labours and Sufferings of Elias Osborn* (1723), 18.

69. Shahar, *Childhood in the Middle Ages*, 19.

70. D. Bergeron, *English Civic Pageantry 1558–1642* (1971), 11–25.

71. For Elizabethan royal entries and Lord Mayor's shows see ibid., 11–65, 125–40; C. Geertz, 'Centers, kings and charisma: reflections on the symbolics of power', in C. Geertz, *Local Knowledge* (New York, 1983), 125–9. For the various meanings and symbols of the Corpus Christi processions and plays, see M. James, 'Ritual, drama and social body in the late medieval English town', *Past and Present*, 98 (1983), 3–29.

72. In the Lord Mayor's show in London in 1566, three young people also gave speeches in which they expressed a hope for the future good government of the city. 'Our Roe by sighte in government / Wee trust shall

Rule so well / That by his doinges suche may Learne as covet to excell.' Quoted in Bergeron, *English Civic Pageantry*, 18, 129.

73. B. Capp, 'English youth groups and the Pinder of Wakefield', *Past and Present*, 76 (1977), 127–33. Historians have also shown that young people themselves could act as the guardians of social morality by demonstrating, petitioning, ridiculing, and even using physical force against nonconformists – Quakers in particular – prostitutes, and other deviant groups. S.R. Smith, 'The London apprentices as seventeenth-century adolescents', *Past and Present*, 61 (1973), 149–61; 'Almost revolutionaries: the London apprentices during the Civil Wars' *Huntington Library Quarterly*, 42 (1979), 313–29, esp. 326–7; B. Reay, 'Popular hostility towards the Quakers in mid-seventeenth century England', *Social History*, 5 (1980), 387–407, esp. 404–6. See also Chapter 8, 203.

74. Ben Jonson, George Chapman, John Marston, *Eastward Hoe* (1605), ed. C.G. Petter (1973), 81–2.

75. Peter Burke, 'Popular culture in seventeenth-century London', *London Journal*, 3 (1977), 156–7; Spufford, *Small Books*, 244–51. For a discussion of the nature of 'thrift', and of the theme of 'poor boys who become wealthy overnight', in the plays and novels of Thomas Heywood and Thomas Deloney, see Stevenson, *Praise and Paradox*, 144–54.

76. For a detailed chronology of the expansion in the market for cheap print (ballads, pictures and chapbooks), see Watt, *Cheap Print and Popular Piety*.

77. Spufford, *Small Books*, 224–50; S.R. Smith, 'The ideal and reality: Apprentice–master relationships in seventeenth century London', *History of Education Quarterly*, 21 (1981), 449–59, esp. 455–7.

78. For discussions of such literature see W.Z. Laqueur, *Young Germany* (1962); R. Wohl, *The Generation of 1914* (Cambridge, Mass., 1979), 42–84.

79. *London's Glory: or, the History of the Famous and Valiant London Prentice* (1700), ch. 4; Spufford, *Small Books*, 224–37.

80. Chappell (ed.), *Roxburghe Ballads*, Vol. I, *passim*.

81. Spufford, *Small Books*, 64, 156–93, 165. For the origins of courtship chapbooks in the 1630s, see Watt, *Cheap Print and Popular Piety*, 294–5.

82. Ibid., 245.

83. Chappell (ed.), *Roxburghe Ballads*, Vol. I, 75–9.

84. Ibid., Vol. I, 208, 265; Vol. IV, 34.

85. Spufford, *Small Books*, 166–7.

86. Ben Jonson *et al.*, *Eastward Hoe*, 8; Smith, 'The ideal and reality', 456.

87. Deloney, *Honourable Prentice*, 2–3.

88. Spufford, *Small Books*, 45–82, esp. 50–75; Watt, *Cheap Print and Popular Piety*, 12–13; 294–5; 301; 323–4.

89. Spufford, *Small Books*, 45–82. See also Burke, 'Popular culture in seventeenth-century London', 143–62; B. Capp, 'Popular literature', in B. Reay (ed.), *Popular Culture in Seventeenth-Century England* (1985), 198–243; Watt, *Cheap Print and Popular Piety*, 13–14.

90. Quotations from Aristotle's *Rhetoric*, Bk. II, chs 12–14, in Burrow, *Ages of Man*, App., 191–4.

91. Ibid., 197–200.

92. 'Thus every day this boy of virtuous disposition advanced': so Alcuin described the early life of Saint Willibrord, 'so that he might transcend the tender years of his boyhood in the seriousness of his behaviour; and he became like an old man in wisdom'. Quoted in Burrow, *Ages of Man*, 99–100.

93. Ibid., 8–9, 107–9.

94. Elyot, *The Boke Named the Governour*, 40–41. According to Elyot, a child was dominated by the power of imagination and the inclination to hear 'things marvellous and exquisite, which hath in it the visage of some things incredible'. As he grew up, 'that reason in him is confirmed with

serious living and long experience', so he could be taught poetry and Greek tragedy, then the great orators, 'from whens an argument for the proof of any matter' could be learned, rhetoric, followed by cosmography, history, and finally, only when he reached the age of 17, philosophy. Assumptions about the late age required for a child to grasp and formulate philosophic arguments must have been very widespread. William Lilly was sent away in his youth to be instructed in Latin and Greek, and he also studied classical texts. In his autobiography, Lilly made a point of the fact that although he had been taught a difficult subject such as Hebrew grammar, his tutor 'never taught logic, but [he] would often say it was fit to be learned in the universities'. William Lilly, *Mr William Lilly's History of his Life and Times from the Year 1602 to 1681* (1715), 5.

95. In his autobiography Alexander Reid inveighed against those of his readers who might doubt his religious conversion in childhood, those 'who may imagine that this was a premature age for serious religious impression'. Richard Norwood also recalled his parental reaction to his fascination with scripture as 'childish'. *Life of Alexander Reid*, 3; *Journal of Richard Norwood*, 8. See also Thomas Melhuish, *An Account of the Early Part of Life and Convincement of* (1805), 7.

96. Edward Chamberlayne, *Anglia Notitia* (2nd edn, 1669), 458–60; F. Pollock and F.W. Maitland, *The History of English Law*, Vol. II, 437; Thomas, 'Age and authority', 224. For confirmation and first communion, see S.J. Wright, 'Confirmation, catechism and communion: the role of the young in the post-Reformation Church', in S.J. Wright (ed.), *Parish Church and People: Local Studies in Lay Religion 1350–1750* (1988), 203–27.

97. Josiah Woodward was critical of the belief that 'when young people arrived at the age of 15 or 16 years, they are fit to be left to their own conduct', a belief he admitted was quite common. Symon Patrick, later bishop of Ely, took it for granted that at the age of 17 he was fit to govern himself. He recorded in his autobiography that in 1644, when he began his university studies, he was 'between seventeen and eighteen years old, and had some discretion to govern myself'. Woodward, *Young Man's Monitor*, 11; *The Autobiography of Symon Patrick*, in the *Works of S.P., D.D. Sometime Bishop of Ely* (Oxford, 1858), Vol. IX, 414. For the medieval use of the term *annis discretionis*, denoting the age of seven years and upwards, see Shahar, *Childhood in the Middle Ages*, 24.

98. *Office of Christian Parents*, 139.

99. Bownas, *Account of Life and Travels*, 2–3; George Brysson, *Memoirs of George Brysson* (1825), 272; Elizabeth Stirredge, *Strength in Weakness Manifest* (1711), 11.

100. Mary Pennington, *Some Account of Circumstances in the Life of Mary Pennington* (1821), 11.

101. As in the story about the young lion who brought destruction upon himself, having disregarded the counsel of his 'aged' father. *An Historie Very Profitable and Delightful for a Youth to Reade and Meditate*, in J[ohn] B[rowne] Marchant, *The Marchants Avizo* (1589) ed. P. M'Grath (Cambridge, Mass., 1957), 57–9.

102. *Barlow's Journal* (1934), 19. Barlow thought that in his younger years, when he decided on a career at sea, this was based on ignorance of what it entailed, and that had he possessed the necessary experience, his decision would have been altered, and the conflict with his parents avoided.

103. Deloney, *Honourable Prentice*, 4–5.

104. It was also not unusual for contemporary observers to justify the statute on grounds that it contributed to the high quality of English products, for if a youth learnt his craft in the space of months or a year, all he

achieved was 'ignorance', as one author put it. S.W., *The Golden Fleece* (1656), in *English Wool Trade: Selected Tracts 1613–1715* (Farnborough, 1968), 75–6. See also Rappaport, *Worlds Within Worlds*, 324–5.

105. N.H., *Complete Tradesman*, 73–4.

106. Keeble (ed.), *Autobiography of Richard Baxter*, 103–19. Quotations from pages 104, 108, 114; italics in the original.

107. E.A. Wrigley and R.S. Schofield, *The Population History of England 1541–1871: A Reconstruction* (1981), 424, Table 10.1. For the importance of marriage in achieving adult status and in the prolongation of youth see also P. Laslett, 'Parental deprivation in the past', in Laslett, *Family Life and Illicit Love in Earlier Generations* (Cambridge, 1977), 163; Thomas, 'Age and authority', 225–6.

108. Caleb Trenchfield, *A Cap of Gray Hairs for Green Head, or, the Fathers Counsel to his Son, an Apprentice in London* (1688), 143.

109. G.E. Mingay, *The Gentry* (1976), 110–12.

110. Warwick, *Autobiography*, 5, 29.

111. *William Lilly's History of his Life*, 19–20.

112. *The Autobiography of William Stout*, 178–9.

113. Armistead (ed.), *Journal of George Fox*, 51.

114. *The Apprentice's Vade Mecum* (1734), 4.

115. *Memoirs of Walter Pringle*, 11.

116. Keeble (ed.), *Autobiography of Richard Baxter*, 108.

117. Burrow, *Ages of Man*, 173.

118. *Office of Christian Parents*, 136.

119. *Barlow's Journal*, 15.

2 *Early Lives: Separations and Work*

1. The first account of the history of child labour, O.J. Dunlop and R.D. Denman, *English Apprenticeship and Child Labour: A History* (New York, 1912), illustrates well the dominance of nineteenth-century perspectives in the history of child labour. The authors chronicle the evolution of child labour from medieval times through the early phase of industrialisation, focusing on the disintegration of guild control and the consequent exploitation of children in the big workshops and early factories. The centrality of the nineteenth-century perspective is also evident in I. Pinchbeck and M. Hewitt, *Children in English Society* (1971), 2 vols. For the importance of child labour in the historiography of early industrialisation and in the controversy over the consequences of industrialisation, see the comments and bibliography in M. Berg, *The Age of Manufactures 1700–1820* (1985), 19–20; 74–6; H. Cunningham, 'The employment and unemployment of children in England c. 1680–1851', *Past and Present*, 126 (1990), 115–16.

2. For assumptions about an early age of departure into service and apprenticeship, see especially P. Ariès, *Centuries of Childhood: A Social History of Family Life*, trans. from the French by R. Baldick (New York, 1962), 365–9. Ariès relied on a description, by now well known to historians, of an Italian traveller in England in 1500, which asserted that Englishmen sent their children to service and apprenticeship from as early as the ages of 7 and 8. For the major findings on the institution of service, see P. Laslett, 'Characteristics of the western family considered over time', in *Family Life and Illicit Love in Earlier Generations* (Cambridge, 1977), 12–49; J. Hajnal, 'Two kinds of preindustrial household formation systems' in R. Wall, J. Robin and P. Laslett (eds), *Family Forms in Historic Europe* (Cambridge, 1983),65–104; R. Wall, 'Leaving home and the process of household formation in preindustrial England', *Continuity and Change*, 2 (1987), 90–97, 77–101, esp. 90–91.

3. In the foregoing analysis, I have used 69 autobiographies whose

authors were born before 1700. In the section on child labour I have used 5 additional autobiographies whose authors were born in the eighteenth century; whenever this has been done I have noted the date in the text.

4. For the age structure of the population between 1541 and 1796, see E.A. Wrigley and R.S. Schofield, *The Population History of England 1541–1871. A Reconstruction* (1981), App. 3, 528–9. For the demographic structure and its impact on labour in general and child labour in particular, see D.C. Coleman, 'Labour in the English economy of the seventeenth century', *Economic History Review*, 2nd ser., 8 (1956), 280–95, esp. 284–8.

5. D.C. Coleman, 'Labour in the English economy', 123. For an emphasis on this aspect of the economy and its greater impact on children than adults, see Cunningham, 'Employment and unemployment of children', 125–50, esp. 116.

6. Thomas Carleton, *The Captives Complaint or the Prisoners Plea* (1688), quoted in M. Spufford, 'First steps in literacy: the reading and writing experiences of the humblest seventeenth-century spiritual autobiographiers', *Social History*, 4 (1979), 417–18; *The Autobiography of William Stout*, 70; *Forman's Autobiography*, in A.L. Rowse, *Simon Forman: Sex and Society in Shakespeare's Age* (1974), 271; Dewsbury, *The First Birth in The Discovery of the Great Enmity of the Serpent against the Seed of the Woman* (1655), 14; *Thomas Sheppard's Memoir of Himself* in A. Young, *Chronicles of the First Planters of the Colony of Massachusetts Bay* (Boston, 1846), 501.

7. For farming systems and the division into the highland and lowland zones, see J. Thirsk, 'The farming regions of England', in J. Thirsk (ed.), *The Agrarian History of England and Wales* (Cambridge, 1967), Vol. IV, *1500–1640*, 2–112; C.G.A. Clay, *Economic Expansion and Social Change: England 1500–1700* (Cambridge, 1984), Vol. I, 53–101, 55.

8. Clay, *Economic Expansion*, Vol. I, 56.

9. Thirsk, 'Farming techniques' in Thirsk (ed.), *Agrarian History*, 177–8.

10. Carleton, *Captives Complaint*; *Autobiography of William Stout*, 70; *Forman's Autobiography*, 271; Spufford, 'First steps', 425. In Hertfordshire, where corn was the major cereal crop, it was claimed in the early seventeenth century that male children were employed 'straining before ploughs in seed time'. Quoted in J. Thirsk, *Economic Policy and Projects* (Oxford, 1978), 110.

11. G.E. and K.R. Fussell, *The English Countryman* (1981), 36.

12. *Tusser's Hundreth Good Poyntes of Husbandrie* (1834; repr. of original edn of 1557), 9.

13. *Barlow's Journal*, 21; E. Robinson (ed.), *John Clare's Autobiographical Writings* (Oxford, 1986), 3.

14. For a description of the specific tasks allocated to children under 12 years of age during the harvest in a nineteenth-century Suffolk village, see G.E. Evans, *Ask the Fellows Who Cut the Hay* (1956), 89. For boys employed in 'outligging', or gathering after the mower, see H. Best, *Rural Economy in Yorkshire in 1641* (Durham, 1857), 48.

15. See Chapter 3, p. 74.

16. For the participation of boys and girls in gleaning, and its importance in the family economy of the poor in the eighteenth and nineteenth centuries, see P. King, 'Customary rights and women's earnings: the importance of gleaning to the rural labouring poor, 1750–1850', *Economic History Review*, 2nd ser., 44 (1991), 461–74. For earlier decades see King's comments on pp. 469–70.

17. Robinson (ed.), *John Clare's Autobiographical Writings*, 3; A. Everitt, 'Farm labourers', in Thirsk (ed.), *Agrarian History*, 431.

18. *Autobiography of William Stout*, 68; Carleton, *Captives Complaint*; *Forman's Autobiography*, 271; Robinson (ed.), *John Clare's Autobiographical Writings*, 56.

19. Richard Norwood remembered being sent 'on an errand two or three miles into the country' during his early childhood. *The Journal of Richard Norwood*, 10. John Jones began to assist his mother in her small shop – this was in the 1770s – 'at a very early age, in going to and fro to Monmouth, about six miles distance, for the necessaries required in her little way of business.' John was seven years old. John Jones, *Attempts in Verse, by John Jones, an Old Servant* (1831), 171.

20. For the importance of children in rural industry, especially in cloth manufacture, knitting, the stocking industry and lace-making, see Thirsk, *Economic Policy and Projects*, 45, 160; Clay, *Economic Expansion*, Vol. II, 31; J.T. Swain, *Industry before the Industrial Revolution: North-east Lancashire c. 1500–1640* (Chetham Society, 3rd ser., Vol. XXXII, Manchester, 1986), 111–12.

21. Houlbrooke pointed out that, in the Norwich census of the poor in 1570, over four-fifths of girls aged between 6 and 12 and living with parents, compared with less than a third of boys of the same ages, were working alongside their parents, who were textile workers for the most part. R. Houlbrooke, *The English Family*, 154. Based on J.F. Pound (ed.), *The Norwich Census of the Poor, 1570* (Norfolk Record Society, 40, 1971).

22. Thirsk, *Economic Policy and Projects*, 80.

23. *Autobiography of William Stout*, 68–9, 110–11. In his adult life, William Stout took under his guardianship a young orphaned girl, Margaret Johnson, whom he provided for in the space of two years, in the course of which he made sure she learnt to 'sawe, knit, and other necessary employ'.

24. A. Everitt, 'Farm labourers', 430.

25. Quoted in Thirsk, *Economic Policy and Projects*, 110.

26. Spufford, 'First steps', 414.

27. Thomas Tryon, *Some Memoirs of the Life of Mr Thomas Tryon* (1705), 12–13; Samuel Bownas, *An Account of the Life and Travels of Samuel Bownas* (4th edn, 1795); *Autobiography of William Stout*, 70.

28. John Jones began to assist his mother in her shop when he was 7 years old but only at age 10 did he begin to drive a plough. Jones, *Attempts in Verse*, 172. See also *Autobiography of William Stout*, 70; Spufford, 'First steps', 425.

29. Evans, *Ask the Fellows*, 89; see also Chapter 3, pp. 74–5.

30. Josiah Langdale, who was reared in a small village in the East Riding in the 1670s, was put to plough and keep horses and oxen at the age of nine, 'being a strong boy, of my years,' as he explained in his autobiography. His father had died some time earlier, and his labour and services were needed to help his widowed mother. Spufford, 'First steps', 425.

31. Robinson (ed.), *John Clare's Autobiographical Writings*, 3; *Barlow's Journal*, 15; *Autobiography of William Stout*, 70.

32. John Clare remembered how his parents despaired of his fondness 'for climbing trees after birds', but nevertheless they 'would not urge me to anything against my will so I lived on at home taking work as it fell'. Thomas Sheppard also recalled that after a period in which he was required to keep geese at a very early age, he was left free for quite a while and was allowed 'to sing and sport, as children do in those parts' (i.e. Northamptonshire). Robinson (ed.), *John Clare's Autobiographical Writings*, 56; *Thomas Sheppard's Memoir*, 501.

33. E.P. Thompson, *The Making of the English Working Class* (1966), 333; D. Vincent, *Bread, Knowledge and Freedom: A Study of Nineteenth-Century Working Class Autobiography* (1981), 75–6.

34. Swain, *Industry before the Industrial Revolution*, 111–12.

35. For the synchronisation between learning technical skills and physical

and social maturation among weavers in northern Ghana, see E. Goody, 'Daboya weavers: relations of production, dependence and reciprocity', in E.N. Goody (ed.), *From Craft to Industry: The Ethnography of Proto-Industrial Cloth Production* (Cambridge, 1982), 50–84, esp. 66–77.

36. J.H. Plumb, *England in the Eighteenth Century (1714–1815)*, (1950; Penguin edn, 1969), 87.

37. Spufford, 'First steps', 414–15; D. Levine, *Reproducing Families: the Political Economy of English Population History* (Cambridge, 1987), 111–15, esp. 112.

38. Tryon, *Some Memoirs*, 14.

39. 'Some days from the first months of fourteen-year-old Thomas Isham', in R. Houlbrooke (ed.), *English Family Life, 1576–1716* (Oxford, 1989), 165, 249. For the professionalism involved in hedging and ditching, see A.H. Smith, 'Labourers in late sixteenth-century England', 21.

40. Spufford, 'First steps', 425–6; Best, *Rural Economy in Yorkshire*, 133.

41. Thomas Hardy, *Tess of the D'Urbervilles* (1891; Penguin edn, 1978), 100.

42. Oliver Sansom, *An Account of Many Remarkable Passages of the Life of Oliver Sansom* (1710), 2.

43. Smith, 'Labourers in late sixteenth-century England', 22, and App. II, 37–42, where a list of names, occupations and wages for specialist labourers in the 1580s is given. In some cases craftsmen appear with two 'sons' or 'boys', and the wage differential indicates that one was a journeyman or an older boy, and the other was a younger trainee, aged about 13 or 14.

44. G. Mayhew, 'Life-cycle service and the family unit in early modern Rye', *Continuity and Change*, 6 (1991), 201–26; esp. 209–10, 213.

45. Based on an analysis of a sample of 1,501 apprentices bound in Bristol between 1600 and 1645, and whose fathers' occupations were recorded. BRO, Register of Apprentices, 04352(3)–(5).

46. J. Burnett, D. Vincent and D. Mayall (eds), *The Autobiography of the Working Class*, Vol. I. *1790–1900* (Brighton, 1984), 152–3.

47. Wrigley and Schofield, *Population History of England*, 207–10; Clay, *Economic Expansion*, Vol. I, 2–3.

48. P. Slack's findings on the poor in Warwick, Ipswich and Norwich shows that a quarter and more of the poor were under 10 years old, while in the population at large they constituted a fifth; for children in the age category 10 to 19, the reverse was true: they composed less than a fifth of the poor, while in the population at large their proportion was more than a quarter. P. Slack, *Poverty and Policy in Tudor and Stuart England* (1988), 78. For the critical effect of the life cycle on poverty, and for the argument that although children played a key part in the family economy their 'net contributions were ambiguous', and they were not necessarily thought of as 'economic assets', see T. Wales, 'Poverty, poor relief, and the life-cycle: some evidence from seventeenth-century Norfolk', in R.M. Smith (ed.), *Land, Kinship and Life-Cycle* (Cambridge, 1984), 351–404, esp. 364–75.

49. *Barlow's Journal*, 21; *Thomas Shepard's Memoir*, 501.

50. Tryon, *Some Memoirs*, 12. In the nineteenth century John Clare also described some agricultural tasks as a pleasant undertaking which involved not only working in the open air and the beautiful countryside, but also communal work and entertainment; so weeding he remembered as a 'delightfull employment, as the old womens memorys never faild of tales to smoothen our labour, for as every day came new Jiants, hobgobblins, and faireys'. Robinson (ed.), *John Clare's Autobiographical Writings*, 3.

51. Dewsbury, *First Birth*, 14.

52. Many agricultural jobs required working alone, and while they sometimes suited Clare's solitary disposition, as he himself described it, at

other times he had to find ways to 'divert melancholy', and on the whole it was 'irksome to a boy to be alone' when required to do agricultural tasks on his own. Robinson (ed.) *John Clare's Autobiographical Writings*, 7.

53. *Journal of Richard Norwood*, 10; Robinson (ed.), *John Clare's Autobiographical Writings*, 8. For his description of his emotional state when out in the forest to gather sticks and losing his way overnight, see also 33–4.

54. Thirsk, 'Farming techniques', 166, 177–8.

55. Robinson (ed.), *John Clare's Autobiographical Writings*, 3.

56. For the expansion of commercial farming and specialisation see Clay, *Economic Expansion*, Vol. I, 67–136. For the growth in the number of schools in this period, and the predominance of sons of the gentry and yeomanry in them, see R. O'Day, *Education and Society 1500–1800* (1985), 25–42.

57. The experience of William Stout was probably the most typical of children of yeomen farmers. When he reached his early teens he was taken to work in the fields, but his father, a Lancashire yeoman, employed on his estate not only his elder brothers and mother, but also agricultural servants and a housemaid. William himself was recruited to work 'especially in the spring and summer season', and he continued to attend school well into his teens. His younger brothers, both under 10, were not required to assist in the routines on the estate. *Autobiography of William Stout*, 70.

58. Clay, *Economic Expansion*, Vol. I, 126. For the variety of cropping schedules and examples of places where more intensive crop rotation occurred – alternating between barley, rye, a spring crop and fallowness; or winter corn and spring corn and fallowness, and so on – see Thirsk, 'Farming techniques', 177–8.

59. Slack, *Poverty and Policy*, 82.

60. Everitt, 'Farm labourers', 430, 436. In some estates of large landowners, ploughboys were employed as day labourers; their wages were lower than those of the ploughmen, and the type of soil on which they were employed was easier to plough. For evidence on the employment of 'harrowing boys', and payments given to hired labourers, both specialists and non-specialists, who also brought their boys (normally under 14 years old), see Smith, 'Labourers in late sixteenth-century England', App. II, 37–42; App. I, 389. For references to wages of boys and to boys spreading marl, see also E.C. Lodge (ed.), *The Account Book of a Kentish Estate 1616–1704* (1927), 134–7, 141, and *passim*.

61. These crops were cultivated on a local rather than a national, or even regional, scale, and they were widespread, especially in the corn-growing areas: in the environs of London, in Kent, Gloucestershire and Oxfordshire. Thirsk, *Economic Policy and Projects*; Clay, *Economic Expansion*, Vol. I, 126–37.

62. In the 1580s, 100 acres of woad cultivated by an Oxfordshire gentleman already provided work for 400 women and children. Thirsk, *Economic Policy and Projects*, 6.

63. For emphasis on the importance of child labour in the expanding rural industries see also H. Medick, 'The proto-industrial family economy: the structural function of household and family during the transition from peasant society to industrial capitalism', *Social History*, 1 (1976), 302, and Levine, *Reproducing Families*, 111–15. Historians diverge on whether this development constituted a distinct, 'proto-industrial' phase which made the Industrial Revolution possible, but they tend to agree, and emphasise, that the expansion of rural industries 'did entail much higher proportions of female and child labour'. For a summary and a critique of the theory of proto-industrialisation see Berg, *Age of Manufactures*, 77–91; 134–9: quotation on p. 136. For a more cau-

tious appraisal of the importance of child labour in industry before the Industrial Revolution, see Cunningham, 'Employment and unemployment of children', 121–2.

64. Clay, *Economic Expansion*, Vol. II, 46–50.

65. Swain, *Industry before the Industrial Revolution*, 170.

66. Thirsk, *Economic Policy and Projects*, 37.

67. Barlow's Journal, 15–16.

68. P. Laslett, 'Parental deprivation in the past: a note on orphans and stepparenthood in English history', in *Family Life and Illicit Love*, 162–5, and 162, note 4.

69. In a sample of 1,945 apprentices registered in Bristol between 1600 and 1645, 618 (31.8 per cent) had lost their fathers by the time they became apprentices. The numbers per decade were: between 1600 and 1604, 36.9 per cent of the apprentices were fatherless; between 1605 and 1609, 34.5 per cent; between 1610 and 1615, 33.3 per cent; between 1621 and 1625, 20.8 per cent; between 1626 and 1630, 28.4; 1631–35, 21.7; 1636–40, 32.6; and between 1641 and 1645, 31.9 per cent. BRO, Register of Apprentices, 1600–45, 04352(3)–(5).

70. A.L. Merson (ed.), *A Calendar of Southampton Apprenticeship Registers, 1609–1740* (Southampton Record ser., Vol. XII, Southampton, 1968), xxxiii.

71. Out of 74 autobiographers, 5 (6.75 per cent) recorded the loss of both parents by the time they had reached the age of 20.

72. For example, Benjamin Bangs had very little to say about his parents' economic standing, family resources or occupations. But he did specify where and when he was born; that his parents were 'reputable'; that he had eight brothers and sisters; and, the concluding detail summing it all up, that his father had died when he was still very young. Benjamin Bangs, *Memoirs of the Life* (1757), 7.

73. Elias Osborn, *A Brief Narrative of the Life, Labours and Sufferings of Elias Osborn* (1723), 16; Bownas, *Account of Life and Travels*, 2; *The Life of Mr Robert Blair, Minister of St Andrews, Containing his Autobiography from 1593 to 1636* (Edinburgh, 1848), 3; Bangs, *Memoirs of the Life*, 7.

74. Thomas Shepard's Memoir, 501; Bownas, *Account of Life and Travels*, 2.

75. *Life of Mr Robert Blair*, 4; *The Life, Experience, and Correspondence of William Bowcock, the Lincolnshire Drillman*, (1851), 7–8; Evans, *An Eccho to the Voice*, 4–6.

76. *Life of Mr Robert Blair*, 4.

77. *Thomas Shepard's Memoir*, 501.

78. Evans, *An Eccho to the Voice*, 5–6.

79. *The Life of Adam Martindale*, 17–19.

80. J.O. Halliwell (ed.), *The Autobiography and Correspondence of Sir Simonds D'Ewes* (1845), Vol. I, 40, 110.

81. *Autobiography of William Stout*, 71–4.

82. For the effect of parental death on the timing of apprenticeship, see also Rappaport, *Worlds Within Worlds*, 295–6 and note 15.

83. Bownas, *Account of Life and Travels*, 7.

84. Ibid., 1; Thomas Chubb, *The Author's Account of Himself*, in *The Posthumous Works of Mr Thomas Chubb* (1748), Vol. I, ii–iii.

85. P. Laslett, 'Clayworth and Cogenhoe', in *Family Life and Illicit Love*, 58, and note 17; Wrigley and Schofield, *Population History of England*, 258–9, and note 101; Houlbrooke, *English Family*, 211–15.

86. *Dr Wallis's Account of Some Passages of His Own Life*, in Thomas Hearne (ed.), *Peter Langtoft's Chronicle* (1725), Vol. I, cxliii.

87. *Thomas Sheppard's Memoir*, 501; Lodowick Muggleton, *The Acts of the Witnesses of the Spirit* (1699), 6; Evans, *An Eccho to the Voice*, 6.

88. For evidence on the behaviour of step-parents as indicated in testamentary litigation, see Houlbrooke, *English Family*, 217–18.

89. For tenuous relations of children with their step-parents, see also McIntosh, *A Community Transformed*, 50. For examples of sons who cooperated with stepfathers and eventually followed their trades and occupations, see Mayhew, 'Life-cycle service and the family unit', 216.

90. Halliwell (ed.), *Autobiography of... D'Ewes* 1–105; *Thomas Shepard's Memoir*, 500–1; Sansom, *An Account*, 2; Mary Rich, Countess of Warwick, *Autobiography* (1848), ed. T.C. Croker (Percy Society, Vol. 22), 1–2.

91. L. Stone, 'The educational revolution in England, 1560–1640', *Past and Present*, 28 (1964), 40–47; K. Wrightson, *English Society 1580–1680* (1982), 184–91; O'Day, *Education and Society*, 25–42, esp. 35–7, 40–2.

92. Matthew Robinson, the son of a Yorkshire gentleman and a barrister in the 1630s, was sent 'abroad when not seven years old to a choice grammar-school'. Young Robinson so excelled in his studies that when he was about 10 years old his father sent him 'to an eminent school the better to fit him for the university'. J.E.B. Mayor (ed.), *Autobiography of Matthew Robinson* (Cambridge, 1856), 6.

93. O'Day, *Education and Society*, 32–3.

94. Ibid., 31.

95. Stone, 'Educational revolution', 44.

96. When Phineas Pett was sent to the free school in Rochester, located about 20 miles from his place of residence in Deptford Strond in Kent, he was boarded there with Mr Webb for the space of a year. Anthony Wood's three brothers sojourned in the house of a vicar, a kinsman, in Thame, while they went to the local school there. Thame, a small market town, was located about 10 miles away from Oxford, where the Woods lived. W.G. Perrin (ed.), *The Autobiography of Phineas Pett* (1918), 1–2; *Life of Mr Anthony A. Wood* (Oxford, 1891–1900), Vol. I, 451.

97. In his diary, John Greene recorded the day when he 'carried [his] eldest son John to school'. Greene lived in London and the school was in the parish of Hadleigh. Young John – he was then 9 years old – was boarded with the schoolteacher. *The Diary of John Greene*, in Houlbrooke (ed.), *English Family Life*, 150.

98. *Life of Adam Martindale*, 11.

99. Fretwell, *A Family History*, 185.

100. Ibid., 185–8.

101. Ibid., 187.

102. This appears to have been the reason why Oliver Heywood, who resided near Halifax, sent his sons to Morley rather then to the Halifax school. In 1669 he commented in his diary that his sons 'having not made their Latin in expectation to go to Halifax', decided to remain at home and avoid going to school. About two years later we find him going to Morley, about 20 miles from Halifax, 'where [my sons] go to school to Mr David Noble, [and] are tabled at Thomas Dawson's.' For excerpts from the diary, see Houlbrooke (ed.), *English Family Life*, 163.

103. D. Cressy, 'A drudgery of schoolmasters: the teaching profession in Elizabethan and Stuart England', in W. Prest (ed.), *The Professions in Early Modern England* (1987), 131–2; O'Day, *Education and Society*, 34–5.

104. Spufford, 'First steps', 434–5.

105. Sansom, *An Account*, 2.

106. *Thomas Shepard's Memoir*, 500–1.

107. *Life of Mr Anthony Wood*, 450–51.

108. For flight from towns during times of plague, see P. Slack, *The Impact of Plague in Tudor and Stuart England* (1985), 166–9. Sometimes there were people in authority who chose not to escape, but under such circumstances they would have made some effort to send their own children away. Slack mentions the example of the rector, William Mompesson, who remained to take care of his villagers

in Derbyshire during the plague of 1665–6. While clearly placing himself at great risk, Mompesson avoided endangering the lives of his children, whom he had sent away early when the plague broke out. Ibid., 20–21.

109. Ibid., 79–110; Wrigley and Schofield, *Population History of England*, App. 10, 645–91, esp. 649–56.

110. Wrigley and Schofield, *Population History of England*, 108.

111. R.S. Schofield and E.A. Wrigley, 'Infant and child mortality in England in the late Tudor and early Stuart period', in C. Webster (ed.), *Health, Medicine and Mortality in the Sixteenth Century* (Cambridge, 1979), 61–95; Slack, *Impact of Plague*, 183.

112. Warwick, *Autobiography*, 1–2.

113. *Thomas Shepard's Memoir*, 501–2. Laslett's findings for resident orphans in 19 English communities in the period 1599–1811 shows only 1 out of 1,383 orphans living with a stepfather or stepmother; or 1 out of 276 orphans whose parents remarried living with a stepfather or stepmother alone. There were 5 orphans living with two steparents, but 46 (3.3 per cent of all orphans) living with persons other than parents or step-parents. Laslett, 'Parental deprivation', 164. The account by William Stout of a girl he took under his care illustrates this well. When his friend and neighbour died, his wife was left with a son of her own and two step-children, the children of the husband's first wife. William Stout 'took the children by the first wife from their stepmother and borded them out [with himself] and kept them to the schoole'. The autobiography leaves the impression that the stepmother was unable to continue providing for the stepchildren, for she had her own child to support. *Autobiography of William Stout*, 110–11. Houlbrooke is also of the opinion that 'the experience of living with step-parents was comparatively rare'. Houlbrooke, *English Family*, 217.

114. Muggleton, *Acts of the Witnesses*, 5–6.

115. Evans. *An Eccho to the Voice*, 4–7, 10–11.

116. Joseph Oxley, *Joseph's Offering to his Children*, in J. Barclay (ed.), *A Select Series . . . of Early Members of the Society of Friends* (1836), Vol. V, 205–8.

117. Thomas Hardy, *Memoir of Thomas Hardy* (1832), 2.

118. William Edmundson, *A Journal of the Life of William Edmundson* (Dublin, 1820), 41–2. For other autobiographers whose fathers died when they were very young and whose mothers were poor, but who were nevertheless placed as apprentices only when they reached about 13 years old, see Bownas, *Account of Life and Travels*, 1; Bangs, *Memoirs of the Life*, 7, 11. Simon Forman, whose mother appears to have wanted her son to leave home following the death of her husband – she 'grudged at his being at home, and . . . suffered him to go to school not longer', as he remembered later on – began to work as an agricultural labourer, and only a few years later left home. Simon was 11 years old when his father died in 1563, and he was 14 when he moved to Salisbury and apprenticed himself to a hosier. *Forman's Autobiography*, 271.

119. P. Sharpe, 'Poor children as apprentices in Colyton, 1598–1830', *Continuity and Change*, 6 (1991), 255.

120. For the low age of parish apprentices in Colyton, compared with other places where children were apprenticed at 13 or 14, see the comments and bibliography in Ibid., 255, 268, note 16.

121. Houlbrooke, *English Family*, 154.

122. As E.M. Hampson noted many years ago, 'the extreme youth and sometimes the weakly constitution of the children' led even the most energetic justice to place children above 10 years, and not younger. Quoted in Pinchbeck and Hewitt,

Children in English Society, 240–41. See also Houlbrooke, *English Family*, 155.

123. BRO, Vestry Minutes, St James, P/St J/V/1–2, 20 June, 1676, fol. 146.

124. As in the case of John Legg of the parish of St John Baptist in Bristol, whose sons were described by the churchwardens as 'now lying on the charge of the parish'. Vestry Minutes, St John Baptist P/St B/V/1–2, 21 December 1696.

125. Out of 95 apprentices bound by the parishes in Southampton between 1609 and 1680, 76 (80 per cent) were aged 10 and above, and 59 (62 per cent) were aged 12 and above. Calculations are based on Merson, *Calendar of Southampton Apprenticeship Registers*, lviii.

126. BRO, Churchwardens' Accounts, Ca 13(2) II, 2 May.

127. For examples of orders for the 'placing out poor children and for the release of sick people', see Temple parish, Bristol, Overseers of the Poor, Da1–3, 1633–34; 1659; 1670; 1673. For payments for the 'placing out' and 'keeping of children', where the names of the children and those paid for their maintenance are recorded, see Churchwardens' Accounts, Temple parish, Ca 13–21, 1582–1668, *passim*; Churchwardens' Accounts, St John Baptist, p/St JB/chw/3/a–b, *passim*; Churchwardens' Accounts, St James, p/St J/chw/1/a–b, 1617, 1621, 1625, 1635, and *passim*.

128. Wales, 'Poverty, poor relief, and the life-cycle', 385, note 66.

129. Laslett, 'Parental deprivation', 164–6; R. Wall, 'The household: demographic and economic change in England, 1650–1970', in R. Wall, J. Robin and P. Laslett (eds), *Family Forms in Historic Europe* (Cambridge, 1983), 498.

130. For the contention that 'temporary movements between households' were likely to have escaped being registered, see R. Wall, 'Leaving home and the process of household formation in pre-industrial England', *Continuity and Change*, 2 (1987), 81, where he also suggested that 'people were credited to their household of usual residence and not to their household of actual residence on a particular night'.

131. For the suggestion that the custom of fostering out, or the 'exporting' of children, was related to lack of affection, see the controversial account of Lawrence Stone, who also assumed that such separations were typical of the adolescent phase, when children departed for service in their mid-teens, rather than earlier. Stone, *Family, Sex and Marriage*, 84.

132. James Fretwell the father, whose son had to walk to school a great distance every day, decided to board him nearer school only after the son had returned home 'weeping'; and he boarded him only on weekdays, so that James came home at weekends and during holidays. Fretwell, *A Family History*, 185.

133. *Autobiography of William Stout*, 76.

134. Bewley, *Narrative of the Christian Experiences*, 7–8; Edmundson, *A Journal of the Life*, 41–2.

135. Of 43 autobiographies in which enough information is provided, 11 entered the university, and 32 were apprentices.

136. For ages of London apprentices, see Rappaport, *Worlds Within Worlds*, 295–6. For ages of entry into agricultural service, see Kussmaul, *Servants in Husbandry*, 70–73. For age of departure in the population at large, see P. Laslett and R. Wall, (eds), *Household and Family in Past Time* (Cambridge, 1972), 57–8; R. Wall, 'The age at leaving home', *Journal of Family History*, 3 (1978), 181–201; McIntosh, 'Servants and the household unit', 11–12. For variation along occupational groups and by sex, see Wall, 'Leaving home and the process of household formation', 90–97. For the suggestion that the age of entering service dropped somewhat – from an average age of 15 to around 13–14 – between the late sixteenth and the late seventeenth centuries, see McIntosh,

'Servants and the household unit', 11, note 4.
137. See Introduction, 1.
138. Bangs, *Memoirs of the Life*, 12.
139. Richard Davies, *An Account of the Convincement, Exercises, Services, and Travels of that Ancient Servant of the Lord, Richard Davies* (1794), 2–3.
140. A.W. Brink (ed.), *The Life of the Late Reverend Mr George Trosse* (Montreal and London, 1974), 49; Disney, *Some Remarkable Passages* (1692), 29; John Shaw, *The Life of Master John Shaw*, in *Yorkshire Diaries and Autobiographies in the Seventeenth and Eighteenth Centuries* (Surtees Society, Vol. 65, 1877), 123; *Life of Adam Martindale*, 24.
141. *Autobiography of William Stout*, 111.
142. See Chapter 6, 151.
143. *Barlow's Journal*, 16.
144. Ibid., 19.
145. Disney, *Some Remarkable Passages*, 29; Bangs, *Memoirs of the Life*, 11.
146. For an extensive review of the findings of sociological research of parent–child relations, see Boyd C. Rollins and Darwin L. Thomas, 'Parental support, power, and control techniques in the socialization of children', in R.B. Wesley, R. Hill, F.I. Nye and I.L. Reiss (eds), *Contemporary Theories about the Family* (New York, 1979), Vol. I, 317–64.
147. *Journal of Richard Norwood*, 15, 31.
148. Boyd *et al.*, 'Parental Support', 322.
149. See also Chapter 1, 30.
150. *Barlow's Journal*, 16; Coxere, *Adventures by Sea*, 5.
151. *Barlow's Journal*, 15.
152. John Whitting, *Persecution Expos'd* (1715), 4.
153. Fretwell, *A Family History*, 185–97.

3 The Mobility of Rural Youth

1. Kussmaul, *Servants in Husbandry*, 11; McIntosh, 'Servants and the household unit', 13–15; R.M. Smith, 'Some issues concerning families and their property in rural England 1250–1800', in R.M. Smith (ed.), *Land, Kinship and Life-Cycle*, 34.
2. R. Wall, 'Real property, marriage and children: the evidence from four pre-industrial communities', in Smith (ed.), *Land, Kinship and Life-Cycle*, 443–79, esp. 457–9; Wall, 'Leaving home and the process of household formation in pre-industrial England', *Continuity and Change*, 2 (1987), 91–2. For the social background of servants, see also Kussmaul, *Servants in Husbandry*, 76. For variations in numbers of servants by occupation, see McIntosh, 'Servants and the household unit', 14–15.
3. Kussmaul, *Servants in Husbandry*, 51–4, 57.
4. McIntosh, 'Servants and the household unit', 15–16.
5. See Chapters 7–9.
6. Kussmaul, *Servants in Husbandry*, 135.
7. A.H. Smith, 'Labourers in late sixteenth-century England: a case study from north Norfolk [Part I]', *Continuity and Change*, 4 (1989), 14–15; McIntosh, 'Servants and the household unit', 12.
8. Smith, 'Labourers in late sixteenth-century England [Part I]', 11–15. For the lack of rigid distinctions between unmarried servants and married labourers in the eighteenth century, see K. Snell, *Annals of the Labouring Poor: Social Change and Agrarian England, 1660–1900* (Cambridge, 1985), 83. For the coexistence of labour with living-in service throughout the period, see also Smith, 'Some issues concerning families', 36.
9. A.H. Smith, 'Labourers in late sixteenth-century England: a case study from north Norfolk [Part II]', *Continuity and Change*, 4 (1989), 370.
10. Kussmaul, *Servants in Husbandry*, 22; Smith, 'Some issues concerning families', 35–6. For a regional study which suggests the relative absence of labourers in pastoral areas, see J.T. Swain, *Industry before the*

Industrial Revolution: North-east Lancashire c. 1500–1640 (Chetham Society, 3rd ser., Vol. XXXII, Manchester, 1986), 50.

11. Kussmaul, *Servants in Husbandry*, 100. For a similar situation in the second half of the eighteenth century, and for the link between rising prices and advantages of labour, see also Snell, *Annals of the Labouring Poor*, 84–7, esp. 86.

12. G.E. Fussell (ed.), *Robert Loder's Farm Accounts* (Camden Society, 3rd ser., Vol. LIII, 1936), 72; Kussmaul, *Servants in Husbandry*, 100–1. For the farming system in the part of Berkshire where Loder lived, see J. Thirsk, 'The farming regions of England', in J. Thirsk (ed.), *The Agrarian History of England and Wales* (Cambridge, 1967), Vol. IV, *1500–1640*, 66.

13. As we shall see in Chapter 9, annual servants and even apprentices occasionally sent or brought home their wages as well. For wages of annual servants paid during the annual term, see Kussmaul, *Servants in Husbandry*, 38, 40.

14. Smith, 'Labourers in late sixteenth-century England [Part I]', App. II, 37–42, Part II, App. I, 382–8, and 389, an explanatory note. For labourers' wages, see Part I, 27, and for his analysis of the working experience of sons and daughters, see Part II, 370.

15. H. Hendrick, *Images of Youth: Age, Class, and the Male Youth Problem, 1880–1920* (Oxford, 1990), 120–1.

16. *Barlow's Journal*, 20–1.

17. Kussmaul, *Servants in Husbandry*, 90.

18. Ibid., 34–5; Smith, 'Labourers in late sixteenth-century England', 16–17.

19. J.J. Bagley (ed.), *The Great Diurnal of Nicholas Blundell of Little Crosby, Lancashire. Vol. I. 1702–1711* (Record Society of Lancashire and Cheshire, 1968), *passim*.

20. For an account based on oral history of village life in the nineteenth century, in which the difficulties and skill involved in learning to thresh properly were recalled, see G.E. Evans, *Ask the Fellows Who Cut the Hay* (1956), 94.

21. On the estate of Nathaniel Bacon, ploughs were taken to the blacksmith for repair, but the routine of work included taking care of ploughs and horses, 'an unremitting job from dawn to dask'. Smith, 'Labourers in late sixteenth-century England', 17. And see also Gervase Markham, *Farewell to Husbandry* (1631), 144–5.

22. A few of Nathaniel Bacon's mowers came from the village of Stiffkey in Norfolk near his estate or from the neighbouring parishes, but some may have come from as far away as Kent. Henry Best was likewise ready to look for skilled and strong mowers in a market some 15 miles away. Smith, 'Labourers in late sixteenth-century England', 18. For Henry Best, and for a discussion of mowing and the skills it required, see M. Roberts, 'Sickles and scythes: women's work and men's work at harvest time', *History Workshop Journal*, 7 (1979), 3–28, esp. 8–13.

23. For a range of diseases and cures of cattle, horses and sheep, see Gervase Markham, *Cheape and Good Husbandry for the Well-Ordering of all Beasts and Fowles* (1657), 48–9, 73–5; 90–92.

24. Smith, 'Labourers in late sixteenth-century England', 20.

25. G.E. and K.R. Fussell, *The English Countryman: His Life and Work A.D. 1500–1900* (1955), 50.

26. 'The shepherd was one of the most skilled and respected members of the old village community. He worked by himself; made his own decisions . . . a farmer would have to be sure of his man before entrusting to him a flock of sheep whose welfare depended solely on the skill and trustworthiness of the shepherd'. Evans, *Ask the Fellows*, 28.

27. The lowest age of 15 appears to have been lower than the lowest age at which farm servants received adult

wages in mid-twentieth-century Europe. Kussmaul, *Servants in Husbandry*, 38–9, and 182, note 40.

28. *The Autobiography of William Stout*, 70.

29. Evans, *Ask the Fellows*, 89–90.

30. Fussell (ed.), *Robert Loder's Farm Accounts*, 90.

31. Roberts, 'Sickles and scythes', 26, note 48.

32. H. Best, *Rural Economy in Yorkshire in 1641* (Durham, 1857), 133.

33. Ibid., 136.

34. Smith, 'Labourers in late sixteenth-century England [Part I]', 19–21. That the responsibilities involved in the management of flocks were not normally given to children before they reached their mid-teens at the least is evident from Thomas Tryon's autobiography. When Tryon was 12, having worked for a neighbouring shepherd for two years, he asked his father to buy a small flock for him to manage on his own. His father, a tiler, refused, arguing that his son was 'too young and inexperienced'. Thomas Tryon, *Some Memoirs of the Life of Mr. Thomas Tryon* (1705), 12–13. For large sheep flocks and cattle herds on some of the largest farms in the north, see Thirsk, 'The farming regions', 26–7. For differences in sizes of herds owned by gentlemen and husbandmen, see Swain, *Industry before the Industrial Revolution*, 44. See also C.G.A. Clay, *Economic Expansion and Social Change: England 1500–1700* (Cambridge, 1984), Vol. I, 116–25.

35. Kussmaul, *Servants in Husbandry*, 14.

36. Best, *Rural Economy in Yorkshire*, 134.

37. Evans, *Ask the Fellows*, 23–7.

38. Ibid., 27.

39. In the eighteenth century, Anthony Errington, of Whickham in Durham, began to work at the colliery; he was 14 years old and quite fearful of the pit. But having been accompanied by his father and brother, 'in a short time the fear of the pit left me'. D. Levine and K. Wrightson, *The Making of an Industrial Society: Wickham 1560–1765* (Oxford, 1991), 328.

40. Johnson, *The Life and Times of William Johnson*, 9. This was in the 1780s, when William Johnson was a boy.

41. Roberts, 'Sickles and scythes', 8–10.

42. Kussmaul, *Servants in Husbandry*, 37; Smith, 'Labourers in late sixteenth-century England [Part I]', 28–9.

43. Roberts, 'Sickles and scythes', 18–19.

44. *Autobiography of William Stout*, 76.

45. A. Everitt, 'The marketing of agricultural produce', in Thirsk, *Agrarian History*, 466–90; P. Clark and P. Slack, *English Towns in Transition 1500–1700* (Oxford, 1976), 8–9; Clay, *Economic Expansion*, Vol. II, 165–73.

46. For Gloucestershire, see ibid., 172. For the occupational structure of sixteenth-century Tewkesbury, see R.B. Pugh (ed.), *Victoria County History of Gloucestershire* (1972), Vol. X, 140–3.

47. C.B. Phillips, 'Town and country: economic change in Kendal *c.* 1550–1700', in P. Clark (ed.), *The Transformation of English Provincial Towns 1600–1800* (1984), 99–132, esp. 104–5; J. Patten, 'Patterns of migration and movement of labour to three pre-industrial East Anglian towns', *Journal of Historical Geography*, 2 (1976), 134–7.

48. Barlow's Journal, 18.

49. Clay, *Economic Expansion*, Vol. II, 101.

50. Ibid., 100.

51. McIntosh, 'Servants and the household unit', 10, Table 2.

52. Based on the evidence on parental occupations of a sample of Bedminster youth who became apprentices in Bristol between 1600 and 1645.

53. McIntosh, 'Servants and the household unit', 13, and note 10.

54. For further information on

migration patterns and distances travelled by apprentices, see Chapter 4, 95.

55. D. Hollis (ed.), *Calendar of the Bristol Apprentice Book 1532–1542* (Bristol Record Society publications, Vol. XIV, Bristol, 1948).

56. Snell, *Annals of the Labouring Poor*, 232–6.

57. Benjamin Bangs, *Memoirs of the Life* (1757), 11; Samuel Bownas, *An Account of the Life and Travels of Samuel Bownas* (4th edn, 1795), 1–2.

58. N. Goose, 'Household size and structure in early Stuart Cambridge', *Social History*, 5 (1980), 373–4; *Barlow's Journal*, 17–18.

59. McIntosh, *A Community Transformed*, 58–9.

60. *Barlow's Journal*, 16–17; Bownas, *Account of Life and Travels*, 1–2; Richard Davies, *An Account of the Convincement, Exercises, Services, and Travels of that Ancient Servant of the Lord, Richard Davies* (1794), 3; Evans, *An Eccho to the Voice*, 7.

61. Evans, *An Eccho to the Voice*, 6–7, 11.

62. Snell, *Annals of the Labouring Poor*, 279–82; B. Hill, *Women, Work, and Sexual Politics in Eighteenth-Century England* (Oxford, 1989), 92–5. For an examination of the skills obtained by women in towns, and some comparison also with the countryside, see Chapter 6.

63. For an abstract of Huntington's autobiography, see J. Burnett, D. Vincent and D. Mayall (eds), *The Autobiography of the Working Class*, Vol. I, *1790–1900* (Brighton, 1984), 164–5.

4 *Urban Apprentices: Travel and Adjustments*

1. For the calculation of proportions of apprentices in mid-sixteenth-century London, see Rappaport, *Worlds Within Worlds*, 232–3. For estimates on the total number and proportions of London apprentices in the early seventeenth century see V. Brodsky Elliott, 'Mobility and marriage in pre-industrial England' (PhD dissertation, University of Cambridge, 1978), 214–15. For late seventeenth-century London, see M.J. Kitch, 'Capital and kingdom: migration to later Stuart London', in A.L. Beier and R. Finlay (eds), *London 1500–1700: The Making of the Metropolis* (1986), 225–6. In calculating the proportions of apprentices in Bristol at any given time, I have followed the method of Rappaport, who took account of the rate of attrition of apprentices through death and emigration. In 1600, 262 apprentices were enrolled in Bristol; seven years later, 57 were registered freemen, a loss of 205 apprentices, or of 26.3 apprentices every year (205: 7.8, the mean length of contracts in the 1600s). Following the same calculation for each consecutive year, between 1600 and 1607 there were 1,381 apprentices, or 11.5 per cent of the 12,000 inhabitants of Bristol at the time. Similar calculations for the late seventeenth century show that the proportion of apprentices dropped to about 8 per cent, a smaller drop than that observed in London.

In other provincial towns the figures are more difficult to obtain, because no systematic registration of apprentices survived, but a rough estimate can be gained through freemen records. In York, between 1590 and 1600, a total of 697 freemen were registered, or 69.7 a year, a rate somewhat higher than in Bristol in the early 1600s. Assuming that the proportion of those among them who had been apprentices was similar to that in Bristol, and since the population of York in 1600 was nearly that of Bristol, then the proportions of apprentices in the town might have been higher than in Bristol. For freemen registrations, see D.M. Palliser, *Tudor York* (Oxford, 1979), 156. For examples of the proportions of apprentices in smaller towns, see

Goose, 'Household size and structure in early Stuart Cambridge', *Social History*, 5 (1980), 374, where the proportion of apprentices in the population was 5.7. For the proportions of apprentices among adult male citizens in London, see Rappaport, *Worlds Within Worlds*, 233.

2. O.J. Dunlop and R.D. Denman, *English Apprenticeship and Child Labour: A History* (New York, 1912).

3. Ibid., 19–20.

4. P. Laslett, *The World We Have Lost* (New York, 1965), 3; G. Schochet, 'Patriarchalism, politics, and mass attitudes in Stuart England', *Historical Journal*, 12 (1969), 413–41; E. Morgan, *The Puritan Family* (New York, 1966); L. Stone, *The Family, Sex and Marriage*, 109–27; K. Thomas, 'Age and authority' in early modern England', *Proceedings of the British Academy* (1977), Vol. LXII, 214–15; J.R. Gillis, *Youth and History* (New York and London, 1981), 22.

5. 'Most apprentices were young men in their twenties but they lived as dependents in their masters' households, occupying a position not unlike that of a child.' Since their labour belonged to their masters, 'the transition to adulthood began for these men when they finished their apprenticeship terms', and when they departed from 'households headed by masters *in loco parentum*'. Rappaport, *Worlds Within Worlds*, 236, 327. For assumptions about the passive role of apprentices in the past, see also K. Snell, *Annals of the Labouring Poor: Social Change and Agrarian England, 1660–1900* (Cambridge, 1985), 261.

Some historians have also described apprentices as possessing solidarity and an adolescent subculture, characterised by the search for identity and a riotous style of living. S.R. Smith, 'The London apprentices as seventeenth-century adolescents', *Past and Present*, 61 (1973), 149–61. For a discussion of this aspect of the culture of youth, see Chapter 8.

6. For the number of migrant apprentices in London, see Rappaport, *Worlds Within Worlds*, 77; Brodsky Elliott, 'Mobility and marriage', 153. In Bristol, 1,396 (79.4 per cent) of all 1,758 apprentices who were registered between 1542 and 1552 were migrants, and in the period 1600–45, 1,314 (68.3 per cent) in a sample of 1,923 apprentices were not natives of the town. Calculation for the mid-sixteenth century is based on E. Ralph and N.M. Hardwick (eds), *Calendar of the Bristol Apprentice Book 1532–1565*, part II, *1542–1552* (Bristol Record Society publications, Vol. XXXIII, 1980), 152. For the seventeenth century, BRO, Register of Apprentices, 04352(3)–(5). For the proportion of migrants among apprentices in other towns, see J. Patten, 'Patterns of migration and movement of labour to three pre-industrial East Anglian towns', *Journal of Historical Geography*, 2 (1976), 122; D.M. Palliser, *Tudor York* (Oxford, 1979), 128–9; A.L. Merson (ed.), *A Calendar of Southampton Apprenticeship Registers 1609–1740* (Southampton Record ser. Vol. XII), xxix; T.C. Mendenhall, *The Shrewsbury Drapers and the Welsh Wool Trade in the Sixteenth and Seventeenth Centuries* (Oxford, 1953), 234.

7. For London, see J. Wareing, 'Changes in the geographical distribution of the recruitment of apprentices to the London companies 1486–1750', *Journal of Historical Geography*, 6 (1980), 241–2. In a sample of 634 apprentices registered in Bristol in the period 1670–1700, 319 (50.3 per cent) were migrants.

8. Quotation in P. Clark, 'The migrant in Kentish towns 1580–1640', in P. Clark and P. Slack (eds), *Crisis and Order in English Towns 1500–1700* (1972), 137. And see also P. Clark and P. Slack, *English Towns in Transition 1500–1700* (Oxford, 1976), 92–3; P. Clark, 'Migration in England during the late seventeenth and early eighteenth centuries', *Past and Present*, 83 (1979), 58–62; P. Clark and D. Souden (eds), *Migration and Society in Early*

Modern England (New Jersey, 1988), introduction, 31. For other references to apprentices as betterment migrants see G.D. Ramsay, 'The recruitment and fortunes of some London freemen', *Economic History Review* (1978), 530; J. Wareing, 'Migration to London and transatlantic emigration of indentured servants, 1683–1775', *Journal of Historical Geography*, 7 (1981), 359. For an emphasis on the heterogeneous, rather than the selective, profile of urban apprentices, see Kitch, 'Capital and kingdom', 225; Brodsky-Elliott, 'Mobility and marriage', 156.

9. Rappaport, *Worlds Within Worlds*, 306; Brodsky Elliott, 'Mobility and marriage', 57–82, esp. 62; R.G. Lang, 'Social origins and social aspirations of Jacobean London merchants', *Economic History Review*, 2nd ser., 27 (1974), 31, 36. In a sample of 339 apprentices in the distributive trades of Bristol between 1600 and 1645, 226 (66.6 per cent) were sons of gentlemen, yeomen, merchants or large-scale traders, and the professions. Only 27 (8.0 per cent) were sons of husbandmen, and only one had a labouring background (BRO, 04352(3)–(5)). For Shrewsbury, see Mendenhall, *Shrewsbury Drapers*, 234. And see also R. Grassby, 'Social mobility and business enterprise in seventeenth-century England', in D. Pennington and K. Thomas (eds), *Puritans and Revolutionaries: Essays in Seventeenth Century History Presented to C. Hill* (Oxford, 1978), 355–7.

10. For the fifteenth century, see S.L. Thrupp, *The Merchant Class of Medieval London* (Ann Arbor, 1948), 214–15, and note 33; Grassby, 'Social mobility and business enterprise', 364–5.

11. Based on a sample of 90 Bristol apprenticeships between 1600 and 1645 in which bonds were paid. Twenty-one (23.3 per cent) were £200 and over, and 51 (56.6 per cent) were £100. Complaints against masters who abused the practice and demanded repayment for these high sums with no justified cause were also presented in the Chancery Court. PRO, C3/289/64, case dated 1595. For complaints about the abuse of bonds by merchants and traders, see also *Relief of Apprentices Wronged by Their Masters* (1687), 2–3.

12. Grassby, 'Social mobility and business enterprise', 365.

13. In the late 1570s a London merchant tailor received only £6 for taking an apprentice; in the mid-1590s one haberdasher received £7, and another London mercer, John Gomersall, received a little over £23. Rappaport, *Worlds Within Worlds*, 306; PRO, C3/289/64.

14. BRO, Register of Apprentices, 04352(4), fo. 292; Quarter Sessions, 04445, fo. 109. Case of William Phelps, a haberdasher, and his apprentice William Phelps, dated 1625. Phelps was registered as an apprentice on 10 September 1622.

15. In a sample of 387 registered between 1600 and 1645, 313 (80.9 per cent) did not have to produce bonds of security.

16. For London, see Ramsay, 'Recruitment and fortunes', 531, where 289 of 493 freemen admitted between 1551 and 1553 had come from the countryside and their fathers had been husbandmen. The number of sons of craftsmen was 289. Calculation for Southampton apprentices is based on Merson, *Calendar of Southampton Apprenticeship Registers*, xxxi, Table E, where 168 (44.4 per cent) of 378 apprentices registered between 1610 and 1648 were sons of husbandmen, craftsmen and labourers, and 110 out of 173 (63.6 per cent) had a similar background in the period 1648–83. Calculation of Bristol apprentices in the 1530s is based on D. Hollis (ed.), *Calendar of the Bristol Apprentice Book 1532–42* (Bristol Record Society Publications, Bristol, 1948), Vol. XIV, 209–11. The data for the period 1600–1645 and the later seventeenth century is based on a sample of 1,512 apprentices in the earlier decades, and 590 in

the later. In the 1530s, 927 (69.3 per cent) of 1,337 apprentices whose fathers' occupations were recorded were from the ranks of craftsmen, husbandmen and labourers. Between 1600 and 1645 these groups still comprised no less than 61.6 per cent of all youth apprenticed in the town.

17. For the distribution of occupations in provincial towns, see D.M. Palliser, *The Age of Elizabeth: England under the Later Tudors 1547–1603* (1983), 242–6, Table 8.1, and App. IV, 392–3. Freemen did not necessarily comprise the whole of the workforce in towns, but they were the masters most likely to take apprentices into their shops, and the distribution of their occupations indicates the types of occupation apprentices were likely to enter.

18. Ramsay, 'Recruitment and fortunes', 534. Rappaport, *Worlds Within Worlds*, 93, and Table 4.2, 92. Of 1,123 freemen, 584 (52 per cent) were engaged in larger victualling companies (bakers, brewers, butchers, grocers, vintners), the cloth trade (drapers, haberdashers, mercers), as well as iron and leather businesses (ironmongers and leather-sellers). But 539 (48 per cent) belonged to occupations and crafts that had to do with the manufacturing of metal products, leatherware and woodwork.

19. A.L. Beier, 'Engine of manufacture: the trades of London', in Beier and Finlay (eds), *London 1500–1700*, 141–67, esp. 148–9; P. Earle, *The Making of the English Middle Class: Business, Society, and Family Life in London, 1660–1730* (1989), 18–26.

20. In the mid-sixteenth century, 957 (66.3 per cent) of 1,444 apprentices entered textile, building, leather, metal and other miscellaneous small crafts. Despite the decline in the textile industry and the recovery and expansion of mercantile activities by the early years of the seventeenth century, the proportion of craftsmen engaged in the manufacturing of products even rose slightly: 1,326 (68.8 per cent) in a sample of 1,926 apprentices registered in the period between 1600 and 1645 were bound with craftsmen involved in building, textile, leather, metal and wood industries. Even by the late seventeenth century, when Bristol entered its most prosperous stage as a centre for overseas trade, these craftsmen provided the training for more than half the apprentices bound in the town. In a sample of 639 apprentices bound between 1670 and 1700, 357 (55.8 per cent) were bound with tailors and clothworkers, leather and metalworkers, and workers in the construction trades; and 282 were apprenticed to merchants and mariners in the distributive trades and the distribution of foodstuffs.

21. Rappaport, *Worlds Within Worlds*, 243; C.G.A. Clay, *Economic Expansion and Social Change: England 1500–1700* (Cambridge, 1984), Vol. II, 8–9. See also below, 102.

22. An Act of 1405–6 for the regulation of apprenticeship included the provision that no person should apprentice his child to an urban craftsman 'except he have land or rent to the value of twenty shillings by the year at the least', but London and Norwich gained exemptions by Acts of 1429 and 1494, respectively. The Statute of Artificers in 1563 repeated these rules, and stipulated a qualification of 40sh. annual freehold income for the parents of those becoming apprentices to merchants, mercers, goldsmiths, ironmongers and clothiers. Town authorities sought to remove such obstacles to labour mobility, and, again, the provision did not apply to London and Norwich. D. Woodward, 'The background to the Statute of Artificers: the genesis of labour policy, 1558–63', *Economic History Review*, 2nd ser., 33 (1980), 32–44, esp. 34–5, 40–42.

23. The list of occupations in which no such qualification was required included smiths, wheelwrights, carpenters, masons, plasterers, sawyers,

lime-burners, brickmakers, tilers, linen weavers, woollen weavers, turners, millers, potters, thatchers, fullers and tuckers. 'The Statute of Artificers', in R.H. Tawney and E. Power (eds), *Tudor Economic Documents* (New York, 1962), Vol. I, 346–7.

24. S.L. Thrupp, *The Merchant Class of Medieval London* (Ann Arbor, 1948), 171–2, 214–15, 218–19.

25. Edmund Wilmott, the son of a husbandman from a small village near Bristol, was apprenticed in 1609 to Thomas Taylor, a Bristol baker. His father 'promised to pay and deliver Thomas Tayler at Michaellmas next for this first year i firkin of good and sweet butter', and for the next year he promised yet another firkin of butter 'or four busshals of wheat at the choice of the said Thomas, and in the third year he was to give a suit of apparel' and the fourth year 'a firkin of butter again, in regard the said Thomas Tayler [takes] . . . nothing else with the said apprentice'. BRO, Register of Apprentices, 04352(3), fo. 285. Indenture dated 23 September 1609.

26. After 1709, when it became obligatory to record the costs of apprenticeships in the indentures, premiums began to be recorded as a normal routine in some urban registers of apprentices. Dunlop and Denman, *English Apprenticeship*, 201; Merson, *Calendar of Southampton Apprenticeship Registers*, xvii.

27. For the relative ease with which some crafts could be learnt, see Chapter 5, 119–24.

28. BRO, Quarter Sessions, 04445, fos 19, 159; Register of Apprentices, 04352(4), fo. 308.

29. Adam Smith, *The Wealth of Nations* (1776, New York, 1937), 105.

30. In mid-seventeenth-century London, Nehemiah Wallington, a turner, probably bargained with all his apprentices for premiums larger than £20. This appears somewhat higher than the amounts many small craftsmen in Bristol took. By the late seventeenth century, London coopers received between £10 and £35, goldsmiths £20–50, and cutlers £10–35. P.S. Seaver, *Wallington's World: A Puritan Artisan in Seventeenth-Century London* (Stanford, 1985), 121; Earle, *Making of the English Middle Class*, 94.

31. For estimates of incomes of labourers and the costs of subsistence see Wrightson, *English Society*, 34; A.H. Smith, 'Labourers in late sixteenth-century England', 31.

32. Case of John Gregorie, from Sulny in Nottinghamshire, whose son was apprenticed to a butcher in Nottingham in 1587. PRO, C3/272/102.

33. BRO, Register of Apprentices, 04352(5)a, fo. 319.

34. *Barlow's Journal*, 20, 30; Bangs, *Memoirs of the Life*, 12–13.

35. Kussmaul, *Servants in Husbandry*, 35–9; McIntosh, *A Community Transformed*, 63.

36. Kussmaul, *Servants in Husbandry*, 76–8.

37. Ibid., 70–73; Rappaport, *Worlds Within Worlds*, 295–6.

38. Ibid., 320, Table 8.9. In Bristol, 1,018 (52.3 per cent) of 1,945 apprentices between 1600 and 1645 signed contracts of between 8 and 15 years. In Southampton, too, about half of the apprenticeships between 1600 and 1630 were for terms of eight or more years. Merson, *Calendar of Southampton Apprenticeship Registers*, xix, Table B, where 48 per cent in 1610–30 signed contracts of between 8 to 10 years or more.

39. Agreements to serve longer than the required seven-year term were also common in all types of trades and industries, including the distributive trades. In the textile industry, the mean length of Bristol apprenticeships in 1600–1645 was 7.8; in construction, it was 7.9; and in the metal industry and the distributive trades the mean number of years was 8.

40. Rappaport, *Worlds Within Worlds*, 321.

41. See Chapter 7, 125–6.

42. Francis Kirkman, *The Unlucky*

Citizen Experimentally Described in the Various Misfortunes of an Unlucky Londoner (1673), 34; *Barlow's Journal*, 15.
43. See Chapter 9, 215–19.
44. In the 1670s, John Smithfield, a Bristol merchant who conducted business mostly in Ireland, accepted an apprentice for only £2. BRO, Quarter Sessions, 04447(2), 1673, fo. 80.
45. BRO, Quarter Sessions, 04445, fo. 159. In London in the late seventeenth century, an apprenticeship with a master who charged no premium could occur as well. James Fretwell recalled that when he began an apprenticeship in London the master took him 'without any premium'. The reason must have been that the master was his cousin, and on agreeing to take James he apparently lost another apprentice who did offer him a premium. Fretwell, *A Family History*, 197.
46. Abraham Jackson, *The Pious Prentice* (1640), 3.
47. For London, see Rappaport, *Worlds Within Worlds*, 77–80. For a comparison with other towns, see ibid., 80, and note 40. In Bristol, 196 (20.5 per cent) of 957 migrant apprentices registered in 1532–42 came from counties in the far north, north Wales, the eastern counties and Ireland. If we add all those coming from the Midlands, as well as from Devon, Cornwall and Dorset, the number rises to a total of 448, or 46.8 per cent of all migrant apprentices. In the period 1542–52, the numbers of those travelling from all these counties was even higher (740 (53 per cent) of 1,396 migrants registered as apprentices). Calculations are based on Hollis (ed.), *Calendar of the Bristol Apprentice Book*, App. B, 197; Ralph and Hardwick (eds), *Calendar of the Bristol Apprentice Book*, App. I, 150.
48. Patten, 'Patterns of migration', 133.
49. E.M. Carus-Wilson, 'The overseas trade of Bristol in the fifteenth century', in *Medieval Merchant Venturers* (1954), 1–97.
50. Between 1532 and 1542, 30 apprentices arrived in Bristol from Lancashire, and only five were from Yorkshire. See also T.S. Willan, *Elizabethan Manchester* (Manchester, 1980), 125.
51. P. Bowden, 'Agricultural prices, farm profits, and rents', in J. Thirsk (ed.), *The Agrarian History of England and Wales* (Cambridge, 1967), Vol. IV, *1500–1640*, 612. On river transport and navigation in early modern England, see T.S. Willan, *River Navigation in England, 1600–1760* (Oxford, 1936).
52. T.S. Willan, 'The movement of goods in Elizabethan England', in *The Inland Trade: Studies in English Internal Trade in the Sixteenth and Seventeenth Centuries* (Manchester, 1976), 19; Carus-Wilson, 'Overseas trade of Bristol', 5.
53. For the importance of road transport as a means of trade from as early as the mid-fifteenth century and throughout the sixteenth and seventeenth centuries, see J.A. Chartres, *Internal Trade in England 1500–1700* (London and Basingstoke, 1977), 39–41.
54. M.D. Lobel, 'Bristol', in *The Atlas of Historic Towns* (Baltimore, 1975), Vol. II, 2; Willan, 'Movement of goods', 7.
55. Chartres, *Internal Trade in England*, 41–2.
56. On contemporary apprehensions of travel by sea, see D. Cressy, *Coming Over: Migration and Communication between England and New England in the Seventeenth Century* (Cambridge, 1987), 146–8.
57. William Lilly, *Mr William Lilly's History of his life and Times from the Year 1602 to 1681* (1715), 7–8; *Barlow's Journal*, 22; Fretwell, *A Family History*, 191–2.
58. Chartres, *Internal Trade in England*, 40–1; J.A Chartres, 'Road carrying in England in the seventeenth century: myth and reality',

Economic History Review, 2nd ser., 30 (1977), 73–8.

59. B.C. Jones, 'Westmorland pack-horse men in Southampton', *Transactions of the Cumberland and Westmorland Antiquarian and Archaeological Society*, 59 (1960), 66.

60. P. Clark, 'Migrants in the city: the process of social adaptation in English towns, 1500–1800', in Clark and Souden (eds), *Migration and Society*, 269–70; Kitch, 'Capital and kingdom', 229; Wareing, 'Changes in the geographical distribution', 241–50. For distances travelled by Bristol apprentices in the period between 1640 and 1658, see D. Souden, '"Rogues, whores and vagabonds"? Indentured servant emigrants in North America, and the case of mid-seventeenth-century Bristol', *Social History*, 3 (1978), 28–9. Calculation for Bristol apprentices in the period 1600–45 is based on identification of a sample of 456 settlements from which apprentices in the town arrived. Calculation for the period 1670–1700 is based on a sample of 319 migrants in the town. Only 18 (5.6 per cent) of these came from Lancashire, the Midlands and Pembrokeshire. I. Krausman Ben-Amos, 'Apprenticeship, the family, and urban society in early modern England' (PhD dissertation, Stanford University, 1985), 137–45.

61. Fretwell, *A Family History*, 191–2; *Barlow's Journal*, 22.

62. Elias Ashmole, *Memoirs of the Life of that Learned Antiquary* (1717), 4; Bangs, *Memoirs of the Life*, 12; *Barlow's Journal*, 23; Thomas Raymond, *Autobiography*, (Camden Society, 3rd ser., Vol. XXVIII, 1917), 22–3.

63. Bewley, *Narrative of the Christian Experiences*, 11; P. Clark (ed.), *The Early Modern Town* (1976), Introduction, 22.

64. In a sample of 210 migrant apprentices in Bristol between 1532 and 1542, 110 were from larger and smaller market towns, and 100 were from villages. In a sample of 1,294 migrant apprentices between 1600 and 1645, 902 (69.7 per cent) were from villages. For London, see Rappaport, *Worlds Within Worlds*, 81; Brodsky Elliott, 'Mobility and marriage', 209; Kitch, 'Capital and kingdom', 234.

65. *Barlow's Journal*, 22, 24.

66. Ibid., 29–31.

67. Lodowick Muggleton, *The Acts of the Witnesses of the Spirit* (1699), 6.

68. See Chapter 7, 159.

69. D. Gardiner (ed.), *The Oxinden Letters 1607–42* (1933), 39–42.

70. For a more detailed analysis of ways of arranging an apprenticeship, see Chapter 7.

71. J. Croker, *Brief Memoir of the Life of John Croker*, in J. Barclay, *A Select Series, Biographical, Narrative, Epistolary and Miscellaneous. Chiefly the Productions of Early Members of the Society of Friends* (1836), Vol. VI, 285.

72. Fretwell, *A Family Journal*, 190, 196–7; *Barlow's Journal*, 1–29.

73. Earle, *Making of the English Middle Class*, 96. For complaints in Bristol Quarter Sessions, see Chapter 5. George Trosse also remembered that when he was apprenticed with a merchant, he served as 'his steward, his butler, his chamberlain, and his shoe-wiper'. A.W. Brink (ed.), Trosse, *The Life of the Late Revered Mr George Trosse* (Montreal and London, 1974), 64.

74. Earle, *Making of the English Middle Class*, 96. This also appears to have been the case of Joseph Oxley, who was relatively young and weak in stature when he began his apprenticeship, and was employed mostly in 'cleaning boots and shoes, and looking after the master's horses'. Joseph Oxley, *Joseph's Offering to his Children*, in J. Barclay (ed.), *A Select Series, Biographical, Narrative, Epistolary and Miscellaneous. Chiefly the Production of Early Members of the Society of Friends* (1836), Vol. V, 208.

75. *Forman's Autobiography*, in A.L. Rowse, *Simon Forman: Sex and Society in Shakespeare's Age* (1974), 271; Kirkman, *Unlucky Citizen*, 35–7. It should be pointed out that this age hierarchy was not all that rigid, and many apprentices formed friendships with fellow apprentices as soon as they entered the shop. See Chapter 7, 178–9.
76. S.R. Rappaport, *Worlds Within Worlds*, 243–4. The evidence on Bristol masters is based on an analysis of 604 masters who took apprentices between 1605 and 1613. For the calculation of the numbers of apprentices taken by woodworkers, I have used an index of all wood-workers in Bristol between 1532 and 1658 prepared for the Bristol Record Office in 1973. The index lists all apprentices in the wood industry in this time span (a total of 3,063), and gives information about their background and, for those who became masters in the town, the number of apprentices they took. Of 566 who eventually became citizens in the town and had apprentices, 356 (62.8 per cent) took only one apprentice.
77. Richard Davies, *An Account of the Convincement, Exercises, Services, and Travels of that Ancient Servant of the Lord, Richard Davies* (1794), 2; *The Autobiography of William Stout*, 74; *The Diary of John Coggs*, Bodleian Library, MS Eng. misc. f78, fo. 65.
78. Martindale, *The Life of Adam Martindale*, 24.
79. Gardiner (ed.), *Oxinden Letters*, 40–42; 59.
80. BRO, 04352(4), fos 129, 236, 238–40, 253, 256.
81. BRO, 04352(4), fo. 103. The apprenticehip was recorded on 16 February 1614. The apprentice, John Price, son of a gentleman from Merionethshire, was bound to a Bristol joiner, Nicholas Easwick.
82. BRO, Register of Apprentices, 04352(4), fo. 184.
83. BRO, Quarter Sessions, 04447(1), fo. 22.
84. BRO, Quarter Sessions, 04445, fo. 159; BRO, 04447(1), fo. 72.
85. BRO, Register of Apprentices, 04352(4), fo. 111.
86. In the years between 1621 and 1625, when the effects of the 1622 depression in the textile industry was most felt, 5 (4.7 per cent) in a sample of 106 apprenticeships were crossed out, a proportion slightly lower than the one observed throughout the whole period.
87. In the sample of 99 apprenticeships which were crossed out between 1600 and 1645, 43 were cancelled within the first year, and 61 within the first two years.
88. In 124 cases of complaints of apprentices and masters which were handled by Bristol's local court in the course of the seventeenth century, some 10 per cent (12 cases) involved abuse or harsh treatment of masters. Among historians, Lawrence Stone was the most extreme in referring to the 'almost limitless sadism' of masters. Stone, *Family, Sex and Marriage*, 120. For a more balanced appraisal of the behaviour of masters, see Houlbrooke, *The English Family*, 175–6; J.A. Sharpe, *Early Modern England: A Social History 1550–1760* (1987), 210.
89. See Chapter 2, 63–4.
90. Fretwell, *A Family Life*, 197.
91. Apprenticeship recorded in November 1621. BRO, 04352(4), fo. 253.
92. Ibid., fo. 185.
93. Gardiner (ed.), *Oxinden Letters*, 40; *Barlow's Journal*, 24, 32, 38, 48.
94. *William Lilly's History of his Life*, 9; *Forman's Autobiography*, 275–6.
95. *Barlow's Journal*, 32; see also Chapter 7, 173–4.
96. BRO, 04352(4), fo. 254; 04352(5), fo. 225.
97. BRO, Quarter Sessions, 04447(2), 49.

5 Urban Apprentices: Skills and Initiatives

1. D. Gardiner (ed.), *The Oxinden Letters 1607–42* (1933), 40, 43.
2. See Chapter 7, 170–5.
3. PRO, Court of Chancery, C3/304/68. Case dated 1620.
4. BRO, case of Elianor Collens, apprenticed to Edward and Luse Jenkins, in 1607. Register of Apprentices, 04352(3), fo. 243.
5. BRO, Quarter Sessions, 04447(1), 61.
6. BRO, Quarter Sessions Recognizances, 04434(1), fo. 501; 498–9; Quarter Sessions, 04447(1), fo. 39. See also P. Earle, *The Making of the English Middle Class: Business, Society, and Family Life in London, 1660–1730* (1989), 96.
7. BRO, 04434(1), fo. 468.
8. In May 1676 Thomas Runitin was apprenticed to a Bristol soapmaker. About a year and a half later, in December 1677, a petition was made at court, according to which 'although [the master] had a considerable sum of money paid him with the said apprentice . . . neither he nor his wife . . . instruct the said apprentice'. BRO, QS Recognizances, 04434(1), fos 498–9.
9. BRO, Register of Apprentices, 04352(3), fo. 202.
10. In the parish of Temple, up to 20d. a week was allocated by the overseers for the maintenance of each of the poor in the first half of the seventeenth century. BRO, Temple Parish, overseers of the poor, Da1, Da2. The findings of Tim Wales on poverty in Norfolk show that in the early 1600s collectioners received between 1d. and 17d. a week, although most received only between 1d. and 5d. a week. T. Wales, 'Poverty, poor relief and the life cycle: some evidence from seventeenth-century Norfolk', in Smith (ed.), *Land, Kinship and Life-Cycle*, 355–6.
11. BRO, The Great Orphan Book, Vol. III, fo. 104; recognizances for orphans, 04423, 15 July 1618. The three Mercer sons, John, Thomas and William, were bound and registered apprentices in August 1614, August 1619 and February 1623. Index to the Register of Apprentices, 1600–30.
12. In 1613 a Bristol haberdasher, John Bush, agreed that his apprentice should supply his own apparel, for which he agreed to give 50sh. a year; and in another case it was agreed that 'notwithstanding the said Thomas Mitchell is bound to find his apprentice clothes and give him double apparel yet it is agreed that [the master] shall give [the apprentice] 30sh. a year to find himself apparell'. Thomas Mitchell paid his apprentice less than John Bush, possibly because he was poorer; he was a whitawer (leather-worker), and his apprentice, bound to him in 1613, was the son of a husbandman from Herefordshire. BRO, Register of Apprentices, 04352(4), fos 77, 95.
13. This is indicated in the indentures of women apprentices who appear with full details of the agreements in the Register of Apprentices. The master promised to give the apprentice the amount of 8d., 10d. or 12d., 'according to the custom of Bristol'.
14. P.S. Seaver, *Wallington's World: A Puritan Artisan in Seventeenth-Century London* (Stanford, 1985), 121.
15. BRO, Register of Apprentices, 04352(3), fo. 243.
16. *Forman's Autobiography*, in A.L. Rowse, *Simon Forman: Sex and Society in Shakespeare's Age* (1974), 271. BRO, Ordinances for City Companies Ratified by the Common Council, 04369(1), fo. 165.
17. See Chaper 4.
18. For the irregularity of employment in the construction industry, and in a shop of a turner, see D.C. Coleman, 'Labour in the English economy of the seventeenth century', *Economic History Review*, 2nd ser., 8 (1956), 288–9; Seaver, *Wallington's World*, 122.
19. See Chapter 7, 172.

20. BRO, 04434(1), 1675, fo. 539; for another similar case, see ibid., fo. 538.
21. Veale was a joiner who had come to Bristol in 1634, when he was bound as an apprentice to a thatcher. Between the time he began to practise the trade of a joiner, probably in the early 1640s, and the time he appeared in court in 1658, he hired and employed in his shop only two apprentices. BRO, Quarter Sessions, 04446, fo. 37. For the apprenticeship of John Veale, and the number of apprentices he took up to 1658, the year he went to court, see Index to Woodworkers, 1532–1658.
22. In 1679 John Brumbele, a Bristol smith, told the court that his apprentice was 'in a present disability of doing his master service . . . by reason of the soreness of one of his legs'. The justices ordered that the apprentice be sent home and that the master pay 2sh. a week for his maintenance. Richard Bough, a whitawer, whose apprentice became sick and was unable to work, was ordered to pay back the full premium of £6. BRO, QS Recognizances, 04434(1), fo. 490; QS, August 1659, 04446, fo. 40.
23. In September 1623 Francis Reade, son of a Bristol merchant, was bound to a Bristol haberdasher. The master and Reade's mother signed a bond of £50, both promising to repay £5 'if the apprentice decease or the said Giles doth decease before the terme of 6 yeares next'. Thomas Luccock, apprenticed to a Bristol gunmaker in 1622, also provided a bond and sureties to secure the repayment if the 'boy shall in the meantime decease'. BRO, Register of Apprentices, 04352(4) fos 261, 292.
24. W.G. Perrin (ed.), *The Autobiography of Phineas Pett* (1918), 3–15.
25. Adam Smith, *The Wealth of Nations* (1776, New York, 1937), 101. For the art of shipbuilding see also C. Singer, E.J. Holmyard, A.R. Hall and T.I. Williams (eds), *A History of Technology* (Oxford, 1957), Vol. III, 486–93.
26. Fretwell, *A Family History*, 187–90.
27. J.R. Harris, *The British Iron Industry 1700–1850* (1988), 21.
28. For sixteenth-century brewhouses in London, see P. Mathias, *The Brewing Industry in England 1700–1830* (Cambridge, 1959), 5–6. For soapboiling, see F.W. Gibbs, 'Invention in chemical industries', in Singer *et al.* (eds); *A History of Technology*, Vol. III, 704.
29. In Bristol between 1532 and 1552, seven young men were apprenticed to bell-founders, and between 1600 and 1645, three in a sample of 1,945 were apprenticed with bell-founders and instrument-makers.
30. For foundry works and cutlery, see *A Universal Dictionary for Trade and Commerce* (4th edn, 1774), article on 'foundry'; Singer *et al.* (eds), *A History of Technology*, Vol. III, 40; P. Smithurst, *The Cutlery Industry* (Shire Album, 195, Bucks, 1987), esp. 18. For coopering, see Singer *et al.* (eds), *A History of Technology*, Vol. III, 128–33.
31. For the tension of the warp, see G.M., *The English Housewife* (1656), 128. In the description of the skills of weaving I have used E.N. Goody (ed.), 'Deboya weavers: relations of production, dependence and reciprocity', in *From Craft to Industry: The Ethnography of Proto-Industrial Cloth Production* (Cambridge, 1982), 66–9; R. Patterson, 'Spinning and weaving', in Singer *et al.* (eds), *A History of Technology*, Vol. III, 151–206; R. Brown, *The Weaving, Spinning, and Dyeing Book* (New York, 1978), 3–18.
32. For the skills and organisation of the industry see L.A. Clarkson, 'The organization of the leather industry in the late sixteenth and seventeenth centuries', *Economic History Review*, 2nd ser., 8 (1960), 245–53, esp. 246–7, 249.
33. Soapmaking was considered 'a tedious operation' which required controlling the process 'by degrees, till the requisite point to the perfection of the soap is hit'. Of the art of the vintner, it was thought that one

should be 'a considerable artist' to master it. *A Universal Dictionary*, article on 'soap'; J. Houghton, *Collection for Improvement of Husbandry and Trade*, Vol. XIV, no. 391 (1669–1700); Gibbs, 'Invention in chemical industries', 704.

34. For the techniques and uses of steel in making cutting tools see Harris, *British Iron Industry*, 41–2; C.G.A. Clay, *Economic Expansion and Social Change: England 1500–1700* (Cambridge, 1984), Vol. II, 56; C.S. Smith, 'Metallurgy and assaying', in Singer *et al.* (eds), *A History of Technology*, Vol. III, 27–71, esp. 34–6; Smithurst, *Cutlery Industry*. The quotation is from a sixteenth-century description of the heat treatment of steel (translated into English in 1658), cited in Smith, 'Metallurgy and assaying', 35.

35. Because the preparation of leather required a long time and great skill, damaged and defective leather frequently found its way to the market. Many shoemakers preferred to buy the tanned leather from the tanner and then take it to the currier, because currying the tanned leather could obscure defects in the material. Clarkson, 'Organization of the leather industry', 251.

36. In the 1540s there were 15 furnaces serving mostly the London smiths and metal-workers; by the 1630s there were 11 furnaces in the Forest of Dean – from where the iron for the use of many Bristol smiths and wiredrawers came – alone. Harris, *British Iron Industry*, 18.

37. Clay, *Economic Expansion*, Vol. II, 84; Patterson, 'Spinning and weaving', 175.

38. In the eighteenth century it was thought that bricklaying 'was not very difficult to be learned', and Adam Smith also thought that 'no species of skilled labour ... seems more easy to learn than that of masons and bricklayers'. *Universal Dictionary*, article on 'bricklayers'; Smith, *Wealth of Nations*, 103.

39. In London in the years 1552–53, the clothworkers already formed 10 per cent of all sworn citizens in the town, and among those involved in the making and distribution of cloth they were the second-largest group, surpassed only by the merchant tailors. At the same time, the number of weavers and dyers was extremely low. The London clothworkers and their apprentices constituted what Ramsay called a 'reservoir of semi-skilled labour'; they 'were needed not only for the fulling and shearing of dyed woollen cloths before they were shipped abroad, but also for finishing the fustians now being imported in quantity, for brushing, trimming, packing, and even storing cloths'. G.D. Ramsay, 'The recruitment and fortunes of some London freemen', *Economic History Review* (1978), 534.

In Bristol in the period between 1532 and 1542, 112 of 211 apprentices in the textile industry (53 per cent) were bound to shearmen and tuckers; by the period 1600–45, 208 in a sample of 330 (63 per cent) apprenticed in the textile industry were bound to shearmen, tuckers, feltmakers and what by now came to be called 'clothworkers'. At the same time the weaver apprentices, who constituted about a third of the textile workforce in the 1530s, had fallen to less than a fifth by the early seventeenth century.

40. In Bristol in the period between 1532 and 1542, there were only four youths (of all 1,444 apprenticed in the town) who were bound to bakers; but by the mid-seventeenth century there were no less than 52 in a sample of 1,945 bound apprentices in the town. Baking required learning to prepare bread and conducting a small shop, but it probably involved less expertise, precision, concentration and understanding than some metal and wood works, for example.

41. In Bristol in the early seventeenth century, apprentices were bound to buttonmakers, platemakers,

lanternmakers and basketmakers – all occupations which had not existed independently a century earlier. In the sample of apprentices in Bristol in the period 1600–45, there were 22 youths who were apprenticed with basketmakers (5), sailmakers (5), platemakers (1), bucklemakers (1), mould-cutters (1), lanternmakers (2), trunkmakers (1), buttonmakers (6). All these were specialised occupations which had not existed among masters taking apprentices in the period 1532–42.

42. For the growth of a consumer society, as well as for the different qualities of goods produced in towns and in the countryside, see J. Thirsk, *Economic Policy and Projects* (Oxford, 1978), 106–32, 109–119. For the growth of London as a centre of consumption in Tudor and Stuart England, see F.J. Fisher, 'London as an "Engine of economic growth"', in P. Clark (ed.), *The Early Modern Town* (1976), 205–15, esp. 206–7.

43. Late medieval London already had some 180 occupations, and the number of individual crafts and occupations continued to grow throughout the sixteenth and seventeenth centuries. By the mid-seventeenth century, occupational categories could be counted in the hundreds. See A.L. Beier, 'Engine of manufacture: the trades of London', in A.L. Beier and R. Finlay (eds), *London 1500–1700: The Making of the Metropolis* (1986), 141–67, esp. 147–51; Earle, *Making of the English Middle Class*, 18–25. For growth in the number of occupations in other towns see also Clay, *Economic Expansion*, Vol. I, 180.

44. For the consumption of fashionable clothing of courtiers and gentlemen, see Thirsk, *Economic Policy and Projects*, 120–1. For the expansion of tailoring and of luxury goods in Norwich, see J.F. Pound, 'The social and trade structure of Norwich 1525–1575', in Clark (ed.), *Early Modern Town*, 138.

45. Of 259 young men bound in the leather industry in 1532–42, 56 (21.6 per cent) were bound to shoe-makers. Between 1600 and 1645 there were 92 shoemaker apprentices (47.9 per cent) in a sample of 192 bound in the leather industry.

46. In Bristol between 1532 and 1542 only one young man was apprenticed with a cutler, and in the following decade eight more became cutler apprentices, comprising together 3.7 per cent of the metal-workers in the town. By the period 1600–45, apprentices who were learning the techniques of cutlery formed nearly 10 per cent of metal-workers in the town. In a sample of 206 apprentices in the metal industry between 1600 and 1645, there were 17 cutlers, or 8.3 per cent. For the expansion of the market and production of knives, whose import by 1700 virtually disappeared, see Clay, *Economic Expansion*, Vol. II, 37.

47. The occupations of brewer, soapmaker, dyer and vintner attracted relatively large numbers of apprentices in Bristol in the period 1600–45. Altogether, they comprised nearly 10 per cent of all apprentices in the town in the period between 1600 and 1645. For Bristol's soapmakers, see D.H. Sacks, *Trade, Society and Politics in Bristol, 1500–1640* (New York, 1985), ch. 10. For the expansion of breweries and the technical innovation and advantages of brewing beer see Mathias, *Brewing Industry*, 3–5.

48. In Bristol the number of those employed in the building trades – mostly carpenters, joiners and shipwrights – more than doubled between the 1530s and the mid-seventeenth century. Apprentices in the building industry comprised 3.1 per cent of apprentices in the town in the 1530s, and 7.7 of the apprentices in the period 1600–45. Coopers were the third-largest occupation in which youths were apprenticed in Bristol in the 1530s; by the early decades of the seventeenth century, barrelmaking was the single largest occupation in which youth became apprentices: no

less than 140 (7.1 per cent) in a sample of 1,945 young people were apprenticed by coopers alone.

49. In Bristol, the percentage of apprentices with dyers in the period 1532–42 was 6.6 (14 out of 211 apprentices). In the period between 1600 and 1645 this rose to nearly 10 per cent (31 in a sample of 330 apprentices in the textile industry).

50. For the techniques involved in the new draperies see D.C. Coleman, 'An innovation and its diffusion: the "new draperies"', *Economic History Review*, 2nd ser., 22 (1969), 422–3. For Norwich bay weavers, dornix weavers, russell weavers, and many worsted weavers, all involved in the making of bays, says, fustians, mockadoes, see Pound, 'Social and trade structure of Norwich' 1525–1575', App. 6.2, 143. See also E. Kerridge, *Textile Manufactures in Early Modern England* (Manchester, 1985), ch. 3.

51. Perrin (ed.), *Autobiography of Phineas Pett*, 3; Joseph Oxley, *Joseph's Offering to his Children*, in J. Barclay (ed.), *A Select Series, Biographical, Narrative, Epistolary and Miscellaneous. Chiefly the Production of Early Members of the Society of Friends* (1836), Vol. V, 208.

52. Perrin (ed.), *Autobiography of Phineas Pett*, 3; *Barlow's Journal*, 29–30.

53. Perrin (ed.), *Autobiography of Phineas Pett*, 10.

54. Smith, *Wealth of Nations*, 103.

55. BRO, Quarter Sessions, 04447(1), fo. 56.

56. Benjamin Bangs, *Memoirs of the Life* (1757), 11; BRO, Register of Apprentices, 04352(5)a, fo. 106.

57. BRO, Register of Apprentices, 04352(4), fo. 118.

58. BRO, Quarter Sessions, 04447(1), fo. 94.

59. Ibid., 04445, fo. 110, 04447(1), fo. 2.

60. See Chapter 4, 104.

61. BRO, Quarter Sessions, 04447(1), fo. 39; 04445, fo. 165; 04445, fo. 109. For the apprenticeship of Walter Marchant, registered in September 1622, see Index to the Register of Apprentices, 1600–30.

62. The ruling at court was made five years after the apprenticeship had begun, but this was at least some time after the apprentice and his master had themselves decided to separate, for Ivy was described in the petition as the 'late apprentice' of Whittorne, the master. BRO, Quarter Sessions, 04445, fo. 40.

63. BRO, Quarter Sessions Recognizances, 04434(1), fo. 514.

64. Rappaport, *Worlds Within Worlds*, 248–9.

65. J[ohn] B[rowne] Marchant, *The Marchants Avizo* (1589), ed. P. McGrath (Cambridge, Mass., 1957), 12–18, and introduction by P. McGrath, esp. xxv–xxvii.

66. Will of Andrew Barker, BRO, Great Orphan Book, Vol. III, fo. 198. For the apprenticeship of Barker see index to the Register of Apprentices, 1600–30; for his father's service as mayor see A.L.B. Beaven, *Bristol Lists* (Bristol, 1899), 195, 222.

67. For a case of a Bristol merchant's apprentice acting as a factor in the Canaries at the age of 21, see deposition of Thomas Wright, apprentice to John Wright, in P. McGrath (ed.), *Merchants and Merchandise in Seventeenth-Century Bristol* (Bristol Record Society, Vol. XIX, 1955), 90–91.

68. Sacks, *Trade, Society and Politics*, ch. 10.

69. BRO, Quarter Sessions, 04447(2), fo. 51. The whole episode would not have reached the court except that Thomas was required by his mistress to return to Bristol and she refused to pay the costs of his voyage back.

70. BRO, Register of Apprentices, 04352(3), fos 26, 32.

71. J. Vanes (ed.), *The Ledger of John Smythe 1538–1550* (Bristol Record Society, Vol. XXVIII, 1974), introduction, 12–13; Ramsay, 'Recruitment and fortunes', 539–40.

72. W.L. Sachse (ed.), *The Diary of Roger Lowe* (New Haven, 1938), *passim*.
73. For an analysis of the details of this apprenticeship and the dispute involved see P. Seaver, 'A social contract? – master against servant in the Court of Requests', *History Today*, 39 (September 1989), 50–6. For thefts and embezzlements in small shops, see also Chapter 9, 212–13.
74. *Forman's Autobiography*, 271–2, 275; *The Autobiography of William Stout*, 74, 79–80, 99. See also Earle, *Making of the English Middle Class*, 98.
75. PRO, Chancery Court, C3/302/ 62, case dated 7 June 1621.
76. Rappaport, *Worlds Within Worlds*, 221, note 16. Calculation of annual wages is based on 5 days a week and 50 weeks a year.
77. In Bristol, wage ceilings ordered in Quarter Sessions in 1654 for the shipbuilding industry made a distinction between 'masters and able workmen' (2sh. a day), 'apprentices that have served two years of their apprenticeship' (18d. a day); and 'labourers and strong bodies' (14d. a day), which suggests that after two years apprentices could be paid as journeymen. The same order includes wage rates for masons, tilers and plasterers, based on the same categories, as well as 'journeymen'. An ordinance of the Company of Tilers and Plaisterers from 1673 includes wage rates for 'master freeman' (2sh. a day); 'journeymen and eldest apprentices' (20d. a day), and 'other apprentices' (16d. a day). BRO, Quarter Sessions, Easter Session, 1654, 04447(1), fo. 3; Ordinances for City Companies Ratified by the Common Council, 04369(1), fo. 83.
78. Rappaport, *Worlds Within Worlds*, 104–10.
79. BRO, Ordinances for City Companies, fo. 56; Quarter Sessions, 04447(2), fo. 60, case dated 1672.
80. In the sample of 1,945 apprentices between 1600 and 1645, there were 140 coopers and 92 shoemakers, comprising altogether 11.9 per cent.
81. See Chapter 4, 102.
82. Case of John Mayes, a Bristol apprentice, who was bound to a weaver in 1619, discharged in 1622, and petitioned the deputy mayor in 1629. BRO, Register of Apprentices, 04352(5)a, fo. 106.
83. PRO, Chancery Court, C3/204/83, case dated 1582; BRO, 04447(1), fo. 77, case dated 1666.
84. Thomas Tryon, *A New Method of Educating Children* (1695), 83.
85. Rappaport, *Worlds Within Worlds*, 311–12.
86. Patten, 'Patterns of migration and movement of labour to three pre-industrial East Anglian towns', *Journal of Historical Geography*, 2 (1976), 121, 130.
87. Rappaport, *Worlds Within Worlds*, 313.
88. A.L. Beier, 'Social problems in Elizabethan London', *Journal of Interdisciplinary History*, 9 (1978), 206–9; 214–17; I.W. Archer, *The Pursuit of Stability: Social Relations in Elizabethan London* (Cambridge, 1991), 206–7; 217–18.
89. I. Krausman Ben-Amos, 'Failure to become freemen: urban apprentices in early modern England', *Social History*, 16 (1991), 155–72.
90. M.J. Kitch, 'Capital and kingdom: migration to later Stuart London', in Beier and Finlay, *London 1500–1700*, 226.
91. Bangs, *Memoirs of the Life*, 13, 22.
92. Rappaport, *Worlds Within Worlds*, 296–7.
93. For the older age of London servants compared with their provincial counterparts, see also J. Boulton, *Neighbourhood and Society: A London Suburb in the Seventeenth Century* (Cambridge, 1987), 134–5. For an average entry age of apprentices in Rye, Sussex, at between 16 and 17 for immigrants and 14–15 for natives, see G. Mayhew, 'Life-cycle service and the family unit in early modern Rye',

Continuity and Change, 6 (1991), 217–19.

6 *Women's Youth: The Autonomous Phase*

1. Thomas Powell, *Tom of all Trades* (1631), 46–7, and *passim.*
2. R. O'Day, *Education and Society 1500–1800* (1982), 183–91.
3. BRO, Orders and Proceedings of Mayor and Aldermen, 1653–73, 04417(1), 3, 85. Instructions dated 2 September 1654; 23 May 1658. For Bristol's schools, see B. Smith and E. Ralph, *A History of Bristol and Gloucester* (Beaconsfield, 1972), 54.
4. Fretwell, *A Family History*, 188–97, 201, 204; *The Life of Adam Martindale*, 6, 24.
5. Studies have shown that London-born daughters tended to remain at home and were married at a relatively young age. V. Brodsky Elliott, 'Single women in the London marriage market: age, status and mobility, 1598–1619', in R.B. Outhwaite (ed.), *Marriage and Society: Studies in the History of Marriage* (1981), 86–90; 97–9; P. Earle, *The Making of the English Middle Class: Business, Society, and Family Life in London, 1660–1730* (1989), 180–1.
6. Earle, *Making of the English Middle Class*, 91–2.
7. For emphasis on relative equality and sexually shared labour before industrialisation, see K.D.M. Snell, *Annals of the Labouring Poor: Social Change and Agrarian England, 1660–1900* (Cambridge, 1985), 309. See also A. Clark, *Working Life of Women in the Seventeenth Century* (1919, new edn, 1982). For a critique of Clark, pointing out the merits as well as the omissions in her account, see Clark, *Working Life of Women*, introduction by Miranda Chaytor and Jane Lewis, esp. xxx–xxxv; M. Prior (ed.), *Women in English Society 1500–1800* (1985), introduction by Joan Thirsk, 11–15; M. Prior, 'Women and the urban economy: Oxford 1500–1800', ibid., 93–4; V. Brodsky, 'Widows in late Elizabethan London: remarriage, economic opportunity and family orientations', in L. Bonfield, R. Smith and K. Wrightson (eds), *The World We Have Gained* (Oxford, 1986), 141–3. For early modern ideas about the subjugation and proper place of women, see S. Amusen, 'Gender, family and social order, 1560–1725', in A. Fletcher and J. Stevenson (eds), *Order and Disorder in Early Modern England* (Cambridge, 1985), 196–217.
8. See Chapter 3, 76–7.
9. Brodsky Elliott, 'Single women', 91.
10. For the numbers of apprentices in these towns, see Chapter 4, 84. For the populations of towns, see E.A. Wrigley, 'Urban growth and agricultural change: England and the continent in the early modern period', *Journal of Interdisciplinary History*, 4 (1985), 684–91.
11. A.L. Merson (ed.), *A Calendar of Southampton Apprenticeship Registers, 1609–1740* (Southampton Record ser., Vol. XII, Southampton, 1968), xli; Snell, *Annals of the Labouring Poor*, 286, 278–83.
12. Thrupp, *The Merchant Class of Medieval London*, 171–2; K.E. Lacey, 'Women and work in fourteenth and fifteenth century London', in L. Charles and L. Duffin (eds), *Women and Work in Pre-Industrial England* (1985), 46–7.
13. Guildhall Library MSS 7351/2, 7357/2, 7358; 5184/2, 5184/3; 3302/1. I am grateful to Paul S. Seaver for pointing out these references to me.
14. For the bibliography on the contraction in long-distance migration to London and other towns, see Chapter 4, 97.
15. The following discussion draws heavily upon I. Krausman Ben-Amos, 'Women apprentices in the trades and crafts of early modern Bristol', *Continuity and Change*, 6 (1991), 227–52.
16. D. Hollis (ed.), *Calendar of the Bristol Apprentice Book 1532–42*

(Bristol Record Society Publications Bristol, 1948), Vol. XIV, 177.
17. For the social background of male apprentices, see Chapter 4, 86–94.
18. Of 1,337 apprentices, 267 (20 per cent) were sons of husbandmen, compared with 14 (15.1 per cent) of 93 women apprenticed who were daughters of husbandmen.
19. Thirty-seven (2.8 per cent) of 1,337 apprentices, and 3 (3.2 per cent) of 93 women apprentices originated in the labouring classes.
20. Of 1,361 apprentices registered between 1532 and 1542, 312 (22.9 per cent) arrived from the Midlands, Wales and the southwest. The comparative number for women was 27 (26.4 per cent) out of 102.
21. In a sample of 1,945 apprentices registered between 1600 and 1645, 618 (31.8 per cent) were men whose fathers had died.
22. Twenty-one (75 per cent) of 28 daughters of gentlemen, yeomen, merchants and traders were orphans; 12 (75 per cent) of 16 daughters of mariners were orphans; but 19 (50 per cent) of 38 daughters of craftsmen, and 7 (58.3 per cent) of 12 daughters of husbandmen were orphans.
23. BRO, Register of Apprentices, 04352(5)a, fo. 2. Indenture dated 4 April 1626.
24. Ibid., 04352(4), fo. 268. Indenture dated 23 August 1622.
25. In 7 out of 28 parish or charity apprenticeships, £3 or £4 were paid, while gifts and charities administered by the town allowed £2 for the apprenticeship of a poor child. BRO, Mayor's Audits, gift of Edward Cox, 04026, 1656–80.
26. For premiums of male apprentices, see Chapter 4, 90–91.
27. D.H. Sacks, *The Widening Gate: Bristol and the Atlantic Economy 1450–1700* (Berkeley, Los Angeles and Oxford, 1991), 24–52.
28. For Bristol's population see Wrigley, 'Urban growth and agricultural change', 684–91.
29. See Chapter 9, 217–18.
30. Although by the seventeenth century the textile industry continued to provide employment for a large segment of the workforce in Bristol – about a fifth of the apprentices and a little less of its freemen entered the textile and clothing industries – employment opportunities in the textile industry, compared with the building or the metal industries, stagnated. While the proportion of apprentices in the building industry doubled – from 3.9 per cent (57 of 1,444) in the 1530s, to 7.9 per cent (152 in a sample of 1,926) in the period 1600–45 – and that of apprentices in the metal industry rose substantially – from 7.5 per cent (109 of 1,444) to 10.8 per cent (208 in a sample of 1,926) in 1600–45 – the proportion in the textile industry rose only from 16.1 in the 1530s to 19.1 in 1600–45.
31. In a sample of 338 apprentices bound in the textile industry between 1600 and 1645, 56 (16.6 per cent) were bound with clothworkers, and 19 (5.6 per cent) with clothiers.
32. Prior (ed.), *Women in English Society*, introduction by Joan Thirsk, 13; BRO, Ordinances of Common Council, 04273(2), fo. 51.
33. BRO, Register of Apprentices, 04352(4), fos 222, 274. Indentures dated 7 July 1620, and 9 November 1622.
34. Merson (ed.), *A Calendar of Southampton Apprenticeship Registers*, xli, li.
35. Based on 32 indentures made in the 1690s by the parishes of St Stephens and St John the Baptist, of which 7 indentures were of young poor women. BRO, P/St S/OP; P/St JB/Misc. 83.
36. For fourteenth-century ordinances in which the admission of women – daughters and widows of freemen in particular – to the freedom of the town is mentioned see E.W. Veale (ed.), *The Great Red Book of Bristol* (Bristol Record Society, Vol.

IV, 1933), introduction, 22; BRO, Information Box, xxv/69.

37. For the period 1558–1600, the records show the admission of four women, none through apprenticeship, to the freedom of the town. BRO, Burgess Books, 1558–98, 04358, fos 22, 35, 77, 100.

38. Snell, *Annals of the Labouring Poor*, 278–94, and Tables 6.1, 6.4; B. Hill, *Women, Work, and Sexual Politics in Eighteenth-Century England* (Oxford, 1989), 89–95.

39. For a discussion of widows' motivations for remarriage, see Brodsky, 'Widows in late Elizabethan London', 121–5; B.J. Todd, 'The remarrying widow: a stereotype reconsidered', in Prior (ed.), *Women in English Society*, 54–83.

40. BRO, Ordinances for the City Companies, 04369(1), fo. 8, article 16; Register of Apprentices, 04352(4), 1609–25, fo. 294.

41. BRO, Quarter Sessions, 1653–71, 04447(1), fo. 39.

42. Earle, *Making of English Middle Class*, 162–3.

43. BRO, Ordinances for City Companies, 04369(1), fo. 129.

44. In the Register of Apprentices there is a record of an indenture, dated 12 November 1627, in which a young man was bound with Samuel Morris, a Bristol saddler, and Margaret his wife, and which specified: 'this boy to be brought up in tobacco-pipe making'. It is possible that the master held two occupations, but it is no less likely that the apprentice was to be taught by the wife. BRO, Register of Apprentices, 04352(5)a, fo. 55. For the women listed in the guild of tobacco-pipe makers, see Ordinances, 04369(1), fo. 129.

45. See Chapter 5.

46. *Autobiography of William Stout*, 90.

47. Based on all cases of craftsmen and traders who obtained freedom of the town through marriage to daughters of freemen, and whose occupations were indicated in the Burgess Books between 1609 and 1645.

48. For patterns of marriage of freemen's daughters compared with those of migrant women in London, see Brodsky Elliott, 'Single women in the London marriage market', 81–100.

49. *The Autobiography of William Stout*, 110–12.

50. Brodsky Elliott, 'Single women', 87, 97–9; R. Wall, 'Leaving home and the process of household formation in pre-industrial England', *Continuity and Change*, 2 (1987), 92–4.

51. 'But having her father's spirit, and her mother's beauty,' her brother later recalled, 'no persuasion would serve, but up she would to serve a ladie as she hoped to do'. *Life of Adam Martindale*, 7.

52. Earle, *Making of the English Middle Class*, 212–18.

53. D. Souden, 'Migrants and the population structure of later seventeenth-century provincial cities and market towns', in P. Clark (ed.), *The Transformation of English Provincial Towns 1600–1800* (1984), 99–132, esp. 142–3, 151, 156–7, 160–1. For the eighteenth century, see Hill, *Women, Work, and Sexual Politics*, 125–47.

54. Earle, *Making of the English Middle Class*, 222–3.

55. *Forman's Autobiography*, in A.L. Rowse, *Simon Forman: Sex and Society in Shakespeare's Age* (1974), 273. See also Earle, *Making of the English Middle Class*, 217.

56. McIntosh, *A Community Transformed*, 61.

57. For bonds allowing the departure of women, see BRO, Register of Apprentices, 04352(4), fos 300, 301, 324, 326, 329; 04352(5)a, fos 23, 99, 106.

58. Brodsky Elliott, 'Single women', 92; Earle, *Making of the English Middle Class*, 225–29; Hill, *Women, Work and Sexual Politics*, 36–7; J.J. Hecht, *The Domestic Servant in Eighteenth-Century England* (1956), 78–83.

59. *Autobiography of William Stout*, 171.

60. *Life of Adam Martindale*, 8.
61. *Barlow's Journal*, 22–3.
62. Earle, *Making of the English Middle Class*, 228–9; Hill, *Women, Work, and Sexual Politics*, 138–9.
63. Francis Kirkman, *The Unlucky Citizen Experimentally Described in the Various Misfortunes of an Unlucky Londoner* (1673), 37–8.
64. *Forman's Autobiography*, 273.
65. Brodsky Elliott, 'Single women', 95–7; M. McIntosh, 'Servants and the household', 21.
66. *Autobiography of William Stout*, 171.
67. *Life of Adam Martindale*, 8.
68. *Autobiography of William Stout*, 157.
69. *Barlow's Journal*, 38–40, 91. For emphasis on the importance of domestic service in the independence with which women entered matrimony, in a late medieval context, see P.J.P. Goldberg, 'Marriage, migration, servanthood and life-cycle in Yorkshire towns of the later Middle Ages: some York cause paper evidence', *Continuity and Change*, 1 (1986), 141–69, esp. 155–61.
70. BRO, Orders and Proceedings of Mayor and Aldermen, 04417(1), fos 9–10; 46.

7 The Widening Circle: The Social Ties of Youth

1. Benjamin Bangs, *Memoirs of the Life* (1757), 7, 29; *Barlow's Journal*, 252; A. Macfarlane, *The Family Life of Ralph Josselin: A Seventeenth-Century Clergyman* (New York, 1970), 112.
2. Stone, *The Family, Sex and Marriage in England*, 81–9, esp. 84–5. For different perspectives on the effects of the departure of children from home during their teens, and for an emphasis on the continuing bond of affection between parents and their children, see Macfarlane, *Family Life of Ralph Josselin*, 110–25; Houlbrooke, *English Family*, 178–88.
3. The conventions regarding assistance of the parish implied that 'relatively little relief was dispensed to individuals in the age range 15–30 years, i.e. after the age of leaving home'. W.N. Brown, 'The receipt of poor relief and family situation: Aldenham, Hertfordshire 1630–90', in Smith (ed.), *Land, Kinship and Life-Cycle*, 419; T. Wales, 'Poverty, poor relief and the life-cycle: some evidence from seventeenth-century Norfolk', ibid., 365. For the 'deserving poor', see also M.K. McIntosh, 'Local responses to the poor in late medieval and Tudor England', *Continuity and Change*, 3 (1988), 210–11.
4. For the flexibility and lack of formalised pattern in the recruitment of servants throughout most of the sixteenth and first half of the seventeenth centuries, see A.H. Smith, 'Labourers in late sixteenth-century England', 14–15; McIntosh, 'Servants and the household unit', 12.
5. K. Wrightson, *English Society*, 44–57; K. Wrightson, 'Kinship in an English village: Terling, Essex 1550–1700', in Smith (ed.), *Land, Kinship and Life-cycle*, 313–32; Houlbrook, *English Family*, 39–58; J. Boulton, *Neighbourhood and Society: A London Suburb in the Seventeenth Century* (Cambridge, 1987), 228–61. For a critique and emphasis on the value and intensity of kin interaction, especially in migration overseas, see D. Cressy, 'Kinship and kin interaction in Early Modern England', *Past and Present*, 113 (1986), 38–69.
6. For the relatively small effects of mobility on neighbourly cohesion in towns, except in the case of apprentices and servants, see R. Finlay, *Population and the Metropolis: The Demography of London 1580–1650* (Cambridge, 1981), 77; Boulton, *Neighbourhood and Society*, 20.
7. S.R. Smith, 'The London apprentices as seventeenth-century adolescents', *Past and Present*, 61 (1973), 149–61; A.L. Beier and R. Finlay, 'Introduction: the significance of the metropolis', in Beier and Finlay (eds),

London 1500–1700: The Making of the Metropolis (1986), 21.

8. *Barlow's Journal*, 16, 21.

9. Ibid., 16.

10. Bewley, *A Narrative of the Christian Experiences*, 10–11; *Barlow's Journal*, 26.

11. Rappaport, *Worlds Within Worlds*, 81. In a sample of 902 immigrant apprentices in Bristol between 1600 and 1645, 392 (43.4 per cent) were from market towns: among those who arrived from places as far away as the Midlands, Wales, the north, and the far south, nearly half were from market towns, while, of those coming from adjacent regions, the vast majority (80 per cent) originated in villages. Identification of market towns was based on A. Everitt, 'The marketing of agricultural produce' in J. Thirsk (ed.), *The Agrarian History of England and Wales* (Cambridge, 1967), Vol. IV, *1500–1640*, 467–75. For the importance of market towns in migration overseas, see also J. Horn, 'Servant emigration to the Chesapeake in the seventeenth century', in T.W. Tate and D.L. Ammerman (eds), *The Chesapeake in the Seventeenth Century* (North Carolina, 1979), 70. For the alehouse as an economic centre and a centre for passing on information and news, see P. Clark, *The English Alehouse: A Social History 1200–1830* (1983), 139.

12. For the links between textile regions and towns, and their impact on the migration of apprentices to towns like Norwich, York and Great Yarmouth, see Patten, 'Patterns of migration and movement of labour to three pre-industrial East Anglian towns', *Journal of Historical Geography*, 2 (1976), 128–9, 132–4; D.M. Palliser, *Tudor York* (Oxford, 1979), 128–9. For patterns of migration to Bristol, and their link to trade routes, industrial regions of textile and the metal (in the Forest of Dean), and agricultural zones of south Somerset, see I. Krausman Ben-Amos, 'Apprenticeship, the family, and urban society in early modern England' (PhD dissertation, Stanford University, 1985), 137–44.

13. For example, Richard Tucker, the son of a clothier from Thornbury, a market town in Gloucestershire, was apprenticed to a Bristol tailor in June 1612; and Francis Tyler, son of a weaver in a Gloucestershire village, was bound to a Bristol weaver in September 1613. (BRO, Register of Apprentices, 04352(3), fos 45, 70). In a sample of 1,512 apprenticeships in Bristol in the first half of the seventeenth century, between 40 and 50 per cent remained within the same category of occupation (distributive trades, food and drink, textiles, metal, wood, and the building industries) as their fathers.

14. Rappaport, *Worlds Within Worlds*, 80; *The Life of Adam Martindale*, 6.

15. *Barlow's Journal*, 22–3.

16. Of the 145 apprentices who also had brothers, 62 (42.7 per cent) were fatherless; among the remaining 688 apprenticed in the same period, only 32.6 per cent were orphaned.

17. For the autobiography of Terril, see E.B. Underhill, *The Records of a Church of Christ Meeting in Broadmead, Bristol, 1640–1687* (1847), 60; *Barlow's Journal*, 19. For Havering's servants, see McIntosh, 'Servants and the household unit', 16.

18. Edward Barlow spent the Christmas holiday with his parents while he was an apprentice in Manchester; and Ralph Josselin's son Thomas also came home during holidays at least twice. *Barlow's Journal*, 19; Macfarlane, *Family Life of Ralph Josselin*, 113.

19. BRO, Quarter Sessions Recognizances, 04434(1), fo. 483, case dated 6 October 1679.

20. Kussmaul, *Servants in Husbandry*, 57. For distances travelled by servants of Havering manor, Essex, see M. McIntosh, 'Servants and the household unit', 16.

21. In a sample of 1,945 Bristol apprentices in the period 1600–45, 609 were natives of Bristol; in addi-

tion, there were about 320 youths who came from adjacent villages and towns (93 settlements) scattered throughout a thin belt of up to 12 miles. Together, they comprised 47.7 per cent of the apprentices registered in the town.

22. PRO, Chancery Court, C3/306/69.

23. BRO, Quarter Sessions Recognizances, 04434(1), fo. 538, case dated 6 September 1675; Quarter Sessions, 04447(1), 1664, fo. 61, case dated 10 January 1664.

24. T. McCrie (ed.), *Memoirs of Mr William Veitch and George Brysson* (1825), 271.

25. John Gratton, *A Journal of the Life of John Gratton* (1720), 18.

26. Macfarlane, *Family Life of Ralph Josselin*, 112–14; *Barlow's Journal*, 48.

27. In his diary, John Coggs, a London apprentice, mentioned that on 7 June 1703 his master went to Kent and on the way back he 'went to see my father and mother'. *The Diary of John Coggs*, Bodleian Library, MS Eng. misc. f78, fo. 7.

28. When Edward Coxere was at sea, his mother received information about her son through her neighbour, who was one of the owners of the ship on which Coxere was apprenticed. Coxere, *Adventures by Sea*, 28. For the information Ralph Josselin received about his daughters in London see Macfarlane, *Family Life of Ralph Josselin*, 113.

29. *The Journal of Richard Norwood*, 30–32.

30. Roger Lowe, an apprentice in Ashton, Lancashire, wrote letters for his neighbours quite regularly, in some cases to their sons. W. Sachse (ed.), *The Diary of Roger Lowe* (New Haven, 1938), 15. Elias Ashmole also received a letter about his father's death, in 1634, when he was a servant in London. Elias Ashmole, *Memoirs of the Life of That Learned Antiquary* (1717), 4. For an example of siblings' letters, see the case of George Bewley, whose sister wrote to him when he was an apprentice, 'being thoughtful of my welfare'. Bewley, *A Narrative of the Christian Experiences*, 12.

31. By the late sixteenth century nearly all apprentices enrolled by ironmongers in London were fully literate. Rappaport, *Worlds Within Worlds*, 298–9. But for the selectivity of literacy rates among urban apprentices, see also Chapter 8, 198–9.

32. *Journal of Richard Norwood*, 30–1; For Woodhouse's letter, see Fretwell, *A Family History*, 205; *The Complete Letter-Writer, Containing Familiar Letters on the Most Common Occasions in Life* (Edinburgh, 1768), 24–8, 34, 44, 47.

33. *Diary of John Coggs*, fos 4, 9, 12.

34. Ibid., fos 9, 12, 13; Gervase Disney, *Some Remarkable Passages* (1692), 31.

35. BRO, Quarter Sessions, 04447(1), 37.

36. D. Gardiner (ed.), *The Oxinden Letters, 1607–42* (1933), 41; Disney, *Some Remarkable Passages*, 45–6.

37. Bangs, *Memoirs of the Life*, 29; Macfarlane, *Family Life of Ralph Josselin*, 112–13; *Life of Adam Martindale*, 207–9. For a case of a seaman's apprentice who went home to his parents at the end of a voyage to Ireland, 'being somewhat sickly', see BRO, Quarter Sessions Recognizances, 04434(1), fo. 546.

38. A.W. Brink (ed.), *The Life of the Late Reverend Mr George Trosse* (Montreal and London, 1974), 64–5. For examples of apprentices who returned to their parents when they became dissatisfied with their apprenticeship, see Fretwell, *A Family History*, 196–7; Macfarlane, *Family Life of Ralph Josselin*, 120.

39. BRO, Quarter Sessions Recognizances, 04434(1), fo. 516.

40. In a sample of 99 apprentices who were formally discharged from their service in Bristol in the period 1600–45, only 46 were transferred at the same time to another master. For Croker's experience in Philadelphia, see John Croker, *Brief Memoir of the Life of John Croker*, in J. Barclay (ed.),

A Select Series, Biographical, Narrative, Epistolary and Miscellaneous: Chiefly the Productions of Early Members of the Society of Friends (1836), Vol. VI, 288–9. For the case of Hyett, see BRO, Quarter Sessions, 04445, fo. 152.

41. Evans, *An Eccho to the Voice*, 7; Robert Persons, *The Memoirs of Father Robert Persons* (Catholic Record Society, Vol. II, 1906), 18.

42. When John Croker's second master in Exeter lost the means to support his family, John 'concluded to return to my father'. Croker, *Brief Memoir*, 303.

43. Macfarlane, *Family Life of Ralph Josselin*, 112.

44. For the autobiography of Joseph Mayett, and the importance of his contacts with his parents, see Kussmaul, *Servants in Husbandry*, 85–93, esp. 86–9.

45. William Gregorie, an apprentice in Nottingham in the 1620s, went back to his father, a poor labourer from a neighbouring village, after he had run away from his master who 'beate, wound and evil entreat the said William Gregorie'; and Samuel Singleton, whose master wanted him to depart from his service, was given 8sh. 'to carry him down to the country to [his parents]'. Another servant was sent to request the carrier of York to 'convey the said apprentice home'. Chancery Court, C3/272/102; C3/289/64, first case dated 29 November 1603; second case dated 24 May 1595.

46. For an analysis of legacies left to children in collections of wills, see Wrightson, 'Kinship in an English village', 326–9, esp. 327, note 18, where reference is also made to customs of inheritance in different rural communities.

47. Joseph Oxley, William Edmundson and John Croker all went, at the end of their apprenticeships, to towns and places where their fathers or brothers made arrangements and helped them to set up. Joseph Oxley, *Joseph's Offering to his Children*, in Barclay (ed.) *A Select Series*, Vol. V, 220–1; William Edmundson, *A Journal of the Life of William Edmundson* (Dublin, 1820), 44–5; Croker, *Brief Memoir*, 303–5.

48. Disney, *Some Remarkable Passages*, 61–3. Gervase's father gave him the following reasons why he should join him in his business and come to live near him in Yorkshire: 'that I [i.e. Gervase] might the better be acquainted with his business'; second, 'that he might in his old age be eas'd in business'; and third, 'that we might, especially, be helpful one to another'. But Gervase decided to settle in Nottingham.

49. Among sons of craftsmen apprenticed between 1600 and 1630, only 14.4 per cent established themselves in the town when their terms came to an end. Among those who were trained in the metal and textile industries, only 9.7 and 12.7 per cent, respectively, became citizens, against between 20 and 27.6 per cent among apprentices trained in commerce, shipbuilding, carpentry, coopering and other crafts involved in the building and wood industries. See also I. Krausman Ben-Amos, 'Failure to become freemen: urban apprentices in early modern England', *Social History*, 16 (1991), 159–63.

50. For an analysis of a variety of bonds and their intensity, see Houlbrooke, *English Family*, 178–88. For a description of a particularly emotional reunion between a youth and his parents, see the autobiography of Croker, *Brief Memoir*, 289–90.

51. Kussmaul, *Servants in Husbandry*, 23. For her discussion of the advantages of taking servants for small nuclear families, see ibid., 22–6. For an example of poverty and lack of employment as a motivation to send all children into service and apprenticeship, see *Barlow's Journal*, 15–16.

52. For the effect parental death had on the timing of service and apprenticeship see Rappaport, *Worlds Within Worlds*, 295–6. For an emphasis on the

importance of orphanage in becoming servants and apprentices, see G. Mayhew, 'Life-cycle service and the family unit in early modern Rye', *Continuity and Change*, 6 (1991), 205–7.

53. This is the only way to explain why so many craftsmen sent their children to learn similar occupations to the ones they themselves held, while at the same time taking other apprentices in their place. An example of the impact periodic economic difficulties could have on the sending of children away is the autobiography of James Fretwell, who recalled that when he reached his mid-teens, his father, a timber-merchant, first suggested that he go to London as an apprentice only for a short while to see if he liked it. But some time later, 'meeting with some disapointments ... in the way of business, [he] was very much concerned upon my account', and so he put a great deal of pressure on young Fretwell to be bound as an apprentice in the town. Fretwell, *A Family History*, 197.

54. K. Wrightson, 'Household and kinship in sixteenth-century England', *History Workshop Journal*, 12 (1981), 155.

55. He was boarded at the age of five with a widow, and later on with a kinsman, another widow, and finally, when he reached the age of 15, with a mercer. Fretwell, *A Family History*, 185–8.

56. Ibid., 185.

57. In London, only 1 per cent of apprentices in the late sixteenth and early seventeenth centuries had the same name as their masters; in Bristol, 44 (2.3 per cent) in a sample of 1,945 apprentices had identical surnames (and 88, or 4.5 per cent, whose masters were fathers, mothers and brothers); in Norwich, less than 4 per cent, and in Salisbury 5 per cent of servants dwelt with kin. Brodsky Elliott, 'Mobility and marriage in preindustrial England' (PhD dissertation, University of Cambridge, 1978), 209; BRO, Register of Apprentices, 04352(3)–(5); Houlbrooke, *English Family*, 46; P. Clark, 'Migrants in the city: the process of social adaptation in English towns, 1500–1800', in Clark and Souden (eds), *Migration and Society in Early Modern England* (New Jersey, 1988), 271.

58. McIntosh, 'Servants and the household unit', 19.

59. Samuel Bownas, *An Account of the Life and Travels of Samuel Bownas* (4th edn, 1795), 1; Trosse, *Life of*, 63; Fretwell, *A Family History*, 197.

60. Fretwell, *A Family History*, 188–90; Disney, *Some Remarkable Passages*, 29.

61. As in the case of Edward Barlow, who refused an offer by his uncle to become his apprentice since he desired to become an apprentice on a ship.

62. A letter copied in Fretwell, *A Family History*, 205.

63. Houlbrooke, *English Family*, 219; McIntosh, *A Community Transformed*, 49.

64. V. Brodsky Elliott, 'Single women in the London marriage market: age, status and mobility, 1598–1619', in R.B. Outhwaite (ed.), *Marriage and Society: Studies in the History of Marriage* (1981), 93–5.

65. Intricate connections between servants or apprentices and their masters, as well as mistresses, could be found. Brodsky Elliott has suggested that if 1 per cent of London apprentices had identical surnames to their masters, there might well have been 10 per cent of all apprentices who were related to their masters. This would raise the numbers of kin-related masters in provincial towns to well over a tenth of the apprentice population, for in towns like Bristol, Norwich and Southampton the proportion of apprentices with identical surnames to their masters was between 2.6 and 5 per cent of all the apprentices. Brodsky Elliott, 'Mobility and marriage', 211.

66. James Fretwell recalled that his

uncle 'was pleased to tell my father that he preferred me without any premium before another with a sum of money'. *A Family History*, 197.

67. Oxley, *Joseph's Offering*, 207–9.

68. McIntosh, *A Community Transformed*, 25–6.

69. BRO, Register of Apprentices, 04352(4)–04352(5), *passim*.

70. Gardiner (ed.), *Oxinden Letters*, 39–42. See also Chapter 5, 107.

71. *Journal of Richard Norwood*, 33.

72. Ibid., 33; *Barlow's Journal*, 24–30.

73. The case of John Godman, a Bristol baker, against his apprentice, John Morgan, in 1628. BRO, Quarter Sessions, 04445, fo. 159. Morgan came from Monmouthshire. His father, a husbandman, was dead when he was apprenticed, and a 'friend' appears to have been present at the court.

74. The case of William Eyton, originally from Horfield, against his master, a Bristol soapmaker, one Richard Baugh, in which it was contended that 'wrongs [were] done' to the apprentice, that his master turned him away and refused to take him back. The court record indicates that William Eyton's uncle appeared on his behalf. BRO, Quarter Sessions, 04445, fos 7, 10, case dated 1620. For his parental origins, see his apprenticeship on 9 November 1614, Register of Apprentices, 04352(4).

75. Trosse, *Life of*, 63; *Diary of John Coggs*, fo. 4; *Journal of Richard Norwood*, 37.

76. His master paid £10, and although it is not clear that the relative took him to his own house, he was obviously well involved on his behalf and his welfare. Blake's father was a Wiltshire yeoman, and he was still alive when Blake was apprenticed a year earlier, in 1653. BRO, 04447(1), fo. 2; Register of Apprentices, 04352(6), fo. 300.

77. BRO, Quarter Sessions, 04447(2), fo. 81.

78. For the importance of kinship ties in migration to towns in the nineteenth century, see M. Anderson, *Family Structure in Nineteenth Century Lancashire* (Cambridge, 1971), esp. 152–61. For the role of kin in migration overseas in the seventeenth century, see Cressy, 'Kinship and kin interaction', esp. 44–53. For the role of kin in migration to London see also P. Clark, 'The migrant in Kentish towns 1580–1640', in P. Clark and P. Slack (eds), *Crisis and Order in English Towns 1500–1700* (1972), 135–9; and also the comments in J. Boulton, *Neighbourhood and Society*, 259.

79. Kussmaul, *Servants in Husbandry*, 59.

80. *Barlow's Journal*, 23.

81. Kussmaul, *Servants in Husbandry*, 31–2.

82. Bangs, *Memoirs of the Life*, 11–12.

83. In Bristol during the depression of 1622, the number of apprentices who were officially discharged (in the Register of Apprentices or at Quarter Sessions) was 24. This was only slightly higher than the number discharged annually during the whole decade, and overall the proportions officially dismissed changed little from year to year during the period between 1600 and 1645. Some of those who were dismissed may not have been recorded in the Register, but the impression given from the records is that, while there was no insurance against such occurrences, most masters did not fire their apprentices during periods of unemployment.

84. M. Pelling, 'Child health as a social value in early modern England', *Social History of Medicine*, 1 (1988), 135–64, esp. 155–62. For cases in which a master was required to pay the apprentice when he was sent to his parents, see Chapter 5, 113.

85. Of 405 patients whom Binn treated and whose occupations he recorded, 71 (17.5 per cent) were ser-

vants. L.M. Beier, *Sufferers and Healers: The Experience of Illness in Seventeenth-Century England* (1987), 56–7; 170–1. The case in Chancery involved the complaint of Benonye Claye against Andrew Quashe in 1620. Chancery Court, C3/304/68.

86. See Chapter 5, p. 111.

87. T.P. Wadley, *Notes or Abstracts of the Wills in the . . . Great Orphan Book and Book of Wills in the Council House at Bristol (1379–1595)* (Bristol, 1886), *passim*. For the will of William Pepwall, see pp. 242–3.

88. Cressy, 'Kinship and kin interaction', 55; McIntosh, 'Servants and the Household unit', 19.

89. BRO, Register of Apprentices, 04352(4), fo. 23, apprenticeship dated 4 December 1626.

90. In 838 of apprentices registered between 1605 and 1609, 374 (44.6 per cent) were promised money at the end of their terms.

91. McGrath pointed out that, according to the *The Marchants Avizo*, an apprentice could receive a commission of 2.5 per cent on each transaction he made. Bristol's apprentices often conducted transactions for a few masters on the same trip, and they were allowed a commission on each one of these. J[ohn] B[rowne], *The Marchants Avizo* (1589), ed. P. McGrath (Cambridge, Mass., 1957), xvii–xviii.

92. PRO, Chancery Court, C3/304/68.

93. BRO, Register of Apprentices, 04352(4), fos 141, 32, 26.

94. When Stout himself finished his apprenticeship, his master gave him information about a shop to rent. *The Autobiography of William Stout*, 88, 119. Joseph Oxley also remembered that after he had finished his apprenticeship he went back to his master to talk 'about some business', and Roger Lowe's master sold him his shop when the term of his apprenticeship ended. Oxley, *Joseph's Offering*, 213; *Diary of Roger Lowe*, 93. See also P. Earle, *The Making of the English Middle Class: Business, Society and Family Life in London, 1660–1730* (1989), 110.

95. *Forman's Autobiography*, 275; *Diary of Roger Lowe*, 50–51; Bangs, *Memoirs of the Life*, 12.

96. Oxley, *Joseph's Offering*, 210; Chancery Court, C3/306/69, case between Walter Davies and James Daniel, dated 1620.

97. Bangs, *Memoirs of the Life*, 12; J. Vanes (ed.), *The Ledger of John Smythe, 1538–1550* (Bristol Record Society, Vol. XXVIII, 1974), 28, 12; Cressy, 'Kinship and kin interaction', 55.

98. Oxley, *Joseph's Offering*, 213; *The Posthumous Works of Mr Thomas Chubb* (1748), iii.

99. Kussmaul cited the case of a Hertfordshire labourer who testified in 1784 that he had worked for one year with one farmer, and the next with the farmer's brother. Kussmaul, *Servants in Husbandry*, 59.

100. For his letter in which the incident was recorded see Fretwell, *A Family History*, 205–6.

101. For an example of an apprentice whose master 'willed him to depart' because of the 'deadness of trade and want of employment for him', see BRO, Register of Apprentices, 04352(5)a, fo. 106. The year was 1622, and the apprentice, John Mayes, was forced to depart from Bristol for several years.

102. Kussmaul, *Servants in Husbandry*, 32.

103. Forty-nine of the wills were made by Bristol inhabitants, and 53 by the inhabitants in villages surrounding the town. The vast majority (51 out of 71 with identified occupations) were widows, single women and small craftsmen (carpenters, masons, weavers, petty chapmen, pointmakers, wire-drawers, etc.). There were also 9 husbandman and 1 labourer; only 11 belonged to higher occupations (5 priests, 2 merchants, 2 yeomen, 1 surgeon, and 1 gentleman). A typescript of the wills, transcribed under the supervision of P. McGrath

and M.E. Williams, is in the BRO, and is entitled *Bristol Wills 1546–1593* (1975), edited with an introduction by P. McGrath and M.E. Williams.

104. For cycles in the demand for annual service see Kussmaul, *Servants in Husbandry*, 97–119. For the elimination of various benefits at the end of apprenticeship, see Chapter 8, 9, 218.

105. For this analysis and for her suggestion that kinship ties were stronger than neighbourly ties in these cases of chain migration, see V. Brodsky Elliott, 'Mobility and marriage', 211–13.

106. E. Robinson (ed.), *John Clare's Autobiographical Writings* (Oxford, 1986), 39–41.

107. N.Z. Davis, 'The reasons of misrule: youth groups and charivaris in sixteenth-century France', *Past and Present*, 50 (1971), repr. in *Society and Culture in Early Modern France* (Stanford, 1975), 97–123. For the view of London apprentices as a 'youth group', see Smith, 'London apprentices', 149–61. For the view that 'nothing in the evidence cited above can compare with the French abbeys in permanence or function', see B. Capp, 'English youth groups and the Pinder of Wakefield', *Past and Present* 76 (1977), 129. For the suggestion that seasonal migration coupled with migration to large towns led to the final extinction of youth groups in nineteenth-century France, see C. Heywood, *Childhood in Nineteenth-Century France: Work, Health and Education among the 'classes populaires'* (Cambridge, 1988), 82.

108. Edward Barlow remembered that his father prevented him from going to church on Sundays, for fear of his neighbours pointing at him in rags, 'which was not seemly'. When he left his master in Manchester and came home to his parents, his neighbours intervened, wondered why, and indirectly allied with his parents in scolding and reproaching him for departing from his master. Edward Coxere wrote similarly that when he deserted his first master and came home and could not settle in his mind what to do next, 'my life began then to be uncomfortable'. *Barlow's Journal*, 16, 19–20; Coxere, *Adventures by Sea*, 5.

109. *Barlow's Journal*, 20.

110. Brodsky Elliott, 'Mobility and marriage', 210–11.

111. Clark, 'Migrants in the city', 273–5.

112. G. Davies (ed.), *Thomas Raymond's Autobiography* (Camden Society, Vol. XXVIII, 1917), 21.

113. For a detailed analysis of a dispute between an apprentice and his master in which neighbours gave long depositions (on behalf of the master), see P. Seaver, 'A social contract?: master against servant in the Court of Requests', *History Today*, 39 (September 1989), 50–6.

114. Lodowick Muggleton, *The Acts of the Witnesses of the Spirit* (1699), 6; *Barlow's Journal*, 18, 22.

115. *Barlow's Journal*, 18; BRO, Quarter Sessions, 04447(1), fo. 61, case between John Wells, mercer, and Walter Escott, his apprentice, dated 1664. For a case in which a series of attempts were made to persuade a master to receive an apprentice back, and in which 'diverse gentlemen and others of his [i.e. the apprentice's father's] good friends' were involved, and another case in which it was alleged the master had been spoken to before a complaint at court was made, see PRO, Chancery Court, C3/272/102; C3/306/69. Cases between John Gregorie, a labourer from Nottingham, and William Widdowson, a Nottingham butcher, dated 1603; and between Walter Davis and James Daniel of the town of Hereford, dated 1620.

116. *Autobiography of William Stout*, 88.

117. *Barlow's Journal*, 18.

118. Oxley, *Joseph's Offering*, 221; Pike, *Some Account of the Life*, 121; Kussmaul, *Servants in Husbandry*,

43; Underhill, *Records of a Church of Christ Meeting*, 59; Bangs, *Memoirs of the Life*, 16; Bewley, *A Narrative of the Christian Experiences*, 14.
119. Kussmaul, *Servants in Husbandry*, 43; Clark, *English Ale-house* 127, 131.
120. Robinson (ed.), *John Clare's Autobiographical Writings*, 41.
121. BRO, Great Orphan Book, Vol. III, fo. 198, will dated 22 August 1622.
122. *Diary of Roger Lowe*, 74–5; 91.
123. Evans, *An Eccho to the Voice*, 5; Anon., *An Account of the Work of Grace upon*, in Charles Doe, *A Collection of Experiences of the Work of Grace* (1698), 13.
124. Adam Martindale recorded the details of a rape of a six-year-old girl by the village fisherman, and his description shows how the community was involved: the girl's mother, Martindale's wife, the neighbour, and other neighbours who testified against the fisherman and eventually appeared as jurors in his trial. *Life of Adam Martindale*, 206–7. For illegitimacy rates, see Chapter 8, p. 204.
125. When Oliver Sansom grew up and came into open conflict with his parents (this was over matters of religious belief), he 'used endeavors to get abroad into service, that I might have been more at liberty, and at my own dispose'. Oliver Sansom, *An Account of Many Remarkable Passages of the Life of Oliver Sansom* (1710), 5–6.
126. H. Best, *Rural Economy in Yorkshire in 1641* (Durham, 1857), 134.
127. P. Slack, *The English Poor Law 1531–1782* (1990), 329–34; 39–40; Clark, 'Migrants in the city', 282–6. For examples of societies' gifts to apprentices see BRO, Register of Apprentices, 1720–70, *passim*.
128. Kussmaul, *Servants in Husbandry*, App. 4, 150–63; J.J. Hecht, *The Domestic Servant in Eighteenth-Century England* (1956), 30–33; Clark, 'Migrants in the city', 285–6.
129. C.W. Brooks, *Pettyfoggers and Vipers of the Commonwealth: The 'Lower Branch' of the Legal Profession in Early Modern England* (Cambridge, 1986). For the presence of an attorney in an apprenticeship case, see BRO, Quarter Sessions, 04447(1), case dated August 1663.
130. For the importance of kinship and, to a lesser extent, neighbourhood ties, in critical life situations (especially unemployment, illness and migration) in the nineteenth century, see Anderson, *Family Structure*, 136–61. Anderson has also shown that bureaucratised forms of assistance (the Poor Law and friendly societies) were either a 'refuge of last resort' to most people, or that they were limited in the amounts they could provide. Ibid., 137–9.

8 Spirituality, Leisure, Sexuality: Was There a Youth Culture?

1. N.Z. Davis, 'The reasons of misrule: youth groups and charivaris in sixteenth-century France', *Past and Present*, 50 (1971), repr. in *Society and Culture in Early Modern France* (Stanford, 1975), 97–123; Smith, 'The London apprentices as seventeenth-century adolescents', *Past and Present*, 61 (1973), 149–61; S.R. Smith, 'The ideal and reality: apprentice–master relationships in seventeenth century London', *History of Education Quarterly*, 21 (1981), 449–59; B. Capp, 'English youth groups and the Pinder of Wakefield', *Past and Present*, 76 (1977), 127–33; B. Reay, 'Popular hostility towards Quakers in mid-seventeenth-century England', *Social History*, 5 (1980), 404–5; R. Thompson, 'Adolescent culture in colonial Massachusetts', *Journal of Family History*, 9 (1984), 127–44; P. Collinson, *The Religion of Protestants* (Oxford, 1982), 225–30; A.L. Beier and R. Finlay (eds), *London 1500–1700: The Making of the Metropolis* (1986), introduction, 21; J.R. Gillis, *For Better, for Worse: British Marriages, 1600 to the Present* (New

York and Oxford, 1985), 11–12, 20–30, 34–7.

2. K.J. Lindley, 'Riot prevention and control in early Stuart London', *Transactions of the Royal Historical Society*, 5th ser., 33 (1983), 109–26; I. Archer, *The Pursuit of Stability: Social Relations in Elizabethan London* (Cambridge, 1991), 1–9; P. Seaver, 'Apprentice riots as social protest' (paper delivered in Moscow, 1991); T. Harris, *London Crowds in the Reign of Charles II* (Cambridge, 1987), 23–4, 82–91.

3. R. Manning, *Village Revolts: Social Protest and Popular Disturbances in England 1509–1640* (Oxford, 1988), 187–219; Seaver, 'Apprentice riots'; Harris, *London Crowds*, 23–4.

4. S. Brigden, 'Youth and the English Reformation', *Past and Present*, 95 (1982), 37–40.

5. Brigden, 'Youth and the English Reformation'. For a psychological interpretation based on E. Erikson's analysis of the adolescent stage of development as characterised by identity confusion or crisis, see Smith, 'London apprentices', esp. 157–8; S.R. Smith, 'Religion and the conception of youth in seventeenth-century England', *History of Childhood Quarterly*, 4 (1975), esp. 506–14. For similar interpretations of the experiences of autobiographers in colonial England, see the comments and bibliography in R. Thompson, 'Adolescent culture in colonial Massachusetts', 128.

6. C. Hill, *The World Turned Upside Down: Radical Ideas during the English Revolution* (Harmondsworth, 1975), 189.

7. Brigden, 'Youth and the English Reformation', 41–2.

8. Ibid.

9. For the suggestion that the fact that the young appeared to be the most active supporters of early lutheranism might be misleading, see R.W. Scribner, *The German Reformation* (1986), 27.

10. Evans, *An Eccho to the Voice from Heaven*, 32. See also Hill, *World Turned Upside Down*, 189.

11. *The Life of Mr Robert Blair, Minister of St Andrews, Containing his Autobiography from 1593 to 1636* (Edinburgh, 1848), 6.

12. St Augustine's *Confessions*, Vol. II, trans. William Watts (1912), *passim*, and esp. 147, 195, 310–11, 325.

13. N.H. Keeble (ed.), *The Autobiography of Richard Baxter* (Everyman's Library, 1974), 10.

14. A.W. Brink (ed.), *The Life of the Late Reverend Mr George Trosse* (Montreal and London, 1974); Oliver Sansom, *An Account of Many Remarkable Passages of the Life of Oliver Sansom* (1710); Disney, *Some Remarkable Passages* (1692); Norwood, *The Journal of Richard Norwood*, 69.

15. Robert Blair began to think about God when he was 'left alone in the house through indisposition' on Sundays; Arise Evans started thinking about God some time after his father's death, and William Bowcock first began to think about the 'terrors of Hell' when he was apprenticed and had 'to work much by myself'. *Life of Mr Robert Blair*, 4; Evans, *An Eccho to the Voice*, 5–6; *The Life, Experience, and Correspondence of Willian Bowcock, the Lincolnshire Drillman* (1851), 8.

16. William Kiffin, *Remarkable Passages in the Life of William Kiffin* (1823), 376. Bangs, *Memoirs of the Life* (1757), 13–23, quotation on p. 23. Among sociologists and social psychologists today there is considerable disagreement about the validity of the Eriksonian model in describing the experience of the majority of contemporary teenagers. For a summary and the literature on the extent of 'adolescent turmoil' in modern American society, see J.J. Conger and A.C. Petersen, *Adolescence and Youth: Psychological Development in a Changing World* (3rd edn, New York, 1984), 19–31.

17. Bangs, *Memoirs of the Life*, 16;

Evans, *An Eccho to the Voice*, 5; Disney, *Some Remarkable Passages*, 38; Lodowick Muggleton, *The Acts of the Witnesses of the Spirit* (1699), 9; Anon., *An Account of the Work of Grace upon*, in Charles Doe, *A Collection of Experiences of the Work of Grace* (1698), 12–13; Thomas Lurting, *The Fighting Sailor Turn'd Peaceable Christian* (1766), 10–11.

18. Although in the end Brysson responded to his father in words which 'did so affect the heart of the old man', that he told his son that 'God forbid!... [if] ever I should hinder you from going where you may get most good for your soul'. George Brysson, *Memoirs of George Brysson* (1825), 271–2.

19. Samuel Bownas, *An Account of the Life and Travels of Samuel Bownas* (4th edn, 1795), 1–3.

20. Anon., *An Account of the Work*, 1. For other autobiographers who emphasised the positive role of their parents, see Bownas, *Account of Life and Travels*, 1–4; Bangs, *Memoirs of the Life*, 8; Elias Osborn, *A Brief Narrative of the Life, Labours and Sufferings of Elias Osborn* (1723), 16–17. For the importance of a godly household in the upbringing of children, see also S.J. Wright, 'Confirmation, catechism and communion: the role of the young in the post-Reformation church', in S.J. Wright (ed.), *Parish, Church and People: Local Studies in Lay Religion, 1350–1750* (1988), 203–4.

21. Bangs, *Memoirs of the Life*, 15–16.

22. Richard Davies, *An Account of the Convincement, Exercises, Services, and Travels of that Ancient Servant of the Lord, Richard Davies* (1794), 3.

23. Charles Doe, *The Experience of Charles Doe*, in *A Collection of Experiences of the Work of Grace* (1698), 30.

24. For references to encounters in the local inn or at the master's shop, see Christopher Story, *A Brief Account of the Life, Convincement, Sufferings, Labours and Travels* (1677), 13–14; William Edmundson, *A Journal of the Life of William Edmundson* (Dublin, 1820), 43; *Memoirs of George Brysson*, 269. Other writers of autobiographies who made references to various people in and around where they lived include Arise Evans, Richard Davies, Elias Osborn and Richard Baxter. For the importance of inns and ale-houses in the dissemination of Protestantism, see P. Collinson, *The Birthpangs of Protestant England: Religious and Cultural Change in the Sixteenth and Seventeenth Centuries* (New York, 1988), 107.

25. Alexander Reid, *Life of Alexander Reid, a Scottish Covenanter* (Manchester, 1822), 4; Disney, *Some Remarkable Passages*, 37; *Memoirs of George Brysson*, 269.

26. Collinson, *Birthpangs of Protestant England*, 106.

27. George Bewley remembered that when he was an apprentice in Dublin, 'a particular visit was appointed by Friends for young people'. Bewley, *A Narrative of the Christian Experiences*, 15.

28. W. Sachse (ed.), *The Diary of Roger Lowe* (New Haven, 1938), 15–18, 22, 25, 29, 33, and *passim*.

29. Story, *A Brief Account*, 14; Bewley, *A Narrative of the Christian Experiences*, 17–18.

30. Reay, 'Popular hostility towards Quakers', 403–7.

31. Anon., *An Account of the Work*, 13.

32. George Fox remembered that, having abandoned his companions in the ale-house, he went home, 'but did not go to bed that night, nor could I sleep but sometimes walked up and down, and sometimes prayed and cried to the Lord, who said unto me, "Thou seest how young people go together into vanity... thou must forsake all, both young and old, and keep out of all, and be a stranger unto all."' *Journal of George Fox* (7th ed. 1852), ed. W. Armistead, 50.

33. BRO, Orders and Proceedings of Mayor and Aldermen, 04417 (1), fo.

135; Wright, 'Conformation, catechism and communion', 202.

34. Collinson, *Birthpangs of Protestant England*, 110.

35. Wright, 'Confirmation, catechism and communion', 201–27; esp. 210–11, 217, 220.

36. Ingram, *Church Courts, Sex and Marriage*, 123, 323–63, esp. 353–5.

37. For examples of conduct books for the young, see Abraham Jackson, *The Pious Prentice* (1640); Burrowes, *Good Instructions for all Young Men and Maids* (1641); Francis Cockin, *Divine Blossoms: a Prospect or Looking-Glass for Youth* (1657). For godly chapbooks and ballads, see T. Watt, *Cheap Print and Popular Piety 1550–1640* (Cambridge, 1991), 101, 298, 304–5.

38. K. Thomas, *Religion and the Decline of Magic* (New York, 1971), 152; K. Wrightson and D. Levine, *Poverty and Piety in an English Village: Terling 1525–1700* (1979), 104, 106, 116, 133; P. Clark, *The English Alehouse: A Social History 1200–1830* (1983), 154, 163, note 28.

39. D. Underdown, *Fire from Heaven: The Life of an English Town in the Seventeenth Century* (1991), 41.

40. Wright, 'Confirmation, catechism and communion', 215.

41. Ibid., 217–20.

42. Ibid., 208.

43. Ibid., 217.

44. For jokes about adults sleeping in church, see Watt, *Cheap Print and Popular Piety*, 321.

45. *Barlow's Journal*, 16.

46. For an emphasis on indifference to religion see Thomas, *Religion and the Decline of Magic*, 159–66; K. Wrightson, *English Society 1580–1680* (1982), 206–21. For views that emphasise 'solid conformity' rather than indifference or religious zeal, see Ingram, *Church Courts, Sex and Marriage*, 84–12. And see also R. Whiting, *The Blind Devotion of the People: Popular Religion and the English Reformation* (Cambridge, 1989); C. Haigh, 'The English Reformation: a premature birth, a difficult labour and a sickly child', *Historical Journal*, 33 (1990), 449–59, esp. 455–6, 458–9.

47. Ingram, *Church Courts, Sex and Marriage*, 120–23.

48. Kussmaul, *Servants in Husbandry*, 43.

49. For the importance of the alehouse in the lives of servants and apprentices, and the predominance of youth in such establishments, see Clark, *The English Alehouse*, 127. See also Kussmaul, *Servants in Husbandry*, 43.

50. *Diary of Roger Lowe*, 28–36.

51. D. Cressy, *Bonfires and Bells: National Memory and the Protestant Calendar in Elizabethan and Stuart England* (1989), 19; C. Phythian-Adams, 'Ceremony and the citizen: the communal year at Coventry 1450–1550', in P. Clark and P. Slack (eds), *Crisis and Order in English Towns 1500–1700* (1972), 66; A. Yarbrough, 'Apprentices as adolescents in sixteenth-century Bristol', *Journal of Social History*, 13 (1979), 71; R.W. Malcolmson, *Popular Recreations in English Society 1700–1850* (Cambridge, 1973), 30, 54.

52. Cressy, *Bonfires and Bells*, 22.

53. Kussmaul, *Servants in Husbandry*, 60–3; Malcolmson, *Popular Recreations*, 22–3.

54. Capp, 'English youth groups', 127–8; Ingram, *Church Courts, Sex and Marriage*, 102–3; Seaver, 'Apprentice riots as social protest', 7.

55. Collinson, *Birthpangs of Protestant England*, 108; Thompson, 'Adolescent culture in colonial Massachusetts', 130.

56. P. Burke, 'Popular culture in seventeenth-century London', in B. Reay, *Popular Culture in Seventeenth-Century England* (1985), 35; Smith, 'London apprentices', 153–6, 158–9.

57. Watt, *Cheap Print and Popular Piety*, 298; M. Spufford, *Small Books and Pleasant Histories: Popular Fiction and its Readership in Seventeenth-*

Century England (Cambridge, 1981), 7–8, 7 1–5.
58. P. Collinson, 'Popular and unpopular religion' in *The Religion of Protestants: The Church in English Society 1559–1625* (Oxford, 1982), 225–8.
59. Willian Lilly, *Mr William Lilly's History of his Life and Times from the Year 1602 to 1681* (1715), 17.
60. Benjamin Bangs also remembered a 'companion' with whom he was 'sometimes a little too jocular in a bantering way'. Disney, *Some Remarkable Passages*, 32; Bangs, *Memoirs of the Life*, 16.
61. Yarbrough, 'Apprentices as adolescents in sixteenth-century Bristol', 73.
62. *Diary of Roger Lowe*; M. Beloff, 'A London apprentice's notebook, 1703–5', *History*, 27 (1942), 38–45. P. Seaver, 'A social contact? – master against servant in the Court of Requests', *History Today*, 39 (September 1989), 54–5.
63. Quoted in Clark, *The English Alehouse*, 127.
64. A.L. Beier, *Masterless Men: The Vagrancy Problem in England, 1560–1640* (1985), 42, 44, 51–5; Archer, *Pursuit of Stability*, 206–8; R.B. Shoemaker, *Prosecution and Punishment: Petty Crime and the Law in London and Rural Middlesex, c. 1660–1725* (Cambridge, 1991), 168–87, esp. 184–6.
65. Clark, *The English Alehouse*, 125; *William Lilly's History of his Life*, 17.
66. Ingram, *Church Courts, Sex, and Marriage*, 103; Malcolmson, *Popular Recreations*, 56. For the importance of cock-fighting in urban rituals, see P. Borsay, 'All the town's a stage: urban ritual and ceremony 1660–1800', in P. Clark (ed.), *The Transformation of English Provincial Towns* (1984), 235.
67. Quoted in Watt, *Cheap Print and Popular Piety*, 13.
68. Cressy, *Bonfires and Bells*, 19; BRO, Orders and Proceedings of Mayor and Aldermen, 04417(1), fo. 15, order dated 26 February 1654.
69. See note 2 above.
70. Cressy, *Bonefires and Bells*, 26–7; Malcolmson, *Popular Recreations*, 60.
71. Malcolmson, *Popular Recreations*, 55–6; Ingram, *Church Courts, Sex and Marriage*, 102.
72. Keeble (ed.), *Autobiography of Richard Baxter*, 6.
73. Phythian-Adams, 'Ceremony and the citizen', 60–62; Phythian-Adams, *Desolation of a City: Coventry and the Urban Crisis of the Late Middle Ages* (Cambridge, 1979), 125–7.
74. Burke, 'Popular culture in seventeenth-century London', *London Journal*, 3 (1977), 148; Borsay, *The English Urban Renaissance: Culture and Society in the Provincial Town 1660–1770* (Oxford, 1989), 118. For Bristol's fairs as recreational sites, see J. Barry, 'Popular culture in seventeenth-century Bristol', in Reay (ed.), *Popular Culture in Seventeenth-Century England*, 79.
75. M. Pelling, 'Occupational diversity: barbersurgeons and the trades of Norwich, 1550–1640', *Bulletin of the History of Medicine*, 56 (1982), 504–5; Barry, 'Popular culture', 78.
76. *Barlow's Journal*, 16.
77. *Diary of Roger Lowe*, 34.
78. *Barlow's Journal*, 38–9.
79. When John Wallington, Senior, came to London in the early 1570s he was put to do household work on Sundays. P.S. Seaver, *Wallington's World: A Puritan Artisan in Seventeenth-Century London* (Stanford, 1985), 187–8.
80. See Chapter 5, 129.
81. London's apprentices complained in one of their petitions that their masters varied in the amount of time they permitted them to absent themselves from work. *The Humble Remonstrance of the Apprentices of the City of London* (1647).
82. *Forman's Autobiography*, in A.L. Rowse, *Simon Forman: Sex and Society in Shakespeare's Age* (1974), 274.
83. M. Rediker, *Between the Devil and*

the Deep Blue Sea (Cambridge, 1987), 11.

84. Yarbrough, 'Apprentices as adolescents in sixteenth-century Bristol', 73. For gold lace on a doublet which was bought by a merchant's apprentice, see Trosse, *Life of*, 56. For a wig bought by a London printer's apprentice, see *The Diary of John Coggs*, Bodleian Library, Ms Eng. misc. fos 9, 78.

85. Trosse, *Life of*, 51–61, quotations on pp. 55, 60, 61.

86. Cressy, *Literacy and the Social Order: Reading and Writing in Tudor and Stuart England* (Cambridge, 1980); Wrightson, *English Society*, 184–91. For literacy rates in Bristol, see Barry, 'Popular culture' 62–3.

87. BRO, Quarter Sessions, 04445, fo. 19; the case of Robert Bennet, a Bristol baker, who in 1614 promised to send his apprentice, John Mercer, to school.

88. Rappaport, *Worlds Within Worlds*, 298–9.

89. Wrightson, *English Society*, 190, 194.

90. Ibid., 190. In Bristol some occupations, especially in the mercantile and distributive trades, were wholly literate by the late seventeenth century; but other crafts, such as the building industry, had well below a 50 per cent literacy rate. Barry, 'Popular culture', 62.

91. Wrightson, *English Society*, 197.

92. *Diary of Roger Lowe*, 15, 16, 19.

93. For examples see BRO, Register of Apprentices, 04352(5)a, fos 12 (apprenticeship of Mathews Maddocks), 54 (Robert Smith), and 81 (John Brigdale).

94. Borsay, *English Urban Renaissance*, esp. ch. 11.

95. For the variety of new high-status leisures which catered to a larger segment of the middling as well as the upper classes, see ibid., 117–196.

96. P. Earle, *The Making of the English Middle Class: Business, Society, and Family Life in London, 1660–1730* (1989), 102–3.

97. *Diary of John Coggs*; see also M. Beloff, 'A London apprentice's notebook', 38–45, esp. 43–4.

98. For apprenticeship premiums in the early eighteenth century in parishes in the south and the east, see K.D.M. Snell, *Annals of the Labouring Poor: Social Change and Agrarian England, 1660–1900* (Cambridge, 1985), 233.

99. Trosse, *Life of*, 58–9.

100. Wrightson, *English Society*, 71–9; Ingram, *Church Courts, Sex and Marriage*, 225–30; 302–4; 261–75; Spufford, *Small Books*, 156–93; Gillis, *For Better, for Worse*, 21–30.

101. Ingram, *Church Courts, Sex and Marriage*, 264–6; 353–5.

102. *Journal of Richard Norwood*, 46; Disney, *Some Remarkable Passages*, 32–3.

103. Archer, *Pursuit of Stability*, 211–15; 207.

104. See note 96 above.

105. Ingram, *Church Courts, Sex and Marriage*, 292–319, esp. 300–3.

106. McIntosh, *A Community Transformed*, 69.

107. *Forman's Autobiography*, 274.

108. Ibid.

109. For the freedom of choice of a marriage partner among London servants, compared with the relative constraint placed on women who were living with kin, see V. Brodsky Elliott, 'Single women in the London marriage market': age, status and mobility, 1598–1619', in R.B. Outhwaite (ed.), *Marriage and Society: Studies in the History of Marriage* (1981), 81–100, esp. 94–6.

110. Ingram, *Church Courts, Sex, and Marriage*, 302–3.

111. Wrightson, *English Society*, 76–7. For the greater control of women who lived with their parents see also Brodsky Elliott, 'Single women', 90–5.

112. Ingram, *Church Courts, Sex and Marriage*, 264–8; Wrightson, *English Society*, 88.

113. Wrightson, *English Society*, 86;

McIntosh, *A Community Tranformed*, 70–1.
114. L. Roper, *The Holy Household: Women and Morals in Reformation Augsburg* (Oxford, 1989), 129–31.
115. Shoemaker, *Prosecution and Punishment*, 185–6; 180, 212–13; Hill, *Women, Work, and Sexual Politics*, 173.
116. Ingram, *Church Courts, Sex and Marriage*, 163–7; M. Ingram, 'Ridings, rough music and the "reform of popular culture" in early modern England', *Past and Present*, 105 (1984), 79–113. For the interpretation – by now classic – of the central role of youths in charivari in France, see N.Z. Davis, 'The reasons of misrule', 97–123.
117. Ingram, 'Ridings, rough music, and the "reform of popular culture"', 103–9.
118. Ibid., 82.
119. Ingram, *Church Courts, Sex and Marriage*, 157, 219–20.
120. P. Laslett, *Family Life and Illicit Love in Earlier Generations* (Cambridge, 1977), 102–59, esp. 137–41. For illegitimacy figures in the manor of Havering, see McIntosh, *A Community Transformed*, 68–9.
121. Wrightson, *English Society*, 86. For a discussion of various interpretations of the reasons and factors underlying low levels of illegitimacy, see Ingram, *Church Courts, Sex and Marriage*, 157–63. For cautious attitudes towards marriage, see also Chapter 9, 230–2.
122. Wrightson, *English Society*, 84–5; Ingram, *Church Courts, Sex and Marriage*, 267.
123. McIntosh, *A Community Transformed*, 68.
124. Gillis referred to comments made in the eighteenth century, by farmers who believed that if they were too strict they would be left with no servants on their farms. Gillis, *For Better, for Worse*, 30.
125. *Forman's Autobiography*, 274.
126. Sociologists emphasise that sharing a common trait, such as a stage in the life cycle, is in itself not a sufficient component of a subculture. Other criteria include association in large numbers, adherence to values and norms that are clearly distinct from those of the larger society, patronising institutions that are exclusive to members sharing the same trait, and possession of a common way of life. For a discussion of the criteria of 'subcultures' in an urban context in modern society, see C.S. Fischer, *To Dwell among Friends: Personal Networks in Town and City* (Chicago, 1982), 194–249, esp. 194–5.
127. For a theoretical analysis which emphasises the differences between youth as a stage in the life cycle and youth as a generation, see A.B. Spitzer, 'The historical problem of generations', *American Historical Review*, 78 (1973), 1353–85. Spitzer emphasises the difference – first formulated by Karl Mannheim – between recurrent collective behaviour associated with a certain phase of the life cycle, and the collective experience which stamps a group of people – a 'generation', or a 'cohort' – and permanently distinguishes them from other people even as they grow up. For a bibliography of the historical literature on generations in the nineteenth and twentieth centuries, see ibid., 1353–4, and notes 1–3. For a discussion of Mannheim's assertion that while men of equal age are drawn together by a natural affinity, this affinity in itself would never produce what he called a 'social generation', see R. Wohl, *The Generation of 1914* (Cambridge, Mass., 1979), 73–84, esp. 79.
128. Ingram, *Church Courts, Sex and Marriage*, 354, 365.
129. See Chapter 7, 178–9.
130. See Chapter 9, 209–15.
131. See Chapter 7, 176–7.
132. For a case which involved an apprentice who was disobedient to his master, and was also 'not true but light fingered and given to pilfering and picking his fellow apprentices' pockets and filching away their

monies', see PRO, Chancery Court, R.I/33, 177.01386, case involving Francis Cuckoe, the son of Rose Cuckoe, and apprenticed to a tanner.

133. See Chapter 7.

134. See Chapter 9, 209–15.

135. For an example in which an apprentice left his master but returned to him some six months later to ask to be taken back, see the case of Peter Bayne. A shoemaker apprentice, Bayne turned to Bristol's court in 1627 when he found that his master was unable to take him back because he now had too many apprentices. BRO, Quarter Sessions, 04445, fo. 144.

136. For the difficulties of a youth confronting a decision whether to remain in the parish where his mother lived, or to go away with his master to look for employment, see Bangs, *Memoirs of the Life*, 12.

137. When he returned home from a service term following his father's death, William Bowcock was to be bound an apprentice by the parish, 'to be a drudge in a farm yard'; for his widowed mother, this was 'a sore trial', as he put it in his autobiography. Bowcock, *Life, Experience and Correspondence*, 8.

9 *'Rites of Passage': Transitions to Adult Life*

1. Ingram, *Church Courts, Sex and Marriage*, 125. For the importance of marriage in an urban context, see C. Phythian-Adams, *Desolation of a City: Coventry and the Urban Crisis of the Late Middle Ages* (Cambridge, 1979), 86; Rappaport, *Worlds Within Worlds*, 327–8. For the importance of marriage in the lives of women, see S. Mendelson, 'Stuart women's diaries and occasional 'memoirs', in M. Prior (ed.), *Women in English Society 1500–1800*, (1985), 181–210; L. Pollock, '"An action like a stratagem": courtship and marriage from the Middle Ages to the twentieth century', *Historical Journal*, 30 (1987), 483–98, esp. 494.

2. For a strong emphasis on marriage as a pre-eminently male rite of passage, see J.R. Gillis, *For Better, For Worse: British Marriages, 1600 to the Present* (New York and Oxford, 1965), 50–52. For comments and criticsm of Gillis's interpretation, see Pollock, '"An action like stratagem"', *passim*. For public ceremonies involving the calling of banns, and more private marriages by licence, see P. Earle, *The Making of the English Middle Class: Business, Society, and Family Life in London, 1660–1730* (1989), 179.

3. J. Croker, *Brief Memoir of the Life of John Croker,* in J. Barclay (ed.), *A Select Series, Biographical, Narrative, Epistolary and Miscellaneous, Chiefly the Productions of Early Members of the Society of Friends* (1836), Vol. VI, 285–302. Other autobiographies also reveal the importance of parents in the initial move from home, followed by moves young people made on their own. See, for example, Bangs, *Memoirs of the Life*, 11–12.

4. Kussmaul, *Servants in Husbandry*, 35–6; McIntosh, 'Servants and the household unit', 12.

5. H. Best, *Rural Economy in Yorkshire in 1641* (Durhan, 1857), 135.

6. Ibid., 135; Kussmaul, *Servants in Husbandry*, 40, and 183, note 59.

7. The apprenticeship was recorded on 20 January 1605. BRO, Register of Apprentices, 94352(3), fo. 202.

8. PRO, Chancery Court, C3/304/ 68. For another example of an orphaned apprentice who turned to court on his own see the case of John Mercer, a Bristol native and orphan, who was bound in 1614 for twelve years with a Bristol baker, and who appeared at the court in 1620 to ask for release, which the court granted. BRO, Quarter Sessions, 04445, fo. 19. For the apprenticeship of Mercer, see Register of Apprentices, 04352(4), 17 August 1614.

9. In 14 out of 35 petitions presented between 1620 and 1675, records show the involvement of a third party, and the wording of many of the remaining petitions suggests that the complaint was made by the apprentice alone rather than by someone on his behalf. These may well have been cases of older apprentices who were 21 or over.
10. Kussmaul, *Servants in Husbandry*, 88.
11. *Barlow's Journal*, 76; BRO, Quarter Sessions, 04445–7(2); 04434(1); R.B. Shoemaker, *Prosecution and Punishment: Petty Crime and the Law in London and Rural Middlesex, c. 1660–1725* (Cambridge, 1991), 174–5.
12. Kussmaul, *Servants in Husbandry*, 34–5; BRO, Ordinances for City Companies, 04369(1), fo. 177; *An Additional Ordinance of the Lords and Commons ... Concerning days of Recreation ... and the Apprentices Petition and Propositions* (1647); *The Autobiography of William Stout*, 80.
13. Best, *Rural Economy in Yorkshire*, 136; Francis Kirkman, *The Unlucky Citizen Experimentally Described in the Various Misfortunes of an Unlucky Londoner* (1673), 35–6.
14. William Bowcock, when he first went into farm service at the age of 11, was 'full of uneasiness, to the barn my feet led me for retirement.... Home now attracted my heart ... while pensive and sad in the barn, my new companions sought and found me sorrowing'. *The Life, Experience, and Correspondence of William Bowcock, the Lincolnshire Drillman* (1851), 7.
15. Kussmaul, *Servants in Husbandry*, 44–7.
16. PRO, Chancery Court, C3/304/68.
17. *The Life of Adam Martindale*, 30.
18. *Forman's Autobiography*, in A.L. Rowse, *Simon Forman: Sex and Society in Shakespeare's Age* (1974), 276.
19. W. Sachse (ed.), *The Diary of Roger Lowe* (New Haven, 1938), 50–51, 65.
20. Kussmaul, *Servants in Husbandry*, 46.
21. BRO, Orders and Proceedings of the Mayor and Aldermen, 04417(1), fo. 46; Tolzey Recognizances, 04434(1), fo. 536.
22. J.A. Sharpe, *Crime in Early Modern England 1550–1750* (1984), 103–4. For an elaborate court case involving large-scale dealings and embezzlement of a master by his enterprising youth, see P. Seaver, 'A social contract? – master against servant in the Court of Requests', *History Today*, 39 (September 1989), 50–6.
23. BRO, Orders and Proceedings, fo. 71. For pilfering in domestic service in the eighteenth century, see B. Hill, *Women, Work, and Sexual Politics in Eighteenth-Century England* (Oxford, 1989), 140–2.
24. BRO, Orders and Proceedings, fo. 99.
25. *Diary of Roger Lowe*, 61, 93; *Barlow's Journal*, 76.
26. For an incident of a runaway apprentice whose master was exceptionally harsh, see the case of John Webb, the son of a weaver in Bedminster, who was apprenticed in Bristol in 1617 to Richard Williams, a cooper. According to the testimony of Webb, and 'by other sufficient proofe', he was so badly beaten by his master and mistress that he nearly became crippled. The master also appears to have failed to provide the youth with his basic needs ('kept him in a most beastly manner'). The justices instructed one of them, A. Kitchen, an alderman who was then responsible for Redcliff ward, to order the master to avoid overworking the apprentice. The master agreed to comply. A year later, however, Webb appeared at court again to ask for an official permit to leave; by this time he had actually already left and was desribed in the record as the 'late' apprentice of Richard Williams. BRO, Quarter Sessions, 04445, fo. 18, case dated 16 April 1621.
27. *The Journal of Richard Norwood*,

40–1.

28. For bonds of security see Chapter 5, p. 87.

29. The episode is recorded in a letter he sent to his cousin, James Fretwell. Fretwell, *A Family History*, 206–7.

30. In 1607 Bristol's Company of Metalworkers (including the smiths, cutlers, gunmakers, sheergrinders, spurriers and girdlers) ordered that no craftsman should 'entice, stir, or provoke any apprentice or servant of any master to depart from his service'. BRO, Ordinances for City Companies, fo. 200, no. 14.

31. T. Nourse, *Compania Felix: Or, A Discourse of the Benefits and Improvements of Husbandry* (1700), 204.

32. Kussmaul, *Servants in Husbandry*, 97–119.

33. Ibid., 55.

34. Edward Barlow recorded in his autobiography that when his brother became an apprentice in London, 'he did not like it very well, and could wish he might go down into the country again, for he . . . loved the country better than the city'. *Barlow's Journal*, 25. For a case of an apprentice who returned to the countryside when plague broke out in London see Disney, *Some Remarkable Passages* (1692), 45–6.

35. *Barlow's Journal*, 63–4.

36. Dod and Cleaver claimed that their readers looked after 'greediness in the world', and that they put their sons with masters 'by whom they may grow into advancement in the world'. John Dod and Robert Cleaver, *A Godly Forme of Household Government* (1630), Q7. See also A.W. Brink (ed.), *The Life of the Late Reverend Mr George Trosse* (Montreal and London, 1974), 57.

37. For the theme of social preferment and ambition in Thomas Heywood and Thomas Deloney, and an intepretation which places them in the context of medieval romance rather than a new bourgeois ethic, see L.C. Stevenson, *Praise and Paradox: Merchants and Craftsmen in Elizabethan Popular Literature* (Cambridge, 1984), 144–58. For the theme of 'poor boy and girl make good' in chapbooks in the seventeenth century, see M. Spufford, *Small Books and Pleasant Histories: Popular Fiction and its Readership in Seventeenth-Century England* (Cambridge, 1981), 244–50.

38. Lodowick Muggleton, *The Acts of the Witnesses of the Spirit* (1699), 8; William Edmundson, *A Journal of the Life of William Edmundson* (Dublin, 1820), 44; *The Journal of Richard Norwood*, 45; Fretwell, *A Family History*, 197.

39. *Barlow's Journal*, 18.

40. In a sample of 113 sons of husbandmen apprenticed in Bristol between 1542 and 1552, 13 (11.5 per cent) entered the distributive trades. In a sample of 274 sons of husbandmen registered between 1600 and 1645, only 27 (9.9 per cent) entered the distributive trades, of whom only 9 (3.3 per cent of the total) entered the top mercantile trades. Of these, perhaps one or two finished their terms and became citizens of the town. For the social origins of London's richest merchants, see R.G. Lang, 'Social origins and social aspirations of Jacobean London merchants', *Economic History Review*, 2nd ser., 27 (1974), 36.

41. Rappaport, *Worlds Within Worlds*, 370; G.D. Ramsay, 'The recruitment and fortunes of some London freemen in the mid-sixteenth century', *Economic History Review*, 2nd ser., 31 (1978), 536–40.

42. C.G.A. Clay, *Economic Expansion and Social Change: England 1500–1700* (Cambridge, 1984), Vol. II, 64–9.

43. Earle, *Making of the English Middle Class*, 106–8.

44. For example, William Stout invested in his shop £50 which had been left to him in his father's will, and nearly £120 which he obtained by selling the land left to him as well. *Autobiography of William Stout*, 89.

45. Rappaport, *Worlds Within*

Worlds, 341.

46. No less than two-thirds of the sons of yeomen who entered a Bristol apprenticeship in the 1540s, and over a half by the early seventeenth century, entered a craft rather than a mercantile business or some large-scale entrepreneurial trade. In the period 1600–45 about a quarter of the sons of gentlemen, merchants and traders likewise entered the crafts rather than the large-scale distributive trades. In a sample of 19 sons of yeomen apprenticed in the 1540s, 13 (68.4 per cent) entered the crafts and only 6 entered the distributive trades; and in a sample of 193 sons of yeomen apprenticed between 1600 and 1645, 110 (56.9 per cent) entered artisanal crafts.

47. The change in the profile of parental occupations of Bristol's apprentices was as follows.

Parental occupations of Bristol apprentices

	1532–42		1600–45	
	no.	%	no.	%
Gentlemen	48	3.6	88	5.8
Yeomen	74	5.5	193	12.8
Traders	244	18.2	250	16.6
Professions	44	3.3	48	3.2
Craftsmen	623	46.6	634	41.9
Husbandmen	267	20.0	285	18.8
Labourers	37	2.8	14	0.9
Total	1337	100.0	1512	100.0

Sources: D. Hollis (ed.), *Calendar of the Bristol Apprentice Book 1532–1565* (Bristol Record Society, Vol. XIV, Bristol, 1948), 209–13; BRO, Register of Apprentices, 04352(2)–(6). The 1532–42 total includes all the entries in the register; the 1600–45 is a sample.

For a detailed analysis of changing patterns of apprenticeship in Bristol, suggesting 'hardening of social boundaries', limited occupational mobility and greater restriction on entry into the top mercantile trades by the seventeenth century, see D.H. Sacks, *The Widening Gate: Bristol and the Atlantic Economy 1450–1700* (Berkeley, Los Angeles and Oxford, 1991), 106–24.

48. In a sample of 634 apprentices registered between 1670 and 1700, 42 (6.6 per cent) were sons of husbandmen.

49. In the mid-sixteenth century the average term that Bristol apprentices signed in their indentures was 8.4 years. In the ensuing decades the terms for which apprentices signed became shorter: they fell from a mean of 8.4 years during the 1550s, and 8.3 in the 1580s, to 7.8 in the first decade of the seventeenth century, 7.9 in the 1620s, 7.4 in the 1630s, and 7.3 in the 1640s. By the mid-seventeenth century the standard term became a seven-year apprenticeship. Poorer youths would have found it increasingly difficult to bargain for a longer term in return for lower premiums. For the likelihood of such bargains, see Chapter 4, pp. 92–3.

50. Cash sums and occasionally the provision of bedding and tools at the end of an apprentice's term were quite common in the sixteenth century, and they were still guaranteed in nearly half of the apprenticeship indentures signed by Bristol youths between 1600 and 1615. From then on, arrangements in which money at the end of a term was promised dropped to a quarter, a fifth, and by the 1640s to less than 10 per cent of all apprenticeship contracts. Between 1600 and 1645, cash sums masters agreed to give to a youth at the end of his term were in the range of 4d. to £20 (most were between 20sh. and 40sh.), and they were more commonly given in industries and crafts, where about a third of those bound between 1600 and 1645 were guaranteed these sums if they finished their terms. The drop in the proportions of such arrangements was as follows:

	%	Sample size
1600–04	48	103
1605–09	44	838
1610–15	41	170
1616–20	27	230
1621–25	14	106
1626–30	21	155
1631–35	17	138
1636–40	14	135
1641–45	8	70

51. If an unmarried journeyman living with his master for the space of three or four years saved around £20 or £30, this could cover a third of the amount required even in shopkeeping, and perhaps half and more of that required in the less costly crafts. Rappaport estimated that in the second half of the sixteenth century journeymen were paid between £2 and £5 a year in addition to room and board. In mid-seventeenth-century London, Nehemiah Wallington, a turner, paid his journeyman £8 a year, in addition to maintenance. Rappaport, *Worlds Within Worlds*, 221, note 16; P. Seaver, *Wallington's World: A Puritan Artisan in Seventeenth-Century London* (Stanford, 1985), 121. For the amounts needed to set up in the lower crafts, see Chapter 9, pp. 220–21.

52. In London, apprentice labour jeopardised journeymen in some trades during periods of unemployment, as was the case in the cloth-working trade in the late sixteenth century. A similar situation would recur a century and a half later in many places in the rural countryside, where complaints of journeymen about low wages and competition from cheap apprentice labour abounded. Rappaport, *Worlds Within Worlds*, 105–6; K.D.M. Snell, *Annals of the Labouring Poor: Social Change and Agrarian England, 1660–1900* (Cambridge, 1985), 243, and note 37.

53. *The Apprentices of London Petition presented to the Honourable Court of Parliament* (1641).

54. I. Krausman Ben-Amos, 'Failure to become freemen: urban apprentices in early modern England', *Social History*, 16 (1991), 155–72, esp. 163–5.

55. A.L. Beier, 'Engine of manufacture: the trades of London', in A.L. Beier and R. Finlay (eds), *London 1500–1700: The Making of the Metropolis* (1986), 156.

56. For London's population growth and expansion within and outside the walls, see ibid., 62, and note 5.

57. Ben-Amos, 'Failure to become freemen', 169; Benjamin Lay, *Memoirs of the Lives of Benjamin Lay and Ralph Sandiford* (1816), 9–10.

58. Rappaport, *Worlds Within Worlds*, 370; Sacks, *The Widening Gate*, 27–8. For better prospects for setting up in Bristol's expanding shipping and building industries in the first half of the seventeenth century, see Ben-Amos, 'Failure to become freemen', 162–3.

59. Edmundson, *A Journal of the Life*, 45.

60. Joseph Pike went to work for his brother-in-law in the textile trade, and Joseph Oxley moved to Norfolk, where his brother found a shop to rent and his grandmother offered him lodging. Ralph Josselin's two sons moved back to Earls Colne, where they set up a grocery shop near their parents, and Gervase Disney's father suggested that he live near him so they could help each other in his business. Pike, *Some Account of the Life*, 121; Joseph Oxley, *Joseph's Offering to his Children*, in Barclay (ed.), *A Select Series*, Vol. V, 220–1; A. Macfarlane, *The Family Life of Ralph Josselin: a Seventeenth-Century Clergyman* (New York, 1970), 118–20; Disney, *Some Remarkable Passages*, 62–3.

61. BRO, Register of Apprentices, 04352(4), fos 132, 261. Apprenticeships dated 19 June 1616 and 2 May 1622. In a sample of 1,945, 648 were given cash payments at the end of their

terms, mostly in the range of £2–£4.

62. Rappaport, *Worlds Within Worlds*, 372–3; Earle, *Making of the English Middle Class*, 110–11; BRO, Loan Book, 1648, 04183(1).

63. *Autobiography of William Stout*, 90; *Diary of Roger Lowe*, 93; Samuel Bownas, *An Account of the Life and Travels of Samuel Bownas* (4th edn, 1795), 113; Oxley, *Joseph's Offering*, 221.

64. Clay, *Economic Expansion*, Vol. II, 67–8.

65. Peter Earle showed, for example, that in late seventeenth-century London the apothecary business could offer the relatively poor apprentice substantial opportunities for upward mobility. Earle, *Making of the English Middle Class*, 108.

66. 'There are no men under the sun that fare harder and get their living more hard and that are so abused on all sides as we poor seamen . . . and so I could wish no young man to betake himself to this calling unless he had good friends to put him in place or supply his wants.' *Barlow's Journal*, 128.

67. For the hierarchy on a ship, see M. Rediker, *Between the Devil and the Deep Blue Sea* (Cambridge, 1987), 83–4.

68. In a sample of 274 apprentices registered between 1600 and 1645, 58 (21.2 per cent) entered trades involved in the distribution of goods and foodstuffs.

69. For the apprenticeship of Christopher Cottrell, see BRO, Register of Apprentices, 04352(5)a, fo. 66. Cottrell became a burgess on 24 June 1637. Burgess Books, 1607–51, 04359(2)a–b.

70. BRO, Register of Apprentices, 04353(1), fo. 53.

71. In the 1630s a third or more of the apprentices eventually established themselves in Bristol, compared with only a quarter or even less in the late sixteenth century; by the late seventeenth century their numbers had risen to half or nearly 60 per cent of all those who had been apprentices in the town. Ben-Amos, 'Failure to become freemen', 157, Table 1.

72. Ibid.

73. BRO, Great Orphan Book, Vol. III, fo. 198. Andrew Barker was apprenticed to his brother, Thomas, and his apprenticeship was recorded in the register on 22 September 1615.

74. McIntosh, *A Community Transformed*, 18–19.

75. William Taswell was the son of a merchant, but he was denied support from his father and considered himself 'poor'. In his autobiography he recalled how he used to give 'something every day to the poor, which I observed for several years with great strictness'. He was then 25 years old, and he also gave assistance to his brother and sister on occasion. G.P. Elliott (ed.), *Autobiography and Anecdotes. By William Taswell* (Camden Society, 1852), 21, 23; William Lilly, *Mr William Lilly's History of his Life and Times from the Year 1602 to 1681* (1715), 17.

76. *Life of Adam Martindale*, 17–18; N.H. Keeble (ed.), *The Autobiography of Richard Baxter* (Everyman's Library, 1974), 12; Edward Coxere, *Adventures by Sea*, 24; Brysson, *Memoirs of George Brysson* (1825), 273.

77. Fretwell, *A Family History*, 202.

78. Kussmaul, *Servants in Husbandry*, 78–82. For a discussion of the question whether servants transferred their incomes to their families, and the suggestion that there was no 'large-scale movement of income from children to parents', see R.M. Smith, 'Some issues concerning families and their property in rural England 1250–1800', in Smith (ed.), *Land, Kinship and Life-Cycle*, 72.

79. *Barlow's Journal*, 50.

80. Ibid., 47–8.

81. Ibid., 45, 48, 75, 91, 129, 139.

82. Kussmaul, *Servants in Husbandry*, 76, 88, and 192, note 21.

83. Coxere, *Adventures by Sea*, 14, 29, 35.

84. C.W. Brooks, *Pettyfoggers and Vipers of the Commonwealth: The*

'Lower Branch' of the Legal Profession in Early Modern England (Cambridge, 1986), 154.
85. *Life of Adam Martindale*, 34–5, 45–6.
86. R. O'Day, *Education and Society 1500–1800* (1982), 58, 170, 173–6.
87. Keeble (ed.), *Autobiography of Richard Baxter*, 8.
88. W.G. Perrin (ed.), *The Autobiography of Phineas Pett* (1918), 6; Edmundson, *A Journal of the Life*, 44.
89. 'No covenant servant, journeyman, or apprentice shall keep any servant or apprentice under him openly . . . until he be enfranchised and made free of the said company.' BRO, Ordinances for City Companies, 04273(2), fo. 247. Ordinance of the merchant tailors, dated 1640.
90. Thomas Aldworth, apprenticed in 1568 to a Bristol cooper, took his own first apprentice in 1576; and Thomas Bourton, apprenticed in 1614, had an apprentice recorded in the register only two years later, in 1616. BRO, Index to Woodworkers recorded in the Bristol Apprentice Register, 1532–1658, 2, 15.
91. *Autobiography of William Stout*, 96, 99.
92. Rappaport, *Worlds Within Worlds*, 327.
93. *Autobiography of William Stout*, 73–4. For entry ages into apprenticeship, see also Chapter 5, p. 131.
94. Fretwell, *A Family History*, 197. When George Trosse found out that his master might decide to discharge him, he decided to leave his apprenticeship sooner, knowing he might well have to start another apprenticeship, and 'having arrived at the age of nineteen'. Trosse, *Life of*, 64.
95. See Chapter 5, p. 3.
96. Kussmaul, *Servants in Husbandry*, 79–80; Snell, *Annals of the Labouring Poor*, 236; BRO, FC/OP/5, collection of indentures in the parish of Frampton Cotterell. There are some 40 indentures for the period between 1738 and 1771, including craft apprenticeships, but also training in husbandry. For the manor of Havering, see McIntosh, 'Servants and the household unit', 11.
97. Kussmaul, *Servants in Husbandry*, 83.
98. McIntosh, 'Servants and the household unit', 19.
99. K. Wrightson, 'Kinship in an English village: Terling, Essex 1500–1700', in Smith (ed.), *Land, Kinship and Life-Cycle*, 327 and note 18, 329; C. Howell, 'Peasant inheritance customs in the Midlands, 1200–1700', in J.R. Goody, J. Thirsk and E.P. Thompson, *Family and Inheritance: Rural Society in Western Europe* (Cambridge, 1978), 145. In his analysis of the effects of holdings on marriage formation, Richard Wall also concluded that 'real property [i.e. landholding] had no measurable impact on the age at marriage'. R. Wall, 'Real property, marriage and children: the evidence from four pre-industrial communities', in Smith (ed.), *Land, Kinship and Life-Cycle*, 443–79, esp. 466–78.
100. McIntosh, 'Servants and the household unit', 11.
101. V. Brodsky Elliott, 'Single women in the London marriage market: age, status and mobility, 1598–1619', in R.B. Outhwaite (ed.), *Marriage and Society: Studies in the History of Marriage* (1981), 94–7; Coxere, *Adventures by Sea*, 32. Richard Davies also finished his apprenticeship in Wales at about the age of 24, moved to London, opened a small shop, and soon afterwards married a London woman. Richard Davies, *An Account of the Convincement, Exercises, Services, and Travels of that Ancient Servant of the Lord, Richard Davies* (1794), 34.
102. Mean age at first marriage in 1750–99 was 26.4, compared with 27.8 in 1650–99, and 28 in 1600–49. E.A. Wrigley and R.S. Schofield, *The Population History of England 1541–1871: A Reconstruction* (1981), 255, Table 7.26.
103. Kussmaul, *Servants in Husban-*

dry, 84, Table 5.4. McIntosh's evidence on careers of apprentices in the manor of Havering in the sixteenth century would also suggest the possibility of a gap between the end of service and marriage. If apprenticeship began at 15 and apprentices married at about 25, and if apprenticeship was normally a seven-year term, then an interval of some three years between the end of apprenticeship and marriage was not unlikely. McIntosh, 'Servants and the household unit', 11.

104. *Journal of Richard Norwood*, 50, 103–4; Thomas Chalkley, *A Journal or Historical Account of the Life, Travels and Christian Experiences* (1751), 3, 29; Disney, *Some Remarkable Passages*, 45–6, 52–3. Of 28 autobiographers who recorded details about exit from apprenticeship and marriage, only 4 left service and married soon after.

105. Bownas, *Account of Life and Travels*, 9, 20, 22.

106. See Chapter 3, pp. 71–2.

107. Kussmaul, *Servants in Husbandry*, 97–9.

108. Rappaport, *Worlds Within Worlds*, 340. In Bristol, more than half in a sample of 262 apprentices who became burgesses between 1660 and 1630 took their freedom of the town only two, three or more years following the end of their terms. Some of them may have spent at least part of this interval as journeymen. For journeywork in Coventry see Phythian-Adams, *Desolation of a City*, 84.

109. Thomas Chubb, *The Author's Account of Himself*, in *The Posthumous Works of Mr Thomas Chubb* (1748), Vol. I, iii–iv.

110. Croker, *Brief Memoir*, 303.

111. Bangs, *Memoirs of the Life*, 22; Muggleton, *Acts of the Witnesses*, 8; *Journal of Richard Norwood*, 50–51; Bewley, *A Narrative of the Christian Experiences*, 17–18.

112. *Diary of Roger Lowe*, 93.

113. Seaver, *Wallington's World*, 115–16.

114. Rappaport, *Worlds Within Worlds*, 327; Earle, *Making of the English Middle Class*, 181–2.

115. Oxley, *Joseph's Offering*, 209.

116. Kussmaul, *Servants in Husbandry*, 73. Brysson, *Memoirs*, 273.

117. For example, 4 out of 36 farmers in Ardleigh, Essex, in 1796 were unmarried, and 3 of them had female servants. Kussmaul, *Servants in Husbandry*, 84.

118. Wall, 'Real property, marriage and children', 443–79, esp. 457–8, 466–72; 478–9.

119. Josiah was 18 years old when his father died, and his mother then had a mature servant to help her manage the estate. Some five years later, however, Josiah–'at an age to manage for himself,' as his brother now described him – had already assumed its management, improving it for the benefit of the family, and especially for the younger brother, Leonard. *Autobiography of William Stout*, 75, 87.

120. Coxere, *Adventures by Sea*, 33.

121. Wrigley and Schofield, *Population History of England*, 402–53, esp. 421–5.

122. Thomas Deloney, *The Pleasant Historic of John Winchcomb, called Jack of Newbery* (1630), 13. Chubb, *Account of Himself*, iv.

123. Muggleton, *Acts of the Witnesses*, 8; *Autobiography of William Stout*, 88.

124. Muggleton, *Acts of the Witnesses*, 8–9.

125. When William Stout decided to retire, he offered his apprentice the opportunity to buy his shop and goods in three instalments to be paid after six, twelve and eighteen months. *Autobiography of William Stout*, 88–9, 118. For longer debts, see Clay, *Economic Expansion*, Vol. II, 68. See also Earle, *Making of the English Middle Class*, 112.

126. Bownas, *Account of Life and Travels*, 13; Bewley, *A Narrative of the Christian Experiences*, 18; *Journal of Richard Norwood*, 51.

127. Although incapacitated from

working in the fields, Elin was helpful in the house throughout her youth in taking care of the younger children, knitting, sewing and spinning. Later on she also helped her brother in his new shop. *Autobiography of William Stout*, 69, 87, 90.

128. Bewley, *A Narrative of the Christian Experiences*, 17–20.

129. Chubb, *Account of Himself*, iii; BRO, Ordinances for City Companies, 04369(1), 157.

130. E. Kerridge, *Textile Manufactures in Early Modern England* (Manchester, 1985), 195.

131. Wrightson, *English Society*, 74–7, 81, 8; Brodsky Elliott, 'Single women', 94–5, 97; Ingram, *Church Courts, Sex and Marriage*, 139, 189–218.

132. Coxere, *Adventures by Sea*, 32.

133. Wrightson, *English Society*, 81–3; 86–8; Brodsky Elliott, 'Single women'. For similar patterns among men marrying daughters of Bristol's freemen, see also Chapter 6, pp. 149–50.

134. Wrightson, *English Society*, 83.

135. Coxere, *Adventures by Sea*, 33.

136. Perrin (ed.), *Autobiography of Phineas Pett*, 10.

137. Disney, *Some Remarkable Passages*, 52; *Life of Adam Martindale*, 71–2; Oliver Sansom, *An Account of Many Remarkable Passages of the Life of Oliver Sansom* (1710), 8.

138. Stone, *The Family, Sex, and Marriage in England*, 136–7; Earle, *Making of the English Middle Class*, 158–60.

139. Bewley, *A Narrative of the Christian Experiences*.

140. Ibid.

141. Coxere, *Adventures by Sea*, 32. For other examples which convey similar attitudes, see Wrightson, *English Society*, 75–7.

142. Ingram, *Church Courts, Sex and Marriage*, 139.

143. Edward Coxere came to ask his future father-in-law for permission to marry his daughter, 'I not doubting his consent...it [i.e. the courting] was not done so privately'. *Adventures by Sea*, 32.

144. Gervase Disney described the way he resisted his father's pressures to come to live near him soon after he had married. Gervase 'considered and debated the Thing deliberately, advis'd with Friends, sought God by prayer, and weigh'd reasons for it and against it'. He then wrote a long letter explaining why he declined his father's offer. 'These reasons fully satisfied my father Disney, and mother,' he wrote later. Disney, *Some Remarkable Passages*, 63–4.

145. Perrin (ed.), *Autobiography of Phineas Pett*, 9.

146. Elias Osborn, *A Brief Narrative of the Life, Labours and Sufferings of Elias Osborn* (1723), 21.

147. Coxere, *Adventures by Sea*, 33.

148. Disney, *Some Remarkable Passages*, 12, 19–21.

Conclusion

1. In the mid-sixteenth century the mean age at marriage for men in early modern English society was about 29. In the final decades of the century the mean age fell to about 28, and thereafter it scarcely changed for the next century. Women married at a somewhat younger age – about 26 years in the mid-sixteenth century – and somewhat older throughout most of the seventeenth century. In the final decades of the seventeenth century there began a trend towards a lowering of the marriage age for both men and women; yet most people throughout the period did not marry before they reached the age of 26. E.A. Wrigley and R.S. Schofield, *The Population History of England 1541–1871: A Reconstruction* (1981), 255, 422–4.

2. *The Autobiography of William Stout*, 87.

3. For a young man who, at the age of 23, had already been the godfather of his cousin, see the will of Andrew

Barker, BRO, Great Orphan Book, Vol. III, 199. The content of the will is discussed in Chapter 9, p. 222.

4. BRO, Orders and Proceedings of Mayor and Aldermen, 04417(1), fo. 23. Order dated 23 February 1655.

5. For examples of adolescents joining their fathers on their ships, see G. Mayhew, 'Life-cycle service and the family unit in early modern Rye', *Continuity and Change*, 6 (1991), 209–10.

6. Bowcock, *The Life, Experience, and Correspondence of William Bowcock, the Lincolnshire Drillman* (1851), 7.

7. *The Life of Adam Martindale*, 8.

8. Abraham Jackson, *The Pious Prentice* (1640), 105.

9. For the ideology of patriarchalism as a response to perceptions of social order, in a period of rapid population growth, see S.D. Amusen, 'Gender, family and the social order, 1560–1725', in A. Fletcher and J. Stevenson (eds), *Order and Disorder in Early Modern England* (Cambridge, 1985), 214–17.

10. Quoted in S.J. Wright, 'Confirmation, catechism and communion: the role of the young in the post-Reformation Church', in S.J. Wright (ed.), *Parish Church and People: Local Studies in Lay Religion 1350–1750* (1988), 205–6.

11. Francis Kirkman, *The Unlucky Citizen Experimentally Described in the Various Misfortunes of an Unlucky Londoner* (1673), 120–21.

12. I. Krausman Ben-Amos, 'Failure to become freemen: urban apprenices in early modern England', *Social History*, 16 (1991), 171–2.

13. K.D.M. Snell, *Annals of the Labouring Poor: Social Change and Agrarian England, 1660–1900* (Cambridge, 1985), 232–3.

14. R.B. Shoemaker, *Prosecution and Punishment: Petty Crime and the Law in London and Rural Middlesex, c. 1660–1725* (Cambridge, 1991), 178–87.

15. *Autobiography of William Stout*, 80.

16. Edward Coxere, *Adventures by Sea*, 8.

Bibliography

Manuscripts

Bristol Record Office

Register of Apprentices,
1566–1592, 04352(2)
1593–1609, 04352(3)
1609–1625, 04352(4)
1626–1636, 04352(5)a
1636–1640, 04352(5)b
1640–1658, 04352(6)
1668–1671, 04357(1)
1670–1684, 04353(1)
1684–1699, 04353(2)
1699–1711, 05353(3)

Burgess Books,
1558–1598, 04358
1607–1651, 04359(2)

Quarter Sessions minute books,
1620–1629, 04445
1634–1647, 04446
1653–1671, 04447(1)
1672–1681, 04447(2)

Quarter Sessions Recognizances,
1673–1693, 04434(1)–(2)

Orders and Proceedings of Mayor and Aldermen,
1653–1673, 04417(1)–(3)

Churchwardens Accounts,
Temple, 1582–1668, P/T/chw/, Ca 1–21,
St John Baptist, 1605–1710, P/StJB/chw/3/a–b
St James, 1566–1701, P/StJ/chw/1/a–b

Overseers of the poor,
Temple, 1633–34, Da1, 1659, Da2 1670–80, Da3(1–2)

Vestry Minutes,
St James, P/St J/1–3, 1623–99
St John Baptist, 1676–1726, P/St JB/1–2

Indentures,
P/StS/OP
P/St.JB/Misc 83
FC/OP/5

Information Box, xxv/69
Mayor Audits, 1656–1680, 04026
Ordinances for City Companies Ratified by the Common Council, 04369(1)
The Great Orphan Book,
1382–1633, 04421(1)

Court of Orphans, recognizances for orphans,
1594–1642, 04423

Loan Book, 1648, 04183(1)

Public Record Office

Chancery Proceedings,
C3/204/83
C3/272/102
C3/289/64
C3/302/62
C3/304/68
C3/306/69

Bodleian Library, Oxford

The diary of John Coggs, MS ENG. misc. f78

Printed Primary Sources

Autobiographies and Diaries

Anon., *An Account of the Work of Grace Upon*, in Doe, Charles, *A Collection of Experiences of the Work of Grace* (1698).

Ashmole, Elias, *Memoirs of the Life of that Learned Antiquary* (1717). Born 1617.

Bangs, Benjamin, *Memoirs of the Life and Convincement of Benjamin Bangs* (1757). Born 1652.

Barlow, Edward, *Barlow's Journal of his Life at Sea in King's Ships, East and West Indiamen, and other Merchantmen from 1659 to 1703* (1934), transc. Basil Lubbock. Vol. I. Born 1642.

Baxter, Richard, *The Autobiography of Richard Baxter* (Everyman edn, 1974), ed. N.H. Keeble. Born 1615.

Bewley, George, *A Narrative of the Christian Experiences of George Bewley* (1750). Born 1684.

Blair, Robert, *The Life of Mr Robert Blair, Minister of St Andrews, Containing his Autobiography* (1848). Born 1593.
Bownas, Samuel, *An Account of the Life and Travels of Samuel Bownas* (4th edition, 1795). Born 1676.
Bowcock, William, *The Life, Experience, and Correspondence of William Bowcock, the Lancashire Drillman* (1851). Born 1790.
Brysson, George, *Memoirs of George Brysson* (1825). Born 1649.
Bunyan, John, *Grace Abounding to the Chief of Sinners* (1688).
Burton, Henry, *The Narration of the Life of Henry Burton* (1643).
Chalkley, Thomas, *A Journal or historical Account of the Life, Travels and Christian Experiences* (1751). Born 1675.
Chubb, Thomas, *The Author's Account of Himself*, in *The Posthumous Works of Mr Thomas Chubb* (1748), Vol. I. Born 1679.
Clap, Roger, *Captain Roger Clap's Memoirs*, in A. Young, *Chronicles of the First Planters of the Colony of Massachusetts Bay* (Boston, 1846). Born 1609.
Clare, John, *John Clare's Autobiographical Writings* (Oxford, 1986), ed. E. Robinson. Born 1793.
Coxere, Edward, *Adventures by Sea* (1945), ed. E.H.W. Meyerstein. Born 1633.
Croker, John, *Brief Memoir of the Life of John Croker*, in J. Barclay, *A Select Series, Biographical, Narrative, Epistolary and Miscellaneous. Chiefly the Productions of Early Members of the Society of Friends* (1836), Vol. VI. Born 1673.
Davies, Richard, *An Account of the Convincement, Exercises, Services, and Travels of that Ancient Servant of the Lord* (5th edn 1794). Born 1635.
D'Ewes, Simonds, *The Autobiography and Correspondence of Sir Simonds D'Ewes, Bart.*, (1845), ed. J.O. Halliwell, Vol. I. Born 1580.
Dewsbury, William, *The First Birth*, in *The Discovery of the Great Enmity of the Serpent against the Seed of the Woman* (1655).
Disney, Gervase, *Some Remarkable Passages in the Holy Life and Death of Gervase Disney* (1692). Born 1641.
Dodshon, Frances, *Some Account of the Convincement and Religious Experience of* (1744). Born 1714.
Doe, Charles, *The Experience of Charles Doe*, in *A Collection of Experiences of the Work of Grace* (1698).
Edmundson, William, *Journal of the Life of William Edmundson* (Dublin, 1820). Born 1627.
Evans, Arise, *An Eccho to the Voice from Heaven. Or a Narration of the Life, and Manner of the Special Calling, and Visions of* (1653). Born 1607.
Forman, Simon, *Forman's Autobiography*, in A.L. Rowse, *Simon Forman: Sex and Society in Shakespeare's Age* (1974). Born 1552.
Fox, George, *Journal of George Fox* (7th edn 1852), ed. W. Armistead. Born 1624.
Fretwell, James, *A Family History*, in *Yorkshire Diaries and Autobiographies in the Seventeenth and Eighteenth Centuries* (Surtees Society, Vol. LXV, 1877). Born 1699.
Gratton, John, *A Journal of the Life of John Gratton* (1720).
Hardy, Thomas, *Memoir of Thomas Hardy* (1832). Born 1752.
Heywood, Oliver, *His Autobiography, Diaries, Anecdote and Event Books* (Brighouse, 1882), ed. J. Horsfall Turner, Vol. I. Born 1630.

Johnson, William, *The Life and Times of William Johnson* (1859). Born 1777.

Jones, John, *Attempts in Verse, by John Jones, an Old Servant* (1831). Born 1774.

Kiffin, William, *Remarkable Passages in the Life of William Kiffin* (1823). Born 1616.

Lay, Benjamin, *Memoirs of the Lives of Benjamin Lay and Ralph Sanford* (1816). Born 1677.

Lilly, William, *Mr William Lilly's History of his Life and Times from the Year 1602 to 1681* (1715). Born 1602.

Lowe, Roger, *The Diary of Roger Lowe of Ashton-in-Makerfield, Lancashire 1663–74* (New Haven, 1938), ed. W.L. Sachse.

Lurting, Thomas, *The Fighting Sailor Turn'd Peaceable Christian* (1766). Born 1646.

Martindale, Adam, *The Life of Adam Martindale, Written by Himself* (Chetham Society, Vol. IV, 1845), ed. R. Parkinson. Born 1623.

Melhuish, Thomas, *An Account of the Early Part of Life and Convincement of* (1805). Born 1737.

Norwood, Richard, *The Journal of Richard Norwood, Surveyer of Bermuda* (New York, 1945). Born 1590.

Muggleton, Lodowick, *The Acts of the Witnesses of the Spirit* (1699).

Osborn, Elias, *A Brief Narrative of the Life, Labours and Sufferings, of Elias Osborn* (1723). Born 1643.

Oxley, Joseph, *Joseph's Offering to his Children. Being Joseph's Oxley's Journal*, in J. Barclay (ed.), *A Select Series, Biographical, Narrative, Epistolary and Miscellaneous. Chiefly the Productions of Early Members of the Society of Friends* (1837), Vol. V.

Patrick, Symon, *The Autobiography of Symon Patrick*, in *Works of S.P., D.D. Sometimes Bishop of Ely* (Oxford, 1858), Vol. IX.

Pennington, Mary, *Some Account of Circumstances in the Life of Mary Pennington* (1821). Born 1616.

Persons, Robert, *The Memoirs of Father Robert Persons* (Catholic Record Society, Miscellany, Vol. II, 1906), ed. A.H. Pollen. Born 1546.

Pett, Phineas, *Autobiography of Phineas Pett* (1918), ed. W.G. Perrin. Born 1570.

Pike, Joseph, *Some Account of the Life of Joseph Pike*, in J. Barclay (ed.), *A Select Series, Biographical, Narrative, Epistolary and Miscellaneous. Chiefly the Productions of Early Members of the Society of Friends* (1837), Vol. V. Born 1657.

Poyntz, Sydnam, *The Relation of Sydnam Poyntz 1624–1636* (Camden Society, 3rd. series, Vol. XIV, 1908), ed. A.T.S. Goodrick.

Pringle, Walter, *The Memoirs of Walter Pringle* (Edinburgh, 1847). Born 1625.

Raymond, Thomas, *Autobiography* (Camden Society, Vol. XXVIII, 1917), ed. G. Davies. Born 1610.

Reid, Alexander, *Life of Alexander Reid, a Scotish Covenanter* (Manchester, 1822). Born 1646.

Rich, Mary, Countess of Warwick, *Autobiography* (Percy Society, Vol. XXII, 1848), ed. T.C. Croker.

Robinson, Matthew, *Autobiography of Matthew Robinson* (1856), ed. J.E.B. Mayor. Born 1630.

Sansom, Oliver, *An Account of Many Remarkable Passages of the Life of Oliver Sansom* (1710). Born 1636.

Shaw, John, *The Life of Master John Shaw*, in *Yorkshire Diaries and Autobiographies in the Seventeenth and Eighteenth Centuries* (Surtees Society, Vol. LXV, 1877). Born 1608.

Shepard, Thomas, *Thomas Shepard's Memoir of his Own Life*, in A. Young, *Chronicles of the First Planters of the Colony of Massachusetts Bay* (Boston, 1846). Born 1604.

Stirredge, Elizabeth, *Strength in Weakness Manifest* (1711).

Story, Christopher, *A Brief Account of the Life, Convincement, Sufferings, Labours and Travels* (1726).

Stout, William, *The Autobiography of William Stout of Lancaster (1665–1752)* (Manchester Chetham Society, 3rd. series, Vol. XIV, 1967), ed. J.D. Marshall.

Taswell, William, *Autobiography and Anecdotes by William Taswell, D.D.*, (Camden miscellany, Vol. II, 1852), ed. G.P. Elliott. Born 1551.

Terril, Edward, *The Records of a Church of Christ Meeting in Broadmead, Bristol 1640–1687* (1847), ed. E.B. Underhill. Born 1638.

Trosse, George, *The Life of the Late Reverend Mr George Trosse* (Montreal and London, 1974), ed. A.W. Brink. Born 1631.

Tryon, Thomas, *Some Memoirs of the Life of Mr. Thomas Tryon* (1705).

Wallis, Dr., *Dr. Wallis's Account of Some Passages of his own Life*, in *Peter Langtoft's Chronicle* (Oxford, 1725), Vol. I, transc. T. Hearne. Born 1616.

Whiting, John, *Persecution Exposed* (1715).

Wilson, Thomas, *A Brief Journal of the Life, Travels and Labours of Love* (Dublin, 1728).

Wood, Anthony, *The Life of Mr. Anthony A. Wood* (Oxford, 1891–1900), Vol. I. Born 1632.

Other Printed Sources

An Additional Ordinance of the Lords and Commons . . . Concerning days of Recreation . . . and the Apprentices Petition and Propositions (1647).

The Apprentice Vade Mecum (1734).

The Apprentices of London Petition Presented to the Honourable Court of Parliament (1641).

Bagley, J.J. (ed.), *The Great Diurnal of Nicholas Blundell of Little Crosby, Lancashire, Vol. I. 1702–1711* (The Record Society of Lancashire and Cheshire, 1968).

Baxter, Richard, *A Breviate of the Life of Margaret, the daughter of Francis Charlton, of Apply in Shropshire, Esq; and Wife of Richard Baxter* (1681).

Best, Henry, *Rural Economy in Yorkshire in 1641* (Durham, 1857).

Bolton, Edmund, *The Citie's Advocate. In this Case or Question of Honour and Armes: Whether Apprenticeship Extinguishes Gentry?* (1629).

Brooks, Thomas, *Apples of Gold for Young Men and Women* (1657).

B[rowne], J[ohn], *The Marchants Avizo* (1589), (Cambridge, Massachussetts, 1957), ed. P. McGrath.

Burrows, Samuel, *Good Instructions for all Young Men and Maids* (1641).

Chappell, W.M. (ed.), *The Roxburghe Ballads* (1871), Vols. I–IV.

Clark, Samuel, *The Lives of Sundry Eminent Persons* (1683).

Cobbet, Thomas, *A Fruitfull and Usefull Discourse Touching the Honour Due from Children to Parents* (1656).

Cockin, Francis, *Divine Blossoms: A Prospect or Looking-Glass for Youth* (1657).
The Complete Letter-Writer, Containing Familiar Letters on the Most Common Occasions in Life (Edinburgh, 1768).
Crouch, Nathaniel, *The Apprentice Companion* (1681).
Cuffe, Henry, *The Differences of the Ages of Mans Life* (1607).
[Christian Parents], *The Office of Christian Parents* (Cambridge, 1616).
Dalton, M., *The Countrey Justice* (1618).
Death's Uncontrollable Summons; Or, The Mortality of Mankind: Being a Dialogue between Death and a Young Man, in W.M. Chappell (ed.), *The Roxburghe Ballads*, Vol. IV, 27–9.
Deloney, Thomas, *The Honourable Prentice... The Famous History of Sir John Hawkwood: Sometime Prentice of London* (1616).
Deloney, Thomas, *The Pleasant History of John Winchcomb, in his younger years called Jack of Newbery* (3rd edn, 1630).
Dod, John and Cleaver, Robert, *A Godly Form of Household Government* (1598, reprinted 1630).
Elyot, Thomas, *The Boke Named Governour* (1531, Everyman ed., 1907).
Evans, G.E., *Ask the Fellows Who Cut the Hay* (1956).
Fleetwood, William, *The Relative Duties of Parents, Husbands, Masters* (1705).
Fussell, G.E. (ed.), *Robert Loder's Farm Accounts* (Camden Society, 3rd ser., Vol. LIII, 1936).
Gardiner, D. (ed.), *The Oxinden Letters 1607–1642* (1933).
Gataker, Thomas, *Davids Instructor* (1620).
H., N., *The Complete Tradesman* (1684).
Hollis, D. (ed.), *Calendar of the Bristol Apprentice Book 1532–1542* (Bristol Record Society publications, Vol. XIV, Bristol, 1948).
Houghton, J., *Collection for Improvement of Husbandry and Trade* (1696/1700).
The Humble Remonstrance of the Apprentices of the City of London (1647).
Jackson, Abraham, *The Pious Prentice* (1640).
Jonson, Ben, Chapman, George, and Marston, John, *Eastward Ho* (1605), ed. C.G. Petter (1973).
Kirkman, Francis, *The Unlucky Citizen Experimentally Described in the Various Misfortunes of an Unlucky Londoner* (1673).
Lodge, E.C. (ed.), *The Account Book of a Kentish Estate 1616–1704* (1927).
London's Glory: or, the History of the Famous and Valiant London Prentice (1700).
Markham, Gervase, *Farewell to Husbandry* (1631).
Markham, Gervase, *Cheape and Good Husbandry for the Well-Ordering of all Beasts and Fowles* (1657).
Markham, Gervase, *The English Housewife* (1656).
McGrath, P. (ed.), *Merchants and Merchandise in Seventeenth-Century Bristol* (Bristol Record Society, Vol. XIX, Bristol, 1955).
Merson, A.L. (ed.), *A Calendar of Southampton Apprenticeship Registers, 1609–1740* (Southampton Records Ser., Vol. XII, Southampton, 1968).
Nourse, Timothy, *Compania Felix: Or, A Discourse of the Benefits and Improvements of Husbandry* (1700).
Powel, Thomas, *Tom of All Trades* (1631).
Ralph, E., and Hardwick, N.M. (eds), *Calendar of the Bristol Apprentice*

Book 1532–1565, part II, 1542–1552 (Bristol Record Society, Vol. XXXIII, Bristol, 1980).
Relief of Apprentices Wronged by Their Masters (1687).
The Prodigal Son Converted; Or, the Young-Man Return'd from his Rambles, in Wm Chappell (ed.), *The Roxburghe Ballads*, Vol. IV, 48–50.
Tawney, R.H., and Power, E. (eds), *Tudor Economic Documents* (New York, 1962), Vol. I.
Trenchfield, Caleb, *A Cap of Gray Hairs for Green Head, or, the Fathers Counsel to his Son, an Apprentice in London* (1688).
Tryon, Thomas, *A New Method of Educating Children* (1695).
Tusser, Thomas, *Tusser's Hundredth Good Poyntes of Husbandrie* (1834, repr. of original edn. of 1557).
A Universal Dictionary for Trade and Commerce (4th edn, 1774).
Vanes, J. (ed.), *The Ledger of John Smythe 1538–1550* (Bristol Record Society, Vol. XXVIII, Bristol, 1974).
Veale, E.W. (ed.), *The Great Red Book of Bristol* (Bristol Record Society, Vol. IV, Bristol, 1933).
W.S., *The Golden Fleece* (1656), in *English Wool Trade: Selected Tracts 1613–1715* (Farnborough, 1968).
Wadley, T.P., *Notes and Abstracts of the Wills in the... Great Orphan Book and Book of Wills in the Council House at Bristol (1379–1595)* (Bristol, 1886).
Williams, Daniel, *The Vanity of Childhood and Youth* (1691).
Woodward, Josiah, *The Young Man's Monitor* (1706).

Secondary Sources

Adelson, J. (ed.), *Handbook of Adolescent Psychology* (New York, 1980).
Amusen, S., 'Gender, family and social order, 1560–1725', in A. Fletcher and J. Stevenson (eds), *Order and Disorder in Early Modern England* (Cambridge, 1985), 196–217.
Anderson, M., *Family Structure in Nineteenth-Century Lancashire* (Cambridge, 1971).
Archer, I.W., *The Pursuit of Stability: Social Relations in Elizabethan London* (Cambridge, 1991).
Ariès, P., *Centuries of Childhood: A Social History of Family Life*, trans. from the French by R. Baldick (New York, 1962).
Beier, A.L., *Masterless Men: The Vagrancy Problem in England, 1560–1640* (1985).
Beier, A.L., and Finlay, R. (eds), *London 1500–1700: The Making of the Metropolis* (1986).
Beier, A.L., 'Engine of manufacture: the trades of London', in A.L. Beier and R. Finlay (eds), *London 1500–1700* (1986), 141–67.
Beier, L.M., *Sufferers and Healers: the Experience of Illness in Seventeenth-Century England* (1987).
Beloff, M., 'A London Apprentice's Notebook, 1703–5', *History*, 27 (1942), 38–45.
Ben-Amos, I.K., 'Failure to become freemen: urban apprentices in early modern England', *Social History*, 16 (1991), 155–72.

Bennett, J.M., *Women in the Medieval English Countryside* (Oxford, 1987).
Berg, M., *The Age of Manufactures 1700–1820* (1985).
Bergeron, D., *English Civic Pageantry 1558–1642* (1971).
Blench, J.W., *Preaching in England in the Fifteenth and Sixteenth Centuries* (Oxford, 1964).
Borsay, P., 'All the town's a stage: urban ritual and ceremony 1660–1800', in P. Clark (ed.), *The Transformation of English Provincial Towns* (1984), 228–58.
Borsay, P., *The English Urban Renaissance: Culture and Society in the Provincial Town 1660–1770* (Oxford, 1989).
Boulton, J., *Neighbourhood and Society: a London Suburb in the Seventeenth Century* (Cambridge, 1987).
Bowden, P., 'Agricultural prices, farm profits, and rents', in J. Thirsk (ed.), *The Agrarian History of England and Wales* (Cambridge, 1967), Vol. IV.
Brigden, S., 'Youth and the English Reformation', *Past and Present*, 95 (1982), 37–67.
Brodsky Elliott, V., 'Mobility and marriage in pre-industrial England', (Ph.D. dissertation, University of Cambridge, 1978).
Brodsky Elliott, V., 'Single women in the London marriage market: age, status and mobility, 1598–1619', in R.B. Outhwaite (ed.), *Marriage and Society: Studies in the History of Marriage* (1981), 81–100.
Brodsky, V., 'Widows in late Elizabethan London: remarriage, economic opportunity and family orientations', in L. Bonfield, R. Smith and K. Wrightson (eds), *The World We Have Gained* (Oxford, 1986), 122–54.
Brooks, C.W., *Pettyfoggers and Vipers of the Commonwealth: the 'Lower Branch' of the Legal Profession in Early Modern England* (Cambridge, 1986).
Brown, W.N., 'The receipt of poor relief and family situation: Aldenham, Hertfordshire 1630–90', in R.M. Smith (ed.), *Land, Kinship and Life-Cycle* (Cambridge, 1984), 405–22.
Burnett, J., Vincent, D., and Mayall, D. (eds), *The Autobiography of the Working Class* (Brighton, 1984), Vol. I, 1790–1900.
Burke, P., 'Popular culture in seventeenth-century London', *London Journal*, 3 (1977), 143–62.
Burrow, J.A., *The Ages of Man: A Study in Medieval Writing and Thought* (Oxford, 1986).
Burton, A., 'Looking forward from Ariès? Pictorial and material evidence for the history of childhood and family life', *Continuity and Change*, 4 (1989), 203–29.
Capp, B., 'English youth groups and the Pinder of Wakefield', *Past and Present*, 76 (1977), 127–33.
Capp, B., 'Popular literature', in B. Reay (ed.), *Popular Culture in Seventeenth-Century England* (1985), 198–243.
Carus-Wilson, E.M., 'The overseas trade of Bristol in the fifteenth century', in *Medieval Merchant Venturers* (1954).
Chartres, J.A., *Internal Trade in England 1500–1700* (London and Basingstoke, 1977).
Chartres, J.A., 'Road carrying in England in the seventeenth century: Myth and reality', *Economic History Review*, 2nd ser., 30 (1977), 73–8.
Clark, A., *Working Life of Women in the Seventeenth Century* (1917, new edn, 1982), with an introduction by M. Chaytor and J. Lewis.

Clark, P., *The English Alehouse: A Social History 1200–1830* (1983).
Clark, P., 'The migrant in Kentish towns 1580–1640', in P. Clark and P. Slack (eds), *Crisis and Order in English Towns 1500–1700* (1972).
Clark, P. (ed.), *The Early Modern Town* (1976).
Clark, P., 'Migration in England during the late seventeenth and early eighteenth centuries', *Past and Present*, 83 (1979), 56–90.
Clark, P., 'Migrants in the city: the process of social adaptation in English Towns, 1500–1800', in Clark and Souden (eds), *Migration and Society*, 267–91.
Clark, P., and Souden, D. (eds), *Migration and Society in Early Modern England* (New Jersey, 1988).
Clarkson, L.A., 'The organization of the leather industry in the late sixteenth and seventeenth centuries', *Economic History Review*, 2nd ser. 8 (1960), 245–53.
Clay, C.G.A., *Economic Expansion and Social Change: England 1500–1700* (Cambridge, 1984), 2 Vols.
Coleman, D.C., 'Labour in the English economy of the seventeenth century', *Economic History Review*, 2nd ser., 8 (1956), 280–95.
Coleman, D.C., 'An innovation and its diffusion: the "new draperies"', *Economic History Review*, 2nd ser., 22 (1969), 417–29.
Collinson, P., *The Religion of Protestants* (Oxford, 1982).
Collinson, P., *The Birthpangs of Protestant England: Religion and Cultural Change in the Sixteenth and Seventeenth Centuries* (New York, 1988).
Conger, J.J., and Petersen, A.C., *Adolescence and Youth: Psychological Development in a Changing World* (3rd edn, New York, 1984).
Cressy, D., *Literacy and the Social Order: Reading and Writing in Tudor and Stuart England* (Cambridge, 1980).
Cressy, D., 'Kinship and kin interaction in Early Modern England', *Past and Present*, 113 (1986), 38–69.
Cressy, D., *Coming Over: Migration and Communication between England and New England in the Seventeenth Century* (Cambridge, 1987).
Cressy, D., 'A drugery of schoolmasters: the teaching profession in Elizabethan and Stuart England', in W. Prest (ed.), *The Professions in Early Modern England* (1987).
Cressy, D., *Bonfires and Bells: National Memory and the Protestant Calendar in Elizabethan and Stuart England* (1989).
Cunningham, H., 'The employment and unemployment of children in England *c.* 1680–1851', *Past and Present*, 126 (1990), 113–50.
Davies, K., 'The Sacred condition of equality – How original were Puritan doctrines of marriage?', *Social History*, 5 (1977), 563–80.
Davis, N.Z., 'The reasons of misrule: youth groups and charivaris in sixteenth-century France', *Past and Present*, 50 (1971), repr. in *Society and Culture in Early Modern France* (Stanford, 1975), 97–123.
Demos, J., and Demos, V., 'Adolescence in historical perspective', *Journal of Marriage and the Family*, 31 (1969), 632–8.
Dunlop, O.J., and Denman, R.D., *English Apprenticeship and Child Labour: A History* (New York, 1912).
Earle, P., *The Making of the English Middle Class: Business, Society, and Family Life in London, 1660–1730* (1989).
Eisenstadt, S.N., *From Generation to Generation: Age Groups and Social Structure* (1958).
Finlay, R., *Population and the Metropolis: The Demography of London 1580–1650* (Cambridge, 1981).

Fischer, C.S., *To Dwell Among Friends: Personal Networks in Town and City* (Chicago, 1982).
Fussell, G.E., and K.R., *The English Countryman: His Life and Work A.D. 1500–1900* (1955).
Gibbs, F.W., 'Invention in chemical industries', in C. Singer *et al., A History of Technology* (Oxford, 1957), Vol. III.
Gillis, J.R., *Youth and History* (New York and London, 1981).
Gillis, J.R., *For Better, For Worse: British Marriages, 1600 to the Present* (New York and Oxford, 1985).
Goldberg, P.J.P., 'Marriage, migration, servanthood and life-cycle in Yorkshire towns of the later Middle Ages: some York cause paper evidence', *Continuity and Change*, 1 (1986), 141–69.
Goody, E.N., 'Daboya weavers: Relations of production, dependence and reciprocity', in E.N. Goody (ed.), *From Craft to Industry: The Ethnography of Proto-Industrial Cloth Production* (Cambridge, 1982).
Goose, N., 'Household size and structure in early Stuart Cambridge', *Social History*, 5 (1980), 347–85.
Grassby, R., 'Social mobility and business enterprise in seventeenth-century England', in D. Pennington and K. Thomas (eds), *Puritans and Revolutionaries: Essays in Seventeenth Century History Presented to C. Hill* (Oxford, 1978), 355–81.
Haigh, C., 'The English Reformation: a premature birth, a difficult labour and a sickly child', *Historical Journal*, 33 (1990), 449–59.
Hajnal, J., 'Two kinds of pre-industrial household formation system', in R. Wall, J. Robin, and P. Laslett (eds), *Family Forms in Historic Europe* (Cambridge, 1983).
Harris, J.R., *The British Iron Industry 1700–1850* (1988).
Harris, T., *London Crowds in the Reign of Charles II* (Cambridge, 1987).
Hecht, J.J., *The Domestic Servant in Eighteenth-Century England* (1956).
Hendrick, H., *Images of Youth: Age, Class, and the Male Youth Problem 1880–1920* (Oxford, 1990).
Heywood, C., *Childhood in Nineteenth-Century France: Work, Health and Education among the 'classes populaires'* (Cambridge, 1988).
Hill, B., *Women, Work, and Sexual Politics in Eighteenth-Century England* (Oxford, 1989).
Hill, C., *The World Turned Upside Down: Radical Ideas During the English Revolution* (Harmondsworth, 1975).
Horn, J., 'Servant emigration to the Chesapeake in the seventeenth century', in T.W. Tate and D.L. Ammerman (eds), *The Chesapeake in the Seventeenth Century* (North Carolina, 1979), 51–95.
Houlbrooke, R.A., *The English Family 1450–1700* (1984).
Houlbrooke, R.A., 'The making of marriage in mid-Tudor England: evidence from the records of matrimonial contract litigation', *Journal of Family History*, 10 (1985), 339–52.
Houlbrooke, R.A. (ed.), *English Family Life, 1576–1716* (Oxford, 1989).
Howell, C., 'Peasant inheritance customs in the Midlands, 1200–1700', in J.R. Goody, J. Thirsk and E.P. Thompson (eds), *Family and Inheritance: Rural Society in Western Europe* (Cambridge, 1978), 112–55.
Ingram, M., 'Ridings, rough music and the "reform of popular culture" in early modern England', *Past and Present*, 105 (1984), 79–113.
Ingram, M., *Church Courts, Sex and Marriage in England, 1570–1640* (Cambridge, 1987).
James, M., 'Ritual, drama and social body in the late medieval English

town', *Past and Present*, 98 (1983), 3–29.

Jones, B.C., 'Westmorland pack-horse men in Southampton', *Transactions of the Cumberland and Westmorland Antiquarian and Archaeological Society*, 59 (1960).

Keniston, K., *Youth and Dissent* (New York, 1970).

Kerridge, E., *Textile Manufactures in Early Modern England* (Manchester, 1985).

Kett, J.F., 'Adolescence and youth in nineteenth-century America', in T.K. Rabb and R.I. Rotberg (eds), *The Family in History: Interdisciplinary Essays* (New York and London, 1973).

King, P., 'Customary rights and women's earnings: the importance of gleaning to the rural labouring poor, 1750–1850', *Economic History Review*, 2nd ser., 44 (1991), 461–74.

Kitch, M.J., 'Capital and kingdom: migration to later Stuart London', in A.L. Beier and R. Finlay (eds), *London 1500–1700: The Making of the Metropolis* (1986).

Kussmaul, A., *Servants in Husbandry in Early Modern England* (Cambridge, 1981).

Lacey, K.E., 'Women and work in fourteenth and fifteenth century London', in L. Charles and L. Duffin (eds), *Women and Work in Pre-Industrial England* (1985), 24–82.

Lang, R.G., 'Social origins and social aspirations of Jacobean London merchants', *Economic History Review*, 2nd ser., 27 (1974), 28–47.

Laquer, W.Z., *Young Germany* (1962).

Laslett, P., 'Mean household size in England since the sixteenth century', in P. Laslett and R. Wall (eds), *Household and Family in Past Times* (Cambridge, 1972).

Laslett, P., *Family Life and Illicit Love in Earlier Generations: Essays in Historical Sociology* (Cambridge, 1977).

Laslett, P., 'Characteristics of the Western family considered over time', in *Family Life and Illicit Love*, 12–49.

Laslett, P., 'Parental deprivation in the past: a note on orphans and stepparenthood in English history', in *Family Life and Illicit Love*, 160–73.

Levine, D., *Reproducing Families: the Political Economy of English Population History* (Cambridge, 1987).

Levine, D., and Wrightson, K., *The Making of an Industrial Society: Wickham 1560–1765* (Oxford, 1991).

Lobel, M.D., 'Bristol', in *The Atlas of Historic Towns* (Baltimore, 1975), Vol. II, 1–21.

Macfarlane, A., *The Family Life of Ralph Josselin: A Seventeenth-Century Clergyman* (New York, 1970).

Malcolmson, R.W., *Popular Recreations in English Society 1700–1850* (Cambridge, 1973).

Manning, R., *Village Revolts: Social Protest and Popular Disturbances in England 1509–1640* (Oxford, 1988).

Mathias, P., *The Brewing Industry in England 1700–1830* (Cambridge, 1959).

Mayhew, G., 'Life-cycle service and the family unit in early modern Rye', *Continuity and Change*, 6 (1991), 201–26.

McIntosh, M.K., 'Servants and the household unit in an Elizabethan English community', *Journal of Family History*, 9 (1984), 3–23.

McIntosh, M.K., 'Local responses to the poor in late medieval and Tudor England', *Continuity and Change*, 3 (1988), 209–45.
McIntosh, M.K., *A Community Transformed: The Manor and Liberty of Havering 1500–1620* (Cambridge, 1991).
Medick, H., 'The proto-industrial family economy: the structural function of household and family during the transition from peasant society to industrial capitalism', *Social History*, 1 (1976), 291–315.
Mendelson, S., 'Stuart women's diaries and occasional memoirs', in M. Prior (ed.), *Women in English Society 1500–1800* (1985), 181–210.
Mendenhall, T.C., *The Shrewsbury Drapers and the Welsh Wool Trade in the Sixteenth and Seventeenth Centuries* (Oxford, 1953).
Mitterauer, M., and Sieder, R., *The European Family: Patriarchy to Partnership from the Middle Ages to the Present* (Oxford, 1982).
Morgan, E., *The Puritan Family* (N.Y., 1966).
Muuss, R.E., 'Puberty rites in primitive and modern societies', *Adolescence*, 5 (1970), 109–28.
O'Day, R., *Education and Society 1500–1800* (1985).
Ozment, S., *When Fathers Ruled: Family Life in Reformation Europe* (Cambridge Mass., 1983).
Palliser, D.M., *Tudor York* (Oxford, 1979).
Palliser, D.M., *The Age of Elizabeth: England under the Later Tudors 1547–1603* (1983).
Patten, J., 'Patterns of migration and movement of labour to three pre-industrial East Anglian towns', *Journal of Historical Geography*, 2 (1976), 119–29.
Pelling, M., 'Occupational diversity: barbersurgeons and the trades of Norwich, 1550–1640', *Bulletin of the History of Medicine*, 56 (1982), 483–511.
Pelling, M., 'Child health as a social value in early modern England', *Social History of Medicine*, 1 (1988), 135–64.
Phillips, C.B., 'Town and country: economic change in Kendal *c.* 1550–1700', in P. Clark (ed.), *The Transformation of English Provincial Towns 1600–1800* (1984), 99–132.
Phythian-Adams, C., 'Ceremony and the Citizen: the communal year at Coventry 1450–1550', in P. Clark and P. Slack (eds), *Crisis and Order in English Towns 1500–1700* (1972), 57–85.
Phythian-Adams, C., *Desolation of a City: Coventry and the Urban Crisis of the Late Middle Ages* (Cambridge, 1979).
Pinchbeck, I., and Hewitt, M., *Children in English Society* (1971), 2 vols.
Pollock, F., and Maitland, F.W., *The History of English Law before the Time of Edward I* (Cambridge, 1895).
Pollock, L.A., *Forgotten Children: Parent-Child Relations from 1500 to 1900* (Cambridge, 1983).
Pollock, L., '"An action like a stratagem" courtship and marriage from the middle ages to the twentieth century', *Historical Journal*, 30 (1987), 483–98.
Prior, M. (ed.), *Women in English Society 1500–1800* (1985).
Prior, M., 'Women and the urban economy: Oxford 1500–1800', in Prior (ed.), *Women in English Society*, 93–117.
Pugh, R.B. (ed.), *Victoria County History of Gloucestershire* (1972), Vol. X.
Ramsay, G.D., 'The recruitment and fortunes of some London freemen

in the mid-sixteenth century', *Economic History Review*, 2nd ser., XXXI (1978), 526–40.

Rappaport, S., *Worlds Within Worlds: Structures of Life in Sixteenth-Century London* (Cambridge, 1989).

Reay, B., 'Popular hostility towards the Quakers in mid-seventeenth century England', *Social History*, 5 (1980), 387–407.

Rediker, M., *Between the Devil and the Deep Blue Sea* (Cambridge, 1987).

Roberts, M., 'Sickles and Scythes: women's work and men's work at harvest time', *History Workshop Journal*, 7 (1979), 3–28.

Rollins, C.B., and Thomas, D.L., 'Parental support, power, and control techniques in the socialization of children', in R.B. Wesley, R. Hill, F.I. Nye and I.L. Reiss (eds), *Contemporary Theories about the Family* (New York, 1979), Vol. I, 317–64.

Roper, L., *The Holy Household: Women and Morals, in Reformation Augsburg* (Oxford, 1989).

Sacks, D.H., *Trade, Society and Politics in Bristol, 1500–1640* (New York, 1985).

Sacks, D.H., *The Widening Gate: Bristol and the Atlantic Economy 1450–1700* (Berkeley, Los Angeles, Oxford, 1991).

Schochet, G.J., 'Patriarchalism, politics, and mass attitudes in Stuart England', *Historical Journal*, 12 (1969), 413–41.

Schofield, R.S., and Wrigley, E.A., 'Infant and child mortality in England in the late Tudor and Stuart period', in C. Webster (ed.), *Health, Medicine and Mortality in the Sixteenth Century* (Cambridge, 1979), 61–95.

Scribner, R.W., *The German Reformation* (1986).

Seaver, P.S., *Wallington's World: A Puritan Artisan in Seventeenth-Century London* (Stanford, 1985).

Seaver, P., 'A social contract? – master against servant in the Court of Requests', *History Today*, 39 (September, 1989), 50–6.

Sharpe, P., 'Poor children as apprentices in Colyton, 1598–1830', *Continuity and Change*, 6 (1991), 253–69.

Shahar, S., *Childhood in the Middle Ages* (1990).

Sharpe, J.A., *Early Modern England: A Social History 1550–1760* (1978).

Shoemaker, R.B., *Prosecution and Punishment: Petty Crime and the Law in London and Rural Middlesex, c. 1660–1725* (Cambridge, 1991).

Shoemaker, W., *The Occult Sciences in the Renaissance: A Study in Intellectual Patterns* (Berkeley, 1972).

Simon, J., *Education and Society in Tudor England* (Cambridge, 1966).

Singer, C., Holmyard, Hall, A.R., and Williams, T.I. (eds), *A History of Technology* (Oxford, 1957), Vol. III.

Slack, P., *English Towns in Transition 1500–1700* (Oxford, 1976).

Slack, P., *The Impact of Plague in Tudor and Stuart England* (1985).

Slack, P., *Poverty and Policy in Tudor and Stuart England* (1988).

Slack, P., *The English Poor Law 1531–1782* (1990).

Smith, A.H., 'Labourers in late sixteenth-century England: a case study from north Norfolk [Part I]', *Continuity and Change*, 4 (1989), 11–52.

Smith, A.H., 'Labourers in late sixteenth-century England: a case study from north Norfolk [Part II]', *Continuity and Change*, 4 (1989), 367–94.

Smith, C.S., 'Metallurgy and assaying', in C. Singer *et al.*, *A History of Technology* (Oxford, 1957), Vol. III, 27–71.

Smith, R.M. (ed.), *Land, Kinship and Life-Cycle* (Cambridge, 1984).

Smith, R.M., 'Some issues concerning families and their property in rural England 1250–1800', in Smith (ed.), *Land, Kinship and Life-Cycle*, 1–86.

Smith, S.R., 'The London apprentices as seventeenth-century adolescents', *Past and Present*, 61 (1973), 149–61.

Smith, S.R., 'Religion and the conception of youth in seventeenth-century England', *History of Childhood Quarterly*, 4 (1975), 493–516.

Smith, S.R., 'Almost revolutionaries: the London apprentices during the Civil Wars', *The Huntington Library Quarterly*, 42 (1979), 313–29.

Smith, S.R., 'The ideal and reality: apprentice-master relationships in seventeenth-century London', *History of Education Quarterly*, 21 (1981), 449–59.

Souden, D., '"Rogues, whores and vagabonds"? Indentured servant emigrants in North America, and the case of mid-seventeenth-century Bristol', *Social History*, 3 (1978), 23–41.

Souden, D., 'Migrants and the population structure of later seventeenth-century provincial cities and market towns', in P. Clark (ed.), *The Transformation of English Provincial Towns 1600–1800* (1984), 99–132.

Spitzer, A.B., 'The historical problem of generations', *American Historical Review*, 78 (1973), 1353–85.

Springhall, J., *Coming of Age: Adolescence in Britain 1860–1960* (Dublin, 1986).

Spufford, M., 'First steps in literacy: the reading and writing experiences of the humblest seventeenth-century spiritual autobiographers', *Social History*, 4 (1979), 407–33.

Spufford, M., *Small Books and Pleasant Histories: Popular Fiction and Its Readership in Seventeenth-Century England* (Cambridge, 1981).

Stevenson, L.C., *Praise and Paradox: Merchants and Craftsmen in Elizabethan Popular Literature* (Cambridge, 1984).

Stone, L., 'The educational revolution in England, 1560–1640', *Past and Present*, 28 (1964), 41–80.

Stone, L., *The Family, Sex and Marriage in England 1500–1800* (New York, 1977, abrdg. edn, 1979).

Swain, J.T., *Industry Before the Industiral Revolution: North-East Lancashire* c. *1500–1640* (Chetham Society, 3rd. ser., Vol. XXXII, Manchester, 1986).

Thirsk, J. (ed.), *The Agrarian History of England and Wales* (Cambridge, 1967), Vol. IV.

Thirsk, J., *Economic Policy and Projects* (Oxford, 1978).

Thomas, K., *Religion and the Decline of Magic* (New York, 1971).

Thomas, K., 'Age and authority in early modern England', *Proceedings of the British Academy* (1977), Vol. LXII, 205–48.

Thompson, R., 'Adolescent culture in colonial Massachusetts', *Journal of Family History*, 9 (1984), 127–44.

Thrupp, S.L., *The Merchant Class of Medieval London* (Ann Arbor, 1948).

Todd, B.J., 'The remarrying widow: a stereotype reconsidered', in M. Prior (ed.), *Women in English Society* (1985), 54–92.

Underdown, D., *Revel, Riot and Rebellion: Popular Politics and Culture in England 1603–1660* (Oxford, 1985).

Underdown, D., *Fire from Heaven: The Life of an English Town in the*

Seventeenth Century (1991).

Vincent, D., *Bread, Knowledge and Freedom: A Study of Nineteenth-Century Working Class Autobiography* (1981).

Wales, T., 'Poverty, poor relief, and the life-cycle: some evidence from seventeenth-century Norfolk', in Smith (ed.), *Land, Kinship and Life-Cycle*, 351–404.

Wall, R., 'The household: demographic and economic change in England, 1650–1970', in R. Wall, J. Robin and P. Laslett (eds), *Family Forms in Historic Europe* (Cambridge, 1983).

Wall, R., 'Real property, marriage and children: the evidence from four pre-industrial communities', in Smith (ed.), *Land, Kinship and Life-Cycle*, 443–80.

Wall, R., 'Leaving home and the process of household formation in pre-industrial England', *Continuity and Change*, 2 (1987), 77–101.

Wareing, J., 'Changes in the geographical distribution of the recruitment of apprentices to the London companies 1486–1750', *Journal of Historical Geography*, 6 (1980), 241–50.

Wareing, J., 'Migration to London and transatlantic emigration of indentured servants, 1683–1775', *Journal of Historical Geography*, 7 (1981), 356–78.

Watt, T., *Cheap Print and Popular Piety, 1550–1640* (Cambridge, 1991).

Willan, T.S., 'The movement of goods in Elizabethan England', in *The Inland Trade: Studies in English Internal Trade in the Sixteenth and Seventeenth Centuries* (Manchester, 1976).

Willan, T.S., *Elizabethan Manchester* (Manchester, 1980).

Wilson, A., 'The infancy of the history of childhood: an appraisal of Philippe Ariès', *History and Theory*, 19 (1980), 132–53.

Wilson, F.P., *The English Drama 1485–1585* (Oxford, 1969).

Wohl, R., *The Generation of 1914* (Cambridge Mass., 1979).

Woodward, D., 'The background to the Statute of Artificers: the genesis of labour policy, 1558–63', *Economic History Review*, 2nd ser., 33 (1980), 32–44.

Wright, S.J., 'Confirmation, catechism and communion: the role of the young in the post-reformation church', in S.J. Wright (ed.), *Parish Church and People: Local studies in Lay Religion 1350–1750* (1988), 203–27.

Wrightson, K., and Levine, D., *Poverty and Piety in an English Village: Terling 1525–1700* (New York, 1979).

Wrightson, K., 'Household and kinship in sixteenth-century England', *History Workshop Journal*, 12 (1981), 151–8.

Wrightson, K., *English Society 1580–1680* (1982).

Wrightson, K., 'Kinship in an English village: Terling, Essex 1550–1700', in Smith (ed.), *Land, Kinship and Life-Cycle*, 313–32.

Wrigley, E.A., and Schofield, R.S., *The Population History of England 1541–1871: A Reconstruction* (1981).

Wrigley, E.A., 'Urban growth and agricultural change: England and the continent in the early modern period', *Journal of Interdisciplinary History*, 4 (1985), 683–728.

Yarbrough, A., 'Apprentices as adolescents in sixteenth-century Bristol', *Journal of Social History*, 13 (1979), 67–81.

Index